THE PEOPLE vs GREED

STEALING AMERICA

MAIN STREET vs WALL STREET

The Continued Erosion of Ethics in Our Professions, Business and Government

JOSEPH W. COTCHETT, JR.

ISBN: 978-0-9975614-0-1

Printed in the United States of America
at **PATSONS PRESS**
Santa Clara, California

To my mother, Jean, and sister, Pat.

Two women who had the greatest influence on my life.

ACKNOWLEDGEMENTS

This book would not be possible without the assistance of many people, including my extraordinary partners, lawyers and staff I have worked with over the past 50 years of law practice. I'm grateful to the many friends who encouraged me to write a follow-up to *The Ethics Gap*, a book I wrote over 25 years ago on the decline of our professions.

The chapters could have been hundreds of pages long covering all the years of cases involving the moral decay and the numerous scams perpetrated on the American public over the past fifty years. We reviewed court documents and press reports, including the incredible work of independent investigative reporters. Lawyers who think they have the inside scoop on the daily scams have little clue of what is going on compared to what our investigative press uncovers.

The researchers, those who edited, reviewed and discussed subjects with me were many. They were reporters, writers, and researchers, including Edward Iwata, Daniel Fost, Deborah Williams, Tema Goodwin, Nicholas DeLuca, and checked and edited by Chuleenan Svetvilas, to name a few of the terrific people who added to the book.

Much of the material came from legal cases and government reports, non-profits and the many outstanding newspapers, blogs and internet news resources. *The New York Times, The Washington Post, Chicago Tribune, The Boston Globe, The Los Angeles Times, The San Francisco Chronicle, The Seattle Times, The Philadelphia Inquirer, The Atlanta-Journal Constitution, The Dallas Morning News, The Denver Post*—to mention a few of the great remaining papers. Some of the information came from former public officials – federal and state – who entrusted me with information on the condition that they remain anonymous. Some of the basic information came from internet search engines for corroboration.

Every book needs people to push the project along. This book could not have been finalized without the untiring work of Nirav Engineer, and my partner, Nanci Nishimura, an active lawyer involved every day helping to make this a better world. My personal assistants, Phyllis Lee, Patrice O'Malley and Karin Yee-Fajardo all deserve recognition for making my life and work possible—without them I could not function as a lawyer. My family, and especially my children, give me the support and education about life I need to make things happen.

Any and all of the small profits from this book will be distributed to the many nonprofits that work every day on our behalf to save our environment and protect the public from corruption and abuse, groups like Public Citizens, Southern Poverty Law Center, Sierra Club, National Resources Defense Fund, animal groups, medical groups, and legal aid societies who work every day for a better and more just America.

Lastly, two women in my life who instilled in me an appreciation for those less fortunate—my mother, Jean, who came out of an orphanage in Ohio to the bright lights of New York and my sister Pat, who had the biggest heart and was probably the smartest person, with great common sense, I have ever known.

ABOUT THE AUTHOR

Joseph W. Cotchett has a legendary reputation for his courtroom accomplishments and is considered one of the country's foremost trial lawyers. *The National Law Journal* has called him one of the 100 Most Influential Lawyers in America. He is the senior partner at **Cotchett, Pitre & McCarthy,** and has been in the top 100 California attorneys selection by the Los Angeles and San Francisco *Daily Journal* for numerous years.

He has authored numerous books on law and ethics. His book, *The Ethics Gap*, was a precursor of today's financial climate. He is active in environmental matters, serving as the past Chair of the California State Parks Commission and as a legal advisor to numerous environmental groups. His book *The Coast Time Forgot* is a historical guide to the California Coast from San Francisco to Santa Cruz.

He received an Engineering degree from California Polytech State University and a Juris Doctor from the University of California, Hastings College of Law. He is a **Fellow** of the American College of Trial Lawyers, the International Society of Barristers, the International Academy of Trial Lawyers, an **Advocate** in the American Board of Trial Advocates, and a former **Master** of the American Inns of Court. He is a member of the prestigious **National Trial Lawyer Hall of Fame** in Philadelphia for his work nationwide in civil rights, and litigation on behalf of the under-privileged in our society. In 2010, he was honored with the **Clarence Darrow Award**. He received the Distinguished Service Award from the Judicial Council of California for years of service to the Judiciary and Courts in California. He was named the **Antitrust Lawyer of the Year** by the Golden State Antitrust Institute as an outstanding lawyer over the years in the field of antitrust competition and honored by the California League of Conservation Voters with the **Environmental Leadership**

Award for his work on behalf of the environmental litigation and the work on the State Parks Commission. He received the **Lifetime Achievement Award** by the California Consumer Watchdog of California for his service in representing consumers across the country. He serves on various boards and commissions.

Following University, he served as an officer in the U.S. Army Intelligence Corps, followed by years as a Special Forces paratrooper and JAG Corps officer in the active reserves. Following active duty, he remained in the Army Reserves for more than 30 years, retiring as a Colonel and serves in a number of veteran organizations. He was awarded the Legion of Merit.

His Cotchett Foundation contributes to educational causes, including assisting teachers to work with inner city children on math and science programs, animal, environmental and social issues of the day. He has five children and "many grandchildren."

TABLE OF CONTENTS

INTRODUCTION

"The truth will set you free, but first it will piss you off."
—Gloria Steinem

"People don't know the corruption unless it's disclosed to them."
—Martin Baron, Editor, Washington Post

"The worst thing that can happen in a democracy – as well as in an individual's life – is to become cynical about the future and lose hope."
—Hillary Clinton

"This is a fight over economics, a fight over privilege, a fight over power. But deep down, it is a fight over values. ... These are America's values. And these are the values we are willing to fight for."
—Senator Elizabeth Warren (D-MA)

There are many quotes you could use to describe the present greed in our Country, but Steinem summarizes it best. Every day we hear people who are mad as hell about the corruption in America and how we have come to accept it as an everyday occurrence. When we read or hear about some new injustice or back-room fraud, we are reminded of Steinem's quote. But no matter how pissed off it makes us, uncovering the truth is the essence of needed change. It is the cover-up by deceit or law that allows such conduct and injustice.

This book is a summary of where we are as a society—it is taken both from the cases my law firm and I have handled and in large part from press reports of greed and scams pushed on our society. The chapters illustrate many reports of our investigative press and in some cases reports and examples with the appropriate attribution—this to give the reader a summary of where our Country is going.

AN INVESTIGATIVE PRESS IS KEY TO A DEMOCRACY
Without a free, open and investigative press, our society echoes the history of all the prior countries that have come and gone due to corruption and powerful forces. Prior to World War II, Germany, Italy, Japan and other countries closed down the open

press. Asia is growing economically and politically at record levels in large part because the press is starting to open doors to information. The awareness comes not only from print media, but from the ubiquitous internet—especially with the new Millenniums and young people. The smart phone has captured the world in terms of people opening lines of communication.

Each of these chapters contains information that will appall you: stories of fraud, theft, bribery and greed in America. But there are also examples of individuals, whistleblowers, doctors, lawyers, accountants, and even members of Congress who have stepped up and made a dent in the wall of corruption. Nothing would be available to us without the investigative press letting the light shine on the conduct. Not only the press, but many recent documentary films such as Michael Moore's films, *Where to Invade Next, Capitalism: A Love Story, Fahrenheit 9/11*, and many other outstanding exposes. One has only to see the movie *Spotlight*, the story of the courageous *Boston Globe* reporters who broke open the entire story of priest abuse of children—a fact that had been hidden for years by money and power of the Catholic Church. Watch the movies *The Big Short, Inside Job* or *Money Monster* to realize the extent of corruption on Wall Street and how it put us into a financial recession in 2008. Ronald Reagan said, "Information is the oxygen of the modern age—it seeps through the walls topped by barbed wire and it wafts across electrified borders."

CHANGE CAN HAPPEN WITH INFORMATION—FLINT, MICHIGAN

Without the passion and belief that we can change the way things are headed, we are lost as a society and nation. Maybe it's the pendulum swinging back the other way, maybe it's that people have access to more information, maybe it's the younger voters, but change is in the wind. The corrupt are more brazen than ever. Yet new voices are speaking out and challenging the corruption in our Country through greater access to information.

A classic example of changes that can be made by public disclosures in the press involves the disclosure of the lead poisoning due to a municipal water system in Flint, Michigan. For years, experts have talked about lead poisoning in children but it did not hit the public in the face until Flint made the front page of newspapers and the evening news in 2015. According to residents of Flint, officials knew about the lead poisoning when they changed the water supply and later tried to cover up the problem. Your good government at its best. In fact, there are areas in our Country that far exceed the potential lead poisoning problem in Flint, including many areas of New York, New Jersey and Pennsylvania.

Only when the media exposed the extent of the lead poisoning in Flint did people speak out. For the first time, the giant of lead poisoning was awakened concerning "a silent epidemic in the United States," as stated by Dr. Philip Landrigan, a professor at the Icahn School of Medicine at Mount Sinai Hospital in New York. None of this would be center stage without the press. Unfortunately, less than 10% of our public information comes from print media.

In 2012, our Congress cut funding for lead poisoning programs due to the influence of major paint companies. These companies had fought regulation of lead for years, including gasoline, while millions of children possibly suffered brain damage. Unfortunately, it is estimated that over 20 million homes in the U.S. have lead paint that is turning to a dust form and possibly absorbed by children resulting in potential brain damage. Thousands of children are now affected by lead poisoning because the problem was kept under the table by lobbyists in Washington, D.C. Hopefully, the free flow of information on the problem will cause our government to better regulate the larger problem of chemical poisoning of our citizens.

EDUCATION FOR ALL

Our education system in this Country takes a backseat to other priorities, particularly when compared to other countries. We have failed to put education first. We spend more money per student than any other Country in the world and we are about close to the bottom of the ladder on producing students who compete globally. War, especially our ongoing role as the global police, take priority over the public's tax dollars when these funds should be directed to our schools and children. Public colleges and universities are no longer public—the students cannot get in because of expense and, if they do get in, they come out with student loan debts that choke them for a decade. When a football coach at a public university makes more than the president of the school or the Governor of the state, our preferences are in serious trouble. Inner city and rural school children deserve as much attention as new fighter jets or new super carriers for the Pacific. In the next few years, India will put over one billion people and students on the internet, not in fighter jets.

HOW DID WE GET HERE—THE POWER SHIFT
Robert Reich, economist, former Secretary of Labor, author, and college professor of the University of California, Berkeley, provides us with a possible answer:

> *The election of 2016 is really all about one thing: power... The fact that most Americans no longer have it and that CEOs, Wall Street, and billionaires have more than ever... The power-shift has occurred over the last forty years, as union membership plummeted from 35% of the private-sector workforce to 6.8%; as industry consolidated (Big Pharma, Big Ag, Wall Street's biggest banks, giant defense contractors, energy, Big Tech); as the Supreme Court became dominated by right-wing Republican justices intent on using the Constitution to disempower most Americans; and as big money inundated American politics... The power-shift has been abetted by Rupert Murdoch's media outlets (Fox News, Wall Street Journal, New York Post), Charles and David Koch's propaganda machine, a Republican Party that fanned racial and evangelical fervor, and a Democratic Party that too often forgot its roots and cozied up to Wall Street and big corporations instead. The result has been the widest inequality of income and wealth in more than a century, a democracy that's turned into a plutocracy (or oligarchy), and widespread frustration and anger.*

Professor Reich is a person of great integrity and foresight, and a street-wise individual who fully understands the orbit of money and greed. He points out the present crucial crossroads in America's history. We face social, political, and economic ills that will worsen if we do not stand up and take action. In fact, the fate of our democracy is at stake if we do not act quickly. One has only to listen to the candidates for President of the United States in 2016 to understand the corporate spectrum of challenges we face. The vast problems facing America require no less than a populist crusade from liberals, conservatives, and independents alike. It will take everyone to revive and sustain a fair and thriving economy for all and to preserve our democratic values that are still the envy of the world. You might well ask what the odds are that this can be turned around.

The charity OXFAM reported that just 60 people own the same amount of wealth as the bottom 3.5 billion people in a world of roughly 7 billion. The inequality is spanning wider every day of the week unless governments stand up. Inequality in the U.S. is much like what is happening around the world. According to the New York Times, Jeffrey A. Winters, a political professor at Northwestern University, has been studying economic integrity for years. Professor Winters determined that the gap between the 1% and everyone else is growing to "unprecedented levels of stratification in all of human history."

WE SHOULD LISTEN TO THE SOUNDS AROUND US

I have spent the last 50 years practicing law and pursuing justice in our Courts. We have seen enough fraud, scams, and stealing from the public to fill many warehouses with documents, transcripts, books and records of the massive swindles.

Over time, we have taken on the rich and powerful, as well as those corporations that scam society. We've taken on the FBI on behalf of Viola Liuzzo, the Bush White House gang for Valerie Plame, Savings and Loan executives for thousands of senior citizens, and Bernie Madoff on behalf of his small investors—along with hundreds of others who were victims of abuse, deception, or corruption. We have taken on those who destroy our environment and seek to help people who cannot speak for themselves, including polluters such as the lead paint industry, chemical companies, and Big Pharma.

As some of our colleagues say, our lawyers sue the big guys for the little guys, or sometimes we represent the big guys who are fed up with the system. You can't always win, but that doesn't mean you don't use the legal system as a platform for change and pursue those who steal from the less fortunate.

We have taken on President Obama and the U.S. Government on behalf of 21 children and a scientist, for failing to protect our environment—you could go on and on—the key is representing those who stand on the right side of what is wrong. As Bob Weissman, President of Public Citizen, has declared, "We the People have not conceded the right to decide our own future." Weissman and Public Citizen represent the very best of our society in taking on those who have abused their privileges.

HERE'S WHAT WE KNOW:
The rich bullies are out of control in Washington, D.C. and our state capitals. They were given the opportunity by a 5—4 Supreme Court decision called *Citizens United,* which basically allows money to control the election of public servants.

Big money infecting government is the root of the problem—lobbyists, hidden dollars, and people who think they can buy the truth have taken the reins. But that doesn't mean it has to be that way. One has only to read Jane Mayer's book, *Dark Money: The Hidden History of the Billionaires Behind the Rise of the Radical Right*, to understand the level of cash that influences elected politicians, especially in Washington, D.C. Greenbacks stopped much of the progressive legislature in the past 20 years, resulting in a major problem of how our Country is actually being governed.

Much of the capital goes to stopping agencies from doing testing or inspections of chemicals used and sold to our citizens resulting in all forms of diseases, and most importantly, brain damage in children. It not only compromises infrastructures like our roads and bridges but more important it directly affects the health of our citizens—people now die and get sick because of a lack of health care and proliferation of chemicals in our environment such as lead, pesticides, PCBs, and mercury. The latter leads to serious brain damage in children and it is reported that chemical companies spent over thousands of dollars on lobbyists to influence members of Congress regarding the oversight of testing chemicals.

Scam artists who abscond with millions of dollars can go to jail, whole most of corporate America skates away from its misdeeds. People are fed up with the slap on the wrist fines handed out to those who have brought down our economy and taken advantage of individuals through their greed.

As many very good prosecutors and judges have said, people who steal from the fabric of our society should go to *JAIL*, not just have their corporation pay a fine without admitting guilt. A change is coming in the prosecution of Wall Street con artists according to some in the Justice Department. Increased enforcement is only because of the outrageous conduct exposed by investigative reporters and courageous whistleblowers. Remember the words of Gloria Steinem as you explore the chapters of the book.

1

Health Care Fraud: Betrayal in a White Lab Coat

"It is horrific and unprecedented, I believe, in the amount of unnecessary treatments to maximize dollars without consideration of the human beings that he was abusing."
—Paul D. Borman, U.S. District Judge sentencing a Michigan oncologist, 2015

"Simple lab work done during a few days in the hospital can cost more than a car. A trip to the emergency room for chest pains that turn out to be indigestion brings a bill that can exceed the price of a semester at college."
—Steven Brill, *Time* magazine, April 2013

"Having an assistant in the O.R. has become an opportunity to make up for surgical fees that have been slashed."
—Dr. Abeel A. Mangi, Professor of Cardiac Surgery, Yale University

Most doctors are reputable and trustworthy, practicing with the utmost integrity, with patient care at the forefront. But opportunities to supplement income are tempting, and for some doctors, their advisors, clinics, and hospitals it can be a slippery slope toward fraud.

Here is but one example of what is going on today in the world of medical fraud that is sweeping the Los Angeles area of California. Using an anonymous name, Maria Gonzales was 47 years old, a mother of four, and a resident of California's San Joaquin Valley. She and her husband, Juan Gonzales, worked in the fields for 25 years. That kind of arduous manual labor can take its toll, and Maria developed chronic back pain. She tried over-the-counter medicines but got no relief. Eventually she visited a chiropractor, who sent her to a nearby clinic to get an MRI. Returning to the chiropractor for the results, Maria got the bad news: She had a degenerative spinal disorder. She would need spinal-fusion surgery to alleviate the pressure on her spinal cord or face the prospect of being paralyzed.

The chiropractor referred Maria to an orthopedic surgeon in Los Angeles. After ordering a second MRI to confirm the diagnosis, he scheduled Maria's back surgery. The operation involved placing three- to four-inch titanium rods along her spine, held in place with screws, cages, caps, and connectors. After a few days in the hospital, Maria went home to recuperate. She faced a lot of pain and severely restricted activity in the ensuing months, and her back would never be as strong or as flexible as it once was. But the surgery was deemed a success. Except that it was all a huge fraud. Maria never needed back surgery.

The local imaging center conspired with the chiropractor, and she was shown a phony MRI scan. The chiropractor received a $10,000 bonus for referring a new patient to the orthopedic surgeon in Los Angeles, who showed Maria a second phony MRI scan. As for the titanium rods and screws placed in Maria's back, they were nonmedical-grade knockoffs produced at a metal machine shop outside San Diego.

The hospital where the surgery was performed billed Maria's insurer nearly $25,000 for rods and hardware that actually cost less than $700. The spinal fusion usually paid by insurers of Medi-Cal is often between $80,000 and $150,000 with a large portion going to the surgeons. This was all done by a law that allowed hospitals and doctors to charge injured California workers full payment for the charges. Through kickbacks and fraudulent billing claims, everyone got what they wanted. Everyone, that is, except Maria. In a few years the crude hardware encasing her spine will deteriorate and she will require another surgery to have the hardware removed. The non-fused parts of her spine caused by the unnecessary operation will result in more pain than she first endured. My partners, Frank Pitre and Bob Hutchinson, are leading the litigation on this tragedy.

There's also the story of Bruce Peterson, who left the U.S. Postal Service after 24 years to fulfill a lifelong dream of opening his own travel agency in Texas. Experiencing chest pains, and having suffered a heart attack ten years earlier, Peterson visited an Austin cardiologist, who told him he needed surgical implants to prop open the arteries in his heart. According to the Texas Medical Board's complaint, over about eight months and several operations the surgeon placed more than 20 metal stents into Peterson's chest, tearing an artery during one of the procedures.

In an attempt to undo the damage, the cardiologist implanted a defibrillator in Peterson's chest. When he was still at Austin's Westlake Medical Center (remember that name), Peterson's heartbeat became erratic, and the defibrillator automatically began to apply shocks to his heart. A nurse at the hospital later reported that Peterson could be heard screaming in pain for two days. After conferring with the family, the cardiologist placed a magnet over Peterson's chest to keep the defibrillator from discharging. Peterson went into cardiac arrest and died.

The Texas Medical Board later ruled that the stents placed in Peterson's heart caused the complete blockage of an artery and decreased the heart's capacity to pump blood. The state medical board also ruled that Peterson was not a candidate for a defibrillator, given his condition and that the unnecessary stents had weakened his heart, which exposed him to serious complications and ultimately his death. While denying any responsibility for his patient's demise, the cardiologist paid a paltry sum to settle the board's complaint over Peterson's treatment. The doctor said he received only $800 per surgery for implanting stents, so profit was not a motivating factor when he performed multiple surgeries on his patients. On average, hospitals nationwide receive about $25,000 per stent case from private insurers, according to Healthcare Blue Book, a website that tracks reimbursements. However, this cardiologist was a major investor in the Westlake Medical Center.

Bruce Peterson's death and Maria Gonzales's painful ordeal are only two of thousands of life-threatening health situations Americans face every day when dealing with medical professionals who have forsaken the Hippocratic oath for the creed of greed. Today "medical entrepreneurs," including therapists, home care providers, pharmaceutical companies, lab technicians, ambulance drivers, hospital administrators, medical-device manufacturers, and insurance executives often choose profits over patients. Pharmaceutical companies are in a league all by themselves, as will be discussed in Chapter7.

All of the above was due to political scams and bribery of state elected representatives in California. The law enabled the above medical scams putting hundreds of innocent people under the knife of a surgeon that was unnecessary. The law was finally changed in 2013 when investigators found out about the surgical scams.

HISTORY OF MEDICAL FRAUD

In 1930 people were closely acquainted with their doctors (40 percent of doctor-patient visits were still house calls), and they usually knew their neighborhood pharmacists by name. In the 1960s medical fraud wasn't considered a serious problem. For the working class, health costs were generally manageable, as hospital rates and insurance premiums hadn't yet exploded, and most expensive technological advances in medicine were still on the horizon.

In 1965 the federal government allocated taxpayer money to establish two major government health insurance programs: Medicare, to help cover the health care costs of Americans 65 and older, and Medicaid to help cover health care costs of Americans with disabilities and those whose income is near the federal poverty level. These programs were fought by those who didn't think big government belongs in our lives—the same song being sung today by many conservatives across the country.

By the 1980s accounts of increasingly fraudulent activity became public, but it was not until the late 1990s that Medicare and Medicaid fraud became a primary concern of the government. By then, billions of taxpayers' dollars had been doled out to health care professionals who had robbed and abused the government's insurance programs.

How many billions are we talking about? Nobody really knows. Because medical fraud is so widespread and undetected among so many health care providers, no official estimate exists as to what percentage of health care expenditures is fraudulent. We know that Medicare annually pays out around $600 billion per year, and Medicaid spends roughly $500 billion.

In 2012 the Centers for Medicare and Medicaid Services (CMS) and the RAND Corporation estimated that medical fraud added as much as $98 billion, or roughly 10 percent, to annual Medicare and Medicaid spending. So if America spends $2.7 trillion on health care in a year, potentially around $270 billion is lost to medical fraud. In fact, it is a lot higher if you count the Maria Gonzales's, the Bruce Petersons, and the many others covered by other forms of private insurance or workers compensation medical programs.

This is not a victimless crime. Siphoning taxpayer dollars from legitimate health care services and pouring it into fraudulent enterprises drives up the cost of medical services for everyone. On an individual level, this means higher insurance premiums and copayments and reductions in coverage. On the national level, medical fraud compromises the safety of millions of patients—one of whom, on any given day, might be you.

YOUR PAIN, THE MEDICAL FRAUDSTER'S GAIN

Here are more examples of unnecessary medical procedures. In 2002 Jonathan Stelly, then 24, was a semipro baseball player in the South. His career was inching toward the big leagues until he fainted one day and ended up in the Louisiana offices of a cardiologist, who told him he wouldn't make it to age 30 without a pacemaker. Surgery was quickly scheduled.

Months after the operation, Stelly caught a TV news report about his doctor, Mehmood Patel, being investigated for performing unnecessary surgeries. He made appointments with three other doctors, and all of them had the same opinion: Stelly hadn't needed a pacemaker; he needed blood-pressure medication.

Stelly says trusting an unscrupulous doctor ended his dreams of becoming a professional ballplayer. Although he had a subsequent surgery to turn off the device, his second career choice—to serve in the armed forces—was denied because he carried a pacemaker in his heart, even though it was nonfunctioning.

In 2012 Dr. Patel was given a ten-year prison sentence after a jury convicted him in a landmark case of 51 counts of health care fraud for performing medically unnecessary operations. Patel's specialty was coronary stenting. He became so good at it that he could insert the metal-mesh tube into an artery in 15 minutes. According to nurses who worked with him, Patel didn't always bother waiting until the anesthetic took full effect before beginning the procedure, which involves jabbing patients with a needle in their groins to insert a catheter. Why the hurry? For each stent implanted, Patel billed as much as $2,600.

Patel increased his profits even more by leasing an 18-wheeler truck and turning it into a cardiac catheterization lab. He parked it next to his office, allowing him to charge fees for facilities as well as for the implants. Patel saw as many as 20 patients an hour, almost always concluding that they needed surgery. At one point, he had nearly 7,000 patients under his care. Patel also set up a virtual assembly line at a hospital in Lafayette, Louisiana, so that he could move from one patient to the next, performing back-to-back surgeries.

At his criminal trial, Patel insisted he had never inserted a stent into a patient that was not needed. However, expert witnesses for the prosecution referred to Patel's angiogram videos, to show jurors that the blockages Patel claimed were at 70 percent or higher (the accepted threshold for surgery) were significantly lower or nonexistent. In court, Patel also claimed he had never harmed a patient. But in civil lawsuits, the 300 plaintiffs who sued him and two of the hospitals at which he worked vehemently disagreed. The suits alleged that at least two people died because of Patel's work, and dozens of others suffered strokes and heart attacks, required blood transfusions, or needed remedial surgery. Unfortunately, the legal system never allowed the plaintiffs to recover the physical harm Patel inflicted on them and thousands of other patients. And all of this happened while hospital officials and other doctors allegedly looked the other way.

One of those patients was Barbara Pellerin, who endured eleven procedures by Patel over a nine-month period, including stenting for a 97 percent–congested artery, according to David Armstrong's 2013 *Bloomberg* report on the case. Continuing to suffer from chest pain, Pellerin went to another cardiologist, who checked her video records on file at the hospital. He told Pellerin she had "crystal-clear arteries" before the stenting but, as a result of the initial stents, a lesion was created, resulting in a need for more angiograms and additional stents for her weakened heart.

The *Bloomberg* article reported that Pellerin's new cardiologist presented his findings to the hospital board at the time and Patel's hospital privileges were suspended, although his license to practice was not revoked. So he continued to operate on hundreds of other patients.

It would take a total of seven years before federal investigators could build a case to support Patel's conviction in 2009—the first in which a doctor was convicted of billing for unnecessary medical procedures. This landmark case was soon followed by convictions of doctors in several other states for performing unneeded cardiac procedures. Pellerin sued as part of a class action suit and collected $89,000—small compensation for her pain and the potential heart problems she will face for the rest of her life.

UNNECESSARY MEDICAL TREATMENTS

Physicians are supposed to consider the well-being of their patients before any other concerns. We trust them with our lives, and most doctors are truly dedicated to helping people. For years the image of the kindly, competent doctor or even the grumpy but gifted doctor has graced our television screens. From *Marcus Welby, M.D.* to "McDreamy" on *Grey's Anatomy*, those TV physicians fought for their patients.

Patients are very vulnerable before their doctors, and when they are truly ill, they may develop an almost religious belief in a doctor's powers of healing. But some doctors are more focused on personal gain than their patients' pain, and the damage they create is both insidious and cruel. Why? Because we fail to police them well through the various medical professional organizations and state agencies established to regulate them.

The most lucrative and perverse way that some doctors bolster their finances involves performing unnecessary operations on unsuspecting patients and then submitting false billing claims to government and private insurers. Cardiac stents, angioplasties, pacemakers, spinal fusions, knee replacements, gallbladder removals, prostatectomies, hysterectomies, and cesarean sections are cited by medical studies as surgical procedures performed much more often than needed. In 2011 a study published in the *Journal of the American College of Cardiology* found that only 36 percent of 24,000 nonemergency angioplasty cases from late 2009 to 2010 met the criteria for the procedure.

FOLLOW THE MONEY TO MEDICAL FRAUD

Anyone who has ever tried to find out what a medical procedure really costs has run up against the arcane maze of insurance codes and the runaround from providers. The health care industry withholds a lot of information about its business practices, including how much doctors are reimbursed for their services from insurance companies.

Recently, however, government officials opened the books on health care financing and revealed just how big a slice of the $64 billion payout pie doctors received from Medicare in 2012. According to those records, 825,000 physicians billed for and received Medicare reimbursements. The median payment was a reasonable $31,000. However, there were 344 doctors who *each* received at least $3 million in Medicare reimbursements, for a total of $1.5 billion.

Some doctors on the list were overpaid in excess of $30 million. On the Medicare billing pyramid, one-third of the top recipients are ophthalmologists. The man at the pinnacle is Dr. Salomon Melgen of West Palm Beach, Florida.

Melgen owns four offices, employs a staff of 30, and caters mostly to senior citizens. In 2012 he received nearly $21 million in payments from Medicare. The doctor insists he conforms to Medicare billing policies and that the "vast majority" of the money reflects the upfront costs of purchasing the drugs he administers as injections into the eye to treat macular degeneration.

Melgen made the same claim in 2009, when Medicare reported overpaying him $9 million. The doctor appealed that finding, claiming that the government program needed to clarify its billing rules. Currently, Medicare pays an ophthalmologist each time he or she administers a drug for macular degeneration; that payment is designed to cover the entire cost of the medication. Melgen, however, saves thousands of dollars by using several doses from the same vial for different patients, even though that presents a risk of infection.

After losing his 2009 case on appeal, Melgen was suspended from receiving further payments from Medicare and ordered to return the $9 million. So he sued the U.S. Department of Health and Human Services. Two months later, Medicare agreed to end

Melgen's payment suspension if he agreed to stop using the disputed method of multi dosing from a single drug vial. Given his $21 million in reimbursements in 2012—more than any other doctor in the nation—Melgen's adherence to Medicare's stipulation may be questionable.

BIG PAYOFFS TO LOOK THE OTHER WAY
Officials in charge of our health care system too often look the other way as fraud and corruption plunge Americans into a medical nightmare from which we may never awaken. Unscrupulous medical professionals often have friends in high places. The health care industry is the top lobbying interest on Capitol Hill, paying out more than three times the amount spent by defense lobbyists last year. In 2015 health care lobbyists delivered $495 million to support political campaigns, sway congressional opinion, and transform their interests into industry-friendly bills. In a familiar unholy alliance, Wall Street financiers partnered with Washington, D.C., lobbyists to create an increasingly corporate health care system that places a premium on CEO bonuses and high shareholder earnings over patients' health care needs. We don't have a patient-centered health care system in America anymore. We have a health care industry.

Melgen's longtime friend was Sen. Robert Menendez, a New Jersey Democrat. Menendez tried to intercede with federal health care officials on Melgen's behalf when the ophthalmologist's overbillings were disputed by Medicare. Not getting the response he wanted from Marilyn Tavenner, the Medicare administrator at the time, Senator Menendez escalated his appeal by approaching then–Senate majority leader Harry Reid to set up a meeting with Health and Human Services Secretary Kathleen Sebelius.

The doctor had contributed thousands of dollars to Menendez's political causes and flew the senator on his private jet. Only after the FBI raided Melgen's practice in 2013—and the senator faced the prospect of a Senate Ethics Committee hearing as well as a possible grand jury investigation—did Menendez pay Melgen $70,000 for the flights. On April 1, 2015, Senator Menendez was indicted on 14 counts of using his office to help Melgen.

Two weeks later Melgen was indicted on 46 counts of health care fraud as well as additional charges of filing false claims and making false statements. The indictment charges Melgen with operating a fraudulent scheme from 2004 to 2013, in which he billed Medicare for more than $190 million, for which he was reimbursed and paid more than $105 million.

You might think that going down the list of doctors getting the highest Medicare payments would be an easy way to spot the bad doctors, but it's not quite that easy. Several doctors on the top-ten list actually represent institutions such as the Mayo Clinic and other legitimate organizations that receive big payments. For example, one doctor's name is frequently used as the reporting physician on Medicare claims submitted by a given institution that may in fact represent hundreds of different doctors and procedures.

However, three of the top ten recipients of significant Medicare payments in 2012 are already under federal scrutiny, and one of them is awaiting trial on fraud charges. Others face payment reviews or have had their licenses suspended. The seventh-highest biller on Medicare's 2012 list, at $10 million, was Farid Fata, an oncologist at Michigan Hematology and Oncology (MHO) in the Detroit area. Ultimately, he was charged with intentionally misdiagnosing his patients and ordering unnecessary procedures for them, including chemotherapy for patients who did not have cancer.

Monica Flagg was 50 years old in July 2012 when Fata diagnosed her with myeloma, a cancer of the plasma cells in bone marrow. She endured multiple rounds of testing, bone marrow biopsies, medication, and one chemotherapy treatment under his care. When Fata gave her the diagnosis, Flagg said he reassured her that they had caught the cancer early but that she would need "a lifetime maintenance dose of chemotherapy." She continued treatment with him over several months.

Almost a year later, she had her first chemo treatment. Later that day she tripped over a suitcase on her bedroom floor and broke her leg, which landed her in the hospital. Another doctor in Fata's practice, Dr. Soe Maunglay, happened to be doing rounds on Fata's patients that Fourth of July weekend and reviewed Flagg's medical chart.

"He read my chart, looked at me very strangely. I'll never forget the look that he had when he looked at me," Flagg told ABC News. "He came back the following day and said to me, 'I want you to know, I work for Dr. Fata. ... You don't have cancer, and you need to not ever go back to Dr. Fata.' "

Newsweek covered the story in 2015, reporting that "Horrified by the [Flagg] incident, Maunglay began to look at Fata's other patient files. He got in touch with George Karadsheh, MHO's practice manager, about his concerns. Afterwards, Karadsheh formally reached out to the FBI with Maunglay's findings, starting the cascade of events that would end in the FBI raiding Fata's offices and arresting him."

An earlier warning had been raised but was dismissed. Angela Swantek, an oncology nurse interviewed for a job with Fata, but as *Newsweek* reported, "she left dismayed over the medical care she saw administered to patients." When she went back to observe a nurse during rounds, "Swantek saw people hooked up to infusion chairs being slowly pumped full of drugs that were meant to be given via a quick injection into an IV, and other treatments like Neulasta, a human growth factor, being administered immediately after chemotherapy, instead of after 24 hours as recommended." The *Newsweek* article continued, " 'That's just the way we do things here,' she recalls being told."

Swantek reported her suspicions to the Bureau of Health Professions that March, but, she says, the state never got back to her.

TOO PROFITABLE TO INVESTIGATE AND JAIL
Is this behavior too profitable to jail? That's the question journalist Ed Cara of the *Medical Daily* asked in July 2015. Was this why Farid Fata got away with his crimes for years? "By the time Fata was apprehended, his practice purchased $45 million worth of drugs annually for a staff of three doctors—the median amount spent by a full-time oncologist is between $1.5 to $1.9 million according to a 2015 report on oncology trends," Cara reported. "He branched out with an in-house pharmacy, Vital Pharmacare; a radiation treatment center, Michigan Radiation Institute; a diagnostic testing facility, United Diagnostics; and his very own charity, Swan for Life."

According to the FBI, Fata fabricated cancer diagnoses and then ordered tests and treatments for cancer-free patients to justify fraudulent billing to the insurance companies for his personal gain. Fata also was accused of paying and receiving kickbacks from home care and hospice workers in return for patient referrals. Arrested in

2013, Fata pleaded guilty in September 2014 to 13 counts of Medicare fraud, 1 count of conspiracy to pay or receive kickbacks, and 2 counts of money laundering.

At the time of Fata's sentencing, U.S. Attorney Barbara McQuade asked for a life sentence or 175 years, because "Fata's crimes demand a sentence commensurate with the momentous suffering he inflicted." In the Department of Justice's sentencing memo, McQuade asserted that "Fata bullied, berated and browbeat patients who dared to question his treatment, telling them they risked death without him or in the case of a patient who could not afford copays, 'It's your life or your money.'"

Ultimately, Fata was sentenced to 45 years in jail. At sentencing, he broke down in sobs, lamenting, "I misused my talents, yes, and permitted this sin to enter me because of power and greed." He apologized to his victims in the courtroom, admitting that they had come to him "seeking compassion and care," but he had "failed them." But Dr. Fata did more than fail his patients; he stole their lives and their family's lives. And he failed the medical profession.

DRIVE-BY MEDICINE
According to the 2015 Medscape Physician Compensation Report, the average pay of a primary care physician is $195,000 a year, compared to $421,000 for an orthopedic surgeon, or $302,000 for a specialist such as an oncologist. That's not bad compared to the U.S. median household salary of about $54,000, although with office rent, staff salaries, equipment, insurance, and other costs, operating a medical practice can be expensive.

"Drive-by doctoring" is a method some physicians employ to offset financial challenges and increase payments from insurance companies. A doctor who is not in a patient's insurance network, and therefore not covered by the patient's insurance, is referred to as "out of network." As the stories of Peter Drier and Patricia Kaufman, profiled in a September 2014 *New York Times* article, demonstrate, out-of-network surgical charges are now being used to increase fees paid to doctors and hospitals.

Peter Drier, 38, of New York City, carefully researched the costs of his upcoming neck surgery for herniated disks, which included a fee negotiated through his insurance company of $6,200 for his surgeon, according to the *Times*. But when Drier received his bill after surgery, he was stunned to see a charge of $117,000 from an assistant surgeon whom Drier never met and who was not in his insurance network.

As the *Times* reports, Patricia Kaufman of Highland Park, New Jersey, had undergone several operations for a chronic neurological condition. In previous operations, salaried resident doctors had sewn up her incisions. But at her last surgery, two plastic surgeons sewed up the incision on her back, at a charge of $250,000!

In an operating room, when a second pair of hands is needed, a hospital resident or a physician assistant usually supports the attending surgeon. But more patients are finding out the hard way that an out-of-network doctor, whose fees are substantially higher than those of in-network doctors, could also serve as an assistant surgeon.

According to Dr. Abeel A. Mangi, professor of cardiac surgery at Yale University, the hiring of out-of-network assistant surgeons by hospitals is becoming a common practice. "The idea of having an assistant in the O.R. has become an opportunity to make up for surgical fees that have been slashed," Mangi told the *Times*. "There's now a whole cadre of people out there who do not have meaningful appointments as attending surgeons, so they do assistant work."

As the use of out-of-network assistant surgeons in operating rooms and on hospital wards increased, insurance companies began filing lawsuits. But the insurers' ability to challenge the out-of-network doctors' higher fees has been tenuous because no insurance representative is on site to dispute a hospital's claim that no residents or in-network doctors were available at the time of the surgeries. Health insurance commissioners from several states are trying to protect patients from these "surprise charges" by out-of-network medical providers who resort to legal action to obtain full payment for their services. But actions by these health insurance commissioners as advocates for patients have been limited as they face off against formidable opponents—health care lobbyists.

"This has gotten really bad, and it's wrong," observed James J. Donelon, Republican insurance commissioner of Louisiana, to the *Times*. "But when you try to address it as a policy maker, you run into a hornet's nest of financial interests."

The difference in costs charged by in-network and out-of-network doctors is significant. According to the online *Healthcare Bluebook* and various insurance plans, an in-network doctor receives $1,781 for a muscle and skin graft and $1,892 to remove a gallbladder. An out-of-network doctor receives $150,500 and $44,000, respectively, for the same operations. Hospitals should be held accountable for using out-of-network doctors when their own medical staff is available. And legislation needs to be put in place to protect patients and private insurers from paying these inflated costs unless they are truly necessary in emergency situations.

SPECIALIZED TREATMENT BY NONSPECIALISTS
The potential for medical fraud involves doctors who routinely bill for providing medical treatments outside their practice specialty and for which they are not qualified. Here is an example of this practice from a June 2014 *Wall Street Journal* article.

Ronald Weaver, a Los Angeles doctor who is not a cardiologist, received more than $2 million from Medicare for providing a rarely used procedure in which patients are attached to large cuffs that inflate and deflate rhythmically to increase blood flow through the arteries. In 2012 only 239 of the thousands of U.S. cardiologists used this questionable cardiology treatment and, even then, on fewer than 5 percent of their own patients. Weaver administered this procedure to 99.5 percent of his patients.

ASSEMBLY LINE MEDICAL PROCEDURES
Massachusetts urologist Evangelos Geraniotis was reimbursed $2.1 million from Medicare—the highest payout to any doctor in his field—for burning possibly cancerous lesions in his patients' bladders. On average, an urologist performs this procedure approximately 38 times a year. In 2012 Geraniotis billed Medicare for 1,757 of these procedures on his patients, according to the *Wall Street Journal* article, citing official Medicare data.

Gary Marder, a dermatologist with an office in Florida, uses radiation to treat melanoma in his predominantly elderly clientele. In 2012 Medicare paid Marder $3.7 million to perform this treatment 15,610 times on 94 patients. That averages 166 treatments per patient when, according to other oncologists interviewed in the *Wall Street Journal* article, the appropriate number of radiation treatments for a patient is only 20. Marder's website displays a photograph of the low-voltage machine used in the process; however, he also allegedly "upcoded" his billings from $22 to $154 per treatment by submitting claims based on the use of a more powerful machine that is typically found only in hospital radiation-oncology units.

"INVESTING" FOR PATIENT REFERRALS

To bolster their incomes, some doctors have acquired ownership stakes in ancillary medical services, such as clinical labs, diagnostic centers, pharmacies, physical therapy centers, and home care companies. Although these kinds of investments by doctors are legal, they create a way for doctors to refer their patients to receive ancillary medical services from providers they have a financial interest in. Such physician self-referrals are ethically suspect, as they may bring high financial returns to the referring doctor. For example, by referring a steady stream of patients to a particular lab, the referring doctor may collect part of the lab's "technical fee" for each test or procedure performed.

Federal and state laws require some transparency concerning a doctor's investments in ancillary medical services. However, even if physicians disclose their financial involvements to patients and provide a list of alternative service providers, they may still refer patients to whichever provider they determine is the best—usually the one they are affiliated with. Not surprisingly, studies also show that physicians who have ownership stakes in diagnostic labs or financial interests in radiation treatment centers order significantly more tests than physicians who have no investments in those ancillary medical services.

DaVita Health Care Partners, one of the largest kidney dialysis providers in the country, had been successfully selling interests in its business at below fair-market value to physicians who referred patients to their clinics. The company recently agreed to settle with the government for $389 million after it was revealed that the company was violating anti-kickback laws from 2005 to 2014.

Testing laboratories provide another lucrative source of ill-gotten money for doctors and others. In 2013 the former owner of a diagnostic lab in New Jersey pleaded guilty to an insurance fraud scheme that reaped $100 million in revenues to his company from patient referrals he obtained by bribing possibly more than 100 doctors. The lab also performed unnecessary tests for which it was reimbursed at least $850,000 from Medicare and private insurers. Twenty-six doctors pleaded guilty in connection with the bribery scheme, and several doctors went to jail.

A 2013 study reported in the journal *Radiology* found that self-referring physicians order more unnecessary knee MRIs than doctors without financial interests in the imaging equipment used for the scans. This problematic connection was articulated by the study's coauthor, Dr. Matthew Lungren of Duke University Medical Center, who noted, "We believe that the inherent conflict of interest present when physicians both order and then perform and collect fees on the basis of the acquisition of MRI imaging examinations is an important factor to consider whenever the matter of health care cost is raised."

DOCTORS PROMOTING MEDICAL DEVICES

In 2013 the Office of Inspector General for the U.S. Department of Health and Human Services (HHS) issued a fraud alert concerning a booming and highly profitable business in implantable medical devices used by surgeons. Physician-owned distributorships, or PODs, buy medical devices such as spinal implants and heart pacemakers directly from the manufacturers—or in some cases, own or have a financial interest in the manufacturer—and then sell the devices to hospitals and surgery centers. For a small investment, surgeons act as distributors and salespeople of these medical devices, aggressively market these devices to the hospitals where they perform the implant surgeries, receive commissions for the sales, and also promote the devices to colleagues at medical conferences and in research journals.

The medical-device manufacturers maintain that PODs control costs and result in savings for patients. But the HHS fraud alert takes a contrary view, explaining, "the financial incentives PODs offer to their physician-owners may induce the physicians both to perform more procedures (or more extensive procedures) than are medically necessary and to use the devices the PODs sell in lieu of other, potentially more clinically appropriate, devices."

Traditional medical-device manufacturers, whose market shares plummeted once PODs were established to sell medical devices, cried foul. Hospitals too question the notion that POD device costs are lower than those from traditional medical-device manufacturers. To avoid any potential legal problems, some hospitals have begun to adopt "no POD" policies.

Concerned about the rapid growth of medical-device surgeries associated with physician-owned distributorships, Congress launched several inquiries into the PODs. Yet it was not until the passage of the 2014 Sunshine Act, part of the Affordable Care Act, that some regulations of PODs went into effect. Distributors who are reimbursed by public insurance now are required to disclose their POD investments and ownerships to Medicare, although such disclosures are not yet required to be made to patients, hospitals, or private insurers.

Since the HHS fraud alert was issued in 2013, the debate over PODs and their legal viability has only increased. PODs generated about 15 percent of the spinal-device market in 2012 and are now seen as a valuable revenue source for surgeons to help offset the decline in their fees due to reductions in Medicare reimbursements. PODs have become increasingly common among hip and knee surgeons, although spine surgeons continue to dominate the POD medical-device marketplace. From 1994 to 2009, sales of spinal devices rose from $250 million to $7 billion, primarily due to price markups by manufacturers, according to *Orthopedic Network News*, an industry newsletter. A spinal screw that cost $60 to make can sell for more than $1,000, and surgeons routinely implant $30,000 worth of hardware inside a patient during a single surgery, such as the one on Maria Gonzales.

In May 2015 Michigan neurosurgeon Aria Sabit (owner and operator of Michigan Brain and Spine Physicians Group) pleaded guilty to four counts of health care fraud after admitting that as an investor in a POD he received kickbacks for the POD spinal devices he sold to the hospital where he implanted the spinal devices.

"Dr. Sabit caused serious bodily injury to his patients by acting out of his own greed instead of the best interests of his patients," U.S. Attorney Barbara McQuade said in a statement following Sabit's guilty plea. "Not only did he steal $11 million in insurance proceeds, but he also betrayed his trust to patients by lying to them about the procedures that were medically necessary and that were actually performed."

Sabit also admitted involvement in a kickback scheme in California in which he convinced a hospital to buy spinal-implant devices from Apex Medical, a company in which he held an undisclosed financial interest. Under the terms of his plea agreement, Sabit faces between 9 years and 11-plus years (135 months) in prison for medical fraud.

SPINAL FUSION CON JOBS

If you want to hear a medical horror story, just ask lawyer Azike Ntephe to show you the metal cage and dozens of rods, screws, and bolts that once held up his spine. Azike is in the same boat as Maria Gonzales described at the outset of this chapter. Suffering from chronic back pain, Ntephe went to see Southern California neurosurgeon Ali Mesiwala, who recommended a spinal fusion. The surgery made things worse, and the pain became excruciating. Eventually, Ntephe sought help from another surgeon, who removed all the hardware, but the damage caused by the cage and rods was irreversible. Ntephe was forced to give up his practice and now must use a walker to get around.

It wasn't until after his second operation that Ntephe learned Dr. Mesiwala had a POD with Reliance Medical Systems, and some of the hardware implanted during his initial surgery was made by Reliance. Had he known this earlier, Ntephe says, he would have refused the surgery and gone with the minimal procedures suggested by two other physicians he had consulted.

From 1997 to 2012, the cost of spinal fusions billed to Medicare rose from $343 million to $3.9 billion, according to a 2013 report released by the Department of Health and Human Services. And as reported in the *Wall Street Journal*, over the course of four years, five surgeons in one Kentucky hospital performed 2,475 spinal fusions on Medicare patients. A 2011 study in *Surgical Neurology International* evaluated 274 patients with complaints of neck and back problems. Of the 50-plus patients who were told they needed surgery, *none* showed any neurological or radiographic evidence suggesting surgery was necessary. According to the study's co-author, neurosurgeon Nancy Epstein, more and more patients today are being told they need operations they simply do not require, including surgeries that carry significant risks.

"If patients have operations they don't need, they risk having major problems—infections, paralysis, heart attacks, strokes," said Epstein in a *USA Today* article on unnecessary surgeries. "Nobody reports the complications, so finding the real morbidity and mortality of these procedures is extremely difficult."

According to government data, more than 465,000 spinal fusions were performed in the United States in 2011. Medical experts say that perhaps as many as half of those complex surgeries were unnecessary.

NATIONAL WEB OF MEDICAL FRAUD

Medicare alone processes about 4.5 million claims a day, and uncovering medical fraud among these claims is not easy. Consider that the pool of potential victims is the entire population of our country, and a fraudulent scheme could involve a vast range of medical conditions and all types of treatments. Add the incentive and ability to include false billings among the glut of statements submitted to public and private insurers, and it's not hard to see how enterprising medical fraudsters have been able to make off with millions of dollars in unlawful payments for decades.

In addition to illegal kickbacks and fraudulent billing for unnecessary treatments, the most common kinds of medical fraud involve billing Medicare, Medicaid, or private insurers for medical services that were never rendered or billing for more costly medical services than the services that were actually provided. Picture a doctor billing for a nonexistent follow-up appointment with a patient, or a doctor billing for a more expensive treatment—referred to as "upcoding"—instead of billing for the actual, less-expensive procedure. While it may not sound like these practices could add up to $270 billion, that's the estimated annual loss resulting from medical fraud, according to 2012 findings by Donald Berwick, a former head of the Centers for Medicare and Medicaid Services, and Andrew Hackbarth of the RAND Corporation. Now imagine these false claims being filed not only by office-based doctors but also by health care professionals in clinics, hospitals, diagnostic labs, MRI and imaging suites, therapy and rehabilitation centers, ambulance services, nursing homes, hospices, and by home care providers. The revenues generated by these false medical claims runs into multimillions of dollars per year.

MEDICARE TAKEN FOR A WILD RIDE

Harris County, Texas, is centered around Houston, with a population of around 4 million. In 2009 the county led the nation in the number of private emergency medical service (EMS) ambulance companies—397. Medicare paid those EMS companies $62 million that year (and more than $300 million over a five-year period). By way of comparison, in the same year, Medicare paid only $7 million to private EMS companies in New York City, with double the population.

By 2010, more than 300 of the 397 EMS companies in Harris County were under investigation for Medicare fraud. Government agencies have charged company owners with filing fraudulent transport orders with Medicare for unnecessary services or services never rendered. Other EMS owners were charged in a $90 million Medicare billing scheme. From April 2012 to July 2013 alone, the U.S. Attorney's office for the Southern District of Texas filed six cases in Houston alleging that EMS companies submitted fraudulent Medicare claims of more than $9.5 million for ambulance transportation. Seven individuals were charged, resulting in three guilty pleas and one conviction after trial. The owner of a company in neighboring Fort Bend County was convicted of fraudulently billing Medicare for more than $1.7 million.

Due to the fraud investigations, and Medicare declaring a moratorium on new ambulance-service providers in the area, the number of private EMS companies in Harris County has dropped to 200 as of August 2014, according to the Texas Department of State Health Services. The moratorium was extended in July 2015.

As the *Houston Chronicle* reported in July 2013, "EMS officials gained the authority to impose the bans through the Affordable Care Act—also known as Obamacare—and are finally exercising one powerful tool that may stop fraud before it starts."

WHISTLEBLOWERS AND MEDICARE FRAUD

Major medical fraud scams can operate undetected for years and might never come to light without the aid of people who have witnessed the abuses firsthand. Medicare has limited funding to investigate alleged acts of fraud and relies on citizen whistleblowers to come forward and file lawsuits on the government's behalf using the qui tam provisions of the federal

False Claims Act. Qui tam is an abbreviation of the Latin phrase *qui tam pro domino rege quam pro se ipso in hac parte sequitur*, meaning "[he] who sues in this matter for the king as well as for himself." What it means in practice is that a private party, called a "relator," brings an action against the person or entity committing a fraud, on the government's behalf. The government, not the relator, is considered the real plaintiff. If the government succeeds, the relator receives a small share of the award. States also have false-claims statutes.

One such suit against National Medical Care in Florida alleged that the company had been bilking Medicare for more than ten years. Several of the company's dialysis centers were accused of billing Medicare for hundreds of thousands of fraudulent blood tests, for submitting fraudulent claims for nutritional-therapy services, and for violating anti-kickback laws. The company's parent corporation, Fresenius Medical Care A.G., paid $486 million to settle civil and criminal charges, and as a result three National Medical Care units were permanently excluded from government health insurance programs.

In another whistleblower case, a speech therapist who had worked at a nursing home in Plymouth, Massachusetts, filed a qui tam lawsuit in 2013 against her former employer, Life Care Centers of America, one of the largest nursing-home chains in the country. Helen Toomey reported that 40 percent of the rehabilitative work she was told to administer at several Life Care facilities was neither reasonable nor necessary by Medicare guidelines. When she attempted to discharge patients, her requests often were denied by management.

Similarly, at a Life Care center in Florida, several employees cosigned a letter stating, "We have been encouraged to maximize reimbursement even when clinically inappropriate," according to court documents. According to other employees, Life Care's chief operating officer told them their job was "to make money for Forrest Preston, the founder, sole shareholder, and Chairman of the Board of Life Care," the government's brief states.

Court documents reveal that from 2006 to 2011 Medicare paid Life Care $4.2 billion. U.S. Department of Justice (DOJ) investigators found the company's facilities regularly billed Medicare almost double the nationwide average for rehabilitation days.

We salute the whistleblowers mentioned in this chapter: Dr. Soe Maunglay, George Karadsheh, Helen Toomey, and employees of Fresenius Medical Care. These people stood up and did what is right by identifying fraudulent medical-service providers. They are critical players in the quest to shut down the exploitation of patients for personal monetary gain by unscrupulous health care providers.

REHAB RIP-OFF

Assisting the elderly with the needs of their daily lives—preparing meals, taking medication, bathing, dressing—is considered custodial care and is not covered by Medicare. In contrast, similar care for housebound seniors just out of the hospital or recovering from an injury is considered rehabilitative care and *is* covered by Medicare. But many home care companies ignore the distinction between these two types of elder care and defraud Medicare of billions in false claims.

In some cases, the circle of fraud widens to include willing Medicare beneficiaries. Contacted by recruiters through local churches and community centers, these senior citizens are aware that they are not entitled to Medicare benefits, yet they agree to join in the fraud in exchange for money or food stamps, or sometimes just for a change in their everyday routines.

Fraudulent billing for home care has become epidemic. For example, the surge in fraudulent billing in Washington, D.C.,'s Medicaid program—from $40 million in 2006 to $280 million in 2013—alerted authorities to scams, but the sheer volume of potential fraud cases around the country is more than the government can handle. In 2014 in Washington, D.C., 25 people were charged with obtaining millions of dollars in fraudulent Medicaid payments. One of the accused was a nurse who had lost her nursing license and was ineligible to receive further Medicaid payments. Yet she billed the city's Medicaid program for $75 million by using different names. In 2014 in Louisiana, home care company Amedisys agreed to pay $150 million to settle government charges of filing false Medicare claims and paying illegal physician kickbacks. Similar fraudulent scams have been reported in Miami, Detroit, and elsewhere.

In Dallas, one doctor was able to mastermind a $375 million home care scam. Medicare regulations require a doctor to certify that home care businesses are providing legitimate services for which they bill the agency. But Dr. Jacques Roy, through his company, Medistat Group Associates, exploited this regulation by selling his certification to 500 home care companies in Texas so their respective patients could bill for receiving Medicare services. With a staff of just four other doctors and 15 nurses, Roy had more beneficiaries under his name than any other medical practice in the country, according to the indictment.

The Roy scam was based on two major components: (1) Most of the so-called patients did not qualify for rehabilitative care (they were not housebound), and (2) no services were ever provided.

The indictment alleges that some patients didn't even have homes for health workers to visit. One nurse from a company in the conspiracy with Roy would park her car outside a homeless shelter and recruit people to bring her Medicare prospects. For every potential patient that came to her car—those with Medicare beneficiary cards—the recruiter got $50.

The nurse's company, as well as 77 other companies associated with Roy, was suspended from Medicare eligibility. Roy's company also was suspended from Medicare, yet he simply created a new company to continue fraudulently billing Medicare until he was finally arrested in 2012. Although suspension may not provide a sufficient disincentive for crooked health professionals to mend their ways, it does raise awareness about the magnitude of fraud in the home care industry.

As for Roy, passage of the Affordable Care Act gave the government another strong tool to fight medical fraud: longer prison sentences. Roy faces one conspiracy count and nine counts of substantive health care fraud. If convicted, he faces life in prison.

MEDICARE AND THE MOB

For criminals, public health insurance programs have created an open season for medical fraud scams in America. Organized crime gangs around the world with a long history of making money through drug running, gambling, and prostitution are now irresistibly attracted to Medicare and Medicaid's easily picked deep pockets. It makes sense that criminals, with their skill set and lack of a moral compass, would be drawn to the world of medical fraud. It's relatively simple to figure out, not dangerous or life threatening, carries moderate prison sentences compared to drug trafficking or murder convictions, and can readily net millions of dollars.

"We've seen organized crime groups use the health care system … setting up a fake medical-supply company, to launder money from another scheme involving real estate," said Lt. Matthew St. Pierre of the Los Angeles Police Department's fraud division in a white paper released by Thomson Reuters in 2012 on health care fraud. "We're also seeing a growing trend of organized crime groups that have been doing health care fraud, teaching street gangs, known for drugs and prostitution, how to do health care fraud," St. Pierre added.

In 2011 the DOJ reported that 102 federal indictments were handed down in Los Angeles, Santa Ana (California), Denver, and Miami to "members and associates of transnational organized criminal groups operating in the United States." Charges include bank fraud, kidnapping, racketeering, and health care fraud. That same year Robert Mueller, director of the Federal Bureau of Investigation, reported to the Senate Judiciary Committee that the "FBI arrested nearly 130 members of La Cosa Nostra in New York, New Jersey, Philadelphia and New England on a number of accounts of illegal activity, including health care fraud." In 2009, 11 members of New York's Bonanno family were indicted for stealing patients' Medicare numbers and using them to submit false claims.

One crime group orchestrated a nationwide medical-fraud scam that billed Medicare $160 million for medical treatments in nonexistent clinics. The group, an Armenian-American organized crime enterprise known as Mirzoyan-Terdjanian, stole identities of doctors along with identities of thousands of Medicare beneficiaries. Using both sets of IDs, the criminals registered their medical clinics with Medicare and then submitted billings for services performed in those phantom clinics by the phantom doctors on the phantom patients.

Clearly, medical fraud does not always require real patients, clinics, or expensive equipment. It can even be pulled off without much medical knowledge. Although it seems obvious that a basic understanding of anatomy would be helpful in perpetuating medical fraud, some of these fraudsters were very bad at playing doctor. Billing invoices were submitted by eye doctors for bladder tests; by ear, nose, and throat specialists for pregnancy ultrasounds; and by dermatologists for cardiac exams. Seventy-three crime members were indicted, including Robert Terdjanian, who directed the New York–based members. In 2013 he was sentenced to ten years in prison and ordered to pay a fine of $1.2 million.

Gang members also often sent "recruiters" to skid rows and homeless shelters in the nation's biggest cities to obtain patient beneficiary numbers. The recruiters told anyone with a Medicare card about a new clinic in the area. The residents knew they were being hustled for what they call their "red, white, and blue"—a reference to their tri-colored Medicare cards—but they also needed to eat. Jimmy Rodgers of San Bernardino, California, told CNN he went to a bogus clinic three times a week—not for medical care but for the $100 he got per visit.

"[There] were no doctors," Rodgers told CNN, "They were just somebody who had their hand out." In another medical scam run out of Los Angeles, a crime gang claimed it was offering health services in a downtown industrial building. Instead of an office, investigators found only a mail drop, where Medicare sent checks for hundreds of thousands of dollars to the scam artists running Medicare frauds—all with taxpayer money.

MEDICAL FRAUD AND RUSSIAN ORGANIZED CRIME

A gang led by Konstantin Grigoryan (a former colonel in the Soviet army), his family members, and immigrants from the former Soviet Union with criminal records operated a string of medical clinics and testing labs in Southern California. The gang drew in senior citizens by advertising free checkups. They then bilked Medicare for $20 million before being caught by law enforcement officials in 2006.

The elderly patients were unaware that their Medicare numbers were used by the criminals to submit claims for a variety of tests and procedures that were never performed. The crime ring later expanded north, and the group bussed hundreds of elderly Vietnamese immigrants from San Jose to Southern California for "free" bogus checkups. Grigoryan was sentenced to four years and eight months in prison; his wife and son-in-law were also convicted and received lesser sentences. The three also forfeited $5.5 million in assets as partial restitution for the medical fraud.

On the East Coast, the Brighton Beach neighborhood in Brooklyn has one of the highest rates of health care fraud in the country. More health care providers with a Brighton Beach zip code are suspended from Medicare programs than in any other region of the nation except southern Florida, according to a 2012 *New York Times* article, which cited official Medicare data. It's also a community with a high percentage of Russian-speaking immigrants, many of whom once lived under a bureaucratic system in which bribery and corruption to obtain goods and services were common occurrences. One organized crime ring of Russian immigrants from Brighton Beach ran nine medical clinics in the area and conspired to bill private insurers $279 million for unnecessary and excessive medical treatments, receiving $113 million in repayments before the perpetrators were arrested in 2012.

Members of a separate network of Russian immigrants who ran three physical therapy clinics in Brooklyn were indicted in 2011 for paying recruiters to bring them elderly patients, and then fraudulently billing Medicare for the senior citizens' physical therapy, which consisted mainly of backrubs. Medicare reimbursed the Russians nearly $57 million for these mini-massages, according to the indictment.

New York University professor Mark Galeotti, an expert on Russian security affairs and transnational organized crime, theorizes that an authoritarian Soviet government conditioned many Russians to finding ways to game the system, including cons, rackets, and bribes. Once in America, some Russian immigrants pursued their "American dream" through medical fraud, while others have been linked to criminal rings back in Moscow: "Organized crime groups in Russia and other former Soviet republics currently send people with no criminal records to the United States ... with seed money, [and] they will operate fraud schemes for a year or two before returning. It's almost like ... you buy into the franchise and you get the three-ring binder and then it's up to you to go apply it," Galeotti told the *New York Times*.

Immigrant mobs ratchet up the violence level in health care fraud, according to Police Lt. Steve Davey, head of the Eurasian Organized Crime Task Force in Southern California. "They don't have the typical structure that we see in Italian mobs," Davey told the *Associated Press*. But they won't hesitate to use scare tactics or physical force to obtain Medicare numbers from elderly patients. "They'll work with whoever can make them money," said Davey. "And if they don't get their way, they won't be ashamed to kidnap somebody, to shoot somebody."

The émigrés may also operate at a more genteel level. An elite Russian ring—current and former diplomats living in New York—made headlines in 2013 when the U.S. Attorney for the Southern District of New York accused 49 of them of underreporting their incomes so they could qualify for Medicaid. The Russian diplomats accumulated nearly $1.5 million in Medicaid benefits, the program paying for 92 percent of the diplomats' childbirth care over a nine-year period. During the time they were receiving Medicaid benefits, the defendants took expensive vacations and bought high-priced goods at stores such as Bloomingdale's and Tiffany & Co. However, the criminal complaint is largely symbolic, as the accused diplomats either have left the country or have immunity from prosecution.

HOME CARE AND MEDICAL FRAUD: THE NIGERIANS
The Nigerian community in Dallas has been linked to home care fraud as well, including several companies in league with the aforementioned Dr. Jacques Roy. Federal indictments allege that hundreds of home care workers in the area profited from Medicare fraud by Nigerian-American ambulance services. Durable medical equipment (canes, walkers, knee braces, and the like) fraud is also on the rise in Texas.

The owner of a medical-device business, Aghaegbuna "Ike" Odelugo, testified before a congressional committee in 2011 about how he learned to defraud Medicare in a matter of weeks. He said, "All of this is right in the computer. You go online, you can see them [descriptions of medical equipment] and how much they pay for it. And you get the correct code and bill it. That's all it takes."

Sentenced to six years for fraud, Odelugo was ordered to pay the government nearly $10 million in restitution. An attorney for Odelugo says that Nigerian émigrés went into the home care business because few other job opportunities were available to them after arriving in Texas in the late '90s. They did not originally intend to defraud the government, he says, but the lure of quick and easy money was too strong a temptation to resist. They did a good job at it. In 2011 the national average spent on home care per Medicare beneficiary was $546. In Dallas, it was $1,624, according to official Medicare data.

A GLOBAL COMMUNITY OF MEDICAL FRAUDSTERS

With the largest population of senior citizens in the nation, Florida has a virtual welcome mat out for medical fraudsters. Elderly Medicare patients are the lifeblood of scams. Medicare benefits can't be revoked—and it's unlikely that senior citizens will face prosecution. More than half of the Medicare-fraud indictments issued in a record-setting takedown by the DOJ in 2012 (107 individuals nationally for $452 million in fraudulent billing) were from the Miami area, a city that one federal agent characterized as "the crown jewel of Medicare fraud."

But even when medical-fraud cases are uncovered, pursuing justice is still tough. Medical companies pop up overnight, bill thousands in false claims, launder their Medicare repayments, and, if law enforcement threatens, they can close their doors as quickly as they opened them. The medical fraudsters then repeat the process by opening a new company and repeating the process. The most-wanted lists of the FBI and the HHS Office of the Inspector General include a global community of criminals who have committed health care fraud and fled before prosecution. Many return to their countries of origin, such as Haiti, India, Nigeria, Pakistan, the Philippines, Russia, South Korea, Sudan, Zambia, and several South American countries. As of 2013, the *Miami Herald* reported, at least 150 fugitives from Medicare-fraud cases in South Florida—"most of them Cuban-born immigrants, have fled to Cuba, Mexico, the Dominican Republic, and other Spanish-speaking countries."

For example, the three Benitez brothers ended up in Cuba, the *Herald* reported. "The brothers used crooked doctors, hired Cuban immigrants to register as clinic owners, and paid $150-per-visit kickbacks to men who had both the AIDS virus and Medicare cards," according to the indictment.

Benitez co-conspirator and clinic director Enrique Gonzalez was a fugitive from justice when he was extradited from Peru in 2012. Gonzalez was sentenced to six years in prison for three counts of health care fraud and ordered to pay $18 million in restitution. Federal authorities seized hotels, apartment complexes, luxury homes, supermarkets, a helicopter, and a pirate-themed amusement park owned by the Benitez brothers in the Dominican Republic, but these assets didn't match the more than $80 million they received in Medicare benefits.

In another case, after serving a five-year stint for dealing crack cocaine, Cuban expatriate Armando Gonzalez applied for a Medicare provider number, according to his indictment. He opened three community mental health centers in Miami-Dade County. Managers of assisted-living facilities for those suffering from dementia and other mental illnesses would bus over their residents to Gonzalez's centers in exchange for kickbacks. Once there, the residents watched TV and DVDs, for which Gonzalez would bill Medicare as "services." When federal agents began investigating him for medical fraud, Gonzalez left Miami and opened new clinics in North Carolina, and he was planning to expand his business to Tennessee. Eventually, he was ordered to pay back the $28 million in payments received as a result of the $64 million he billed Medicare, and he also received a 14-year prison sentence.

TURNING UP THE HEAT ON MEDICAL FRAUD

The DOJ and HHS have worked together to create multiagency teams known as Medicare Fraud Strike Forces, a division of the Health Care Fraud Prevention and Enforcement Action Team (HEAT). The HEAT strike forces operate out of nine hot spots: Los Angeles, Dallas, Houston, Baton Rouge (Louisiana), Miami, Tampa Bay (Florida), Chicago, Detroit, and Brooklyn. They identify Medicare providers and suppliers who have filed suspicious billing claims, verify that medical company licenses and accreditation are in order, and often make unannounced visits to medical-service providers.

In May 2012 HEAT strike forces joined federal, state, and local law enforcement agencies in a one-day, seven-city takedown of 107 health care professionals, including doctors, nurses, social workers, and health care company owners. All were charged with cheating the Medicare system out of $452 million through fraudulent billing. Five months later, the strike forces assisted Medicare again when another raid netted indictments against 91 people in multiple cities. Those charges included a range of fraud schemes involving psychotherapy, ambulance services, physical therapy, home health care, mental health services, durable medical equipment, and occupational therapy. Fraudulent Medicare billings amounted to nearly $430 million this time around.

By May 2014 the HEAT strike forces coordinated their seventh national Medicare fraud takedown, charging 90 health care professionals in fraud schemes that involved $260 million in false billings. Since they began operating, the HEAT strike forces have charged more than 1,900 defendants involved in approximately $6 billion worth of medical fraud. According to government reports, every dollar the DOJ and HHS spend fighting health care fraud has returned an average of $8 to the U.S. Treasury and the Medicare Trust Funds. Defendants convicted by juries are facing more jail time than they would have if sentenced just a few years earlier. Yet, our agencies are still understaffed and underfunded in relation to the scope of the problem.

In addition to going after the medical fraudsters and recouping billions of dollars through False Claim Act cases, the Centers for Medicare and Medicaid Services (CMS) is fighting back with another powerful tactic: CMS stops the money before it reaches the criminals. For decades CMS operated by the "pay and chase" method. It routinely paid every bill that came in and attempted to recoup the money only when it became clear a billing claim was fraudulent. But given the dramatic rise in medical fraud, a shift in payment practices was needed.

Over the past five years, CMS followed the lead of credit card companies and used data-analysis software to detect suspicious claims. Prepayment reviews, both automatic and manual, have been put in place to deny claims the agency determines should not be paid, while post-payment reviews are made in an attempt to recover improperly paid claims. The Affordable Care Act expanded the government's ability to suspend a reimbursement until a fraud investigation can be completed. These tools will help CMS identify millions of dollars in fraudulent activity each year, though that's still a small fraction of the billions pouring out because of undetected false claims.

BATTLING MEDICAL FRAUD: AN UPHILL FIGHT

Identifying medical fraud and recovering ill-gotten gains from medical fraudsters are two separate matters. However, in 2013 CMS Deputy Administrator Shantanu Agrawal reported that in its second year of operation, the new Fraud Prevention System identified $210 million worth of improper payments, double the amount of the previous year. However, in a speech to an oversight panel of the House Energy and Commerce Committee, Agrawal conceded that only $54 million of those unlawful payments are likely to be recovered. That equates to a return on investment of only $1.34 for every $1 spent. And the potential $54 million estimated recovery is even less impressive once you subtract the $23 million mistakenly paid to deceased patients in 2011, the $25 million paid to deceased doctors, and the $29 million improperly paid to illegal immigrants from 2009 to 2011. Where do you begin to track down those payments?

Jail time as punishment for medical fraudsters has not occurred as often as warranted to be a measurable deterrent. Although the HEAT strike force is determined to show that medical fraud is no longer going to be the easiest get-rich-quick scam in town, courts are overburdened with criminal cases. Some judges look at these scams as nonviolent white-collar crimes. As an unfortunate consequence, medical fraud is not treated as a high-priority crime or the harmful conduct that it really is. So medical fraudsters continue to act with impunity, to the detriment of all people and the waste of taxpayer dollars.

FLYING THROUGH UNPREDICTABLE AIRSPACE

Conceptually, managing a hospital may be analogous to running an airline. In addition to dealing with air traffic control issues, airlines are faced with the difficulty of predicting weather conditions and how many passengers will actually show up for a flight. Hospital administrators face a similar vortex of conflicting concerns, chief among them balancing patient care and satisfaction with the vagaries of state and private insurance rules. The ongoing challenges to operating a hospital are enormous, and they include the cost of uncompensated care (the responsibility to provide health care for those with no insurance), budgets and maintenance, staffing and schedules, equipment and technology upgrades, and the need to make a profit.

Like the airlines, some hospitals have responded to the challenges of increasing operating costs with the equivalent of providing narrower seats and adding fees for incidentals. For example, passengers and patients both wait longer for services and care, and they face unexpected charges for various add-ons.

Meanwhile, while some CEOs walk away rich.

Stephanie and Sean Recchi own a small technology business in Ohio and spend around $500 a month on health insurance, which comes to about 20 percent of their income. When Sean, then 42, became ill in 2012 with non-Hodgkin's lymphoma, the couple flew to Houston so he could be treated at the University of Texas MD Anderson Cancer Center.

When the hospital would not accept their "discount insurance," Stephanie was forced to come up with $83,900 *in advance* before the hospital would give her husband his initial medical plan and treatment.

In March 2013 *Time* magazine devoted most of that week's issue to the rising costs for health care, particularly the high prices for hospital services. Author Steven Brill's award-winning article, "Bitter Pill: Why Medical Bills Are Killing Us," investigated several nonprofit hospitals and found how little power consumers and patients have in the health care marketplace when they struggle to comprehend and navigate the medical bureaucracy they are caught in.

As Brill recounts, the first line of Sean Recchi's hospital bill set the tone for the remaining 342 charges: "1 ACETAMINOPHE TABS 325 MG." The product was generic Tylenol; the charge was $1.50 for one pill, the same pill you can buy in a 100-pill bottle from Walmart for $1.97. What followed were dozens of dramatically marked-up items and procedures, including a $238 simple chest X-ray that Medicare pays out at $20.44, and $13,702 for the cancer drug injected into Recchi that cost MD Anderson about $3,500, almost a 400 percent markup. Such exorbitant prices show how this so-called nonprofit hospital can book a 26 percent profit margin on revenues of more than $2 billion, and how it can reward its president with a compensation package of $1.85 million in 2012, Brill notes. This financial scam is repeated daily on vulnerable and desperate patients at thousands of hospitals throughout America.

MEET THE CHARGEMASTER AT HOSPITALS

Every hospital has its own chargemaster, or charge description manager (CDM). A CDM is an internal price list, or a mammoth computer file that assigns a cost to everything. Chargemaster prices at one hospital are not the same as prices at other hospitals. According to Brill, hospitals don't like to talk about CDMs because they don't appear to have an objective process for determining their prices. In other words, as Brill put it, "there seems to be no process, no rationale, behind the core document that is the basis for hundreds of billions of dollars in health care bills." The only near consistency Brill found among hospital chargemaster prices was that each hospital routinely marked up the cost of expensive implantable devices, such as a spine stimulator, to achieve a profit of 150 percent for the hospital.

When Brill asked a hospital executive to explain how chargemasters work, he was told, "They were set in cement a long time ago and just keep going up almost automatically." Forty percent of chargemaster programs are purchased from outside vendors and are rarely reviewed by hospitals, Brill noted. One hospital spokesperson told Brill the chargemaster prices were irrelevant, as very few people actually paid those prices once their insurance company rates were applied.

Yet even patients with private insurance are affected by chargemaster pricing. Brill points out that insurance companies with the most leverage—those with the most patients to offer a hospital—can negotiate their prices above Medicare's set rates. Insurance companies with less leverage have to negotiate discounts from chargemaster prices. For the patient, Brill notes, paying a 30 percent markup on a lab test that costs $13 is better than getting a 30 percent discount for the same lab test when it costs $200. "That so few consumers seem to be aware of the chargemaster demonstrates how well the health care industry has steered the debate from why bills are so high to who should pay them," Brill concludes.

Brill's article shows that comparing how often standard stress tests versus more advanced CT scans are ordered for the same patient (or for the same diagnosis in many patients) is an example of when testing can veer into overtesting. It is also a good example of the chargemaster system at work. Although many doctors may initially order standard stress tests that do not require added technology and cost less—$1,200 at the chargemaster price, $96 at the Medicare price—they often order more advanced follow-up stress tests that record the progress of an injected radioactive dye with a CT scan.

According to a McKinsey & Company report, health care

providers in the United States conduct far more stress tests than those in any other country. Ensuring that the ability to freely order those tests continues, again according to Brill's article, the American College of Radiology is aggressively lobbying Congress to pass the Diagnostic Imaging Services Access Protection Act to block efforts by Medicare to discourage doctors from ordering multiple stress tests or CT scans on the same patient.

A new trend in dealing with the chargemaster system, Brill explains, is to hire a medical-billing advocate, a growing online cottage industry. Hospitals are now paying outsiders to set the prices, and patients have to hire outsiders to decode them. A former appeals coordinator in a hospital billing department remarked to Brill that, "The hospitals all know the bills are fiction, or at least only a place to start the discussion, so you can bargain with them."

But not all attempts to negotiate bills are successful, Brill relates. Emilia Gilbert, a school bus driver, was 61 years old in 2008, when she slipped and fell in the backyard of her Connecticut home. After six hours in the E.R. at Bridgeport Hospital in Connecticut, where she received three CT scans and a few other tests, Gilbert's bill came to $9,418. On it were charges for items neither Medicare nor any for-profit insurance company would cover (such as bandages, tubing, and basic instruments), as those items are regularly included in the overall facility charge.

Although Gilbert's employer provided her with Cigna health insurance, it was a policy designed for low-wage earners and covered only $2,500 of her bill. And with her $1,800-a-month salary, Gilbert did not qualify for Medicaid. When she was unable to pay her bill, the hospital sued her. As a consequence, a Bridgeport Superior Court judge ordered Gilbert to pay all but $500 of the charges, and he put her on a payment schedule of $20 a week for six years.

Brill's accounts of patients who've had to spend several nights in a hospital also provide a sobering lesson in economics for the working class. For example, Brill reports that a patient's bill he investigated included charges for a blanket ($32), surgical gown ($39), and the strap that held the patient onto the operating table ($31). In many instances, the trade-off is your life or your life savings.

Hospitals prey on the vulnerability of patients and their family members. Whether it's a crisis that lands you in an emergency room, a scheduled procedure, or the need to support a loved one in the hospital, the experience is fraught with stress and fear. And then there is the mind-boggling paperwork. If you survive your hospital encounter, you may still suffer pain from the aftereffects, including billing nightmares. After living through a surgery or serious illness, who would question a 1,000 percent markup on intravenous bags of saline solution? Who has any idea of the exorbitant costs of out-of-network lab tests? Who even knows about chargemaster prices, let alone knowing that they're negotiable?

HEALTH CARE: A MATTER OF LIFE OR DEBT

Many hospitals—private or public—aggressively pursue ways to lower their costs and increase their revenues, and to avoid federal regulators or criminal investigations in the process. To safeguard profits, hospitals estimate the number of patients expected on a given day and manipulate nursing schedules to cover those approximations. This process can lead to insufficient staffing, even in critical-care units. Hospitals also negotiate lower prices for equipment and supplies from vendors, but often they don't pass the savings on to patients. These business decisions might not meet the criminal definition of fraud, but they involve conduct that is detrimental to patients.

Hospital Corporation of America, or HCA—the nation's largest for-profit hospital chain, with 163 hospitals from New Hampshire to California—paid a record $1.7 billion (at that time, 2003) in federal fines and repayments. The federal charges against HCA included making illegal kickback payments to physicians and filing false claims to federal health care programs, including Medicare.

The chief executive officer of HCA at the time of the fraud investigation was Rick Scott, who later became governor of Florida. Although not personally accused of wrongdoing, Scott was forced to resign his post under pressure from HCA board executives. According to a tweet by *New York Times* investigative reporter Kurt Eichenwald, Scott sent a note to his HCA staff that read: "The law is simply a device used by people trying to stop those who seek change."

Well, change came in 2006, when HCA was acquired by three private-equity firms, including one cofounded by former Massachusetts governor Mitt Romney. Whenever "private-equity firm" appears as a participant in a transaction, it is unlikely to mean that the acquired entity will provide better service or lower costs to consumers. In fact, since its acquisition, profits at HCA have soared, raising the value of the firms' holdings to nearly three and a half times its initial investment.

However, a 2012 *New York Times* investigation found that after an earlier 2000 fraud settlement, and even after HCA was acquired, several HCA hospitals were suspected of submitting false claims to Medicare for unnecessary treatments, particularly for risky cardiology procedures involving stents and catheters. Corporate memos that the *Times* obtained show HCA conducted an internal investigation into the alleged improprieties using an outside consulting company and found long-term evidence that cardiologists in at least ten of the chain's hospitals could not justify the procedures they performed. In one HCA hospital, as many as 43 percent of angioplasties performed were deemed unnecessary, according to a confidential HCA memo reviewed by the *Times*. Also, at that facility, medical records indicating that patients had up to 90 percent arterial blockage were later found to be closer to 53 percent arterial blockage, well below the guideline for requiring surgery.

Upon being presented with these alarming findings, HCA declined to present evidence to the *Times* that it did any of the following:

- Inform state or federal authorities of any illegalities;
- Reimburse Medicare for fraudulent billings;
- Notify patients who might have been entitled to compensation;
- Suspend all doctors accused of performing the unnecessary surgeries; and
- Investigate whether patients were injured or died as a result of the unnecessary surgeries.

However, HCA officials *did* ask for information on "how the physicians' activities affected the hospitals' bottom line," according to internal documents reviewed by the *Times*. This exemplifies how choosing to protect profits over patients can easily turn deadly.

A growing number of hospitals have screening policies to turn away emergency room patients if they appear to have nonurgent conditions unless they make copayments in advance. In one case at Northside Hospital in Florida, a patient with a fever who had been screened as nonurgent and sent away was readmitted two days later suffering from severe respiratory problems. He died the next day. In 2013 the Office of the Inspector General of HHS settled with Donalsonville Hospital in Georgia after one patient suffering from "shortness of breath and chest pain" was turned away when he could not pay the $100 fee for treatment. Each year, the inspector general of HHS settles with hospitals for hundreds of thousands of dollars for violating the patient antidumping statute, which is supposed to prevent hospital emergency departments from refusing to treat people based on their ability to pay.

PAYING FOR HEALTH CARE: VALUE OF CARE

In general, chargemaster prices seem to be based on what hospitals can get away with, not on what services actually cost. The chargemaster codes are so arcane and convoluted as to be impenetrable. In September 2015, *New York Times* writer Gina Kolata wrote about how the Affordable Care Act is trying to change that situation, by showing what services actually cost. This shows why, in part, so many health care providers invested heavily in trying to defeat the Affordable Care Act and now trying to get it repealed.

According to Kolata, the Affordable Care Act, and Medicare too, are "setting new goals for payments based on the value of care. Under such a system, if a hospital does additional tests and procedures or if patients get infections or are readmitted, the hospital bears the cost." That means that now medical centers have to figure out what their services really cost.

Kolata's article points out that hospitals have focused on what insurers would pay, and knew very little about their actual costs. Dr. Vivian Lee of the University of Utah Health Care set up a groundbreaking study on the topic. The study employs an evolving computer program that already has 200 million cost items. The effort is already succeeding in getting answers to how much goods and services actually cost at hospitals and other medical institutions—and those answers are saving money and improving care. MD Anderson Cancer Center in Houston and the Mayo Clinic are conducting their own studies of accurate health care costs. Perhaps these studies are the forerunners to eliminating chargemasters.

DENYING COVERAGE FOR PROFITS

"My name is Linda Peeno .... I am here primarily today to make a public confession. In the spring of 1987, as a physician, I denied a man a necessary operation that would have saved his life and thus caused his death. No person, and no group, has held me accountable for this because, in fact, what I did was I saved the company a half a million dollars for this.

And furthermore, this particular act secured my reputation as a good medical director, and it insured my continued advancement in the health care industry ... I went from making a few hundred dollars a week to an annual six-figure income. In all my work, I had one primary duty, and that was to use my medical expertise for the financial benefit of the organization for which I worked ... And I was repeatedly told that I was not denying care. I was simply denying payment.

... I know how managed care maims and kills patients. So I am here to tell you about the dirty work of managed care ... . I'm haunted by the thousands of pieces of paper in which I have written that deadly word, 'denial.' "

—Testimony of Linda Peeno, former HMO director, before a House Subcommittee on Health and Environment, 1996

Anthem (formerly known as WellPoint), Cigna, Aetna, Humana, and UnitedHealthcare—the largest for-profit medical insurers in the country—along with their competitors, are known as the most avaricious companies in the health care industry. While millions of American families and businesses struggle to deal with skyrocketing health insurance costs, these companies reap billions of dollars in profits. And a 2010 study predicted that private health insurers would earn $1 trillion in new revenue by providing health insurance to millions of previously uninsured Americans. This expanded consumer base of newly insured

Americans is the result of the passage of the Affordable Care Act. Ironically, according to a 2012 *National Journal* "Influence Alley" article, health insurers secretly spent more than $102 million in an attempt to defeat the act.

And to be sure, a sizeable chunk of the increased profits will end up in the pockets of health insurance company executives, who are paid even more than most executives in other industries.

TO INCREASE HEALTH CARE PROFITS, CUT DOCTORS
Enhancing the role of for-profit health insurance companies helped ensure passage of the Affordable Care Act, but it came at a high price. Health insurers are dropping thousands of doctors from their Medicare Advantage plans, a privately run option to Medicare that covers 13 million people. The health insurers cite cuts in government payments as the reason for terminating the doctors and claim that reducing the number of approved doctors will curb increases in insurance premiums.

Health insurers are not explaining why some doctors were cut and others were not. Some critics of the move point out that many of the terminated doctors have private practices in rural or suburban areas, so the insurance companies are economizing by herding people into larger, hospital-affiliated physician groups. Others note that UnitedHealthcare began terminating doctors after its parent company acquired its own physician practices in Florida, California, and other states.

Many of the patients who were treated by their physicians for years are senior citizens who now need to find new doctors. In 2013 a 79-year-old woman in Ohio lamented to CNN that four of her six regular doctors, with whom she had a trusting relationship, would no longer be covered by her Medicare Advantage plan. On the practitioner's end, Arthur Vogelman, a New York doctor who was terminated in late 2013, appealed to UnitedHealthcare for reinstatement, according to the *Washington Post*. But he was denied without any explanation. "It is an outrage," Vogelman told the *Post*. "I have patients in their 80s and 90s who have been with me 20 years, and I'm having to tell them that their insurer won't pay for them to see me anymore. The worst thing is I can't even tell them why."

TO LIMIT INSURANCE CLAIMS, DUMP THE SICK

Doctors aren't alone in being terminated by health insurance companies. For years, insurers have routinely canceled individual health policies through a practice known as rescission. Before terminating policyholders, the insurer must prove the policyholder "materially misrepresented" their medical history or previous conditions when the patient applied for insurance. In 2007 California regulators began investigating Blue Cross of California and its parent company WellPoint (now Anthem) after the insurer began dropping policies held by women diagnosed with breast cancer, pregnant women, and chronically ill patients. Regulators examined a random sampling of 90 cases involving canceled policies and found that the insurer had violated state law in every case. The company ultimately paid millions in fines and restitution to settle the matter.

That same year, then–California Insurance Commissioner Steve Poizner sought a $12.6 million fine against Blue Shield. He said that the company had committed "serious violations that completely undermine the public's trust in our health care delivery system," according to the *Los Angeles Times*, including improper rescissions, failure to pay claims, failure to provide information when claims were denied, and mishandling of member appeals. Despite the fines and reprimands, WellPoint continued canceling the policies of sick patients.

In 2008 a lawsuit was filed against Anthem Blue Cross by the city of Los Angeles. In answering the lawsuit, City Attorney Rocky Delgadillo criticized Anthem, stating, "The company has engaged in an egregious scheme to not only delay or deny the payments of thousands of legitimate claims but also to jeopardize the health of more than 6,000 customers by retroactively canceling their health insurance when they needed it the most."

In 2009 former Cigna insurance executive Wendell Potter admitted that the company's decision to deny health coverage to sick policyholders was motivated by profit. Potter testified at a U.S. Senate hearing that Cigna would routinely "dump the sick" so it could "satisfy their Wall Street investors." Potter also faulted insurance companies for misleading consumers through deceptive marketing practices and for encouraging them to purchase "what essentially is fake insurance" with high costs and limited benefits. After the passage of the Affordable Care Act, it became more difficult for insurers to deny coverage outright. But by terminating doctors, many patients will follow those doctors out of network, which will achieve the same outcome.

Since 2010 and after passage of the Affordable Care Act, it has been illegal for insurance companies to cancel coverage except under limited circumstances: nonpayment, fraud (based on proof of knowingly committing fraud), misrepresentation (based on proof of willful misrepresentation), or the insurance plan isn't ACA compliant and the insurer stops offering it.

UnitedHealthcare has been charged with engaging in illegal practices by consumers, doctors, and government agencies. In one case, New York regulators determined that it used a database that consistently understated the "usual, customary, and reasonable" reimbursement rates. The database used by the UnitedHealthcare to calculate reimbursement rates for out-of-network charges was developed by health data company Ingenix, which was owned by, yes, UnitedHealthcare.

As a result of that investigation and a subsequent $350 million class action settlement with medical associations, UnitedHealthcare was required to close Ingenix and pledged to establish a new independent database. In 2011 UnitedHealthcare rebranded its database company, and it's now doing business as OptumInsight.

For-profit insurance companies have limited constraints on the way they do business and make profits. In large part, this is because under the 1945 McCarran-Ferguson Act, for-profit companies engaged in the "business of insurance" are exempt from having to compete in the marketplace. Insurance companies profit from consumers not only by what they charge them for insurance premiums, but also by what conditions they avoid covering and by what they avoid paying out to medical providers through manipulating deductibles. Insurance companies also pile lavish rewards on their executives and put their shareholders' and Wall Street's interests ahead of patient care. They operate in one of the most profitable and least transparent markets in the country, and they do so with few, if any, checks and balances.

U.S. HEALTH CARE: UNIVERSAL SCAM

"You know, when we see a good idea from another country, we grab it. If they build a better car, we drive it. If they make a

better wine, we drink it. So if they've come up with a better way to treat the sick ... to take care of their babies ... then what's our problem? Why can't we do that?

They live in a world of 'we,' not 'me.' We'll never fix anything until we get that one basic thing right. And powerful forces hope that we never do. And that we remain the only country in the western world without free, universal health care."
—Michael Moore, filmmaker

The United States ranked number 37 among the world's health care systems in the World Health Organization's World Health Report, published in 2000. France was number 1. In most health services categories, the United States scores devastatingly low. In 2015 the National Center for Health Statistics reported the U.S. infant-mortality rate as stalled, giving Americans one of the worst rates in the developed world. Six out of every 1,000 U.S. babies died at birth or in the first year of life, triple the rate of Japan or Norway, and double the rate of Ireland, Israel, and Italy, according to the Central Intelligence Agency's 2015 World Factbook data.

America spends almost one-fifth of its yearly gross domestic product on health care, according to official estimates. That's $3 trillion. If you add up the annual health care costs of ten major countries—the United Kingdom, Germany, France, Italy, Spain, China, Japan, Australia, Canada, and Brazil—the combined total is still less than what America spends annually on health care. Almost every medical procedure costs Americans more than in other developed countries. For-profit health care providers argue that we should be grateful to have better health care than people in those industrialized nations. But the fact is, we don't.

THE UNITED STATES: LAST IN HEALTH CARE IN THE DEVELOPED WORLD
The Commonwealth Fund compares health care systems around the world. On their 2014 list, the United States ranked last compared to Australia, Canada, France, Germany, the Netherlands, New Zealand, Norway, Sweden, Switzerland, and the United Kingdom. The United States was also last in 2004, 2006, and 2010. We remain the only country in the developed world without universal health care.

In a 2015 *Forbes* article, Avik Roy noted, "Many American conservatives oppose universal health insurance because they see it as fundamentally antithetical to a free society. ... But according to the Heritage Foundation, a leading conservative think tank, ten nations [with more economic freedom] than the United States have achieved universal health coverage. It turns out that the right kind of health reform could cover more Americans while increasing economic freedom."

EUROPE: HEALTH CARE IS A BASIC HUMAN RIGHT

According to *Politifact*, "nearly every European nation has signed and ratified the European Social Charter. That treaty's section on health care casts health care as a right." Under the charter, notes *Politifact*, "The system of health care must be accessible to the entire population. To that end, states should take as their main criterion for judging the success of health system reforms effective access to health care for all, without discrimination, as a basic human right."

Countries follow different paths to make good on the promise to provide health care. For example, Great Britain has its national health service, where the government runs the hospitals and pays the doctors and nurses. It may not provide 100 percent quality health care, but it sure takes a lot of the excessive profit out of a basic right. Germany and France have a more complicated mix of highly regulated public and private insurance companies, and—as in America—a law that makes insurance mandatory for everyone.

OUR ELECTED OFFICIALS

When will our elected representatives in Washington, D.C., stand up for people concerning such a basic right as health care and stop allowing the medical and insurance industries to continue stealing from us? The candidates for the 2016 U.S. presidential election on the Republican side have *all* railed against the Affordable Care Act while failing to propose any solutions to the health care crisis. Why? They are beholden to the health care industry because of millions of dollars in political contributions. Only Democratic presidential candidate Bernie Sanders proposes a single-payer system to cover all people in the United States. Hillary Clinton proposes additional consumer protections to the

Affordable Care Act to make it more effective. Both believe strongly that our country's first priority is the health of its citizens.

Eliminating health care fraud and abuse in the future depends on electing committed people to political office, people who are not beholden to lobbyists and political contributors with ties to the health care and medical industries. The issue is whether our elected public servants will choose to stand up to the onslaught of millions of dollars of contributions from the health care industry and defeat its agenda of valuing profits over patients. We will see, starting with a new President and new Congress in 2017.

The real challenge to the new Congress will be strengthening the Federal False Claims Act to allow public spirited lawyers, doctors and whistleblowers to pursue corrupt practices in our health care system to be eliminated. Lawyers like Niall McCarthy, and many others, take on these cases regularly and fight the battle on a daily basis. The real issue in the coming years is how far the health care industry can push Congress to cut back on the FCA.

2

Thugs of Wall Street

"Back in 2000, before they almost ruined the economy and had to be bailed out, the five biggest banks on Wall Street held 25 percent of the nation's banking assets. Now they hold more than 45 percent."
—Robert Reich, professor, former Secretary of Labor

"If crimes are committed they are committed by people, they are not committed by some free-floating entity. These companies and other entities don't operate on automatic pilot. There are individuals that make decisions—and some make the right decisions and some make the wrong decisions."
—Jed S. Rakoff, U.S. District Judge, Southern District of New York

"I don't think anyone went [to] the polls and said, I am casting my vote to make sure that Wall Street has better chances to make bigger profits off the backs of the American people."
—Senator Elizabeth Warren (D-MA)

"I am concerned that the size of some of these institutions becomes so large that it does become difficult for us to prosecute them ..."
—U.S. Attorney General Eric Holder, speaking to the Senate Judiciary Committee in March 2013

Too big to hold accountable?! That statement, or rationale, uttered by Eric Holder, the country's former top law enforcement officer, encapsulates one of the great betrayals in American history. Not only did Wall Street almost bring down the entire world's economy, but it will also never fully be called to account for the ruin of millions of lives, or for the crimes that precipitated the near collapse of the global financial market, or for the abuses that were committed by those who took advantage of the crisis of 2008.

Why? Because the statutes of limitation on those crimes, or the deadline for prosecutors to file criminal charges for crimes committed mostly in the early 2000s, have run out. As a feeble gesture of atonement, just a few months before he left his post in April 2015, Holder gave his deputies 90 days to identify any individuals who could be brought before the U.S. Department of Justice for their actions contributing to America's worst economic crisis since the Great Depression. Still, to this day, there have been no serious prosecutions even though over 9 million people lost their jobs and trillions of dollars of assets were lost in the 2008 recession.

LEHMAN BROTHERS, THE INVESTMENT BANK
The stories are filled with arcane financial terms—derivatives, capital accretion, dark pools. But behind the scenes, it's a drama of greed. Matt Taibbi, writer for *Rolling Stone* and author of *The Divide: American Injustice in the Age of the Wealth Gap,* describes what happened at Lehman Brothers, the 158-year-old investment banking firm that went bankrupt in September 2008:

"That last Sunday evening some of the remaining executives and board members were still unconvinced that the government would actually ... [let] Lehman fail .... When the grim reality ... finally sank in, the company shifted gears.

" 'Traders have no loyalty to anybody,' one former high-ranking Lehman executive explained. ... 'The writing is on the wall: Lehman is dead. So one nanosecond later they're looking for the next trade. How can we make money? And the way we can make money is by marking everything down and getting Barclays to give us big bonuses.'

"The next morning all the principals from both sides ... started working on a deal. Well, two deals actually."

The fake deal was concocted for show and seeming equitability dressed in language about "obligation to Lehman employees." The other deal was done "in the manner of a political coup d'état ... before dawn." In the middle of the night nine

Lehman insiders were paid to move from one team bench to the other. The Lehman board "never had a clue that many of the people who [were] working on the fine print of the pseudomerger were already, in effect, working for Barclays," according to Taibbi. Barclays was the acquiring firm in the deal.

Seventy-six thousand institutions and individuals lost money in the Lehman collapse, among them missionaries in Africa, a lawyer representing a wine workers' union that lost $180,000 in pension money, comedian Bill Maher, and the city of Long Beach, California which two weeks earlier had invested $20 million.

The nine Lehman insiders were the winners in the deal, receiving more than $300 million, essentially for one night's work that made it possible for Barclay's to misappropriate $5 billion.

Also, relief was denied in court to the Lehman creditors. Although the judge agreed that the disclosure problems were real, he coined a term—"the fog of Lehman"—to describe the "confusion, ambiguity, and uncertainty" of the events of the time, which made it impossible to confirm a crime had been committed.

As Taibbi summarized the situation, "The creditors were thrust face-first into the immovable principle that underlies everything modern that Wall Street does: if a crime is complicated enough, and sanctified by enough 'reputable' attorneys and accountants, then American law enforcement will inevitably be too slow or too weak to stop it." There were zero fines and zero prosecutions for the losses caused by the collapse of Lehman Brothers.

LIBOR MANIPULATION

Meanwhile, Wall Street and London insiders conspired to manipulate LIBOR, the London Interbank Offered Rate. LIBOR effectively sets the interest rate for about $800 trillion worth of transactions around the world. This affects the finances of ordinary citizens in everything from their savings to mortgage payments, as well as auto, home, and student loans. It has long been a benchmark of world finance. Almost all mortgages are tied to LIBOR.

Nevertheless, behind the scenes, via text messages and phone calls, the world's interest rate was being bent to the will of hedge funds and big investment banks. Transcripts featuring Jezri Mohideen (Royal Bank of Scotland [RBS] head of yen products in Singapore), revealed the collusion:

Mohideen: What's the call on the LIBOR?

Trader 2: Where would you like it, LIBOR that is?

Trader 3: Mixed feelings, but mostly I'd like it all lower so the world starts to make a little sense.

Trader 4: The whole HF [hedge fund] world will be kissing you instead of calling me if LIBOR move[s] lower.

Trader 2: OK, I will move the curve down 1 basis point, maybe more if I can.

RBS trader Tan Chi Min told colleagues that his bank could move global interest rates. He stated that the bank knew of LIBOR manipulation and supported such actions. In instant messages, a cartel of traders at RBS extensively discussed manipulating the rates.

In March 2008 Tan wanted RBS to raise its LIBOR submission. He complained that his team had lost £200,000 on an earlier lower figure. The year before, Tan had a conversation with traders at other banks, including Mark Wong of Deutsche Bank. The conversation went like this:

Tan: It's just amazing how LIBOR fixing can make you that much money, or lose if opposite … It's a cartel now.

Wong: Must be damn difficult to trade man, especially [if] you [are] not in the loop.

An example of someone hurt by the manipulation is Annie Bell Adams, a 65-year-old American woman who lost her home in the credit crunch. She is the lead plaintiff in a class action suit against 12 of the world's major banks for manipulation of LIBOR which made mortgage payments more expensive than they should have been. The suit alleges the LIBOR was artificially changed, at times when it would have an impact on adjustable rate loans to the detriment of borrowers. If the class action succeeds, it could mean damages in the billions of dollars.

In 2012 Barclays Bank was fined $200 million by the U.S. Commodity Futures Trading Commission, $160 million by the U.S. Department of Justice, and £59.5 million by the United Kingdom (U.K.) Financial Services Authority in London for its role in the scandal. As of mid-2015, JPMorgan Chase, Citigroup, and Bank of America were still under investigation for involvement in the fraud.

THE LONDON WHALE

In Las Vegas the high rollers are referred to as whales. They get free rooms, limousines, plane rides, interesting social playmates, and sometimes are granted exceptions to the rules. They bet large amounts and take risks that other gamblers would not. Bruno Iksil was a trader for JPMorgan Chase and was called the "London Whale." But he didn't go to Las Vegas. He was in London, working at JPMorgan Chase's Chief Investment Office (CIO). Here's how *Bloomberg QuickTake* explained his actions:

"[The] job ostensibly was to hold down the bank's risk level. Instead, the CIO used the $350 billion it had to invest (much of it from federally insured deposits) to become a moneymaker, with its London office focused on complex derivative trades that had less and less to do with hedging." They were pretty good at it. According to *Bloomberg,* for example, one of Iksil's 2011 trades generated $400 million for the firm.

"The trouble came in early 2012, when the bank decided to reduce risk in the swaps portfolio by making more offsetting bets," *Bloomberg* continues. "As the strategy unraveled, Iksil's positions grew so big that they disrupted the thinly traded markets he worked in—earning him the nicknames of *Whale* and *Voldemort.* It made his group's hard-to-unwind trades a target for hedge funds. After the trades collapsed, regulators found that Iksil's colleagues had been keeping two sets of books to minimize the projected size of the losses."

His bets lost $6.2 billion in 2012 for shareholders of the bank—held by many pension funds.

There were many victims of the London Whale scandal. Despite the fact that as much as $51 billion of shareholder value was erased, investors' lawsuits claiming executives and directors of JPMorgan could have prevented the losses were dismissed.

Internally, heads rolled. As Taibbi reported in *Rolling Stone*, "Their first move was to make sure people outside the penthouse boardroom took on all the pain, laying off 7,500 employees and freezing salaries for the non-CEO class of line employees." *Reuters* reported that "most of JPMorgan'[s] job cuts were from positions handling mortgage loans. Some tellers in bank branches were also replaced with financial advisors selling investment products."

Still, JPMorgan Chase CEO Jamie Dimon gained from the whole affair, as the company's board doubled his take-home pay. *Naked Capitalism,* a finance and economics blog, said the board "... thought he bought the bank's way out of trouble on the cheap, disproving the wailing in the financial firm toadying media that the Morgan bank had been ill-treated by the Administration."

Although JPMorgan did have to pay a fine of more than $1 billion levied by U.S. and U.K. regulators in 2013, a negligible sum compared to the losses, there were no prosecutions. And the whale swam away free as U.S. regulators dropped their case against Iksil in 2013.

Iksil's former boss, Javier Martin-Artajo, and a junior trader, Julien Grout, were both indicted by a U.S. grand jury. However, neither face prosecution. Spanish courts refused to extradite Martin-Artajo, a Spanish citizen, and Julien Grout lives in France, which does not extradite its citizens for such actions.

In April 2013, *Bloomberg* summed up the situation this way: "To critics of Wall Street, the real lesson of the London Whale is that megabanks such as JPMorgan are not only too big to fail—they may also be too big to manage and too big to regulate."

WALL STREET SCANDALS ARE TOO COMPLICATED

Since 2008, the public has been inundated with recurring Wall Street scandals. There's so much complex discussion about capital accretion, derivatives, credit default swaps, residential mortgage-backed securities, high-frequency trading, and hedge funds to make even the most well-informed financial wonk feel overwhelmed. This plays nicely into Wall Street's favorite pose when presenting itself to the public and regulators alike, namely, "This is too complicated for you to understand. Leave it to us." It is a culture of self-serving insiders vouching for each other. This is in conjunction with the practice of keeping two sets of books to provide cover for multiple crimes. The bankers employed the advice of an ancient Chinese war strategist who said, "The whole secret lies in confusing the enemy, so that he cannot fathom our real intent."

MRS. WARREN GOES TO WASHINGTON

Sometimes a woman on a mission can bring light to a pool of darkness. In November 2008, Harvard law professor Elizabeth Warren was surprised to pick up the phone and hear Democratic Senate Majority Leader Harry Reid invite her to be part of a Congressional Oversight Panel (COP) monitoring the $700 billion Troubled Assets Relief Program. She was even more surprised when she arrived in Washington and discovered that the COP had no powers but was merely expected to write a report. As Warren wrote in her book, *A Fighting Chance,* "The country was awash in news programs featuring financial experts who spoke about the crisis using language that to most people sounded like gibberish. Collateralized debt obligations, special-purpose entities, synthetic derivatives—whatever the topic, the explanations offered by the talking heads all had the same subtext: *Only the insiders were smart enough to understand what's really going on, so just trust us."*

Warren wrote, "I didn't buy that. In fact I thought it was the oversight panel's job to make sure that *everyone* could understand what was going on." So she and her colleagues on the COP delivered the report—37 pages, with ten specific questions for the Treasury Department to answer including these three:

- Is your strategy helping to reduce foreclosures?
- What have financial institutions done with the taxpayers' money received so far?
- Is the public receiving a fair deal?

What was the answer they got from then– U.S. Treasury Secretary Henry Paulson? As Warren describes it, in the simplest terms, "a big nothing sandwich."

Furthermore, Warren recalls in her book how *ABC News*

summarized the situation: "Rather than write original answers to questions posed ... by a congressional oversight panel, U.S. Treasury officials appear to have creatively repurposed old testimony and even Web site copy into a 13-page report that left some questions entirely unanswered."

She also explains how the COP created another report: The COP listed each question from the first report in one column and the Treasury Department's corresponding response in another. "In the end, out of ten questions, Treasury gave no response or only partial responses to all ten," she wrote. Treasury continued to ignore the committee, but the media picked up on the new report, with the *Boston Globe* commenting, "If taxpayers are spending billions to bail out banks, they deserve to know how that money is used."

Warren says that Treasury Secretary Paulson never did respond to the report, leaving his job two weeks later. President Obama's new team arrived in January 2009, with Timothy Geithner heading Treasury to replace Paulson, Larry Summers as Director of the National Economic Council, and Eric Holder as Attorney General.

ABDICATION OF DUTY BY THE DEPARTMENT OF JUSTICE

To fully investigate the financial malfeasance, the Department of Justice (DOJ) granted immunity to those providing testimony and evidence. But what the DOJ really went after is what was presumed to be important to the banks—their money. Attorney General Holder says he thought fines worked well in dealing with the banks' actions. Citing the multibillion-dollar settlements of recent years, Holder told the *Financial Times* in July 2015, "People tend to undervalue what we did with the banks. Given the nature of the penalties that were extracted, given the interactions that we had with people at the banks, with those attorneys who represented the banks, I think the cultures have changed." This is an extraordinary statement from someone sworn to prosecute criminals as the nation's top cop. And worse, now he is back at a law firm defending those same banks.

THE TALLY

Since 2009, the 25 largest banks in the United States and

Europe have paid $260 billion in fines, according to a Morgan Stanley analysis in August 2015. Bank of America tops the field with $65.6 billion in fines, with another $2.5 billion forecast to come. JPMorgan Chase is in second place with $42.4 billion paid and an estimated $4.5 billion to be set aside for future settlements. The other megabanks comprise most of the rest of the list. These fines and penalties (including $2.6 billion for Morgan Stanley itself) are for actual *crimes*—from mortgage malfeasance and securities fraud to interest and foreign exchange rate rigging and money laundering.

Here are a few recent highlights of such criminal activity: The Consumer Financial Protection Bureau (CFPB) reportedly recovered roughly $10 billion for consumers, mainly through debt cancellation and principal reduction on consumer loans. The CFPB and 47 state attorneys general and the District of Columbia charged JPMorgan Chase with selling millions of dollars of "zombie debts" (debts discharged, not owed, and not collectible) to third-party debt buyers, and with illegal "robo-signing" of court documents to go after consumers for unsubstantiated debts. JPMorgan Chase is on the hook for at least $216 million in fines and penalties for these matters, according to the CFPB.

In another example, Citigroup agreed to pay a $180 million fine to settle charges by the U.S. Securities and Exchange Commission (SEC) of engaging in a municipal bond scam that bilked investors of an estimated $2 billion. The 4,000 well-heeled investors involved were assured their money was safely stowed in a few well-capitalized hedge funds. The extremely risky funds went belly-up during the financial crisis, which Citigroup allegedly knew was a distinct possibility, if not inevitable. In agreeing to pay the fine, Citigroup "neither admitted nor denied wrongdoing" in the matter—the standard get-out-of-jail-free card routinely issued by the SEC in exchange for settlements. Of course, neither the fund manager nor any other employees involved in the fraud was charged. And just two days after Citigroup was hit with a bid-rigging penalty, it was fined another $15 million to settle charges that it failed to enforce policies designed to prevent and detect insider trading.

The truth is, the banks readily accept such fines. Besides being viewed as just a cost of doing business, it's actually part of the game: As in sports, penalties and fouls can be a strategy. The banks are not really paying with their own money, it is shareholders, who are mostly pensions. In the fine print of the settlement documents are tax benefits that greatly reduce the fines and the public is never told this.

THE FACE OF BILLIONAIRE BANKING

JPMorgan Chase CEO Jamie Dimon is a man of charm, charisma, and good looks. It has been said that if there ever were an award for the "Teflon CEO" of the early 21st century, Dimon would win. He also happens to be one of the highest-paid bank CEOs in the world, earning more than $27 million in 2014—a 134 percent increase over the previous year—making him one of the newer members of the $1 billion–plus net worth club.

Under Dimon's leadership, JPMorgan Chase has been charged with an amazing range of criminal and civil misdeeds, which have cost his bank (including its insurance company) billions of dollars in fines. According to reports and filings, the misbehavior includes auto finance deception; "unfair" credit card billings; "check sequencing" (processing consumer checks by size, not chronology, to impose overdraft fees); energy-market manipulation (shades of Enron, whose executives went to prison); fraudulent security marketing; illegal accounting; illegal robo-signing; and faulty foreclosure processing, as well as the previously discussed LIBOR interest rate manipulation.

But the list of misdeeds goes on: money laundering involving drug cartels, mortgage fraud, mutual bond bid-rigging, obstruction of justice, overcharging or wrongfully foreclosing on active-duty men and women in the armed services, shoddy loan servicing, violating trade embargoes against sanctioned countries such as Iran, and violations of the Bank Secrecy Act (in the role as banker for Bernard Madoff's Ponzi scheme). There's also the London Whale matter and many other banking scams.

Through all this Dimon somehow maintains a particular talent. According to the *New York Times*, his defenders explain that much of Dimon's support derives from "his active role in negotiating a string of government settlements that helped JPMorgan move beyond some of its biggest legal problems. ... Just hours before the Justice Department was planning to announce civil charges against JPMorgan over its sales of shaky mortgage investments in September [2013], Mr. Dimon personally reached out to Attorney General Eric H. Holder Jr.—a move that averted a lawsuit and ultimately resulted in the brokered deal." Acting as JPMorgan's chief negotiator, Dimon "worked out a string of banner government settlements," the *Times* reported.

Chummy relationships between Wall Street executives and government officials are common—and settlements worked out in boardrooms and over dinners in private clubs among people who all know how to game the system.

WHEN JAMIE MET ELIZABETH

In early 2013 newly elected Sen. Elizabeth Warren of Massachusetts ran up against Jamie Dimon. He came to her temporary office (located in a trailer) and complained to her about the burdensome rules his bank had to follow. As she recounts in the afterword to the paperback version of her book *A Fighting Chance*:

> "I couldn't believe he was complaining about regulatory constraints less than a year after his bank had lost billions in the infamous London Whale high-risk trading episode. I said I thought the banks were still taking on too much risk and that they seemed to believe the taxpayers would bail them out—again—if something went wrong.
>
> Our exchange heated up quickly. By the time we got to the Consumer Financial Protection Bureau ... we were definitely raising our voices. At this point—early in 2013— [acting director] Rich Cordray ... hadn't yet been confirmed by the Senate, which meant that the agency was vulnerable to legal challenges over its work.
>
> Dimon told me what he thought it would take to get Congress to confirm a director, terms that included gutting the agency's power to regulate banks like his. By this point I was furious.
>
> Dodd-Frank had created default provisions that would automatically go into effect if there was no confirmed director, and his bank was almost certainly not in compliance with those rules. I told him that if that happened, 'I think you guys are breaking the law.'

Suddenly Dimon got quiet. He leaned back and slowly smiled. 'So hit me with a fine. We can afford it.' "

Can you imagine if a member of your family committed a serious crime and you could resolve it by simply paying a fine?

WE'VE BEEN HERE BEFORE: THE ROBBER BARONS

It's easy to compare the actions of Wall Street to the age of the robber barons in the late 19th century when the big trusts controlled the oil, steel, tobacco, and railroad industries. The countervailing action in the early 20th century was the development of strong antitrust legislation and the establishment of the Federal Trade Commission in 1914. The strong will of the public forced the breakup of Standard Oil and other monopolies. But today, those laws have been weakened and are regularly challenged by corporate America.

MIT economics professor Charles Kindleberger, in his classic book *Manias, Panics, and Crashes: A History of Financial Crises,* tracked waves of financial crises over time and defined the symptoms of dysfunctional monetary arrangements. Says Kindleberger, "In a boom, fortunes are made, individuals wax greedy and swindlers come forward to exploit that greed." He advances the opinion that "swindling is demand determined."

Dealing in billions of dollars, the goal becomes clear—as stated by Iago to Roderigo in Shakespeare's *Othello,* "Fill thy purse with money ... Make all the money thou canst." And when the guy at the next desk is getting away with theft and prospering as well, even the most honest person can be tempted and find a way to justify larceny.

As Kindleberger observed, "There is nothing as disturbing to one's well-being and judgment as to see a friend get rich." Janis Joplin put it another way, singing, "Oh Lord, won't you buy me a Mercedes Benz. My friends all drive Porsches, I must make amends."

And talk about rich, Steve Schwarzman, CEO of Blackstone Group, is on his way to being the first head of a public company to be paid $1 billion in a single year. In 2014 he earned (that is to say, "was paid") $690 million, itself a record for a public-company CEO. Assuming the stock market remains in good order and Blackstone offloads more of its properties bought on the cheap,

$1 billion doesn't look that far away, as predicted by *Crain's New York Business*. By comparison Goldman Sachs CEO Lloyd Blankfein earned a mere $24 million that same year.

Schwarzman made a lot of his money through leveraged buyouts during the Great Recession (usually resulting in significant job losses for the unfortunate employees of the acquired companies), and sold securities high in the high-flying stock market of the early 2010s after the recession.

THE RICH GET RICHER

"Bigness is the prejudice of American life ... the axiom being that when something is big it is automatically better .... Thus, we prefer our Big Macs and our Whoppers, our food portions supersized, our big cars and sprawling cities, our enormous football players ..., our big breasts and big penises and big houses ..., our big armies with big reach. ... That we allow corporations to grow to outrageous size is just another symptom of the disease."

—Christopher Ketcham, *Orion Magazine*, March 2010

Financial ethics may be a paradoxical concept in the rarified atmosphere of private-equity firms, which invested $112 billion in the second quarter of 2015 alone. This is the second-highest-recorded level of deal making since 2007. These firms also held $467 billion in "dry powder" (capital on tap). An SEC examination of 150 private equity firms in 2014 found "violations of laws or material weaknesses in controls" relating to hidden fees, poor disclosure, and other problems "50 percent of the time ... a remarkable statistic," said Andrew Bowden, then director of the SEC's Office of Compliance Inspections and Examinations.

With few exceptions, such abuses remain rampant, according to a speech given by Bowden's successor, Marc Wyatt, at a private-equity conference in New York in May 2015. For example, such practices include shifting fees and expenses away from funds created for insiders, friends and family, and "preferred investors" to charge to parallel funds marketed to the less privileged who don't know any better.

"Many managers still seem to take the position that if

investors have not yet discovered and objected to their expense-allocation methodology, then it must be legitimate and consistent with their fiduciary duty," said Wyatt in his speech. "This practice can be difficult for investors to detect, but easy for our examiners to test."

Taking a closer look at the handling of real estate equity funds, the SEC discovered some specific sector-related abuses, especially in what investors are told (and not told) about fees relating to property upkeep. For example, investors are assured that the fees are "at market rate or lower" when such claims are unsubstantiated. "We have seen that the manager collects no data to justify their fees at all," said Wyatt in his conference remarks. "Other times, the data is collected informally through calls to other industry participants and is not documented. Or, when the information is collected, what is presented to investors can be misleading."

In his 2015 speech, Wyatt put the entire industry on notice, concluding: "It is reasonable to assume that the next year may bring additional private-equity actions by the SEC's Division of Enforcement, and so we anticipate heightened awareness of reputational and headline risk by the investor community."

The SEC has already started to move on this. In June 2015, investment firm Kohlberg Kravis Roberts & Co. (KKR) agreed to pay $30 million, plus $24 million in penalties and disgorgement, for "misallocating" $338 million in expenses to investors. In other words, the firm admitted to perpetrating an accounting scam play on investors.

TOOLS OF ENFORCEMENT: THE DODD-FRANK LAW
Enacted in July 2010 in response to the financial crisis of 2008, and cosponsored by Senator Christopher Dodd and Congressman Barney Frank, the Dodd-Frank Wall Street Reform and Consumer Protection Act, includes:

- The Consumer Financial Protection Bureau, an agency to combat abusive mortgage lending practices, simplify documents, and receive consumer complaints;
- Whistleblower incentives, such as monetary rewards (up to 30 percent of the monetary proceeds), for those instigating a lawsuit against a financial company; and

- "funeral plans" and orderly liquidation procedures for "systemically important" banks.

Currently, 33 banks in the United States, Europe, and Asia are listed as systemically important. They include Bank of America, Citigroup, Goldman Sachs, JPMorgan Chase, Morgan Stanley, and Wells Fargo, all of which benefitted from the government's bail-out from the $431 billion Troubled Asset Relief Program, called TARP.

These financial institutions are now required to make "living wills" or "funeral plans" describing how they will shut down—without any financial assistance from the government—if their business goes *kaput*. If you believe they have plans that will actually work, you are one of the few who do.

The Volcker Rule, a provision of Dodd-Frank, outlaws proprietary trading by banks in private-equity and hedge funds, and should curtail some of the more than $40 billion in Wall Street revenue that comes from "market making," which, according the SEC, occurs when a firm "stands ready to buy and sell a particular stock on a regular and continuous basis at a publicly quoted price." It also should prohibit transactions such as those executed in JPMorgan Chase's London Whale episode.

Dodd-Frank also gets personal for Wall Street CEOs—with a couple of key stipulations. The "pay-ratio" provision requires public companies to disclose a CEO's compensation compared to the median pay of the company's employees. This rule was adopted in August 2015 and won't fully go into effect until January 2017, but some data are already available on CEO-to-employee pay ratios. For example, in 2013, Citigroup's CEO salary, $90.8 million, was 132-times more than the median pay of the bank's employees ($73,200). Wells Fargo, the world's biggest bank by market capitalization in 2013, had a CEO-to-employee pay ratio of 141:1. Morgan Stanley's is 93:1 Other megabanks, including JPMorgan, have yet to disclose their pay ratios.

Wall Street doesn't actually lead the pack in compensation for CEOs, which for all CEOs rose 937 percent from 1978 to 2013, while workers' pay barely grew and real incomes declined. For example, drugstore chain CVS's CEO Larry Merlo made $123.1 million in 2013, compared to his employees' average salary of $28,700. That's a ratio of 422:1. Goodyear Tire and

Rubber's ratio is 323:1, and Twenty-First Century Fox's CEO Rupert Murdoch, made $27.7 million, a ratio of 268:1.

"CEOs should not receive outsized pay when their companies underperform," said law professors Steven Bank and George Georgiev in a 2015 report from UCLA. "Company boards, shareholders and policymakers have been trying, and largely failing, to put this simple principle into effect for decades." Shareholders continue to approve stratospheric executive pay regardless of their companies' performance. Successful pushbacks on compensation have been miniscule, despite campaigns by activist shareholders and institutional proxy advisers. And the fact that such resolutions are nonbinding on company boards doesn't help the effort.

Dodd-Frank also gives shareholders "say on pay" for all senior executives, and the right to "claw back" executive bonuses if they are based on false accounting. Bonuses and dividends on Wall Street depend on how well the company performs in the stock market. Jamie Dimon knows all about that. JPMorgan's stock price, which fell as low as $17 a share during the Great Recession, has been in the high-$60 range throughout the first half of 2015. Profits for the company hit an all-time high in the same period; the year 2015 closed at nearly $24 billion.

One notable attempt in 2015 was a shareholder resolution to reduce Dimon's pay package and split up his dual role of CEO and chairman of JPMorgan. The resolution failed, but it got nearly 40 percent of the vote—as well as a contemptuous sneer from Dimon.

"God knows how any of you can place your vote based on ISS or Glass Lewis [proxy adviser firms that backed the resolution]," Dimon told some investors at a conference in May 2015. "If you do that, you are just irresponsible .... And you probably aren't a very good investor, either. I know some of you here do it because you're lazy."

Huge bonuses and executive pay are sure indicators of corporate bloat and signs that someone is making off with someone else's money. Adding insult to injury is the fact that the already high-paid CEOs get to keep a higher percentage of their income thanks in part to a tax ruse called "carried interest," which taxes profits on income from the firm's investments at the significantly lower capital gains rate than the rate for normal income.

For example, $570 million of Blackstone CEO Steve Schwarzman's income in 2014 was taxed at the lower 23.8 percent capital gains rate. This has proven to be a big advantage for other private-equity titans who were also taxed at this rate, such as KKR's co-chairmen and CEOs Henry Kravis ($219 million) and George Roberts ($229 million); CEO of Apollo Capital Management Leon Black ($331 million); and CEO of Carlyle Group, William Conway ($343 million).

Coming out of the Great Recession, the Obama administration suggested, as part of much-needed tax reform, that perhaps the Schwarzmans of the world should be taxed like most of the rest of us. Schwarzman took it personally, and as reported by *Newsweek* in August 2010, he famously expressed his views by telling a nonprofit board that, "It's a war. It's like when Hitler invaded Poland in 1939."

Democratic presidential candidate Hillary Clinton has seen the inside of plenty of boardrooms but says she will go where Obama did not. "There's something wrong when hedge fund managers pay lower tax rates than nurses or the truckers that I saw on I-80 as I was driving here," she told a group of Iowa voters in April 2015.

Even Republican presidential candidate Donald Trump would likely agree. "I would take carried interest out, and I would let people making hundreds of millions of dollars a year pay some tax, because right now they are paying very little tax and, I think it's outrageous," Trump said when his campaign was picking up steam in August 2015. This could, of course, be Trump blowing hot air, as his team most likely saw a Pew Research Center poll in April 2015 that showed 61 percent of Americans feel that "some wealthy people don't pay their fair share" of taxes.

TODAY'S CULTURE OF GREED

Attorney General Holder's prediction about changing the culture in the banking industry turns out to be flat-out wrong. You'd think that he would have known better from his experience representing some of the same clients that he saw being fined. He and his former Justice Department colleagues at the law firm of Covington & Burling may well have the opportunity to represent them again. According to a May 2015 survey of

financial professionals in the United States and the United
Kingdom, "Attitudes toward corruption within the industry have
not changed for the better."

The authors of the report found that more than one-third of
those making $500,000 or more annually say they have seen or
learned of wrongdoing in the workplace. An even higher number,
38 percent, "disagree that the financial services industry puts
the best interests of clients first," according to the report. One-
quarter of the 1,200 financial professionals surveyed overall said
that they "would likely use non-public information to make a
guaranteed $10 million if there was no chance of getting arrested
for insider trading" and 33 percent believe the industry hasn't
changed for the better since the financial crisis. Many of these
numbers are higher than a similar survey conducted in 2012.

THE ASSAULT ON DODD-FRANK

The billion-dollar banking industry is not about to stand quietly
by and let Washington, D.C., dictate to them. Wall Street is
contributing millions of dollars to political candidates who will
work to repeal or greatly eviscerate Dodd-Frank, the law passed
after the 2008 financial meltdown. U.S. Senator and presidential
candidate Marco Rubio is one Dodd-Frank opponent who says
that law has to go. "We need to make America fair for all
businesses, but especially for small biz," he said at a debate in
August 2015 in Cleveland, Ohio. Citing the concerns of small
business while protecting big business is a common theme of
most Republican politicians.

Since its passage in 2010, Congress faced 139 separate
attempts to repeal or amend Dodd-Frank, according to numbers
collected by New York law firm Davis Polk & Wardwell. Some
Dodd-Frank provisions have already been weakened, while
others are being challenged in court, and dozens of specific rules
still remain to be drafted. The way things work in Washington,
for every enforcement rule enacted by Congress, a countervailing
maneuver arises in the halls of finance. Dodd-Frank's
restrictions on derivatives—which were dubbed "financial
weapons of mass destruction" by Warren Buffett—have already
been repealed. This action, tacked on as a provision of the 2010
$1.1 trillion omnibus spending bill, with the help of many elected
Democrats, was a notable win for the banks against taxpayers.

Although some financial executives have tried to stay under the radar in their activities, the biggest money guys, such as Jamie Dimon, seem to openly challenge anyone to stop them. Publicly, the big time CEOs say that their main responsibility is to their stockholders, having long ago jettisoned responsibility to consumers and employees. But now they seem to display growing disdain for even their shareholders. For example, Jamie Dimon scoffs at shareholders who want to reduce his pay, while the Bank of America board of directors decided to ignore theirs.

The Bank of America story goes like this: In 2009, BofA shareholders voted to require an independent chairman, but the board made a few bylaw changes and circumvented the action, leaving CEO and Chairman Brian Moynihan with both jobs, saying that it was in the best interest of the company to retain power in one person. Then in September 2015, a new vote was taken. While shareholders such as New York City's $165 billion pension funds and other large investors voted to strip Moynihan of his chairman title, the bank announced after a 15-minute shareholder meeting that 63 percent of votes cast had supported its move to allow Moynihan to keep both executive positions. "We're happy with the results," Moynihan said after the meeting, which was attended by a crowd of fewer than 100 people.

WHEN JAMIE MET ELIZABETH: ROUND 2

In another example of corporate arrogance that smacks of the assaults on Dodd-Frank, in June 2015, Jamie Dimon disingenuously told a group at the Executives' Club of Chicago "I don't know if [Elizabeth Warren] fully understands the global banking system." The *Huffington Post* reported this under the banner headline: "Jamie Dimon Wants To Mansplain Banking To Elizabeth Warren." It seems clear that Dimon would prefer the former Harvard professor and member of the Senate Banking Committee to not be seen as an expert in the field. It's certainly true that he would prefer for her to see things his way—or just shut up. But thankfully, it looks like that isn't going to happen anytime soon.

Citing the London Whale loss at JPMorgan Chase as a reason to bring back the division between commercial and investment banking, Senator Warren, in July 2015, joined forces with Senator John McCain to introduce a bill to reinstate certain provisions that were in the repealed Glass-Steagall Act.

Then, in September 2015, the Truth in Settlements Act, a Warren-sponsored bill to ensure transparency in government settlement cases, unanimously passed in the Senate.

"The idea behind this bill is straightforward," said Warren in a statement. "If the government is going to cut deals on behalf of the American people, the American people are entitled to know what kind of a deal they're getting." She pointed to a 2013 settlement with mortgage servicers accused of illegal foreclosure practices in which federal regulators claimed the settlement totaled $8.5 billion. However, more than half the value of the settlement—about $5.2 billion—was in the form of credits the servicers could get for agreeing to modify or forgive loans. According to the *Boston Herald,* the undisclosed method of calculating credits could cut the overall value of the $8.5 billion settlement by almost 60 percent. Such details call into question the efficacy of many of the fines and settlements imposed on Wall Street by the DOJ.

JUSTICE MUST GET SERIOUS

In new guidelines announced in September 2015, the DOJ will begin to pursue charges against individuals, not just their employers, in civil and criminal Wall Street investigations. In an interview with the *New York Times,* the memo's author, U.S. Deputy Attorney General Sally Q. Yates, said, "Corporations can only commit crimes through flesh-and-blood people. It's only fair that the people who are responsible for committing those crimes be held accountable. The public needs to have confidence that there is one system of justice, and it applies equally regardless of whether that crime occurs on a street corner or in a boardroom." This echoes the frustration of countless jurists, consumer watchdogs, and ordinary citizens.

In 2010, before signing off on a deferred-prosecution agreement between the DOJ and Barclays Bank, which was guilty of laundering millions of dollars from American-sanctioned countries— including, Iran, Cuba, and Libya—U.S. District Judge Emmet Sullivan in Washington, D.C., angrily declared, "No one goes to jail, no one is indicted, no individuals are mentioned as far as I can determine ... there's no personal responsibility."

In another ruling, U.S. District Judge Jed S. Rakoff in New York reluctantly signed off on a settlement between the SEC and Bank of America that was revised after he had previously rejected it. The judge said he accepted the settlement but was very disturbed because it advocated "very modest punitive, compensatory, and remedial measures that are neither directed at the specific individuals responsible for the nondisclosures nor appear likely to have more than a very modest impact on corporate practices or victim compensation." Rakoff added, "While better than nothing, this is half-baked justice at best." He also faulted a "modest" $150 million fine, which he said "penalizes the shareholders for what was in effect, if not in intent, a fraud by management on the shareholders."

Daniel Tarullo, a governor of the Federal Reserve, said at a gathering in June 2015 at the Council on Foreign Relations in New York, "Once you've had the issues around consumer protection—or lack of protection—over a number of years, when you've had the LIBOR problems, when you've had the Forex problems [foreign exchange rate rigging], it's difficult to say, 'Gee, we just have a few bad apples down there somewhere.'

"There's no substitute for punishing and seriously punishing individuals who have transgressed the law," added Tarullo.

BIGGER THAN EVER

Ironically, the financial crisis and bailout has led to the consolidation of the large banks and financial institutions, making them bigger than ever and securing even more power for financial leaders. As economist James W. Brock noted in a 2008 article he wrote in the *Christian Science Monitor,* what has resulted is:

> "Survival of the fattest, not the fittest—survival of the biggest, not the best. ... A better way—and a more conservative one—would be to prevent such giantism in the first place. ... Instead of celebrating mega-mergers that combine corporate giants, perhaps we should see these combinations as bailout time bombs waiting to explode—and challenge them under US antitrust laws.
>
> We should consider antitrust as more than a policy to promote competition and the economic benefits that flow from

it. We should also value it as a vital instrument for upholding principles of private enterprise ... by preventing too many economic eggs from being consolidated into too few, too big baskets. When those gigantic baskets fail, everyone gets splattered."

THERE IS A MADOFF HAPPENING EVERY DAY

For over forty years, our law firm has represented victims of Ponzi schemes. We have seen a high school football coach defrauded by his former players, graduates of Stanford University defrauded by fellow alumni who were their golfing buddies, and other con men who have defrauded senior citizens, doctors, professional athletes, and other small-time investors.

Banks and Wall Street help people like Bernie Madoff, the man thought to have orchestrated the largest Ponzi scheme in history. For over 40 years, Madoff was well-respected on Wall Street for his brilliant investment strategy known as "split strike conversion." In December 2008, he knew facts were getting out and he turned himself in to the authorities admitting that his company Bernard L. Madoff Investment Securities LLC ("BMIS") was "basically, a giant Ponzi scheme" and that there was "no innocent explanation" for his fraudulent conduct. The truth was that for decades Madoff had not purchased a single security, but instead had used the funds from new investors to pay interest to pre-existing investors. On June 29, 2009, District Court Judge Denny Chin sentenced Madoff to 150 years in prison. Judge Chin called Madoff's actions "extraordinarily evil."

Immediately after Madoff turned himself in, our firm was inundated with telephone calls from people who had been defrauded by Madoff. For the next few months, we met with victims of this massive fraud and filed lawsuits on behalf of the victims. As part of litigating the case, my law partner Nancy Fineman and I were able to negotiate an interview with Madoff's lawyer and were the first and only lawyers to interview Madoff in prison.

On July 28, 2009, Nancy Fineman and I spent four hours in the visitors' room at the Butner Federal Penitentiary in North Carolina interviewing Madoff. In his prison uniform and tennis shoes, Madoff still had his arrogant demeanor as he tried to convince us that he never intended to defraud anyone and that no one else assisted him in the fraud. His story was not believable, but connected some dots in identifying those who aided and abetted in the fraud.

A number of Madoff's cohorts, including Madoff's brother Peter Madoff, his right-hand man Frank DiPascali, lawyer and accountant Paul Konigsberg, and others who worked for Madoff, pled guilty to involvement in the fraud. Prosecutors convicted 15 others. Yet these individuals could not have accomplished the fraud alone. It took accountants, banks, and others to move the money around and allow the Ponzi scheme to flourish for as long as it did.

One key to Madoff's success was the "feeder funds," large institutions, like Tremont and Fairfield Greenwich Advisors, who conducted minimal due diligence, and continued to invest their clients' money into BMIS even though, as Madoff told us in our prison interview and we later confirmed, Madoff never let these companies see any documentation supporting the investments.

A key to Madoff's success was his London operation, Madoff Securities International, Ltd. ("MSIL") where Madoff laundered money back and forth between New York and London through his JP Morgan Chase account to create the illusion that BMIS was a successful business. As Madoff stated at his sentencing:

> "There were also times in recent years when I had money, which had originated in the New York Chase Manhattan bank account of my investment advisory business, transferred from the London bank account of Madoff Securities International Ltd. to the Bank of New York operating bank account of my firm's legitimate proprietary and marketing making business. That Bank of New York account was located in New York. I did this as a way of ensuring that he expenses associated with the operation of the fraudulent investment advisory business would not be paid from the operations of the legitimate proprietary trading and mark making business."

These transfers through the JP Morgan account violated

money laundering laws and other banking requirements. In January 2014, JP Morgan agreed to pay $2.6 billion to resolve criminal and civil claims related to Madoff.

While Madoff's Ponzi scheme was one of the largest, it was not unique and there is another Madoff scheme occurring every day. Con men and women who convince unsuspecting investors, with no way to discover the fraud of their own, to invest in a fraudulent scheme, a scheme which could be stopped by the bankers, accountants, and lawyers who remain silent to reap financial rewards rather than performing their duties and conducting adequate due diligence.

MEGA-MERGERS: A BILLION DOLLARS IN FEES TO SAVE TAXES

As the holiday season rolled around at the end of 2015, Pfizer (maker of Viagra) and Allergan (maker of Botox) announced a mega-merger. *ThinkProgress*, an independent news site, reported, "After more than 160 years, America's second-largest drug company is moving out—and taking tens of billions in unpaid tax dollars with it, forever. Pfizer will merge with Dublin-based Allergan and relocate its executive offices to Ireland to minimize its U.S. tax liabilities, the companies announced... . At about $160 billion, Pfizer's inversion deal will be the largest ever. ... The Wall Street advisors that help shepherd such deals to completion have raked in about a billion dollars in fees from such mergers in recent years."

One such advisor is former U.S. Representative and Republican House Majority Leader Eric Cantor, now vice chairman and managing director of investment bank Moelis & Co. Moelis, is part of the team advising Pfizer; JPMorgan Chase and Morgan Stanley are advising Allergan. The banks advising Allergan stand to earn collectively between $140 million and $180 million in the deal, while banks advising Pfizer could make between $80 million and $100 million in total, depending on the final purchase price, according to estimates by consultancy Freeman & Co.

So it's more bonuses for Cantor and Dimon, while the country loses tens of billions of dollars in tax revenue. It's tragic when you consider what that kind of money could be used for in the public interest.

As these companies get ever bigger, the American public suffers. Alan Pyke, author of the *ThinkProgress* article, has a cogent analysis: "In general, companies that fixate on minimizing their tax liability contribute far less to real economic growth and job creation than those that don't spend as much time on accounting gimmicks. The Fortune 500 companies with the highest tax rates from 2008 to 2010 added about 200,000 jobs on net from 2008 to 2012, while the firms that achieved the lowest tax rates laid off a net 51,289 people in the same window. The divergence there is between companies that are looking to manufacture healthy financial reports for shareholders and those that are actually growing their business's production capacity and customer base."

The above is just the tip of the iceberg. Google saved $2.4 billion in the worldwide taxes in 2014 by shifting $12 billion in international revenues to a Bermuda shell company, Alphabet Inc. The story goes on and on and only a few elected officials want to take them on—why—read chapter 3 and the story of the case of *Citizens United*.

GOING FORWARD

The forces of big money on Wall Street are well financed and well entrenched. The concept of "too big to fail" may be hard to shut down, even if the majority of people oppose it and more responsible leaders are elected to run our country. Whether Democrat or Republican, our congressional representatives will never really take on reform unless we change campaign contribution laws and reverse rulings such as *Citizens United*. Money is power, and the looting of America will continue until the people responsible go to jail. Individuals must be held accountable, and until we remove the "fog of Wall Street" and elect or appoint responsible prosecutors and legislators, the rigged game will continue.

We cannot let government lawyers rotate in and out of big law firms to make the big dollars from clients they formerly agreed to regulate. Eric Holder was but one small example of the revolving door that protects Wall Street. Holder is now ensconced at the prestigious law firm of Covington & Burling in

Washington, D.C., where he worked before he became U.S. attorney general. As the *New York Times* reported the week Holder rejoined the firm in July 2015, "Covington already employs a number of former Justice Department officials, including Lanny Breuer, the former assistant attorney general for the department's criminal division under Mr. Holder; Mr. Breuer's successor, Mythili Raman; and Michael Chertoff, a former assistant attorney general and secretary of Homeland Security."

We must appoint more federal judges like Jed Rakoff, Emmet Sullivan, Charles Breyer, Dean Pregerson, Thelton Henderson, Susan Illston, David Carter, Claudia Wilkin, Beth Freeman, Lucy Koh, Vince Chhabria, Maxine Chesney, Ed Chen, Denise Cote, Marianne Battani, Marsha Pechman, Michael Fitzgerald, Jacqueline Nguyen, Shira Scheindlin and William Young and the many other federal and state judges who stand up and speak out on the many abuses—particularly financial ones—of our society. Failing to do so will put our country at great risk of further financial upheaval in the future. CEOs with their Wall Street money and their Wall Street lawyers should not be allowed to overrun our judiciary. It may be the only branch of our government left to protect the American people against the thugs of Wall Street.

According to the *Washington Post*, even Donald Trump said, "hedge fund managers are getting away with murder under the current corporate tax code" and blames the megabanks for the financial crisis of recent years. He once called Jamie Dimon the worst banker in the United States.

Hillary Clinton has been pulled in the direction of taking on Wall Street by people like Bernie Sanders, Elizabeth Warren and many others in our Senate and House who are willing to stand up against the money. The time to stop the influence of Wall Street money is in the election of 2016 and the appointments made by our next President. The world will be watching the United States to see if wealthy people will continue to dominate our government. Our country's future is in the hands of our young people when it comes to the thugs of Wall Street. We have almost 50 million people living in poverty and this can't continue in a nation with such wealth.

3

Money Equals Free Speech: The Case of *Citizens United*

"The rich have the right to buy more cars, more vacations, more leisure, but they don't have the right to buy more democracy."
—**Bill Moyers**

"Where enough money calls the tune, the general public will not be heard ... And a cynical public can lose interest in political participation altogether."
—**Justice Stephen Breyer, from his dissenting opinion in *McCutcheon v. FEC***

"Citizens United *was about me. Think how that makes me feel. A lot of people don't know that, but the backstory is eye-opening."*
—**Hillary Rodham Clinton**

Politics today comes down to one thing—Money.

CITIZENS UNITED: UNITED AGAINST DEMOCRACY

When it comes to the landmark 2010 U.S. Supreme Court case *Citizens United,* Hillary Clinton knows all too well that the genesis of the case was about her. It was founded on sleaze, at a level that was remarkable, even for politics in today's world. One could argue that the 2016 Presidential Primary topped all sleaze but the road to *Citizens United* case is unmatched.

Floyd Brown made his reputation on an infamous TV commercial featuring Willie Horton, the convicted murderer released from prison under a weekend furlough program supported, though not initiated, by Michael Dukakis, who was then the governor of Massachusetts. After Horton raped a woman and knifed her fiancé while on furlough, his story became a hammer to clobber Dukakis for being weak on crime. The commercial was the brainchild of Lee Atwater, the controversial Republican campaign operative, but it came to life through Americans for [George H. W.] Bush, an independent campaign committee, and its political director, Floyd Brown.

In 1988 Brown founded a new organization, Citizens United. In 1992 the group took on the Clinton campaign, publishing the book *Slick Willie: Why America Cannot Trust Bill Clinton*. The organization worked tirelessly on all fronts to attack Bill and Hillary Clinton. It issued a barrage of stories about the Clintons' failed real estate investments and offered a 1-900 number to callers who wanted to pay to hear alleged edited selections of telephone conversations between Bill Clinton and model/actress/singer Gennifer Flowers.

President George H. W. Bush called the Flowers phone line "the kind of sleaze that diminishes the political process," reported the *New York Times*, while Mike McCurry, Clinton's press secretary, accused Brown of being "personally responsible for some of the sleaziest politics this country has seen."

David Bossie, who had worked as Brown's chief researcher, took over as president of Citizens United in 2000. Writing for the *New Yorker,* Jeffrey Toobin described a pivotal move that would prove to change the course of political events. "Bossie's epiphany came in 2004, when he saw advertisements for Michael Moore's movie *Fahrenheit 9/11.* He recognized that a documentary could be a twofer. *Fahrenheit 9/11* and the television commercials promoting it were ammunition aimed against President Bush's re-election and also a potential source of profit. Bossie decided to turn Citizens United into a movie studio, to produce conservative documentaries."

In 2007 Brown and Bossie, along with Clinton's disgruntled former campaign manager and adviser, Dick Morris, created a 90-minute film titled *Hillary: The Movie* with the tagline "If you thought you knew everything about Hillary Clinton, wait 'til you see the movie." The documentary is heavy on commentary from Morris, Newt Gingrich, and others.

The strategy was to release the movie at the beginning of 2008, as Democratic primary voters began choosing between Clinton and Obama. But the Federal Election Commission blocked Citizens United's plan to promote the movie in television advertisements, saying the commercials amounted to an election-time message that would require disclosure of the group's donors to federal regulators and a message disclaimer at the end of each ad. The group hired attorney James Bopp, Jr., and sued.

CITIZENS UNITED ROUND 1: DISTRICT COURT

"In January 2008, James Bopp got laughed out of court—literally," according to a 2011 story in *Mother Jones* magazine. "The white-haired lawyer from Terre Haute, Indiana, was appearing before a federal three-judge panel in Washington, D.C., to argue that his client, a small conservative nonprofit named Citizens United, should be able to air *Hillary: The Movie* on on-demand TV during the Democratic presidential primaries. Citizens United had produced the film to show that Hillary Clinton was a 'European socialist' and ruthless political schemer—a cross between Machiavelli and Lady Macbeth...."

However, the *Mother Jones* article continued, "The Federal Election Commission (FEC) told Citizens United that it couldn't air or advertise the film during primary season, because it amounted to a 90-minute campaign ad that didn't identify who'd paid for it. In court, Bopp argued that the movie wasn't so different from what you'd see on *60 Minutes,* and its creators deserved First Amendment protections."

U.S. District Court Judge Royce Lamberth said in response, "You can't compare this to *60 Minutes*. Did you read this transcript?"

A three-judge appellate panel agreed with the FEC, ruling that Citizens United was prohibited from broadcasting *Hillary: The Movie* because it was akin to paying to have the film shown on television within 30 days of the 2008 Democratic primaries. For the well-funded Citizens United, it wasn't over, and the fight continued.

CITIZENS UNITED ROUND 2: REVIEW BY THE U.S. SUPREME COURT

Citizens United disagreed with the district court's backing of the FEC and sought review by the U.S. Supreme Court. In an unexpected turnaround, the Supreme Court reversed the district court, striking the prohibitions in the Bipartisan Campaign Reform Act that prohibited corporations, including nonprofits and unions, from making independent expenditures and "electioneering communications." In other words, in a 5-4 decision, the nation's high court said the rights of corporations, nonprofits, and labor unions to spend money on federal political causes is protected by the First Amendment's right of free speech. The following highlights key questions and answers during oral argument before the Supreme Court in March 2009.

Cast of Characters

Lawyer for Citizens United: Former Solicitor General Theodore Olson

Lawyer for the FEC: Malcolm L. Stewart, Deputy Solicitor General

The Court: Associate Justices Ruth Bader Ginsburg, Stephen Breyer, David Souter, John Paul Stevens, Clarence Thomas, Anthony Kennedy, Antonin Scalia, and Samuel Alito, and Chief Justice John Roberts.

ALITO: That's pretty incredible. You think that if ... a book was published, a campaign biography that was the functional equivalent of express advocacy, that could be banned?

STEWART: I'm not saying it could be banned. I'm saying that Congress could prohibit the use of corporate treasury funds and could require a corporation to publish it...

Justice Anthony Kennedy, considered a "swing" justice in some areas but a reliable conservative vote on campaign-spending cases, later interrupts Stewart, interjecting: "Well, suppose it were an advocacy organization that had a book. Your position is that under the Constitution, the advertising for this book or the sale for the book itself could be prohibited within the 60- ... the 30-day period?

STEWART: If the book contained the functional equivalent of express advocacy. That is, if it was subject to no reasonable interpretation.

ROBERTS: If it has one name, one use of the candidate's name, it would be covered, correct?

STEWART: That's correct.

ROBERTS: If it's a 500-page book, and at the end it says, "And so vote for X," the government could ban that?

STEWART: Well, if it says "vote for X," it would be express advocacy and it would be covered by the preexisting Federal Election Campaign Act provisions.

According to Adam Winkler, UCLA constitutional law professor and commentator on the Supreme Court, that was the "gotcha" moment, turning what might have been a fairly dull case about campaign finance into a battle over government censorship. Unwittingly, Stewart seems to be supporting the idea that the government can censor a book based on a single phrase. Stewart tried to backtrack, but to many legal pundits the government's case was over at that point.

CITIZENS UNITED: BEHIND THE SCENES
At the time the decision in *Citizens United* was still pending following oral argument, Associate Justice David Souter was in the process of retiring from the Court and is said to have written a stinging dissent that documented behind-the-scenes machinations in the case. *New Yorker* writer Toobin claims to have seen Souter's original dissent on the case, which he describes as "including an accusation that [Chief Justice] Roberts violated the Court's procedures to get the outcome he wanted."

Toobin described Souter's intended dissent as "an extraordinary, bridge-burning farewell to the Court" that Roberts felt "could damage the Court's credibility."

As a result of internal wrangling among the justices over the outcome of *Citizens United*, Chief Justice Roberts proposed re-argument of the case six months later. This time, however, the question to be addressed by both sides was broader than the original. It was, moreover, a rare re-argument. When the case was first heard in March, it centered on whether the restrictions on corporate spending in the 2002 McCain-Feingold campaign finance law applied to the documentary *Hillary: The Movie*. This time, the Court raised the much broader question of whether it should abolish all restrictions on political spending by corporations under the freedom of speech rationale.

CITIZENS UNITED ROUND 3: SIX MONTHS LATER

By September 2009 when the case came up for re-argument, the cast of characters had changed. Associate Justice Sonia Sotomayor had just been appointed to the Supreme Court in August, and Elena Kagan was the newly appointed Solicitor General representing the Federal Election Commission (she would not be appointed to the Court until August 2010).

The stakes were higher now, with the Court considering a broader question of whether all restrictions on political spending should be abolished on the basis of freedom of speech.

According to the *New York Times*, Kagan said, " 'The government's answer has changed' and the Federal Election Commission had never tried to regulate the book distribution."

It came down to this exchange between Kagan and Justice Roberts as reported by the *Times:*

> "Ms. Kagan all but said that a loss for the government would be acceptable, so long as it was on narrow grounds.
>
> "She suggested to the justices that Citizens United might not be the sort of corporation to which some campaign finance restrictions ought to apply. What the Supreme Court should not do, she said, is overrule two earlier decisions and thereby allow all kinds of corporations to spend money to support or oppose political candidates, principally through television advertisements.
>
> "Chief Justice Roberts Jr., on hearing the government's position, accused it of engaging in strategic behavior.
>
> " 'So you want to give up this case,' Chief Justice Roberts said to Ms. Kagan, 'change your position, and basically say you lose solely because of the questioning we have directed on re-argument?'
>
> "Ms. Kagan did not go that far. But she said, 'If you are asking me, Mr. Chief Justice, as to whether the government has a position as to the way it loses, if it has to lose, the answer is yes.' "

A 5–4 decision with an opinion written by Associate Justice

Kennedy representing the majority with Chief Justice Roberts and Justices Thomas, Alito, and Scalia. Justice Stevens dissented, joined by Justices Ginsburg, Breyer, and Sotomayor. Stevens felt so strongly that he read 20 minutes of dissent from the bench, a rare move that traditionally signifies severe disagreement with the majority.

In part Justice Stevens said in his dissent:

> "The real issue in this case concerns how, not if, the appellant may finance its electioneering. Citizens United is a wealthy nonprofit corporation that runs a political action committee (PAC) with millions of dollars in assets. Under the Bipartisan Campaign Reform Act of 2002 (BCRA), it could have used those assets to televise and promote *Hillary: The Movie* wherever and whenever it wanted to. It also could have spent unrestricted sums to broadcast *Hillary* at any time other than the 30 days before the last primary election. Neither Citizens United's nor any other corporation's speech has been "banned" ....
> All that the parties dispute is whether Citizens United had a right to use the funds in its general treasury to pay for broadcasts during the 30-day period. The notion that the First Amendment dictates an affirmative answer to that question is, in my judgment, profoundly misguided. Even more misguided is the notion that the Court must rewrite the law relating to campaign expenditures by *for-profit* corporations and unions to decide this case."

CITIZENS UNITED: UNINTENDED CONSEQUENCES

"The thing that they're [Citizens United] most famous for is something they never set out to do," said Fred Wertheimer, president of Democracy 21, a group advocating stricter campaign finance rules, in an *AP* story. "They're proud of the super PAC world that they never intended to create. Their lawsuit just became a vehicle for five justices hostile to campaign finance laws." But in taking the credit for the Supreme Court decision, the group claimed they intended this outcome all along.

"The movie was created with the idea of establishing a vehicle to chip away at the decision," said Nick Nyhart of Public Campaign in the *Washington Post*. "It was part of a very clear strategy to undo McCain-Feingold." Bossie himself confirmed that contention in the *Post*, saying: "We have been trying to defend our First Amendment rights for many, many years. We brought the case hoping that this would happen ... to defeat McCain-Feingold." And James Bopp, the legal strategist behind *Citizens United,* has dedicated much of his career to removing restrictions from campaign finance law.

SUPERPACS: UNLEASHING GREAT SUMS OF MONEY

In the wake of the *Citizens United* decision, Super PACs emerged with the potential to fundamentally alter the landscape of money in politics. That's because as of July 22, 2010, the FEC green-lighted Super PACs, all but eliminating previous limitations on political donations. Thanks to the FEC ruling, individuals, corporations, and unions can now contribute unlimited cash to Super PACs, which essentially means there is no ceiling on how much money can be injected into elections.

The main prohibition placed on Super PACs, aside from having to report their expenditures and contributors to the FEC, is that they cannot coordinate directly with the campaign staff of individual candidates. (Regular PACs have to abide by these same mandates as well.) There is another key difference: Super PACs can't contribute directly to candidates the way PACs do. The money Super PACs raise can only be used for such things as creating TV or radio ads supporting or excoriating particular candidates.

SETTING UP A SUPER PAC: ASK A COMEDIAN

> *"Not even the actual news reporters want to cover campaign finance. We decided that we would just see how far we could go. And it turns out that, like everyone else raising money in politics, we can pretty much do what we want."*
> **—Employee of *The Colbert Report* who declined to be named in the *New York Times,* in keeping with the secrecy of Super PAC-hood**

In 2011, in the wake of the *Citizens United* decision, comedian Stephen Colbert described the $60 million spent by Super PACs as a "megaphone of cash." To understand the situation from the inside, he started one himself. In May 2011, the *New York Times*'s media columnist David Carr reported that Colbert applied for Super PAC status with the Federal Elections Commission and was approved the following month. "This is 100 percent legal and at least 10 percent ethical," Colbert told the *Times*.

It was quintessential Colbert. He had mocked conservative talk show hosts by pretending to be one for nine years, and now he was making fun of Super PACs by actually creating one. The *Times* article reported that more than 165,000 fans of his Comedy Central show *The Colbert Report* signed up, "many of them sending along money to finance his evil plot to make fun of campaign finance abuse."

Colbert's Super PAC, Americans for a Better Tomorrow, did what Super PACs do. His committee spent money on advertising in Iowa during the run-up to the Ames straw poll in August 2011, suggesting "all the soft-money ads with their soft-focus shots of rural tableaus were exposing the children of Iowa to "cornography," reported Carr in the *Times*.

Colbert's committee "paid for broadcast ads that criticized spending on behalf of the Texas governor, Rick Perry, who had multiple Super PACs raising money for him even before he declared his candidacy for the Republican nomination," noted the *Times*. One ad "suggested that participants in the straw poll should write in the name 'Richard Parry,' saying the rogue 'a' 'stands for America' and for 'IowA.' Two television stations in Des Moines ran the ad, while a third, WOI-TV, refused, saying that it would confuse voters."

Carr described Colbert's actions this way: "Mr. Colbert has taken the equivalent of a political homework assignment and sprinkled a little silly sauce on top, and people seem happy to dig in."

Carr also reported a few other people's responses. Sheila Krumholz, executive director of the Center for Responsive Politics, said Colbert was "taking on a serious subject that many Americans find deadly dull and is educating the broader public on why it matters and what is at stake." And University of Maryland broadcast journalism professor and investigative reporter Mark Feldstein said that Colbert's Super PAC was "hilarious and very effective" and that he has taken "advantage of loopholes to set up an organization that is not a legitimate political action committee, if there is such a thing, to make the point that the current system is a form of legalized bribery."

SUPER PACS: SOMETHING OLD, NOTHING NEW
You might be surprised to know that the first Political Action Committee was formed in 1944 by the Congress of Industrial Organizations. Its purpose was to re-elect President Franklin Delano Roosevelt. The union used the PAC to dodge Congress's extension of the corporate money ban to unions. They weren't using dues, so it wasn't illegal.

Taft-Hartley came along in 1947 and banned both corporations and unions from making independent expenditures to federal political campaigns. Candidates could campaign with publicly funded dollars so long as they promised not to use their primary money during the general election or collect private donations. Those promises must have been good enough because it wasn't until about 20 years later that Congress decided to finally collect campaign finance reports.

SLOW GOING: CAMPAIGN FINANCE REFORM
Campaign finance reform moved slowly and incrementally through the 1970s. We got the little box to check on tax forms to donate $3 to the Presidential Election Campaign fund from the 1971 Revenue Act. That same year the Federal Election Campaign Act (FECA) became law and provided restrictions on and clarifications of campaign finance laws. Post-Watergate, Congress amended the FECA in 1974 to set limits on contributions, facilitate disclosure, and manage the public funding component. It also established the FEC to enforce the laws.

In 1976, in a foreshadowing of *Citizens United,* the Supreme Court struck down some of the campaign finance restrictions in the five-year-old FECA in its *Buckley v. Valeo* decision, stating that FECA restrictions violated the First Amendment. According to a *Washington Post* article on campaign finance reform, this decision lifted caps on "campaign spending and candidate and family contributions to their own campaign," and corporations and unions could do "electioneering for 'issue advocacy,' as long as they didn't say words like 'elect.' "

The see-saw wrangling on campaign finance meandered through the '90s. The Supreme Court upheld Michigan's law banning corporations from using company money for independent expenditures, ruling that Michigan had a compelling state interest in stopping corruption. On the other hand, President George H. W. Bush vetoed a bill that would have provided partial public financing for congressional candidates.

The win for those who wanted to keep big money out of elections was the McCain-Feingold Bipartisan Campaign Reform Act (BCRA) in 2002. As the *Washington Post* article on campaign finance reform noted, the law's goal was to limit use of "soft money," which grew after FECA was put in place. Soft money was the kind "raised by national parties and political actions [*sic*] committees for 'get-out-the-vote' campaign efforts and other organization-building activities," the *Post* article continued. "Because the money's purpose is sort of mushy, the laws regulating it were equally vague. Parties were raising unlimited funds for these activities and using them for wider purposes than just voter registration. After BCRA, this type of fundraising was deeply curtailed." Federal fundraisers "didn't know what things they'd been doing for decades were now illegal."

Since 501(c)'s and 527s were exempt from the soft-money ban, interest in these groups escalated. However, as the *Post* noted, they were banned from certain types of electioneering, notably for the *Citizens United* case, ads were not allowed 30 days before a primary or 60 days before an election. Direct advocacy for a candidate was also prohibited.

Political entities of several stripes went after the BCRA. Senator Mitch McConnell, the California Democratic Party, and the NRA challenged the law in court as too broad and limiting their First Amendment rights. In 2003, the Supreme Court upheld the law. At that time Justice Stevens wrote, "money, like water, will always find an outlet."

CITIZENS UNITED RIPPLE EFFECT

As part of the 2010 *Citizens United* case, "the Supreme Court held that independent expenditures by corporations and labor unions were protected by the First Amendment," noted the *Washington Post* in its campaign finance reform article, striking down the previous BCRA prohibitions against those campaign expenditures. Later in the year, the article continued, the D.C. Circuit Court of Appeals applied the *Citizens United* ruling to another case, *Speechnow.org v. FEC*. The federal judges ruled any argument "that unlimited independent expenditures would lead to corruption were invalid" and in the chief judge's words, " 'plainly have no merit after *Citizens United.*' "

REMOVAL OF SPENDING LIMITS ON INDIVIDUALS

Shaun McCutcheon, CEO of Coalmont Electrical Development in Alabama and self-described Republican Party activist, had generously donated to Republican candidates for more than a decade when in 2012 he ran up against a limit. He had given $33,088 to 16 federal candidates and more than $25,000 in noncandidate contributions during the 2011–2012 election cycle. But he wanted to give more. He intended to donate to an additional 12 federal candidates, bringing his contribution total over the federal-aggregate limit. McCutcheon filed suit against the FEC, joined by the Republican National Committee.

The resulting ruling in 2014 opened the floodgates. The U.S. Supreme Court ruled that aggregate contribution limits—caps on the amount of money any single donor can give to candidates and party committees—infringed on First Amendment rights. In many states, aggregate limits were already nonexistent. In other words, the biggest impact of this case was the removal of aggregate spending caps on PAC contributions.

Time magazine calculated that "[a] single donor can now theoretically spend up to $3.5 million supporting each and every candidate for the House and Senate ... a figure that doesn't include contributions to political action committees." Since there is no limit to the number of PACs that can exist, donors could up their contributions to certain candidates through multiple PACs.

NEW AGE OF PACS: DELUGE OF DOLLARS

Here's how Trevor Potter (Colbert Super PAC advisor) explains the situation to the *Washington Post*, "Donors now essentially have a choice as to whether their contributions will be disclosed. They can give directly to Super PACs, which disclose their donors, or they can give to a 501(c)(4) or (c)(6) or other "non-political" organization, which does not publicly disclose its donors. The 501(c) organizations can spend money on the very same campaign ads that a Super PAC can, or it can even give to a super PAC."

By 2014 the effect of *McCutcheon* was already making itself felt. According to the Center for Public Integrity, outside groups spent more than $220 million in U.S. Senate races just for television ads. Meanwhile parties spent more than $43 million on TV ads that year.

Americans for Prosperity, the organization of billionaire industrialists Charles and David Koch (who are also the well-known forces behind political spending for many conservative candidates), spent at least $125 million for Republican politicians in 2014 races, according to a story in Politico. For the 2016 election cycle, it has been widely reported that the Koch brothers have budgeted $889 million. Some have estimated that this could go up to $1 billion.

DARK MONEY: U.S. LEADS IN HIDDEN POLITICAL SPENDING

In the United States "there is the unusual spectacle of secret money finding its way into elections," reported the Sunlight Foundation in 2014. "During the midterms, independent groups spent almost $770 million on elections. Of that, at least $145 million was made up of dark money—contributions hidden from the public, but almost certainly known to the politicians who are the beneficiaries of it. The amount of dark money the U.S. spent in an off year was almost three times as much as the 31 million pounds (about $50 million) Great Britain spent during the entire general election in 2010."

The nonprofit, nonpartisan Sunlight Foundation's goal is to use technology and journalism to make government and politics more transparent. Its article on U.S. political finance points out that other countries may have secret money in elections, "but even among the most corrupt countries..., such transactions are technically illegal, even if the laws are not enforced."

In contrast, the article continues, in the U.S., "anyone who has the resources and the will to influence elections and elected officials need not risk violating the law with under the table transactions. Instead, they can engage in legalized bribery by funneling money through so-called "social welfare" organizations.

Influence peddlers can set up their own nonprofits to pay for election ads, but if that's too much work, they can take advantage of one of the many dark money organizations already in existence."

THE U.S. CHAMBER OF COMMERCE: POLITICAL
COVER FOR SALE

The U.S. Chamber of Commerce is the most powerful business lobby in the country. It is a 501(c)(6) tax-exempt organization that spent more than $30 million on the 2014 midterm elections and has made keeping its donors secret a marketing tactic. As noted by the *Washington Monthly*, "A large part of what the Chamber sells is political cover. For multibillion-dollar insurers, drug makers, and medical device manufacturers who are too smart and image conscious to make public attacks of their own, the Chamber of Commerce is a friend who will do the dirty work. 'I want to give them all the deniability they need,' says [the Chamber's president and CEO Tom] Donohue.

Prior to Donohue's arrival in 1997, the chamber "used to be a trade association that advocated in a bipartisan manner for narrowly tailored policies to benefit its members," according to *SourceWatch.org*, a collaborative encyclopedia published by the Center for Media and Democracy. The chamber's budget in 2010 budget was approximately $200 million, and as a trade organization, its donors can remain anonymous, reported *SourceWatch*.

The *New York Times* in October of 2015 revealed Donohue's longtime advocacy for the tobacco industry, reporting, "After taking over the chamber, Mr. Donohue fought the Justice Department's tobacco litigation, personally lobbied against antismoking legislation in the Senate and promised 'a unique role in determining the future direction of the U.S. Chamber of Commerce' to a big cigarette maker in a letter.

"In the early 2000s, Donohue publicly vowed to fight 'outrageous tobacco settlement fees in state after state.' Chamber lawyers filed briefs on behalf of cigarette makers that challenged class-action suits, punitive damages awards and the validity of racketeering claims."

His latest effort is having the chamber and its foreign affiliates pressure "governments around the world to turn back antismoking legislation," the *Times* continued. "That pits Donohue against groups like the World Health Organization, whose officials refer to the Chamber as a tobacco industry front group." This move by the chamber has led to some defections, notably CVS Health.

Green Chamber of Commerce, a business network that supports the development of sustainable business practices, often characterizes the U.S. Chamber of Commerce as an organization that is "dominated by oil companies, pharmaceutical giants, automakers and other polluting industries." The *New York Times* reported in October 2010 that almost half of the U.S. chamber's $140 million in contributions in 2008 came from only 45 big-money donors, and that "many of those large donations coincided with lobbying or political campaigns that potentially affected the donors." "Revenue at the chamber has grown to $164 million in 2013, from $76 million a decade earlier," reported an October 2015 *Times* article. "Including its various affiliates, the total rises to $260 million."

"Show me the Money" proclaims a plaque on Mr. Donohue's desk. The October 2015 *Times* article says, "It could refer to his predilection for chauffeured Lincolns and chartered flights, or his $5.5 million paycheck in 2013, more than 10 times what his predecessor earned in his last full year ... . It is also a reminder that under his watch, the chamber has become a fund-raising juggernaut."

The latest targets for the chamber is the Consumer Financial Protection Bureau and its champion Elizabeth Warren. The *Times* reported in November 2015 that the Chamber wanted to block the agency "by lobbying lawmakers to attach a rider to the federal budget bill that would force the bureau to conduct a new study before issuing any rule."

" 'If the Chamber of Commerce thinks they are going to slip a provision into a spending bill that cuts off consumer rights without a fight, they are very much mistaken,' Senator Warren said," the *Times* article continued.

THE LEWIS POWELL MEMO: PRECURSOR TO *CITIZENS UNITED*

The Chamber of Commerce has a long history and strategy, much of it dating from to the 1971 Lewis Powell Memo. Then a corporate lawyer and board member of 11 corporations (including Philip Morris), Lewis Powell wrote a memo to his friend Eugene Sydnor, Jr., director of the U.S. Chamber of Commerce. It was dated August 23, 1971, about two months before Powell's nomination by President Richard Nixon to the U.S. Supreme Court.

The Powell Memo did not become known to the public until after his confirmation to the high court, when it was leaked to Jack Anderson, a liberal columnist. According to an article on *Reclaim Democracy*'s website, Anderson warned that Powell "might use his position on the Supreme Court to put his ideas into practice ... in behalf of business interests."

"Though not the sole influence, the Chamber and corporate activists did take Powell's advice to heart and began building a powerful array of institutions designed to shift public attitudes and beliefs over the course of years and decades," reported the *Reclaim Democracy* article. "The memo influenced or inspired the creation of the Heritage Foundation, the Manhattan Institute, the Cato Institute, Citizens for a Sound Economy, Accuracy in Academe, and others."

The article notes that "evidence is mixed" on whether Powell's political views influenced his judicial decisions. On social issues, he proved to be a moderate, often surprising his supporters. But he was in favor of expanding corporate privilege in his 1978 majority opinion in *First National Bank of Boston v. Bellotti*. The decision effectively created a First Amendment "right" for corporations to influence ballot questions. Which brings us right back to *Citizens United*—and to the Chamber of Commerce's ongoing interest in the activities of our Supreme Court.

POST-*CITIZENS UNITED:* RISE OF THE MEGADONORS

"Five years after the Supreme Court's *Citizens United* ruling ditched decades of campaign finance laws and ushered in an era of mega-donors ..., the flood of big money into the 2016 elections has been unprecedented—and unpredictable," noted a 2015 op-ed by longtime political journalist Peter H. Stone in the *Sacramento Bee*. "Altogether, Republican and Democratic super PACs in the first half of 2015 roped in almost $255 million," Stone continued, "almost double the $130 million raised by all the candidates' campaigns in the same period, according to the nonpartisan Center for Responsive Politics. Overall, GOP super PACs pulled in $235 million, while Democratic ones raised just $19 million." Here are some examples:

Right to Rise USA, a super PAC backing Jeb Bush for president, raised more than $118 million by the time he dropped out of the race.

Unintimidated, a super PAC for Wisconsin Governor Scott Walker, a favorite of the billionaire Koch brothers' donor network, had raised $20 million before he terminated his run for president.

Opportunity and Freedom, the super PACs using different variations of this name, raised a total of $16 million for former Texas Governor Rick Perry before he ended his run for president.

Keep the Promise. Senator Ted Cruz of Texas benefits from four affiliated super PACs—all with variations of the same name. One of the super PACs, Keep the Promise I, got $11 million from hedge fund executive Robert Mercer and then turned around and donated $500,000 to Carly Fiorina. As of January 2016, Keep the Promise III, has raised nearly $16 million.

CITIZENS UNITED: THE BACKLASH

A September 2015 *Bloomberg* poll found that although the ruling was fashioned by the Court's conservative majority, registered Republicans oppose *Citizens United* 80 percent to 18 percent and Democrats oppose the decision 83 percent to 13 percent. Independents also oppose the ruling 71 percent to 22 percent.

The American people have expressed their rejection of *Citizens United* in multiple ways. Petitions from such groups as moveon.org, People for the American Way, and democracyisforpeople.org expressed opposition to the decision; almost 700 cities and towns from California to the east coast, have asked Congress to pass a constitutional amendment to overturn *Citizens United;* and 16 states have already issued statements and resolutions calling for an end to *Citizens United*.

BACKLASH AGAINST CORPORATE FREE SPEECH: PUBLIC MATCHING FUNDS

"If we throw up our hands at any attempt to seek solutions,

saying it's too late, there is too much money, we'll never fix it," said a 2014 article on the Sunlight Foundation's website, "U.S. election spending will continue to run ahead of everyone else, leaving our democracy very much behind." The *Citizens United* and *McCutcheon* decisions have lit a blaze under the opposition to unfettered political spending. Lawmakers and public-interest groups are pushing legislation and proposing constitutional amendments to slow and reverse the corporate free speech movement. The Brennan Center for Justice is urging the finest legal minds in the land to build "a new jurisprudential movement" and "a vision of the Constitution as a charter for a vibrant democracy."

According to the National Conference of State Legislatures, several states—Arizona, Connecticut, Florida, Hawaii, Maine, Maryland, Massachusetts, Michigan, Minnesota, New Mexico, Rhode Island, Vermont, and West Virginia—have their own forms of publicly financed elections for some or all statewide and legislative offices. Maine has probably been the most successful to date, with a majority of Maine legislative candidates of both parties using public funding since 2000, when it was first available.

LAWRENCE LESSIG'S MOONSHOT: TO OVERTURN *CITIZENS UNITED*

Lawrence Lessig, an American academic, attorney, and political activist, became a candidate for the Democratic Party's nomination for president in 2016. He was running on one issue— overturning *Citizens United*. In April 2014 he explained in the *Atlantic* why a public figure should run a campaign with a mandate of reform:

> "We want reform. We just don't trust that we can actually get it. We believe we have a corrupt system. But we don't believe insiders when they tell us they will fix it.
>
> "This is the politics of resignation. ... We are resigned precisely because we view the very process by which we would effect change as corrupt. ... Yet the reformers I know ... think small. They call their thinking "realistic."
>
> "But it is precisely this "realism" that begets our resignation. If we're going to crack it, we need escape

velocity. A Saturn V, not a belief in Flubber. A thunderclap, not a few more reformist members of Congress. We must show Americans something unlike anything they've seen before. We must give them a reason to believe—plausibly—that something fundamentally different is possible.

"A moonshot takes a president ... ."

Lessig stated that, if a well-respected public figure—such as David Souter, Christine Todd Whitman, or Michael Bloomberg—were to take up this issue and were elected, he or she should use that mandate to pass Lessig's proposed reforms, and then immediately resign from office and transfer power to the vice president. Four months after his *Atlantic* article, Lessig announced that he was running for president. Unfortunately, Lessig's moonshot was aborted because he was unable to qualify for the Democratic debates. Still, the campaign of Bernie Sanders, and Hillary Clinton have stood strong against *Citizens United* in the face of old guard Republicans.

THE 28TH AMENDMENT: USING THE CONSTITUTION FOR POLITICAL CAMPAIGN SPENDING REFORM

In April 2015, Linda Greenhouse wrote in an op-ed in the *New York Times* about Justice John Paul Stevens, "In his final term on the court, Justice Stevens was a vigorous dissenter from the *Citizens United* decision, ... and in his Senate testimony in April [2014] he repeated his longstanding view that 'while money is used to finance speech, money is not speech.' He told the senators that the problem stemmed from the 'fundamental error' in the 1976 decision in *Buckley v. Valeo,* in which the Court held that while campaign contributions could be capped, the First Amendment barred restrictions on so-called independent expenditures."

Stevens's 2014 book, *Six Amendments*, proposes a constitutional amendment to guard against unchecked campaign spending by corporations, and help preserve truly democratic elections for future generations. Greenhouse notes that Stevens had testified to the Senate that the Supreme Court's *Buckley v. Valeo* decision was in error and should be corrected: "Neither the First Amendment nor any provision of this Constitution shall be construed to prohibit the Congress or any state from imposing reasonable limits on the amount of money that candidates for public office, or their supporters, may spend in election campaigns."

GOING FORWARD

There is little doubt about what the decision in *Citizens United* is doing to our democracy. Everyone has to get onboard to rid our country of this vehicle that allows Wall Street thugs and corporate money to overwhelm our elections. As with Wall Street money and influence, the only branch of government that can determine the future of our elections is the judiciary. The appointments to our Supreme Court by future presidents will determine the future of our country—that is—if they have the integrity and guts to take on big money.

4

The Public's Money

"You can't just take the public's money and give it to yourself or give it to your friendly employees or members of the city council, just because you want to."
—Jerry Brown, California Governor and former Attorney General

"This case is the age-old tale of abuse of political power …. Should a politician and his family be entitled to more just because they have power?"
—Assistant U.S. Attorney Tatiana Martins, opening statement in the trial of former New York State Senator Dean Skelos

"Corrupt public officials undermine our country's national security, our overall safety, the public trust, and confidence in the U.S. government, wasting billions of dollars along the way."
—Patrick Bohrer, FBI Special Agent

PUBLIC MONEY THEFT

As Democratic Speaker of the New York State Assembly, Sheldon Silver was the second-most-powerful politician in the state of New York. But apparently that wasn't enough. A 35-page charge sheet compiled over 15 years detailed how he enriched himself with millions worth of bribes and kickbacks until his arrest and resignation in 2015.

In exchange for delivering public grants to a New York mesothelioma doctor, Silver received the names of potential clients, which he passed on to an asbestos litigation law firm. Asbestos claims are very big business and can be worth significantly more in damages than other toxic exposure cancers because mesothelioma is usually very painful and fatal. Silver was on the law firm's payroll and although Silver did no actual legal work for the firm, the kickbacks came to him masked as legal fees.

And still that was not enough. Silver became impatient with how long it took for his kick-back checks to get to him in the mail. So the managing attorney at the firm took it upon himself to deposit the checks directly into Mr. Silver's account. Clearly a testament to how valuable a resource he was.

The investigation into Silver stems from the Moreland Commission, the New York State anticorruption probe that was looking into several Albany lawmakers before Governor Andrew Cuomo abruptly shut it down. Preet Bharara, a very courageous U.S. attorney for the Southern District of New York, took the commission's files and said his office would continue the work. In an October 2015 radio interview, he described New York's government as "a little bit of a corruption disaster." *New York* magazine called arresting Silver "a bold move by Bharara, and right now many Albany lawmakers must be worried that it's just the first of many."

In November 2015, a New York jury found Silver guilty on charges of corruption in a scam to make almost $5 million in fees from a cancer doctor and local developers. Prosecutors told the jury that Silver gave public money in return for client referrals to his law firm.

In December 2015, the Republican president of the New York Senate, Dean Skelos, and his son were convicted of numerous felonies, including bribery, after only eight hours of deliberation by a jury.

Skelos stepped down in May 2015 after being charged with alleged extortion and bribery involving various businesses, the proceeds of which he allegedly passed on to his son, who was also charged. Silver and Skelos had control over a New York budget of almost $150 billion. It took a very dedicated U.S. Attorney, Preet Bharara, and his assistants to crack these top people.

That makes 30 New York lawmakers who have been charged with various forms of criminal or ethical (mostly criminal) misconduct, in the past 15 years, according to the *Associated Press*. That's an average of two a year, for everything from bribes to sexual corruption. New York is not unlike many other states in our country, all of which have corrupt public officials. At least in government, money corrupts, it seems, and leads to the exercise of undue influence and coercive power. It happens in many small cities, towns, and even local school boards across the country every day of the week.

BELL, CALIFORNIA: CROOKS AND SCANDAL

In Los Angeles County there is a small, blue-collar town of 35,000 called Bell, where Robert Rizzo, the city's administrator, found a way to get rich. A man with a penchant for gambling and Cadillacs, expensive cigars and booze, according to the *Los Angeles Times,* he only had limited means. But through the clever use of a loophole in a state law and a little creative voter fraud, Rizzo was able to indulge in his vices, and along with others in Bell's government, were able to live in luxury.

Rizzo paid himself $1.5 million in annual compensation and paid six-figure salaries to the part-time city council members. In comparison, the president of the United States earns $400,000 per year and the Los Angeles County Chief Executive Officer earns $355,000. Rizzo also received an unusually large package of benefits, including paid vacation, sick, and personal time totaling 28 weeks per year.

In contrast, Bell laid off employees, cut services, illegally increased property and sewer taxes, and raised money by unfairly towing and impounding cars. Meanwhile, a state investigation revealed, city officials raised Rizzo's salaries 16 times by double-digit percentages and gave themselves yearly raises of 16 percent beginning in 2001. They billed the city for enormous amounts of overtime and vacation allowances and for board meetings that lasted a few minutes or didn't happen at all. They also racked up huge retirement guarantees from the state's public pension funds. By the time the fraud was revealed, Bell was carrying $77 million in debt—three times its annual revenue—and its credit rating was in junk territory mainly as a result of a failed land deal engineered by Rizzo and approved by the city council.

Bell's chief of police, Randy Adams, was paid a salary of $457,000 and was looking for a pension of nearly half-a-million dollars a year after declaring himself disabled. And he seemed to know what he was getting into and perhaps even had a sense of what the market would allow. In the process of negotiating his salary while being hired he emailed his old friend, Angela Spaccia, Bell's assistant city manager, "I'm looking forward to see you and taking all of Bell's money?! Okay ... just a share of it.!!"

Spaccia wrote back: "LOL ... well you can take your share of the pie ... just like us!!! ... We will all get fat together.... Bob has an expression he likes to use on occasion ... Pigs get Fat ... Hogs get slaughtered!!! So as long as we're not Hogs ... All is well!"

Rizzo pillaged city funds to give himself and other city officials loans. He used his city loan to buy a second home and other expensive diversions, including a gelding named "Depenserdel'argent," which is French for "spend money." After years of investigation and great delay, in March 2013, five members of the Bell city council were found guilty of giving themselves inflated salaries. In October 2013, Rizzo pleaded no contest to 69 corruption felonies, and the following year, he pleaded guilty to federal tax charges related to him claiming more than $770,000 in phony losses, mostly on his horse ranch. In April 2014, Rizzo was sentenced to 12 years in prison and ordered to pay $8.8 million in restitution for the state charges, as well as sentenced to 33 months in prison for the federal charges. In December 2013, Spaccia, Rizzo's second-in-command, was convicted of 11 corruption felonies.

The Bell scandal was uncovered because *Los Angeles Times* investigative reporters Jeff Gottlieb and Ruben Vives, were suspicious about the neighboring city of Maywood, which was in such dire financial straits that it had outsourced many of Maywood's city services to Bell. That put the reporters on the track and they discovered that Bell city officials were receiving unusually large salaries, perhaps the highest in the nation.

Though we usually picture Los Angeles as a city teeming with cars and millions of people, some adjacent towns, like Bell and Maywood, are quite small, which made them ripe targets for the plucking. And pensions were the popular fruit to go after.

Just five miles south of downtown L.A. is the tiny city of Vernon, population 113 (not a misprint). The CalPERS (California Public Employees' Retirement System) caught up with Vernon's former city administrator, Bruce Malkenhorst, and cut his pension from $551,000 to $115,000 after he pleaded guilty to misappropriating public funds in 2011. He was convicted of misappropriating public funds to pay for golf, massages, meals, and political contributions and sentenced to three years' probation. He was also ordered to pay $95,000 in penalties and restitution. His successor, Eric Fresch, made about $1.6 million a year and was looking at an estimated pension of $300,000. In June, one month after CalPERS informed Fresch that his expected pension had been cut to zero and when a state audit threw the book at Vernon city administrators, Fresch was found dead in a state park in the Bay Area. The Marin County coroner ruled his death an accidental drowning.

The second season of HBO's *True Detective* is loosely based on the City of Vernon, and a number of the scenes were shot there. One of the key plot points in the series revolves around the gruesome murder of the fictional city chief administrator. Bell, Maywood, and Vernon are the tip of the iceberg when it comes to small town corruption around the country—with many officials simply looking the other way.

PUBLIC CORRUPTION: OLD AS TIME

Corruption makes for great drama and it's certainly not new—from the Egyptian pharaohs and corrupt senators in ancient Rome, to European monarchs living lavishly thanks to taxation without representation. America has added its own colorful scandals: the Teapot Dome, in which during U.S. President Warren Harding's administration, Secretary of the Interior, Albert Fall, gave oil leasing rights to private oil companies without competitive bidding; the political patronage of New York's Tammany Hall; and ABSCAM, which took place in the early 1980s and involved the investigation of 30 political figures. Among those 30 politicians, a total of seven Congressmen—six members of the U.S. House of Representatives and one U.S. Senator—were convicted of taking bribes from FBI agents posing as Arab businessmen. The story was turned into the comedy/drama feature film *American Hustle*.

Corruption continues, despite anticorruption laws, prosecutorial fervor—and surely by now the knowledge that one is highly likely to get caught (didn't they see the movie?). Avarice is alive and well and running strong through the veins of too many elected and appointed officials, from Washington to our local governments.

"When they call the roll in the Senate, the Senators do not know whether to answer 'Present' or 'Not Guilty.' "
—Theodore Roosevelt

BETTER OR WORSE TODAY?

Is the situation getting better or worse? If you are a glass-half-empty pessimistic kind of person you are probably overwhelmed with outrage by the limited number of investigations and convictions. If you are a glass-half-full optimistic kind of person you might point to the conviction count as evidence that we are finally catching some of these corrupt officials, and in record numbers. Whatever your perspectives, there is no doubt that the situation has been exacerbated by the economic challenges of the past decade.

FINANCIAL TAPEWORMS

Tax revenues are hitting all-time lows and public pension systems that rely on tax revenues as a source of funding are being depleted. No less a sage than Warren Buffett, the billionaire "oracle of Omaha," declared in a shareholder letter: "Local and state financial problems are accelerating, in large part because public entities promised pensions they couldn't afford. Citizens and public officials typically under-appreciated the gigantic financial tapeworm that was born when promises were made that conflicted with a willingness to fund them."

You would think, for instance, that California public pension administrators would have caught Rizzo and his co-conspirators in Bell when they learned about the Bell officials' massive salaries that were wholly inconsistent with the norm in small working class cities like Bell. Those salaries, after all, promised to put a big drain on the pension system. The pension administrators were apparently asleep while Bell officials were busy milking the system with enhanced benefits schemes, government-sanctioned tax avoidance plots, and pay-to-play scams. Everyone in Bell knew their turn to make money would come if they could just keep the carousel spinning long enough.

As the toll of the 2008 financial meltdown shrunk assets in public pension funds across the nation, and pension administrators realized they would not have enough income to meet their obligations to retirees, public scrutiny and audits revealed a disturbing picture of problems with pension officials, public employee unions, and government workers themselves. It was, as one columnist put it, "an economic [Hurricane] Katrina" waiting to happen.

In some cases, it is all about mismanagement of pensions, leaving the working and middle classes to struggle in the future. Many states, counties, and cities are in the same situation.

HOW PENSIONS ARE SCAMMED

Some employees have figured out how to game the system. Here are some of the ways they have increased their personal pensions.

Manipulate the "high three." Federal and state government pensions are typically based on years of employment and the highest average pay earned during three consecutive years, which might or might not be that of the final three years. The *Los Angeles Times* reported in 2014 that CalPERS hasn't allowed so-called salary spiking since 1993. However, 20 of California's 58 counties don't participate in CalPERS so those employees who are close to retirement can strategize how to inflate the "three consecutive years" rule by legally racking up overtime, bonuses, car allowances, and deferred paid vacation and sick days to receive hugely inflated pensions for the rest of their lives. In an outrageous rationale, "Ventura County officials have defended the practice, arguing that some pension boosts were meant to make up for pay freezes during lean years," according to the paper.

Government leaders at every level know what's going on but do nothing to control and limit the pension obligations that our grandchildren will be paying for.

Get a "Public Safety" pension. City administrators in Vernon, California, inflated their pensions to get more generous benefits afforded police officers and firefighters for their service to "public safety," according to the *Los Angeles Times*. CalPERS found that Vernon erroneously awarded "public safety" pensions to staff attorneys, including Eric Fresch, who already earned as much as $1.6 million as city administrator and city attorney. Similar examples of this ploy have taken place in Florida and Oregon.

Fake disabilities. And the Oscar goes to … New York City police and fire department retirees. Coached by a couple of ex-cops, more than 100 former civil servants—over a 26-year period—learned an artful script that netted them lucrative Social Security payouts totaling $21 million. The *New York Post* reported how retired police officer Joseph Esposito would coach other retirees to receive a "psychiatrics infirmity" diagnosis: "You're gonna tell them, 'I don't sleep well at night. I'm up three, four times. Usually I nap on and off during the day,' " Esposito was recorded telling defendant Jacqueline Powell in January, according to a phone wiretap. At some point, "they're liable to say ... 'Spell the word *world*,' so you go '*W-R-L-D*.' Then, they're gonna say, 'Spell it backwards.' You think about it, and you can't spell it backwards."

Manhattan's district attorney estimated that as many as 1,000 people could be involved in the scam and that the total tab could run to $400 million. According to New York news accounts, the four instigators, including an ex-FBI agent and an 89-year-old pension adviser, taught retirees how to get anywhere from $20,000 to $50,000 a year in fake claims.

The *Post* also reported that about half of the 102 defendants falsely claimed that they suffered post-traumatic stress from working at Ground Zero after the terrorist attacks of 9/11. Some of them said they "couldn't sleep, do simple arithmetic, or even leave their own home—but investigators found that they'd been piloting helicopters, riding Jet Skis, teaching karate, deep-sea fishing, and even running half-marathons."

The King-for-a-Day Scam. The New Yorker scam artists seemed to take their cues from the Boston Fire Department, where the practice of faking an injury and then retiring, often on the same day that a firefighter was filling in for a supervisor, had sent the rate of disability retirement soaring to 74 percent of all retirements, according to a *Boston Globe* investigation, more than twice the rate in similar-size cities. And with a disability retirement, the bulk of a firefighter's pension is tax-free.

According to the *Boston Globe*, 167 Boston firefighters between 2003 and 2008 reported career-ending injuries while working, and a majority of them claimed they were injured on the same day they were filling in for a supervisor. Firefighters become eligible to receive a pension at a supervisor's pay level if they are injured while filling in for their supervisor, a practice known as "king for a day."

U.S. District Judge Edward F. Harrington blasted the disability pension system, saying it is "patently flawed and abuses the taxpayers of the City of Boston .... It should not be allowed to continue in its present form. The United States Government deserves great credit for exposing this travesty of a disability system to public scrutiny."

"Pay-to-Play." In several states, including California and New York, enormous pay-to-play schemes rewarded middlemen or "placement agents"—some former pension advisers or board members—for steering pension dollars to certain investment firms. Pension funds are multibillion-dollar enterprises that need to invest their money to generate retirement income for pensioners, such as with—hedge funds, private equity firms, and others need that money ... badly.

And placement agents are willing to pay people big bucks if they can steer the money in their direction. But it's not always good for the pension funds. They can often wind up investing with firms that charge excessive fees or don't offer the best returns, or worse.

In New York, for instance, the private equity firm Riverstone Holdings was accused of paying a placement agent $5 million to steer the state pension fund to invest $530 million with Riverstone, according to the *New York Times*. A Riverstone co-founder even invested $100,000 of his own money to finance a low-budget movie, entitled *Chooch*, that was being made by the brother of the pension fund's chief investment officer. Then-Attorney General Andrew Cuomo's major investigation, which began in 2007, eventually netted multiple convictions and settlements, including $30 million from Riverstone two years later.

As the scandal widened, former New York State Comptroller Alan Hevesi pleaded guilty in 2010 to approving $250 million in pension fund investments in exchange for almost $1 million in gifts. He was the sole trustee of New York's vast pooled pension system—valued at more than $125 billion, the third largest in the United States. Hevesi essentially admitted to selling pension investment contracts to money managers, for which he served 20 months in a medium-security prison. (He had already resigned from the comptroller's job in 2006 after pleading guilty to using state employees to act as chauffeurs for his wife.)

Hevesi's top political consultant, Hank Morris (who was also the placement agent who took the money from Riverstone), pleaded guilty to violating securities law, served more than two years in prison, and paid the state pension fund $19 million. Six others also pleaded guilty in the scandal, and other firms involved paid hefty sums to settle civil suits.

However, it seems that a $30 million fine isn't enough of a deterrent for Riverstone. Just a few years after paying the fine in the New York investigation, Riverstone, along with its parent company the Carlyle Group, and others, was sued by two police and firefighters' pension funds for alleged misconduct resulting in multibillion dollar investment losses. The misconduct? Bribery in Angola by a Riverstone energy company to get oil drilling rights and falsely claiming that a well had oil reserves when it didn't.

Targeting pension funds is big business for Riverstone, and paying fines appears to be just part of the cost of doing business.

STATES LEADING IN CORRUPTION

When something happens in the Big Apple it gets full media attention and people everywhere shake their heads as though acknowledging that those New Yorkers are expected to engage in something newsworthy. But while New Yorkers may brag about being the biggest and best at everything, it's still a contest for crookedness.

Writer Harry Enten, who covers politics for the website *FiveThirtyEight,* had this to say about corruption in the 50 states:

"We can look at the absolute number of public officials convicted in federal court on corruption. On that score, New York was No. 1 from 1976 to 2010 with 2,522 convictions. California was No. 2, Illinois No. 3, Florida No. 4 and Pennsylvania No. 5. Yet it's clear from this list that the most corrupt states are also the states with the biggest populations."

On a per capita basis, "Louisiana is the most corrupt state, followed by Mississippi. New York drops to No. 11 on the list, and California falls to 34th. The least corrupt states are Washington and Oregon. This way of measuring corruption also has problems. Remember, these are only federal crimes. Plenty of corruption falls outside the purview of U.S. authorities. Some acts are technically legal but clearly unethical. We don't know how many corrupt officials are never caught."

Oguzhan Dincer and Michael Johnston of Harvard University's Center for Ethics were concerned that federal prosecutors have a lot of leeway in what they investigate, so they surveyed 280 state political reporters to ask them how corrupt they thought the branches of their respective state governments were.

Here's how the Harvard authors of the survey categorized and defined Harvard state corruption:

(1) **Illegal corruption.** "Private gains in the form of cash or gifts by a government official, in exchange for specific benefits to private individuals or groups."

(2) **Legal corruption.** "Political gains in the form of campaign contributions or endorsements by a government official, in exchange for providing specific benefits to private individuals or groups, by explicit or implicit understanding."

Aggregating their results across the branches of state government and for both legal and illegal corruption, Kentucky emerges as the most corrupt state, according to an analysis of the Harvard data by *FiveThirtyEight*'s Enten. "Mississippi drops to No. 7, and California rises to No. 9. New Mexico, which was in the 30s in per capita federal convictions emerges as fifth. The least corrupt state, according to local reporters, was Massachusetts, even though in terms of federal convictions per capita it ranked in the top 25," Enten wrote.

MAYORS MARCH TO PRISON

In recent years, the rogues' gallery of corruption has grown faster than their portraits can be hung.

Former New Orleans Mayor Ray Nagin, a national and local hero after Hurricane Katrina in 2005, fell into disgrace in 2014 with his conviction on 20 counts of corruption. The feds said Nagin took more than $200,000 in bribes, as well as personal services and free travel, in a kickback scheme in which businessmen sought contracts and favorable treatment from the city in the aftermath of the devastating natural disaster. He was sentenced to ten years in prison.

Although it may have surprised people outside Louisiana who bought into the one-time mayor's image as a reformer, Nagin's conviction couldn't have elicited much shock in the Bayou State, which federal records show as possibly the most corrupt in the nation. According to the *Times-Picayune,* Department of Justice data reveals that between 2002 and 2011, Louisiana convicted 403 government officials of crimes "involving abuses of the public trust," nearly nine convictions per 1,000 residents.

It's a fitting modern twist on the Bayou State's colorful history, which ranges from "The Kingfish," Governor Huey Long, one of the masters of political machines in the 1930s, to four-term Governor Edwin Edwards, who was convicted of extortion during his last term in office, eventually serving eight years in prison.

But data shows that Louisiana is not the most corrupt state. Not to be outdone by Louisiana, Florida led the country in convictions of public officials, with 781 between 2000 and 2010. Maybe it was something in the water: Three suburban Miami mayors were arrested within a month of each other in 2013, two in a kickback and bribery scheme and one on charges of taking under-the-table payments from a company that wanted to build a health clinic.

The following year, in 2014, North Carolina Mayor Patrick Cannon was arrested on suspicion of taking $48,000 in cash, plus other gifts, as bribes. Unfortunately for him, the gifts were in exchange for using his office to help FBI agents, who were posing as real estate investors. What's that they say about real estate? Location, location, location. Well, Cannon was certainly in the wrong place. He was convicted and sentenced to 44 months in federal prison.

In 2014, former state senator, Leland Yee, was charged with racketeering, accepting bribes from FBI agents, and other crimes. What brought Yee down was an FBI investigation into a Chinatown gang leader, Raymond "Shrimp Boy" Chow. As the FBI probed Chow's dealings in illegal guns, liquor, and cigarettes, it also found evidence of money laundering—and a trail that led to Yee. After a five-year investigation, Yee and 25 other people, including Chow and former San Francisco School Board president Keith Jackson, were charged in March 2014.

Yee's downfall is attributed to his unsuccessful run for mayor in 2011 that left him with $70,000 in campaign debt. He would have to leave his state Senate seat in 2014 because of term limits. Next was a campaign for statewide office that would surely run up even higher bills. Like all politicians in our broken system, he found himself beholden to his campaign donors and desperate for more cash to run more races.

The *San Francisco Chronicle* reviewed Yee's voting record and revealed that the legislator's votes often happened in lockstep with his campaign contributions. Usually the contributions came after the vote, big-money backers rewarding the lawmaker as if they were training a puppy. The *Chronicle* reported that it found "more than 30 instances dating back to 2003 where he cast votes that were arguably counter to his stated positions or the interests of his constituents in San Francisco and San Mateo counties, and then received large campaign contributions from the industries that benefited." Sadly, in 2015, Yee pleaded guilty to one count of racketeering and, in 2016, was sentenced to eight years in prison.

GOVERNORS GO TO JAIL

In January 2015, *USA Today* reported, "Bob McDonnell [was] about to join an exclusive but infamous club." As the first Virginia governor ever to be convicted of a felony, McDonnell was sentenced to two years in federal prison. He and his wife, Maureen McDonnell, were convicted of public corruption after accepting gifts, expensive vacations, and loans in exchange for favors.

In Illinois, four of the past seven governors have ended up in prison:

- Rod Blagojevich (governor from 2002 to 2009) was the first Illinois governor in history to be impeached. He was convicted of numerous corruption charges in 2011, including allegations that he tried to sell or trade President Barack Obama's old Senate seat. He was sentenced to 14 years in prison.
- George Ryan (governor from 1999 to 2003). After leaving office, Ryan was convicted of racketeering and other corruption charges for actions while he was governor and secretary of state; he was sentenced to six-and-a-half years in federal prison.
- Dan Walker (governor from 1973 to 1977) pleaded guilty in 1987 to bank fraud and other charges related to his business activities after leaving office. He

spent about a year-and-a-half in federal prison.

- Otto Kerner (governor from 1961 to 1968) resigned to become a judge and then was convicted of bribery related to his tenure as governor; he was sentenced to three years in prison.

DISCOVERY OF THE FRAUDS

Investigative Journalism. There are still investigative journalists out there who spend years of their lives, wear down a considerable amount of shoe leather, and put in a lot of keyboard time to probe, ask questions, and stay on the case until the story is uncovered. Conspiracies are hard to keep quiet—someone always wants to brag, complain, or spill the beans. "Three can keep a secret, if two of them are dead," said Benjamin Franklin. It's just as true today. And crooks with oversize egos who think they are entitled to big payoffs often have a habit of showing off just a little too much and giving themselves away.

Unfortunately, newspapers are on their way to becoming obsolete, and the funding for investigations has been severely curtailed. Good journalism can be drowned out by the day-to-day and even hour-by-hour, or minute-by-minute scandal and innuendo that informs the news today through social media. Sometimes that "news" is made up out of whole cloth by pseudo-experts and pundits.

Tough Law Enforcement. After some bad years at the Justice Department, where fines and slaps on the wrist were common for bad actors in big crimes while little guys had the book thrown at them, the tide seems to be turning. Aided by whistleblowers and some new legislation, U.S. Attorneys in New York, Detroit, and other cities are taking on corrupt politicians, healthcare, and pension fraud as well as corporate crimes.

Transparency of Public Monies. Ultimately, the cure is "sunshine," a reference to public transparency—to provide a clear view of where the public's money is going. New technology makes it possible to track both funds and communications in ways that were not previously possible. Hiding documents becomes a bit more difficult when digital copies and emails exist. Many municipalities post their budgets and expenditures online, giving citizens access to the information.

The Sunlight Foundation (sunlightfoundation.com) has

developed government transparency agendas with suggestions on how to make changes in both the executive and legislative branches.

Informed Voters. Today we have a more savvy and cynical electorate. Although some decry what they see as a lack of involvement among millennials, this is a group that disdains hype and hoopla while demanding a higher level of authenticity in the products and people they support. And they talk to each other, at least online. Watchdogs and activists have taken to communicating on blogs and social networks, and they are able to spread their disclosures at an incredibly rapid rate. Let a thousand whistles blow and a million tweets be sent.

WHAT ABOUT ANTICORRUPTION LAWS

It makes you wonder if one state has better anticorruption legislation than another. The State Integrity Investigation (an assessment conducted by the Center for Public Integrity) asked experienced journalists in 2015 to grade each state government's transparency and accountability. They were given 245 specific measures in 13 categories, which covered campaign finance, ethics laws, lobbying regulations, and management of the states' pension funds.

"The scores on these laws had little correlation with the other measures of corruption. Georgia took home the honors as having the least stringent anticorruption laws," concluded Harry Enten with the *FiveThirtyEight* website. "Somehow, New Jersey was rated as having the best anti-corruption laws, even though it ranked as the third and eighth most corrupt state, according to the reporter rankings and federal corruption convictions per capita. Illinois ranked in the top six across all the other categories, except it had some of the best anti-corruption laws on the books."

The lack of connection between laws and actual corruption is not necessarily surprising. Some of the most corrupt states recently passed anticorruption laws simply because corruption has come to light. Less corrupt states may not need the stricter anticorruption laws.

UNDERMINING THE RETIREMENTS OF MILLIONS, FOR MILLIONS

New York is not alone when it comes to pay-to-play. CalPERS (the California Public Employees' Retirement System) is the country's largest pension fund. With about $280 billion in investable assets, CalPERS represents a particularly lucrative target for investment fund managers. The news media reported in 2010 that those private investment firms paid more than $125 million to placement agents, including former CalPERS board members, to steer investments their way. One former board member, Alfred Villalobos, was paid nearly $60 million for securing CalPERS investments in several private equity firms before he was charged with corruption in an alleged pay-to-play scheme.

According to federal prosecutors, Villalobos conspired with former CalPERS chief executive Federico Buenrostro to defraud the private equity firm Apollo Global Management, a $160 billion investment management firm that has owned in whole or in part many well-known companies, from Coldwell Banker Real Estate to the fast food chains Hardee's and Carl's Jr. Authorities claim that Buenrostro and Villalobos created fake investor disclosure documents so Villalobos could earn fees from Apollo for acting as a middle man. Prosecutors said that Apollo paid Villalobos at least $14 million to help secure an investment from CalPERS. All told, CalPERS paid Villalobos $48 million, and CalPERS invested at least $3 billion with Apollo, including paying $600 million in 2007 for a 9 percent stake in the firm.

In 2011, CalPERS's internal investigators found sources who claimed Villalobos was using Buenrostro as "a puppet" to steer CalPERS investments to his clients. Villalobos made sure his buddy Buenrostro received a share of bribes and gifts, including trips on private jets and gambling junkets to Nevada casinos, according to the investigation. Villalobos, who was also the former deputy mayor of Los Angeles, committed suicide in January 2015, weeks before he was scheduled to go on trial.

TIPPED INTO UNSUSTAINABILITY

Under the weight of these scams and through the potentially lethal combination of demographic and financial trends and political mismanagement, many public pension systems now face questions about their very viability. To see how the problems of a pension system can affect the workings of government, just take a look at Detroit. According to the *New York Times:*

"Detroit's municipal pension fund suffered severe losses on real estate investments, among other problems ... . In some cases, certain Detroit pension trustees were taken on junkets dressed up as investment site inspections. And in one instance, an investment promoter paid a bribe to win pension money for real estate projects in the Caribbean but then spent the money building an $8.5 million mansion in Georgia."

And look where these pension problems got Detroit: bankruptcy.

Detroit is not alone, or at least it might not be for very long. Pension funds across the country are struggling because they cannot fund their obligation to pensioners. *Governing.com* referenced a 2014 report from Morningstar Municipal Credit Research that calculated the totals for unfunded pension amounts per resident in 25 major U.S. cities and Puerto Rico. Chicago tops the list at $18,596 per capita, including public schools and county pensions. Puerto Rico comes in next at $9,987, followed by New York City at $9,842, and Boston at $7,802. (The median amount of unfunded pension liability per resident was $3,550.)

So it's not surprising that some cities are trying to find other ways to deal with their pension debt. In 2010, a San Diego grand jury proposed that the city convene a bankruptcy panel to explore that option for getting out from under more than $3 billion in unfunded pension and health care liabilities. (San Diego came in tenth in the 2014 Morningstar report, with a liability of $5,973 per resident.)

The problem is magnified at the state level. The Pew Charitable Trust noted in its July 2015 brief on state pensions that the "nation's state-run retirement systems had a $968 billion shortfall in 2013," an increase of more than $50 billion from the year before.

THE NEED FOR REFORMS

A handful of brave public officials are showing a willingness both to wrestle with the tough issues surrounding the sorry state of America's pension funds and to crack down on the fraudsters who are unconscionably seeking to personally enrich themselves off of those funds.

Guardians of public pension funds must take heed and learn from Detroit. "The recent financial difficulties in Detroit serve as a stern wake-up call, demonstrating why strong oversight of New York's public pension funds is so important," said Benjamin M. Lawsky, the New York financial services superintendent, in letters he sent in 2013 to the trustees of the top state and city public plans, according to local media.

When Lawsky issued subpoenas to investment firms to make sure they weren't fleecing the pension funds, his colleague, New York City Comptroller Scott Stringer, sought a wider ban on placement agents and stiffer financial disclosure rules.

Yet not all reforms are successful. Some in New York sought to change the rules that allowed New York State comptroller Hevesi's corrupt dealings, particularly by doing away with the absurd notion that a single person—instead of a board of trustees—should be in charge of the state pension's investments. New York is one of the few states that still rely on a sole trustee. Yet, even after seeing firsthand how such an arrangement can cause significant financial problems, the attempted reform to abolish a sole trustee was shot down. Still, the *New York Times* reports that Hevesi's successor, comptroller Thomas DiNapoli, "instituted a number of reforms and control measures intended to ensure that investments were chosen on the merits instead of secret payments."

COST OF CORRUPTION

Political corruption can carry a higher price tag than just bilking voters. A 2004 study by the University of Connecticut found that corruption can cost a state jobs—perhaps the most valuable commodity in today's economic environment. The study found that for each federal conviction for misconduct per 100 elected officials, job growth dropped by 1.1 percentage points—more than double the 0.5-point decline attributed to a $100 increase in per-capita state taxes.

"The outcome makes sense," said then-Connecticut State Representative Demetrios Giannaros in the *Hartford Courant*. He was also an economics professor at the University of Hartford at the time. "Some international investors might say, 'I'm not going to move to a corrupt state.' Businesses want stability, and corruption implies instability in government. It doesn't matter who it is [committing the corruption]. Corruption is bad for the economy. It's not a level playing field. Some people are favored over others. You're inflating the costs [of doing business]".

GOING FORWARD

People are mad as hell and willing to call out the corrupt public officials because people are fed-up having their backs pushed up against the wall. The fat cats have become so blatant and greedy that they have rubbed the public's nose in the evidence of their ill-gotten gains. The public is watching, and it is an informed citizenry.

Unfortunately, much of the above comes in the pension area and not with the average working person who deserves a pension. It's the so-called executives who get a bump up of their pensions every time a lower working employee gets a well-deserved increase in salary. Some public executives get an equity pay bonus every time the people below them get a pension raise. Some senior executive public employees have made better than $500,000 per year when they retire—all public tax dollars.

The key is getting people involved and getting prosecutors to act boldly and forcefully when public money is at stake. Once again, it all comes down to the prosecutors, the courts, and the judges who have the guts and integrity to put public officials in jail once they have been convicted. Unfortunately, too many walk free. It also takes private lawyers with guts like one of my partners, Steve Williams, to take on the global cartels that regularly take the public's money.

Years ago, I was the lawyer who led the trial against Charles Keating, Jr. As one of the individuals that brought about the Savings and Loan scandals of the 1980s, Keating had a reputation for using politicians and one of his candid statements was, "As to the question of whether my financial support in a way influenced several political figures to take up my cause. I want to say in the most forceful way I can: I certainly hope so." Not much has changed in the past thirty years.

5

The Changing Climate:
Drought, Drowning, and Denial

"The time to find global solutions is running out .... There is therefore a clear, definite and urgent ethical imperative to act."
      —Pope Francis, 266th Pope of the Roman Catholic Church

"I am suing the Federal Government because it's the right thing to do. Our future survival depends on our leaders taking dramatic action on climate change NOW, for the sake of future generations and all life on Earth."
      —Journey Zephier, 15, Our Children's Trust

"Because we keep hearing that 2014 has been the warmest year on record, I ask the chair, you know what this is? It's a snowball. And it's just from outside here. So it's very, very cold out."
      —Senator James Inhofe (R-OK), Chair of the Senate Committee on Environment and Public Works

The year 2015 was the warmest in the history of recorded temperatures, with climate changing around the world. In that year, three distinctive voices told us much about what we face, what is to be done, and what is to be overcome: Pope Francis, the first Pope from the developing world; 21 kids suing the United States government for failing to act on climate change; and a senator with a snowball.

THE SHOES OF THE FISHERMAN
As the U.N. Climate Summit was about to begin in Paris in

December 2015, authorities banned demonstrations as a precaution after the November terrorist attacks. Demonstrations had been planned, however, so to stand in for those who now could not march, climate change activists set out more than 20,000 shoes in the Place de la République. Among them, a pair of plain black shoes sent by Pope Francis.

There is much that is new about this Pope: He is the first Pope from anywhere in the Americas; he is the first Pope from a country in the Southern Hemisphere; he is the first Pope from outside Europe in more than 1,000 years; and he is the first Pope to speak directly and passionately about our role in causing, and stopping, climate change.

"Every year the problems are more grave," the Pope said at the start of the United Nations–sponsored environmental summit in Paris. "We are at the limit. We are at the limit of a suicide, to say a strong word." Politicians have generally "done little" to deal with the growing problem, Francis said, according to the *National Catholic Reporter*.

But "I have trust …. I am sure they have the good will to do it. And I wish that it will be so, and I pray for this," he said.

In a 184-page papal encyclical issued in June 2015, the Pope "called for a radical transformation of politics, economics and individual lifestyles to confront environmental degradation and climate change," reported the *New York Times*, "blending a biting critique of consumerism and irresponsible development with a plea for swift and unified global action. The vision … is sweeping in ambition and scope: He describes relentless exploitation and destruction of the environment and says apathy, the reckless pursuit of profits, excessive faith in technology and political shortsightedness are to blame."

"He places most of the blame," the *Times* article continues, "on fossil fuels and human activity, while warning of an 'unprecedented destruction of ecosystems, with serious consequence for all of us' if corrective action is not taken swiftly. Developed, industrialized countries are mostly responsible, he says, and are obligated to help poorer nations confront the crisis."

Francis took his papal name in honor of Saint Francis of Assisi, and Pope Francis drew on the message of Saint Francis in his encyclical: "Saint Francis of Assisi reminds us that our common home is like a sister with whom we share our life and a beautiful mother who opens her arms to embrace us .... This sister now cries out to us because of the harm we have inflicted on her by our irresponsible use and abuse of the goods with which God has endowed her. We have come to see ourselves as her lords and masters, entitled to plunder her at will. The violence present in our hearts, wounded by sin, is also reflected in the symptoms of sickness evident in the soil, in the water, in the air and in all forms of life. This is why the earth herself, burdened and laid waste, is among the most abandoned and maltreated of our poor; she 'groans in travail' (Rom 8:22). We have forgotten that we ourselves are dust of the earth (cf. Gen 2:7); our very bodies are made up of her elements, we breathe her air and we receive life and refreshment from her waters."

In September 2015 Pope Francis addressed Congress. He spoke on many subjects: abortion, same-sex marriage, the death penalty, and protecting the poor and vulnerable. But just once, reported the *Washington Post*, did he call Congress to specific action. " 'I am convinced,' Francis said, 'that we can make a difference, and I have no doubt that the United States—and this Congress—have an important role to play.' The subject: climate change.

"I call for a courageous and responsible effort to 'redirect our steps,' " he said, "and to avert the most serious effects of the environmental deterioration caused by human activity. ... Now is the time for courageous actions and strategies, aimed at implementing a 'culture of care' and 'an integrated approach to combating poverty, restoring dignity to the excluded, and at the same time protecting nature.' ... In this regard, I am confident that America's outstanding academic and research institutions can make a vital contribution in the years ahead."

TWENTY-ONE KIDS (AND A GRANDFATHER)

In August of 2015, Our Children's Trust, an Oregon-based nonprofit, sued the United States, to force our government to protect the environment. The lawsuit was filed by my law firm, Cotchett Pitre & McCarthy, led by partner Phil Gregory, and by Julia Olson, the executive director and chief legal counsel for Our Children's Fund. The plaintiffs are 21 young Americans (and renowned climatologist James Hansen). Ranging in age from 8-year-old Levi Draheim in Florida to 19-year old Kelsey Juliana in Oregon, they come from ten states, including Alaska, Arizona,

Colorado, Hawaii, Louisiana, New York, Pennsylvania, and Washington.

"At first glance," *Slate* reported in November 2015, "the circumstances surrounding this lawsuit read like a storyline straight out of a Disney movie: On one side is a group of energetic kids, joined by a wise and genial grandfather who is fond of fedoras (James Hansen's 17-year-old granddaughter Sophie Kivlehan is one of the plaintiffs)."

Fourteen-year-old Nick Venner of Colorado says on the Our Children's Trust website, "Climate impacts in the U.S. are real and getting worse. We're running out of water, we're faced with record-setting heat waves, and wildfires and superstorms are becoming common. We must act now to protect our planet and our civilization."

So will the kids save the world? The fossil fuel industry is apparently afraid they just might. Not surprisingly, the Obama administration moved to dismiss the suit, on the grounds that the kids had no standing to sue, and the court had no power to decide the issue.

But, as reported in *Slate*, November 2015 "brought an interesting twist in the plot." Three of Washington, D.C.'s most powerful trade groups, each representing major players in the fossil fuel industry, including ExxonMobil, Shell, Chevron, Koch Industries, and BP, "joined the federal case as intervenors, arguing that the lawsuit is 'extraordinary' and 'a direct threat to [their] businesses' and that, if the kids win, 'massive societal changes' and an 'unprecedented restructuring of the economy' could result.

"That means the American Petroleum Institute (API), the American Fuel and Petrochemical Manufacturers (AFPM) and the National Association of Manufacturers (NAM) would make their case side-by-side with the Obama administration," continued the *Slate* piece, "using their own lawyers—including Roger Martella, the former general counsel of George W. Bush's EPA—to argue against the youths and Hansen."

" 'It's fairly common for trade associations to move to participate in lawsuits that could affect their interest,' says Michael Gerrard, a professor at Columbia Law School and the director of the Sabin Center for Climate Change Law. 'I think it shows that they're not utterly certain it will be dismissed,' " as reported in *Grist,* a website that covers environmental news, in November 2015.

Cotchett Pitre & McCarthy is squarely in this fight. CPM partner Phil Gregory, who is taking point on the case, summed it up this way in an interview with *SustainableBusiness.com* "The largest, best-funded fossil fuel heavyweights want the court to protect their wallets over ensuring a habitable country for these young plaintiffs and future generations."

But the courts are the place to fight this fight, according to Mary Christina Wood, the Philip H. Knight Professor of Law at the University of Oregon. She explained to *Moyers and Company:* "The fact is we have only three branches of government. So from a lawyer's perspective, you have to look at the structure we have and ask which part is functional and which part of it has become corrupted through big industry money. Two of the branches have become essentially corrupted because of the campaign contributions to those two branches of government. And so the third branch—while it's not perfect, by any means—the federal judiciary is as close to insulated from that big money influence as you can get."

Thirteen-year-old Isaac Vergun on the Our Children's Trust website said, "The courts have the ability to impact the lives of future generations and our lives in the future. I am speaking for the future generations, and they would want to have a livable planet as they grow up."

The children's campaign has already had some success. Last year, the group filed a separate petition in the state of Washington, to require emission reductions there. That got the attention of the state's governor, Jay Inslee, and a meeting with him for five of the plaintiffs (ranging from 11 to 15 years old). And the result *was* a result: Inslee told his people to get to work on a plan to cap emissions.

In that same Washington case, *Moyers and Company* reported that although the judge did not order the state to act (in part because the governor was already acting), the judge did say about the young people bringing the suit that their "very survival depends upon the will of their elders to act now, decisively and unequivocally, to stem the tide of global warming ... before doing so becomes first too costly and then too late." Our Children's Trust and its allies say the judge's agreement with the idea that America's youth have a right to a clean environment is a victory.

Lawsuits on these same issues have been successful in other countries. "In June, a high court ordered the Dutch government to cut emissions after plaintiffs successfully argued that business as usual would violate the human rights of future generations. And in Pakistan last month, a farmer went before the high court in Lahore arguing that climate change threatened his future, and the court agreed: 'The delay and lethargy of the state in implementing the [climate change] framework offend the fundamental rights of the citizens,' " as reported on *Moyers and Company*.

THE SNOWBALL OF JIM INHOFE

In February 2015, Oklahoma Senator James Inhofe brought a snowball onto the Senate floor to make his point on climate change, saying, "Because we keep hearing that 2014 has been the warmest year on record, I ask the chair, you know what this is? It's a snowball. And it's just from outside here. So it's very, very cold out.

This might just be an amusing political interlude except that Inhofe is the chairman of the Senate Committee on Environment and Public Works and the biggest and loudest denier of climate change in Congress. In addition to his empirical evidence—the snowball—he also cited his own book, *The Greatest Hoax*.

In turn, his book cited a still-higher authority: "[This] is what a lot of alarmists forget: God is still up there, and He promised to maintain the seasons and that cold and heat would never cease as long as the earth remains." Or as one of Inhofe's favorite Bible verses, Genesis 8:22, says,

"As long as the earth remains,
There will be seed time and harvest,
Cold and heat, winter and summer, day and night."

In a subsequent radio interview hawking his book, Inhofe told Voice of Christian Youth America, "The arrogance of people to think that we, human beings, would be able to change what he is doing in the climate is, to me, outrageous."

Oddly, the religious senator is apparently unfamiliar with the story of another religious man who also was certain he knew just what God was thinking about the climate (a story that, coincidentally, also features rising floodwaters):

"In the face of a flood, that man climbed up onto the roof of his house and trusted God to rescue him.

"A neighbor came by in a canoe and said, 'The waters are rising. Hop in and we'll paddle to safety.' 'No thanks,' replied the religious man. 'I've prayed to God and I'm sure he will save me.'

"A short time later a police boat came by. 'The waters will soon be above your house. Get in and we'll take you to safety.' 'No thanks,' replied the religious man. 'I've prayed to God and I'm sure he will save me.'

"A little time later a helicopter flew overhead and let down a rope ladder. 'Come up the ladder. We'll fly you to safety.' 'No thanks,' replied the religious man, 'God will save me.' Finally, the floodwaters rose over the roof and the man drowned.

"When he arrived at heaven, the man demanded to see God. 'Lord, why am I here? I prayed for you to save me; I trusted you to save me from that flood.' 'Yes,' replied the Lord. 'And I sent you a canoe, a boat, and a helicopter. But you never got in.' "

Which should remind us that it is dangerous for even the holiest of mortal men and women to think they know just what God thinks and wants (about climate change, or anything else).

I AM NOT A SCIENTIST, BUT I AM RUNNING FOR OFFICE

Inhofe is not alone in his party however. "I'm not a scientist" was a familiar line from Republicans on climate change during the 2014 election, as Republicans like John Boehner (former House Speaker) and Senate Majority Leader Mitch McConnell chose ignorance over science.

Former Republican presidential candidate and New Jersey governor Chris Christie took it a step further. While the U.N. climate change conference was underway in Paris, Christie told MSNBC's *Morning Joe*, "I don't buy the fact that it's a crisis. I just don't." And why wasn't Christie buying? "That's my feeling. I didn't say I was relying on any scientist."

Former GOP presidential candidates Jeb Bush and Rick Santorum (former senator from Pennsylvania) chided the Pope for his comments to Congress on climate change. They said he should stick to religion and "leave science to the scientists" (perhaps forgetting that Francis actually *has* some scientific background, having studied chemistry before becoming a priest).

In North Carolina's 2014 Republican primary, the four

candidates running for U.S. Senate were asked during a debate, "Is climate change a fact?" The answers were "no," "no," "no," and "no." In fact, both the audience and the candidates thought the question was funny. (Those candidates, incidentally, included Thom Tillis, who today represents North Carolina in the U.S. Senate.)

FOOLS ON THE HILL

In fact, denying climate change has certainly been no barrier to getting elected. According to *ThinkProgress,* as of January 2015, more than 50 percent of the Republican members of the House of Representatives do not accept the idea that human action is causing global warming, and 70 percent of Senate Republicans agreed. As Senator Joni Ernst of Iowa put it in the same *ThinkProgress* piece, "I don't know the science behind climate change. I can't say one way or another what is the direct impact, whether it's man-made or not. I've heard arguments from both sides.

A number of these lawmakers hold prominent positions in the 2015 Congress—68 percent of the Republican leadership in both the House and Senate are climate change deniers. At the committee level, the "just say no to science" crowd includes 62 percent of the Republican members of the House Committee on Science, Space, and Technology, joined by 67 percent Republican members of the House Energy and Commerce Committee (number-crunching from *ThinkProgress.org*).

In addition to Senator Inhofe (Mr. Snowball), who chairs the committee, all but 1 of the 11 Republicans on the Environment and Public Works committee, according to *ThinkProgress.org,* have said either that the climate is not changing, or if it is, humans aren't responsible.

EVERYTHING WE KNOW (WE LEARNED FROM THE FOSSIL FUEL LOBBY)

You can follow the fossil fuel money on *ThinkProgress:* "The members of the 114th Congress who have publicly misrepresented the science behind global warming have accepted their fair share of contributions from the fossil fuel industry. The 38 climate [change] deniers in the Senate have taken $27,845,946 in donations from the coal, oil, and gas industries, while the 62 Senators who haven't denied the science have taken $11,339,967 in career contributions, ... On average, Senate deniers took $732,788 from fossil fuel interests while other Senators took $182,902.

"On the House side, the 131 climate science deniers have taken $35,702,245 in fossil fuel industry contributions while the remaining voting members who haven't denied the science have only taken $24,268,787 in career contributions. On average, House deniers took $272,536 from coal, oil and gas interests while other members took $80,095."

Twelve-year-old Jayden Foytlin of Louisiana, one of the plaintiffs in the Our Children's Trust federal lawsuit, summed it up on OCT's website, "Our government seems to care more about money for the fossil fuel industry than our futures. But money isn't going to matter if we can't fix our planet."

OUTSIDE WASHINGTON, D.C.: A MIXED PICTURE

New Scientist, a print and digital publication covering current scientific issues, reported on Americans' view of climate change in November 2015: "interest of US citizens in climate change decreased sharply in 2009 to 2010 when people were more worried about their jobs and mortgages. But since 2010, there has been a long, slow increase in concern." After Pope Francis's visit to the United States "the percentage of Catholics who said they were 'very worried' about global warming more than doubled over the numbers this [past] spring. And those who denied the scientific consensus that human-caused climate change is happening declined 10 percentage points for Catholics and 6 points for the US population in general .... [A]uthors of the survey ... dub the shift in public opinion 'the Pope Francis effect.' "

A *New York Times/CBS News* poll published in the *New York Times* at the end of November 2015 showed, "A solid majority of Americans say the United States should join an international treaty to limit the impact of global warming, but on this and other climate-related questions, opinion divides sharply along partisan lines .... Two-thirds of Americans support the United States joining a binding international agreement to curb growth of greenhouse gas emissions, but a slim majority of Republicans remain opposed, the poll found. Sixty-three percent of Americans—including a bare majority of Republicans—said they would support domestic policy limiting carbon emissions from power plants.

" 'If you just look over the past five or six years ... there's been a shift,' " David Waskow, director of the International Climate Initiative at the World Resources Institute, told the newspaper. " 'There's much more awareness of issues like sea level rise, water scarcity and climate instability.' "

The *Times* found that, "Seventy-five percent of Americans polled said that global warming was already having a serious environmental impact or would in the future. Nine in ten Democrats agreed, compared with 58 percent of Republicans. One-third of Republicans said they believed it would never have much of an impact on the environment."

(AND YET) THE U.S. LEADS IN CLIMATE DENIAL

At the same time, (and just a week after a report that the United States is lagging behind other developed countries in energy efficiency), an international survey found that our nation leads the world in denying the existence of climate change, according to an article on *EcoWatch*. The *EcoWatch* data comes from United Kingdom–based research company Ipsos MORI, as part of its study on global trends. The study polled 16,000 people in 20 countries and asked more than 200 questions about eight topics, including the environment.

Of all the countries surveyed, says *EcoWatch,* the U.S. was the country with the fewest people agreeing that the primary cause of climate change is human activity. On the other hand, in countries as diverse as Argentina and France, China and Italy, and India, Turkey, and Spain, at least 80 percent of those surveyed said we humans are the ones responsible. But perhaps that difference reflects who is telling Americans about climate change, and who is paying for that message.

AMERICANS ARE INTENTIONALLY MISINFORMED

Just as the economic interests behind climate change denial have poured plenty of money into influencing Congress, those same wealthy interests have been working hard to mislead the American people.

The leading wealthy interests? ExxonMobil and the Koch Brothers. Their money goes to a web of more than 4,500 individuals, connected in various ways to more than 160 organizations—and these groups and individuals are the leading messengers of climate change denial in the United States, according to a paper published in *Nature Climate Change* and reported by *Bloomberg.*

"Corporate funding influences the actual language and thematic content of these polarization efforts ... . These effects were visible over time," Justin Farrell, assistant professor of sociology at the Yale School of Forestry and Environmental Studies, wrote in a separate paper for the *Proceedings of the National Academy of Sciences.*

"The report," the *Washington Post* wrote of Farrell's work, "a systematic review of 20 years' worth of data, highlights the connection between corporate funding and messages that raise doubts about the science of climate change and whether humans are responsible for the warming of the planet."

" 'The contrarian efforts have been so effective for the fact that they have made it difficult for ordinary Americans to even know who to trust,' " Farrell told the *Washington Post.*

"Numerous previous studies have examined how corporate-funded campaigns have helped shape individual views about global warming," the *Washington Post* reported. "But the Yale study takes what Farrell calls the 'birds'-eye-view' using computer analytics to systematically examine vast amounts of printed matter published by 164 groups—including think-tanks and lobbying firms."

The *Post* continued, "The results, Farrell said, revealed an 'ecosystem of influence' within the corporate-backed groups. Those that received donations consistently promoted the same contrarian themes—casting doubt, for example, on whether higher levels of man-made carbon-dioxide in the atmosphere were harmful to the planet. There was no evidence of such coordination among the non-funded groups."

THE GRANDFATHER WITH THE FEDORA

In his own measured and precise (and fedora-sporting) way, James Hansen, former director of NASA's Goddard Institute for Space Studies in New York, has been a voice for science, and for the reality of climate change, over more than 30 years. His participation as a plaintiff, along with the children, in the Our Children's Trust lawsuit comes out of a deep belief that he didn't want his grandchildren to think that with his knowledge he hadn't done more. His 2009 book, *Storms of My Grandchildren: The Truth About the Coming Climate Catastrophe and Our Last Chance to Save Humanity,* tells about his mission and his attempts over time to be the "Paul Revere" of climate change, as Robert F. Kennedy, Jr., wrote of Hansen's book.

Sometimes his own scientific caution and meticulousness tripped him up, making it possible for people to misuse his words. He berates himself for not being a better communicator, struggling to find accurate and compelling language that will make a difference. But he also tells a chilling story of being ignored, dismissed, and muzzled by his employer, NASA, at the behest of the George W. Bush White House and his manipulator-in-chief, Vice President Dick Cheney.

In his book Hansen writes that "Bush came into office carrying a pledge to treat carbon dioxide as a pollutant. When EPA administrator Christine Todd Whitman testified on February 27, 2001 to a Senate Committee on Environment and Public Works subcommittee, she advocated for a plan for regulating carbon dioxide emissions under the Clean Air Act. At an international meeting the following week, Whitman said that 'she assured [her] G8 counterparts that the president's campaign commitment to seek a mandatory cap on carbon dioxide emission was solid,' according to her book, *It's My Party, Too.*"

Within 30 days the ground had shifted. As Hansen tells the story, U.S. Senators Chuck Hagel, Jesse Helms, Pat Roberts, and Larry Craig wrote to President Bush. "[Their] letter drew attention to Whitman's remarks and asked the president to clarify the 'Administration's position on climate change, in particular the Kyoto Protocol, and the regulation of carbon dioxide under the Clean Air Act.'

"Bush responded with a March 13 letter in which the president reversed his position on carbon dioxide, stating that it was not a pollutant under the Clean Air Act. He claimed that important new information warranted the reevaluation, specifically a Department of Energy report concluding that caps on carbon dioxide emissions would reduce the use of coal and raise the price of electricity."

Hansen writes that Mark Bowen's book *Censoring Science: Inside the Political Attack on Dr. James Hansen and the Truth of Global Warming,* and *The Price of Loyalty: George W. Bush, the*

White House, and the Education of Paul O'Neill by Ron Suskind, analyzed what happened.

Hansen continues, drawing on Mark Bowen's account: "O'Neill notes that the tone and much of the substance of the letter from the four senators seemed to have come 'right out of Dick Cheney's mouth' and that he believes the letter from the president in response was prepared by the vice president ... . Whitman went to the Oval Office on the morning of March 13, 2001 hoping to argue her case, but instead Bush read to her portions of the letter reneging on his pledge to regulate carbon dioxide. As Whitman left the Oval Office, Cheney arrived expressly to pick up the letter—which he pocketed and took to his weekly policy meeting with Republican senators .... Bowen [described] the episode [as] a 'knockout punch to facts-based consensus-building decision-making.' The decision not to regulate carbon dioxide had been made two weeks before the first meeting of the Climate Task Force, which was supposed to consider the evidence."

In July 2003, Hansen "received a request from the Director's Office at the NASA Goddard Space Flight Center, in Greenbelt, Maryland, to give a presentation to NASA administrator Sean O'Keefe ... a friend and protégé of Vice President Dick Cheney." Mark Bowen describes O'Keefe (an accountant by training) as "openly and unapologetically partisan. As one senior insider at the agency puts it, 'In came Sean, and then it became very clear that NASA belonged to Sean, who belonged to Cheney.' " In preparation for an O'Keefe visit to NASA, Hansen sent a copy of a document entitled "Can We Defuse the Global Warming Time Bomb?." The Goddard director in charge of escorting O'Keefe decided to change the title to make it less "incendiary." In its final presentation was "something about 'climate change.' "

Hansen writes that when he showed O'Keefe a chart with the headline "What Determines Dangerous Anthropogenic Interference?," "O'Keefe interrupted me to say that he did not think I should use the 'dangerous' phrase."

"Of course by 2005 I was well aware that the NASA Office of Public Affairs had become an office of propaganda," Hansen continues. "In 2004 I learned that NASA press releases related to global warming were sent to the White House, where they were edited to appear less serious or discarded entirely." And an even more sweeping clampdown on information was coming.

David Mould was promoted from Assistant Administrator of Public Affairs to Press Secretary for NASA. He had been at the agency only six months, but, as Bowen writes in his book, "during George W. Bush's 2000 presidential campaign, Mould held senior positions in public and media relations at the Southern Company of Atlanta, the second-largest holding company of coal-burning utilities in the United States and for that simple reason the nation's second greatest emitter of carbon dioxide. ... That year, Southern's contributions to the Republican Party were exceeded only by Enron's."

New rules came down—scientists could only talk to the press with the approval of the Public Affairs unit. Anything put up on NASA's website had to be approved beforehand. And speeches, releases, anything that might get the attention of a reporter— had to be reported to Public Affairs well in advance.

A few days later National Public Radio wanted to interview Hansen for its On Point program. The message came back to him that NASA did not want him to go on NPR because it was "the most liberal news outlet in the country." He heard that there would be "dire consequences" if he went ahead and did the interview. In the end, NPR dropped the interview, because they had specifically wanted to talk to Hansen.

TO UNDERSTAND AND PROTECT

While completing an annual government "training exercise" on NASA standards of conduct, Hansen found himself bolstered in his resolve when he re-read the agency's mission statement. The opening phrase was "to understand and protect our home planet." He put this together with language from NASA's core values: "integrity—defined as honesty, ethical behavior, respect and candor" and the first principles of government ethics— "public service is a public trust"—and he fed them back to Goddard management as a rationale for why they should fight the restrictions of public affairs. He began emphasizing the mission statement in his public talks. But, in the spring of 2006 he got an email from a colleague warning him to stop because the phrase "to understand and protect our home planet" had disappeared from the NASA mission statement. "The second thing to disappear," according to Hansen, "was 20 percent of the

NASA earth science research and analysis budget."

DON'T MENTION CLIMATE CHANGE HERE

Apparently there really is a trickledown effect—from Washington to the states. To Florida, for example, where *Mother Jones* reported in March 2015 that "former staffers with the [Florida] Department of Environmental Protection alleged that senior officials, under the direction of Gov. Rick Scott (R), had instituted an unwritten ban on using the phrases 'climate change' and 'global warming.' Scott denied the claim."

In April that year, it was Wisconsin's turn, as *Bloomberg Business* reported:

"Discussing climate change is out of bounds for workers at a state agency in Wisconsin. So is any work related to climate change—even responding to e-mails about the topic.

"A vote on Tuesday by Wisconsin's Board of Commissioners of Public Lands, a three-member panel overseeing an agency that benefits schools and communities in the states, enacted the staff ban on climate change.

"The move to ban an issue leaves staff at the Board of Commissioners of Public Lands in the unusual position of not being able to speak about how climate change might affect lands it oversees."

The agency's director *had* done some climate-change-related work, at the direction of the governor of Wisconsin, back in 2007 and 2008. The ban was the work of two newly elected Republicans, the state treasurer and the attorney general.

The third member of the commission, Secretary of State Douglas La Follette, a Democrat, who voted against the ban, said in a conference call with *BloombergBusiness*, "Having been on this board for close to 30 years, I've never seen such nonsense. ... That's as bad as the governor of Florida recently telling his staff that they could not use the words 'climate change.' "

YOU CAN'T FOOL ALL THE PEOPLE ALL THE TIME

In 2016, the Federal Emergency Management Agency (FEMA) is about to put climate-denying governors on the spot. The agency will now only approve disaster preparedness plans for states that plan for the effects of climate change. A number of Republican governors may have to choose between their political beliefs and hundreds of millions of dollars in disaster preparedness aid from FEMA.

Over the past five years, the agency has awarded an average $1 billion a year in grants to states and territories for taking steps to mitigate the effects of disasters. "If a state has a climate denier governor that doesn't want to accept a plan, that would risk mitigation work not getting done because of politics," Becky Hammer, an attorney with the Natural Resources Defense Council's water program, told *Inside Climate News*. " 'The governor would be increasing the risk to citizens in that state,' because of his climate beliefs."

Republican governors who may be in just that position include Rick Scott of Florida, Chris Christie of New Jersey, Greg Abbott of Texas, and Pat McCrory of North Carolina. Their states are all on the frontline because they face immediate threats from climate change. As FEMA put it, "The challenges posed by climate change, such as more intense storms, frequent heavy precipitation, heat waves, drought, extreme flooding, and higher sea levels, could significantly alter the types and magnitudes of hazards impacting states in the future," *Inside Climate News* reported in March 2015.

As of October 2014, according to data released by the Georgetown Climate Center, 14 states had "fully fledged adaptation plans with specific goals in place. Nine more have adaptation plans in the works," *Mother Jones* wrote in its coverage of the Georgetown Climate Center data. "The rest have not developed statewide plans (though a number of these states do have plans in place at the local or regional level). Of the 14 states with concrete plans, California is clearly out front: The Golden State has the highest number of completed climate adaptation goals, and the highest number in the works." The *Mother Jones* headline says it all: "The rest of you are screwed." (Especially if you live in a state with a Republican governor.) Unfortunately, the next president elected in 2016 will have a lot to say on the subject.

DITHERING WHILE THE PLANET BURNS
"Imagine a giant asteroid on a direct collision course with Earth," James Hansen said in a TED talk. "That is the equivalent of what we face now [with climate change], yet we dither."

For Hansen, who has been aware of the problem and potential solutions for years without being able to achieve the actions he feels are not just necessary but critical, this is clearly a case of "fiddling while Rome burns." As a country we are barreling along toward destiny in our fossil-fuel mobile, on the verge of redlining that engine. And when we hit that redline, we are in...

THE DANGER ZONE

Temperature Redline. "The world is on course for 2.7 degrees of warming, far higher than the upper threshold of two degrees Celsius that climate scientists have encouraged governments to hit. (We've already warmed the planet by one degree Celsius.) As we pass the two-degree threshold, researchers have warned, we pass more and more tipping points triggering climate change's most catastrophic effects," according to a November 2015 article on *Moyers and Company*.

Carbon Dioxide Redline. CO2 levels first hit 400 parts per million (ppm) in 2013 at the National Oceanic and Atmospheric Administration's (NOAA) measuring station in Hawaii. It hit that mark again in May 2015, and the number was around 398 ppm at the end of 2015. Unfortunately, the goal was 350 ppm. The group *350.org* takes its name from this goal. They spell out where we are headed on their website: "We're adding 2 ppm of carbon dioxide to the atmosphere every year. Unless we are able to rapidly turn that around and return to below 350 ppm this century, we risk triggering tipping points and irreversible impacts that could send climate change spinning truly beyond our control."

Sea Ice Redline. "In the summer of 2012, roughly half of the Arctic's sea ice went missing (some scientists estimate that the total volume of summer sea ice loss may be as high as 80 percent). The entire Arctic region is undergoing drastic changes, threatening vital habitat for countless species ... and the livelihoods of many indigenous communities," according to *350.org*. "This is also bringing us closer to dangerous tipping points, like the breakdown of the Greenland ice sheet and major methane releases from quickening permafrost melt."

Disease Redline. The World Health Organization set out the picture: Between 2030 and 2050, climate change is expected to cause approximately 250,000 additional deaths per year, from malnutrition, malaria, diarrhea, and heat stress. But we won't have to wait that long to start seeing the impact of climate change on human health. Warmer weather means mosquitoes and other bugs can live longer, and move farther. The latest development on that front? The mosquito-borne Zika virus. As the Sierra Club said in a statement in February 2016: "The tropical disease and disease-carrying mosquitoes are currently present in some Latin American countries, but climate disruption could cause the risks of the outbreak to spread ... [and] the resulting spread of the virus is an unpredictable and looming."

"The urgency is mind-blowing," University of Oregon School of Law professor and activist Mary Christina Wood told *Grist*. The Our Children's Trust plaintiffs argue that the atmosphere should be considered a "public trust." As one of those plaintiffs, 17-year-old Sophie Kivlehan, said on the OCT website, "I know climate change is going to have the biggest impact on my generation and generations to come. Our government isn't taking action and we have a very small window to turn this around. I feel a sense of responsibility to take action."

NOW WE SEE IT EVERY YEAR

"People used to say, 'I don't care, it's not in my back yard.' But now it's in everyone's back yard," actor Robert Redford, a trustee of the National Resources Defense Council, told *Time* magazine.

At some point the effects of climate change get pushed in your face and become harder and harder to dismiss as normal cycles of weather. Like a fish on a street. Swimming.

In Miami Beach, Mayor Philip Levine said Al Gore "spotted the fish [swimming in the street] on Indian Creek Drive, a state road that routinely floods during seasonal tides," according to the *Miami Herald*.

And while the fish are not coming out of the sea in large numbers, Florida has seen reports of "street fish" in Delray Beach, Hollywood, and Fort Lauderdale, especially in high tide conditions.

Californians also have a front row seat to climate change. While dealing with drought that caused the earth to sink in places, threatened farmers, and changed toilet-flushing habits throughout the state, some on the coast are also making plans for sea level rise and the threat of floods and evacuations due to El Nino–driven storms. And if that weren't enough, the crab season was cancelled along much of the West Coast due to an algae bloom some say was brought on by climate changes.

Even so, Californians have it good compared to residents of the Marshall Islands. The *New York Times* tells the tale in a special report, "The Marshall Islands Are Disappearing": Located halfway between Hawaii and Australia, "most of the 1,000 or so Marshall Islands, spread out over 29 narrow coral atolls in the South Pacific, are less than six feet above sea level—and few are more than a mile wide. For the Marshallese, the destructive power of the rising seas is already an inescapable part of daily life. Changing global trade winds have raised sea levels in the South Pacific about a foot over the past 30 years, faster than elsewhere."

Kwajalein, the largest of the Marshall atolls, is home to an American military base. As the *Times* describes it, "The 1,200 Americans who live on the base launch missiles, operate space weapons programs and track NASA research, supported by an annual budget of $182 million.... In 2008, a tidal wash flooded the base and destroyed all the freshwater supplies on the island. The military responded with expensive desalination machines and heavy-duty sea walls....

"On other islands, the wash of saltwater has penetrated and salinated [the] underground freshwater supply. On Majuro, flooding tides damaged hundreds of homes in 2013. The elementary school closed for nearly two weeks to shelter families. That same year, the airport temporarily closed after tides flooded the runway."

Neither leaving nor staying is an easy choice for many. The *Times* told the story of Linber Anej. Thirty years old, he lives with his family of 13, including parents, siblings, and children, in a four-room house on Ebeye. "I'm the oldest—I can't leave my parents. But I don't want my kids to drown here."

PICTURES FROM ALASKA

Perhaps Alaska is one of the best places to see the challenge of climate change and the need for climate action. It is part of the United States yet still exotic and far away to many. President Obama's trip there in September 2015 was revealing on many levels. *Rolling Stone* writer Jeff Goodell captured the significance:

"Obama could not have picked a better place to make his point than Alaska. Climatewise, it is the dark heart of the fossil-fuel beast. On one hand, temperatures in the state are rising twice as fast as the national average, and glaciers are retreating so quickly that even the pilot of my Delta flight into Anchorage told passengers to 'look out the window at the glaciers on the left side of the aircraft—they won't be there for long!'

"The very week of Obama's visit, 35,000 walruses huddled on the beach in northern Alaska because the sea ice they used as resting spots while hunting had melted away; in the Gulf of Alaska, scientists were tracking the effects of a zone of anomalously warm water that stretches down to Baja California and which has been named, appropriately enough, 'the blob.'

"On the other hand, the state is almost entirely dependent on revenues from fossil-fuel production, which, thanks to the low price of oil and exhausted oil and gas wells on the North Slope, are in free fall—the state is grappling with a $3.7 billion budget shortage this year. Alaska Governor Bill Walker had flown from Washington, D.C., to Anchorage with the president at the beginning of his trip; according to one of the president's aides, Walker asked the president to open more federal lands to oil and gas drilling to boost state revenues. 'Alaska is a banana republic,' says Bob Shavelson, executive director of Cook Inletkeeper, an environmental group in Alaska. 'The state has to pump oil or die.' "

Accompanying the president to Alaska, Goodell saw both the beauty and the danger at hand:

"When we were hiking at the glacier in Seward the other day, one of the rangers who works for the park said that more and more people are making pilgrimages to see the glacier before it vanishes. Some people even kiss it goodbye. And she said there's a sadness in a lot of the people who go there because they know the world is changing so quickly as a result of climate change."

"Our government continues making today's profit a priority over protecting our right to a sustainable future."
—Nathan Baring, 15, Fairbanks, Alaska
(Our Children's Trust website)

LAST CHANCES

"There is such a thing as being too late. And when it comes to climate change, that hour is almost upon us."
--President Barack Obama

Since Obama's trip to Alaska in the first week of September 2015, a few things have happened that give hope that climate action can snatch us away from the jaws of disaster.

"Royal Dutch Shell [announced it would] end exploration in off shore Alaska 'for the foreseeable future,' after an exploratory well in the Chukchi Sea failed to yield the oil and gas that was hoped for."—USA Today, September 28, 2015

"The Obama administration canceled offshore drilling in Alaska's Arctic Ocean for the coming two years after scrapping current and future drilling plans in the Chukchi and Beaufort seas."—UPI, October 17, 2015

"President Obama on Tuesday vetoed legislation authorizing construction of the Keystone XL oil pipeline."—The Hill, February 24, 2015

And in the last year of his term President Obama is pushing hard to make climate action part of his legacy. Maybe he has a chance before his time runs out. As he said to *Rolling Stone*, "Historically, politics catch up when the public cares deeply. And when people couldn't breathe in L.A., the state of California starts saying, 'You've got to get catalytic converters.' When the river catches fire in [Cleveland], the people of Ohio and, eventually, the people nationally, say, 'That's getting kind of out of hand.' "

He might also be getting a little help.

FUNDING THE FUTURE

"Bill Gates, Mark Zuckerberg, Richard Branson, Jeff Bezos, and pretty much every other tech leader you can imagine have announced that they're banding together to combat climate change with a new partnership called the Breakthrough Energy Coalition. Their timing couldn't be better—or more telling. Through the partnership, the group's members have committed to use a substantial portion of their hundreds of billions of dollars in collective net worth to invest in early-stage clean energy companies.

"There's no word yet on just how much the members of the coalition—which also include Jack Ma, Meg Whitman, George Soros, and Tom Steyer—plan to invest. But they say they will fund startups in a range of industries, from agriculture to transportation to electricity storage.

"They'll also focus the investments on the countries that are part of Mission Innovation—a consortium of 20 countries, including the U.S [along with China, Brazil, Germany, and Saudi Arabia among others] that have committed to doubling their investment in clean energy over the next five years." *Wired*, November 30, 2015

Zuckerberg announced his involvement on Facebook (naturally). "Solving the clean energy problem is an essential part of building a better world," he wrote. "We won't be able to make meaningful progress on other challenges—like educating or connecting the world—without secure energy and a stable climate.

"Our primary goal with the Coalition is as much to accelerate progress on clean energy as it is to make a profit," Bill Gates wrote on his website.

Talking to *Mic*.com, an online news aggregator, in December 2015, Tom Steyer, founder of NextGen Climate, laid down the challenge,: "If you set up the right framework for American business, they are the most innovative, creative force in the world, and we can solve this problem in ways that no one's imagined. ... To me, the ironic part of this whole conversation is that the so-called 'Party of American Business' is sitting there and loudly screaming that American business can't solve this problem. They have absolutely no confidence in America's ability to innovate, drive down costs and come up with better solutions. And we're sitting here, and saying, 'We always have done that! That's what we do!' "

THE WILL OF THE PEOPLE: WHO'S IN

"The fact is you cannot get an international agreement until domestic will is in place, because it would be meaningless."
—Mary Christina Wood, University of Oregon law school

Islanders, tech investors, pediatricians, farmers, and lawyers have all spoken up in favor of climate action. All have brought something of their own to the mix—traditions and art, analytical tools and organizing techniques. During the Paris climate talks, representatives from indigenous tribes from the Arctic to the Amazon paddled their canoes and kayaks and took to the water of the Bassin de la Villette (since demonstrations on land were forbidden).

But as *Think Progress* put it, "Few things strike fear into the hearts of politicians like a disgruntled grandparent entering a voting booth. Seniors wield immense political power in the United States, a fact made plain by their voting record. In the 2014 midterm elections, a year of historically low voter turnout, nearly 59 percent of adults aged 65 and older pulled the lever on Election Day. Just 23 percent of 18- to 24-year-olds bothered to do the same. It's numbers like these that have made Social Security and Medicare the third rail of American politics. So, what happens when America's seniors find out what climate change means for their grandkids?"

"We represent a very big block of voters," John Sorensen, co-founder of the Conscious Elders Network told *Think Progress*. Speaking of his group, which was in Washington to meet with their representative. Sorensen said, "There's a lot of people that don't want to go play shuffleboard and bingo. They want to go do stuff." (In fact, doing "stuff" on that visit also included forming a senior flash mob in a House cafeteria, livening up the lunch hour with a musical case for climate change.)

As *ThinkProgress* reported, "For the seniors in attendance, that means fighting to safeguard an uncertain future. Sunny Thompson, a small business owner from Ashford, Washington, said, 'If you have children or grandchildren, or you are an aunt or an uncle, or you just care about life in general, it upwells within you to make sure you're leaving it in good standing, and we're not.' It was a sentiment echoed by many of those in attendance.

"Erv DeSmet, a retired lawyer from Woodinville, Washington, said, 'A special sense that I have is I'm a grandfather. I have four grandkids.' He added, 'I've come to understand that it's time for me to open my big mouth and talk about these things.' DeSmet expressed his frustration at the dearth of meaningful climate legislation at the federal level. 'A majority of people want some action on the climate.' "

And on climate change, young people are saying "Me too." Xiuhtezcatl Martinez from Colorado put it like this on the Our Children's Trust website, "Climate change is the defining issue of our time. The actions those in power take and decisions they make today, will determine the kind of world future generations will inherit.

More and more voices are calling for climate action from outside the Beltway, and from inside the Capitol. Remember Senator Inhofe and his snowball? One of Inhofe's colleagues, Rhode Island's Senator Sheldon Whiteside, stepped up to the podium with the needed dose of common sense:

"You can believe NASA and you can believe what their satellites measure on the planet, or you can believe the Senator with the snowball. The United States Navy takes this very seriously ... Admiral Locklear, who is the head of the Pacific Command, has said that climate change is the biggest threat that we face in the Pacific... you can either believe the United States Navy or you can believe the Senator with the snowball ... [E]very major American scientific society has put itself on record, many of them a decade ago, that climate change is deadly real. They measure it, they see it, they know why it happens. The predictions correlate with what we see as they increasingly come true. And the fundamental principles, that it is derived from carbon pollution, which comes from burning fossil fuels, are beyond legitimate dispute ... so you can believe every single major American scientific society, or you can believe the Senator with the snowball."

And from the top: "'Climate change is no longer some far-off problem; it is happening here, it is happening now,' President Obama said in his remarks to an international conference on the Arctic in Anchorage.... Obama warned that unless more was done to reduce carbon pollution, 'we will condemn our children to a planet beyond their capacity to repair: Submerged countries. Abandoned cities. Fields no longer growing.' His impatience was obvious: 'We're not moving fast enough,' he repeated four times in a 24-minute speech," as reported in *Rolling Stone*.

The need for quick and decisive work to take on climate change has never been greater—on the political front and on the legal front, in cities and in states, in the U.S. and around the world. But even though that work may be done in courtrooms and capitals, the pressure to do the work must come from the grassroots. From us

And never has the word "grassroots" been so apt, since the very grass itself, along with the rest of our natural world, is in grave danger. From us.

Or as Miko Vergun, age 14, said on the Our Children's Trust website, "This is our future we're talking about. We have to stop going about our lives as if nothing is happening."

THE FUTURE OF DEALING WITH THE CLIMATE

Virtually everything is going to depend on the next several elections, especially 2016 and the next President of the United States and appointments to our Supreme Court. While we are facing a global challenge, a lot of the leadership has to come from the U.S. because of the economics we influence and control. The global energy producers and manufacturers are largely directed or influenced by Wall Street and energy producing countries. Until we elect leaders that do not use snowballs as "scientific evidence," our future for our children is in deep trouble. Global warming continues and we need elected officials and judges that understand the problems. Big oil and fossil fuels have to give way to clean energy now—not tomorrow—it will be too late.

The immediate need to take global warming seriously was highlighted in a March 2016 article in *The New York Times*, referring to new research findings released by a group of leading climate scientists led by James Hansen. According to the new report published in the European Science Journal, *Atmospheric Chemistry and Physics*, Dr. Hansen and his colleagues warn that at the current rate we are burning fossil fuels, even reducing greenhouse gases to previously agreed-upon limits "would actually be highly dangerous." The scientists basic claim is that "by burning fossil fuels at a prodigious pace and pouring heat-trapping gases into the atmosphere, humanity is about to provoke an abrupt climate shift." This is already occurring. "The Earth has already warmed by about half that [agreed-upon] amount, with the consequence that virtually all land ice on the planet has started to melt and that the oceans are rising at an accelerating pace." According to Dr. Hansen, the sad fact is that

"We're in danger of handing young people a situation that's out of their control."

6

Chemicals for Breakfast, Lunch, and Dinner

"Monsanto should not have to vouchsafe the safety of biotech food. ... Our interest is in selling as much of it as possible. Assuring its safety is the FDA's job."
          —Phil Angell, director of corporate communications, Monsanto

"It used to be we had a review process at the [FDA]. Now we have an approval process. I don't think the FDA is doing good, honest reviews. They've become an extension of the drug industry."
          —Richard Burroughs, former FDA reviewer and veterinarian

"It was a spring without voices. On the mornings that had once throbbed with the dawn chorus of robins, catbirds, doves, jays, wrens, and scores of other bird voices there was now no sound; only silence lay over the fields and woods and marsh."
          —Rachel Carson, *Silent Spring*

THE EARLY SENTINELS

From the early 1900s until the mid-1980s, coal miners brought caged canaries into the mines with them. As the birds were more sensitive than humans to noxious gasses. Any sign of sickness in the canary was an early warning to the miners.

In 1957 the birds were dying at Olga Huckin's bird sanctuary in Duxbury, Massachusetts. She sent a letter to her friend Rachel Carson, a marine biologist and the author of *The Sea Around Us*. As the birds had been subject to aerial spraying of the pesticide DDT. During World War II DDT was used against insects that carried diseases such as malaria and yellow fever. It had long-term potency and was able to kill some insects upon contact, without being ingested. This opened a new era in pest control and led to the development of new, more powerful synthetic poisons.

Carson had heard of DDT, but her concern about the birds was soon outstripped by her growing awareness of the permanent effects of pesticides. She decided to write a book because, as she said, "There would be no future peace for me if I kept silent."

That book, *Silent Spring,* was well received, and in 1963—a year after the book's publication—*CBS Reports* presented a special called "The Silent Spring of Rachel Carson." The audience was estimated at 10 million to 15 million viewers.

In Carson's obituary one year later, the *New York Times* described how Monsanto and other chemical companies attacked her. "The Monsanto Company, one of the nation's largest chemical concerns, used parody as a weapon. ... Without mentioning her book, the company adopted her poetic style in an article labeled 'The Desolate Year,' which began: 'Quietly, then, the desolate year began ... and wove its own apocalyptic word picture—but one that showed insects stripping the countryside and winning."

Carson biographer Linda Lear recounts that Ezra Taft Benson, U.S. secretary of agriculture from 1953 to 1961, said Carson was "probably a Communist" because she was unmarried despite being physically attractive. American Cyanamid biochemist Robert White-Stevens called her "a fanatic defender of the cult of the balance of nature."

As the pesticide controversy grew, Carson's views received increasing support. President John Kennedy's Science Advisory Committee largely backed Carson's claims, and Supreme Court Justice William O. Douglas declared the need for "a Bill of Rights against the 20th century poisoners of the human race." The general public joined the battle as well.

A POLICY OF BIG FARMS

Under Presidents Richard Nixon and Gerald Ford, Secretary of Agriculture Earl Butz encouraged farmers to "get big or get out" and to plant "hedgerow to hedgerow." In 1973 the government started subsidizing corn, and it became big business. Since that time farms have in fact become large, capital-intensive operations fueled by subsidy policies promoted by Butz at the expense of small- and medium-size family farms.

"The percentage of Americans living on farms diminished from nearly 25 percent during the Great Depression to about 2 percent today," according to the 2015 book *Local Food Environments: Food Access in America,* edited by Kimberly Morland. Less than 1 percent of that tiny population works at farming full time, In contrast, U.S. farms have turned into tax havens for some 50 billionaires, who received $11.3 million in farm subsidies from 1995 to 2012, according data from the Environmental Working Group published in *Forbes* magazine in November 2013. $13,000 over 17 years is a pittance to a billionaire, but coupled with taxpayer funded federal insurance subsidies for crop loss, farming is big business for big investors. And to indicate just how big big farming has become, according to OpenSecrets.org, which reports research gathered by the Center for Responsive Politics, agribusiness spent more than $130 million in 2015 on lobbying.

HOW YOU GONNA KEEP 'EM DOWN ON THE CAFOs?

Concentrated animal feeding operations (CAFOs) aka "factory farming," started in 1926, according to the website factory-farming.com, as "the result of a surplus delivery of 450 chicks to a small farm on the Delmarva Peninsula on the East Coast. Instead of returning the overage, the farmer/housewife decided to keep them indoors through the winter. The chicks survived and almost ten years later, she had increased her flock to 250,000."

In the early 1970s one California farm had 3 million hens in one location and with so many animals in a confined space, disease spread easily. The entire flock had to be destroyed. Nevertheless, by the early 2000s more and more companies were keeping millions of hens. Cal-Maine, headquartered in Jackson, Mississippi, is one of the largest egg producer in the country. A Cal-Maine 2016 investor presentation reported that the company had more than 34 million egg-producing hens in 2014.

BIG PIG AND THE SENATOR

By 1997 the pork industry had made North Carolina state senator Wendell Murphy a *Forbes*-certified billionaire. The magazine's profile reported on Murphy's role in the expansion of industrial hog farms, most significantly by sponsoring legislation that "denied counties the right to zone livestock operations, regardless of size."

In less than a decade North Carolina's hog production rose from less than 3 million animals to about 13 million. The number of small hog farms decreased, with many going out of business, and by 2001 most small pig farms were gone. By 2007 giant industrial farms were raising 97 percent of all the hogs, according to Farm Forward, a nonprofit advocacy group.

BIG PIG LEADS TO BIG BEEF

Erik Marcus's book *Meat Market: Animals, Ethics, and Money* notes that between 1950 and 1980 the number of U.S. farms with dairy cows declined from 3.65 million to 278,000. By 2001 there were only 97,460 such farms left. Wenonah Hauter, in her 2012 book, *Foodopoly: The Battle Over the Future of Food and Farming in America,* tracks the massive consolidation of the meat industry, which is controlled from top to bottom by a handful of giant multinational companies, including Cargill, Tyson, Smithfield, and the Brazilian meat company JBS S.A.

One hallmark of this massiveness is enormous feedlots. Hauter notes that the conditions on these huge feedlots are appalling. Jammed in steel pens, the cows stand without shelter, shade, or grass. They sleep on their own waste, which forms a hard-as-concrete surface that is dusty when dry and sewer-like in the rain. The cattle are squeezed together tightly to minimize the number of calories lost to movement, and they're forced to eat a high-calorie diet of soy and corn byproducts, which can bloat their stomachs and even lead to suffocation.

Not surprisingly, crowding of more and more animals into less and less space increases the opportunity for the spread of disease and infection. Huge amounts of antibiotics are then used to control the problem. That's when farmers discovered that low doses of antibiotics caused the animals to grow faster, and thus the use of antibiotics for nontherapeutic uses skyrocketed.

In addition to drugs (including growth hormones) protein supplements, and corn as the main source of food, genetic engineering also came into widespread use with big farming, transforming animals into living production machines. Beef cattle, which two generations ago took four or five years to get big enough to slaughter, now reach a ready-for-slaughter size of 1,200 pounds in 14 to 16 months, according to a 2002 article by food writer Michael Pollan in the *New York Times Magazine.*

The website factory-farming.com says that a newborn piglet today weighs in at about 2 pounds, but in six months it tips the scales at 260, far more than six-month-old pigs weighed 50 years ago.

SUPER CHICKENS

The Truth About Chicken website notes that in 1925 it took 16 weeks to raise a chicken to 2.5 pounds; today it takes just 6 weeks to double that weight. Chickens have become far bigger than they were in the '50s, with much of the increase occurring in their breasts, making it difficult for them to support their own weight.

San Jose resident Rick Schiller almost died after eating a Foster Farms chicken in September 2013. He had a run-in with a "superbug," a bacterium that has built up resistance to antibiotics because of the avalanche of drugs administered to chickens to make them grow fast.

Wyl S. Hilton told a chilling tale in a 2015 *New Yorker* article of how over the next several days after eating the chicken, the 51-year-old developed classic symptoms of *Salmonella* poisoning: severe diarrhea, vomiting, and painful stomach cramps. Eventually the illness got so bad that Schiller's leg turned purple and swelled to twice its normal size. He was rushed to the emergency room, where doctors struggled to bring down his 103-degree fever. They gave him antibiotics, but the drugs were not effective and his illness, which included an inflamed colon and an acute form of arthritis, persisted for weeks.

Doctors were finally able to treat Schiller effectively with other antibiotics—once he tested positive for *Salmonella heidelberg,* a potent new drug-resistant version of the bacteria that sends about 40 percent of its victims to the hospital. Later, in Schiller's freezer at home, U.S. Department of Agriculture (USDA) inspectors found more chicken with the Foster Farms label that likely originated from one of three California processing plants linked to the outbreak of the superbug.

Once it was able to determine the direct link, the USDA asked Foster Farms to voluntarily recall the contaminated chicken products—but not before scores of people in 29 states and Puerto Rico became sick from eating the tainted meat. Schiller, who says he's lucky to be alive, is suing Foster Farms.

Schiller's case might seem like an isolated horror story, but it's really just one chapter in an entire volume of tales of innocent people suffering from food-borne illnesses caused by the agricultural and livestock industries' hunger for more efficient production and greater profits.

FDA AND USDA'S USELESS RESPONSE

In 2012, under court order to act on the use of antibiotics in livestock production, the Food and Drug Administration (FDA) asked pharmaceutical companies to voluntarily remove labels stating that antibiotics may be used to "promote growth." The agency also requested that animal drugs no longer be available over the counter at feed stores, requiring farmers to get prescriptions from veterinarians. The agency also asked that farmers use antibiotics "judiciously" for therapeutic reasons, or to treat illnesses in their animals, but not to use them to enhance growth—what a joke.

The FDA expects the drug companies and farmers to follow these guidelines, the first steps in phasing out the use of growth-promoting antibiotics in livestock. Consumer groups remain skeptical of requests and guidelines as opposed to what they believe is needed—a full stop to the indiscriminate use of antibiotics in livestock. Representative Louise Slaughter of New York, who is a microbiologist, told *Food Safety News* in 2015, "Certainly one of the reasons that we believe that the American agribusiness uses so many antibiotics is that they keep the livestock in despicable, filthy, dirt-ridden conditions. And then they try to make up for that."

Since 1999 Slaughter has cosponsored legislation to end the overuse of antibiotics in livestock, and she has been the bill's main sponsor since 2007. Her latest bill would require large-scale animal producers and drug companies to disclose the amount of antibiotics being used in food-producing animals. All her previous bills have been killed after intense lobbying efforts by the agricultural and pharmaceutical industries, which benefit from the huge sale of antibiotics for animal feed.

Every day, 51 tons of antibiotics are administered in the

United States, and about 80 percent of that is used by the agricultural industry, according to a December 2013 report in the *New England Journal of Medicine.* An estimated 30 million pounds of these drugs were dumped into animal feed in 2011, reported the news website TakePart.com. Large amounts of nonpharmaceutical-grade antibiotics are routinely sold in feed stores and online without a prescription. Low-dosage antibiotics given to animals kill the weakest bacteria and allow the strongest to flourish, creating superbugs, which are difficult to wipe out. But the lobbyists continue to shower Washington, D.C. with money.

THE SUPERBUG IN MEAT PRODUCTION

The Centers for Disease Control and Prevention (CDC) calls superbugs a "potentially catastrophic" problem. The CDC estimates that more than 2 million people in the United States are sickened by antibiotic-resistant infections each year, and *at least 23,000 people a year die* of them—a high price to pay for an increase in meat production. Just to put that number in perspective, that's about *twice* the number of gun homicides each year from 2009 to 2014, according to Pew Research Center data. In part because of all the drugs given to livestock, many doctors worry that whole classes of antibiotics might one day become useless and make treating humans almost impossible, whether for anything such as minor infections all the way up to organ transplants.

From March 2013 to July 2014, the CDC reported that 634 people became infected with *Salmonella heidelberg,* the super bug that almost killed Rick Schiller in San Jose. But studies suggest that for every documented illness, nearly 30 cases go unreported, meaning this single outbreak may have sickened thousands of people eating Foster Farms chicken. Fortunately for the food-poisoning victims in the Foster Farms case, effective antibiotics were available for this strain of *Salmonella.* But nearly 40 percent of those infected required hospitalization, and 15 percent developed serious bloodstream infections, though no deaths were reported.

So why did it take so long to resolve this epidemic? Unlike *E. coli, Salmonella* bacteria are not classified as an adulterant in meat—even the potent antibiotic-resistant *Salmonella heidelberg* escapes that classification. As a result, the USDA maintains it did not have the power to order a recall of the Foster Farms chicken or to shut down the packing plants contaminated with this version of *Salmonella*. Instead, the agency could only ask Foster Farms to submit a plan to deal with the problem. The company didn't comply until July 2014, *more than a year after the outbreak started.*

Even more dangerous than *Salmonella heidelberg* are antibiotic-resistant staph infections, known as MRSA or "methicillin-resistant *Staphylococcus aureus.*" MRSA does not respond to many types of antibiotics, so it's very difficult to treat. These voracious infections start with standard flu-like symptoms, then they produce large boils that refuse to heal. They spread rapidly through the body, shutting down kidneys and other organs; they can kill victims within hours of when the first symptoms appear. Originally, these super-staph infections were seen only in hospitals, but new clusters of infections have cropped up outside hospitals. Several recent studies have tied them to pig-farming practices. A study in the *Journal of the American Medical Association* found that people who work with pigs, or live near pig farms or fields where pig manure is used as fertilizer, have a higher risk of contracting potentially deadly MRSA infections than the general population. The study's author theorizes that because most of the antibiotics used in breeding pigs pass into their manure, the animals' dung could be a breeding ground for the MRSA superbug.

Treating sick animals with antibiotics is a humane practice, but using drugs to fatten up animals for food production or to help them survive the brutal living conditions of factory farming are unconscionable acts. The FDA and the American Medical Association have joined animal rights groups and consumer-safety organizations in calling for an end to the indiscriminate use of antibiotics in livestock for nonmedical purposes. Yet efforts to ban the practice have been stamped out by agribusiness and pharmaceutical lobbies again and again—the profits reaped by those industries using the drugs are just too big.

BIG COWS YIELD MORE MILK

In 1950, according to factory-farming.com, "an average dairy cow produced 665 gallons of milk per year but now they [*sic*] produce over 2,320 gallons per year." The difference is due to artificial growth hormones. The genetically engineered recombinant bovine growth hormone (rBGH)—also known as recombinant bovine somatotropin or rBST)—is injected into dairy cows to increase milk production, sometimes by as much as 15 percent. Yet the health risks to both livestock and humans are hotly debated.

Forced to produce more milk than they would naturally, rBGH-treated cows become more susceptible to mastitis, a painful udder infection, than their non-treated bovine counterparts. Mastitis results in an increase of pus and blood secretions into the milk and requires treatment with antibiotics, residues of which can remain in the milk—or cheese, or yogurt, or ice cream—they produce.

Genetically modified growth hormones in cows also significantly increase the animals' production of insulin-like growth factor 1 (IGF-1).

BANNED AROUND THE WORLD BUT APPROVED IN THE UNITED STATES

Use of rBGH is banned in all countries within the European Union, plus Japan, Canada, Australia, and New Zealand. Ignoring two decades of mounting opposition from scientists, health professionals, food-safety organizations, organic farmers, and consumers, the FDA remains resolute in its approval of rBGH, which has been linked to carcinogens. In declaring that no material difference exists between milk from rBGH-treated cows and milk from non-treated cows, the FDA is shirking its responsibility by refusing to label milk products containing the potentially lethal rBGH hormone. It doesn't matter if it is a Democratic or Republican administration—the lobbyist dollars are just too big to give up.

Former veterinarian Richard Burroughs was one of the FDA reviewers for the growth hormone. His concerns about the safety of the hormone brought about his dismissal for "slowing down the approval process." Burroughs told the *New York Times* that the FDA was so eager to approve rBST that administrators overlooked flaws in safety studies submitted by the drug manufacturers and did not fully consider potential hazards. He alleges that the FDA knew of the higher-than-normal rate of udder infection and infertility in treated cows but did not require any further study into these issues.

Burroughs also charges that no tests were conducted on the drug's potential effects on humans so as to avoid further delay in regulatory approval of the hormone. "It used to be we had a review process at the [FDA]," Burroughs told the *New York Times*. "Now we have an approval process. I don't think the FDA is doing good, honest reviews. They've become an extension of the drug industry."

Damning research on the synthetic bovine growth hormone was made public even before 1993, when the FDA decreed that rBGH posed no health problems and needed no regulating. In fact, two years earlier, Rural Vermont, a nonprofit farm advocacy group, revealed that rBGH-injected cows used in a study being financed by Monsanto were experiencing serious health problems. The group also found a substantial rise in the number of deformed calves birthed by the rBGH-treated mothers in the study.

A few years later, a report by Health Canada, Canada's health department, confirmed these findings and added that the use of rBGH can lead to reproductive problems in cows, increase the risk of clinical lameness by approximately 50 percent, and even lead to their premature death. (Canada has banned the use of rBGH.) The Health Canada report admonished the FDA for seemingly rubber-stamping its approval of rBGH.

The Canadian report also criticized the manufacturer, Monsanto, for not performing any long-term toxicology studies, for providing sketchy data, and for not explaining how the corporation reached the conclusions it did in its supporting material, including its claim that there were no safety concerns for humans.

Finally, the report took Monsanto to task for its bullying behavior, stating, "There are reports on file that Monsanto pursued aggressive marketing tactics, compensated farmers whose veterinary bills escalated due to increased side effects associated with the use of rBST, and covered up negative trial results."

One of the scientists from the Canadian health department testified before a Canadian Senate committee that Monsanto had attempted to bribe regulatory scientists by offering them up to $2 million to approve rBGH without further tests. The scientist also recounted the theft of notes and files critical of Monsanto's research from her locked office. (Monsanto officials denied the allegations.) In 1999 Health Canada denied Monsanto's application for approval of rBGH.

A United Nations food-safety commission refused to endorse the safety of rBGH, prompting several countries to ban sales of U.S. milk within their borders. Shortly thereafter, American family-owned dairies, major retailers, hospitals, schools, and consumers also began changing their rules to become rBGH-free.

A November 2015 survey of likely 2016 voters by the Mellman Group reported that nearly 90 percent say they are in favor of mandatory labels on "foods which have been genetically engineered or containing genetically engineered ingredients." However, the FDA, Monsanto, and the American Dairy Association have been successful in thwarting legislation to require this step. But they have been unsuccessful at preventing rBGH-free milk providers from marking their milk products as originating from cows not treated with artificial growth hormones. Labels on those products, however, are required to contain the following line: "The FDA has said there is no significant difference between milk from cows treated with rBGH and milk from untreated cows."

In 2008 Monsanto—in what we can only hope was a sign of throwing its hands in the air—sold the worldwide rights of rBGH to Elanco, a division of Eli Lilly. Elanco president Jeffrey Simmons said he was looking forward to providing dairy farmers with options and giving consumers affordable choices. "Critically, we remain focused on the health and care of the cow in working with farmers to increase global milk supply," Simmons declared.

Good luck, Bessie. You're gonna need it.

ROUNDUP: THE NEW POTENTIAL DDT?

Although the pesticide DDT is a thing of the past in the United States, the latest chemical herbicide under scrutiny is glyphosate, the active ingredient in Monsanto's Roundup. In March 2015 the World Health Organization's International Agency for Research on Cancer released its assessment of five organophosphate pesticides, classifying glyphosate as "probably carcinogenic to humans." Monsanto issued a press release saying that the IARC's "conclusion is inconsistent with the decades of ongoing comprehensive safety reviews by the leading regulatory authorities around the world that have concluded that all labeled uses of glyphosate are safe for human health" and that the result was "a clear example of agenda-driven bias." Monsanto soon demanded that the WHO issue a retraction.

In addition, a 2013 article in *Interdisciplinary Toxicology* reported on the growing epidemic of celiac disease, also known as gluten intolerance, and associated it with the Roundup chemical glyphosate, which has been sprayed for decades over millions of acres of our nation's crops. In fact, from 1992 to 2012 an estimated 2.6 billion pounds of Monsanto's glyphosate-based herbicide was used on America's agricultural land, according to a U.S. Geological Survey study.

The good news is that in February 2016, the FDA announced that it would begin testing for glyphosate in corn, soybeans, milk, and other foods sold in the United States. *Newsweek* noted that the "FDA's action comes two years after the U.S. Government Accountability Office chastised the agency in a report for not sufficiently monitoring residues of the chemical on foods." Monsanto responded to the announcement by *Newsweek*, "If FDA does move forward with residue testing in a scientifically rigorous manner, we are confident it will reaffirm the safe use of this vital tool used safely and effectively by farmers, landowners and homeowners around the world."

THE NEW CANARIES: CHILDREN

Like canaries in the coal mines, children today are frequently on the front line of bigger dangers in our environment. Studies show that children with high exposure to pesticides are at increased risk of developing attention deficit hyperactivity disorder (ADHD), autism, and other developmental disorders, according to a December 2012 article published in *Pediatrics*, the journal of the American Academy of Pediatrics. The article also noted that a review of several studies of childhood cancer concluded that exposure to pesticides in utero increased the risk of children developing brain cancer and leukemia. A 2013 survey by the Centers for Disease Control and Prevention found that food and skin allergies among children had increased since the late 1990s. Asthma cases in children have also skyrocketed over the past three decades, according to a 2011 article in *Scientific American*. Furthermore, the number of autism cases and related disorders is far higher today than it was in the 1980s.

It's probably not a coincidence that the time line of genetically modified organisms entering our food system corresponds with these sharp spikes in illnesses and diseases. Children's genes haven't changed in such a short time, but the food that they and their mothers eat has. The scientific community has begun to connect the dramatic uptick in children's health issues to biochemical changes in our food supply.

GMO: GLOBAL SCIENCE EXPERIMENT

In the early 1990s, the chemical giants Monsanto, Dow, and DuPont announced that their newly bioengineered seeds and plants would require fewer pesticides, produce more food, benefit the environment, and end world hunger. Two decades later, the U.S. Department of Agriculture's report on genetically engineered crops in the United States says that more than 90 percent of the acres devoted to soy, corn, and cotton are genetically modified organisms (GMOs). Most require higher levels of pesticides than conventional crops do, few produce significantly higher yields, all have an adverse effect on the environment, and none have helped cure world hunger.

Unless you eat only organic fare, as much as 80 percent of the food you consume has been genetically modified, according to WebMD. It's estimated that the average American eats more than his or her weight in GMOs every year. And while you can check nutrition facts on the labels of packaged food for the amount of calories per servings or the percentage of trans fat, you will not find any information designating that the product contains GMOs. This omission is the direct result of the strong influence of biotech and chemical corporations and the passivity of the FDA.

To create GMOs, biotech engineers—known as "pharmers"—transfer DNA from one or more genes present in one organism into a second organism. Inserting a bacterium into the host's cells infuses pieces of DNA into an organism that contains desired traits. The modified seed can then be programmed for tolerance to a particular herbicide, allowing farmers to spray their fields with a pesticide that kills the weeds without killing the genetically modified (GM) crops. Other seeds can be genetically altered to produce a protein that makes the crop resistant to pests and/or viruses.

All GM crops are programmed to be used in conjunction with some of the most toxic herbicides and insecticides available on the planet, including Monsanto's Roundup. The chemical company reports that the pesticide's active ingredient, glyphosate, passes all safety standards. What it doesn't add is that glyphosate is only one of many ingredients in the proprietary pesticide.

A 2011 health study in the journal *Reproductive Toxicology* was one of the first to detect this dangerous chemical in humans. Glyphosate was found in 5 percent of the 39 nonpregnant women sampled, but none was detected in the 30 pregnant women in the study. GM corn, produced by Monsanto and other companies, has a gene injected into it to kill certain insects.

In addition, a 2014 article published in the *International Journal of Environmental Research and Public Health* reported that "there is consistent evidence that pesticide exposures experienced in occupational agricultural settings may be important determinants of [non-Hodgkin lymphoma]."

Even before GM crops were being considered for commercialization, opponents contended that the process of transferring genes between organisms could cause unexpected and undesirable changes in the altered species. Science and health organizations called for more rigorous studies than those provided by the chemical industry. Memos by scientists at the FDA noted the possible hazards of genetic engineering from "high concentrations of plant toxicants" and warned of "unique animal and food safety concerns."

Yet even as FDA scientists called for Monsanto to supply them with additional research, agency administrators chose to ignore their warnings. Administrators at the agency agreed with Monsanto that GM products were "substantially equivalent" to non-GM products. The FDA affixed its "Generally Regarded As Safe" (GRAS) (things are either GRAS or non-GRAS) label to GMOs, which allows them to be marketed without any testing by the regulatory agency.

Monsanto and the FDA maintain that GM crops are the equivalent of their traditionally grown counterparts, but the fact is that the company holds patents on these GMOs that it can and does profit from.

Canadians are also concerned about how their government has handled GMOs. Geneticist, author, and environmental activist Dr. David Suzuki said in an essay on the David Suzuki Foundation website, "Pressured by companies like Monsanto, the

Canadian government has acted as cheerleader for the biotech industry, approving new strains with little regard to the urgent questions that have been raised. Unlike chemical pollutants or radioisotopes which degrade or decay, GE plants and animals reproduce and mutate, so once released into nature, they cannot be recalled."

MONSANTO TAKES ON FARMERS

The patents on Monsanto's bioengineered seeds make the seeds twice as expensive as conventional seeds, so farmers end up paying much more for a product they are forbidden to reuse the following year. And Monsanto aggressively pursues any farmers who attempt to reuse its seeds. The company has even pursued farmers who didn't even buy Monsanto seeds but whose fields were contaminated by pollen blown from GM crops in nearby farms. This results in a new breed of modified plant, for which Monsanto holds the patent. Of 147 lawsuits Monsanto has filed against U.S. farmers since 1997, only 9 have gone to trial and the company won every case. According to the Center for Food Safety, since 2012 Monsanto has won 72 judgments that total nearly $24 million. The company also won damages in 27 other lawsuits that ended in confidential settlements.

The battle lines have been drawn, and the biotech companies have the connections and funds to fight strenuously to expand their markets. Still, scientists, health professionals, and environmentalists are speaking out about the potential risks GMOs carry for humans, animals, and our increasingly fragile ecosystem. The Non-GMO Project says, "Most developed nations do not consider GMOs to be safe. In more than 60 countries around the world, including Australia, Japan, and all of the countries in the European Union, there are significant restrictions or outright bans on the production and sale of GMOs."

Despite the warnings, it's clear that U.S. regulatory administrators will continue to shower their blessings on genetically engineered products. For example, in March 2015 the FDA approved apples designed not to turn brown when sliced open, and potatoes that resist bruising. Eight months later, the FDA announced that the genetically engineered salmon produced by AquaBounty Technologies was as safe and nutritious to eat as non GM Atlantic salmon.

THE FIGHT FOR LABELING

A coalition of organic farmers and health and consumer-rights advocates hopes that the American public will fight for the labeling of any foods containing genetically engineered material. In 2012 a ballot proposition that would have required such labeling was narrowly defeated in California, thanks in no small part to the more than $20 million contributed by the big food manufacturers opposed to it. That loss was followed by a similar defeat in the state of Washington, as well as the rejection of a labeling amendment in the U.S. Senate.

Opponents of GMO labeling argue that it would add another layer of government bureaucracy and increase costs for farmers and manufacturers for food products that, as Monsanto and the FDA point out, have already been declared safe. But the pivotal point that biotech corporations and food conglomerates are careful not to bring up is that many consumers won't buy foods identified as genetically engineered. In a 2013 *New York Times* survey, 93 percent of consumers favored mandatory food labels on GM products, while more than half of those responding said they would avoid foods labeled as GMOs.

The FDA dropped the ball on this issue—in fact it never even took the field. It appears that any changes involving the labeling or banning of GMOs must come from consumers and legislators who are willing to take on big money. As it turns out, consumers have a pretty good track record on such issues. Still, it has been a struggle to maintain it for the last four decades in the face of entrenched corporate influence.

Science writer Philip Shabecoff spent 14 years at the *New York Times* as chief environmental correspondent. Since then he has written strongly about the environment, including two books on the effect of toxins. In *Earth Rising* (2001) he talked about the back and forth between the government and environmentalists and consumers:

> "The golden age of environmentalism, if such it was, came to an abrupt end in 1980 when Ronald Reagan entered the White House. ... His goal was to get government off the backs of the people. In practice, this generally meant easing or removing regulatory requirements, particularly environmental regulatory requirements. He appointed environmental officials,

notably Secretary of the Interior James G. Watt and Environmental Protection Agency administrator Anne (Burford) Gorsuch, who devoted their energies to reducing the ability of their agencies to protect natural resources and public health.

"At the same time, corporate America, which had been caught off guard by the militant environmentalism that emerged in the 1960s and 1970s, began to mount an effective resistance. The business community, which had originally viewed anti-pollution efforts as a temporary if annoying fad, began to employ sophisticated skills ... to fight environmental regulation and to counter the warnings and accusations leveled against it by the environmentalists.

"In large part because the American people, alerted by the environmentalists through the news media, were paying attention to what was happening in Washington, President Reagan and his administration were unable to roll back the gains made over the course of the century. In fact, the membership rolls and treasuries of the environmental groups swelled to unheard-of levels as Americans demonstrated their concern by joining in record numbers. Gorsuch and Watt were forced to resign. And George Bush, Reagan's vice president, pledged to be the 'environmental president' during his successful first run for the White House."

BIG CHEMISTRY IS NOW THE BIG BOSS

Meanwhile, the chemical companies have grown into chemical conglomerates, now reaping trillions of dollars by bio-industrializing agriculture. According to Sourcewatch, the "Big 6"—BASF, Bayer, Dow, DuPont, Monsanto, and Syngenta (formerly Novartis)—"dominate" the agrochemical field; they "own the world's seed, pesticide, and biotechnology industries." Monsanto has a distinctly high-profile production history; it is known for manufacturing DDT; Agent Orange, the notoriously dangerous defoliant used during the Vietnam War; Roundup; and a sterile seed known as the Terminator seed, whose use forces farmers to purchase additional seed each year.

These corporations are aided by federal agencies that turn a blind eye to the harmful practices they engage in at the expense of the public's health. They have grown used to sidestepping regulations and bulldozing any scientist or advocacy group that gets in their way. What's truly remarkable is that in less than 20 years they have supplanted the country's agricultural industry as well as the prevailing livestock breeding culture. They own the rights to the gene traits in crop seeds. They fill the fields with heavier doses of increasingly lethal poisons. They cause suffering to farm animals and shorten their lives. They spread sickness in people through bioengineered food and chemical food additives. Somewhere, Rachel Carson is turning in her grave.

THE PESTICIDES INSIDE US

America is celebrated for the astounding diversity of its ethnic, social, and cultural groups. But now all Americans share a common bond: No matter what part of the country you live in, what kind of job you have, what you like to do for fun, all of us have dozens of chemicals in our bodies.

We're exposed to chemicals on a daily basis. They're in the air we breathe, the food we eat, the water we drink. We absorb them through our skin by touching everyday items in our houses, workplaces, and backyards. Most are benign, but many pose serious health risks.

In a study conducted in 2000 by the Mount Sinai School of Medicine in New York and published two years later in the journal *Public Health Reports*, a total of 167 chemicals, including industrial compounds and pollutants, were found in the blood and urine of nine volunteers. Of those elements—which included mercury, arsenic, PCBs (banned in 1976), pesticides, and fuel additives—researchers found the following in the participants: 76 carcinogens, 94 chemicals that were toxic to the brain or nervous system, and 77 chemicals that cause reproductive damage. Yet none of the volunteers had ever worked with chemicals or lived close to industrial complexes. Perhaps naively, we expect our state and federal governments to safeguard us from deadly chemicals like these. But, sadly, the system is broken, so it's up to us to protect each other, and the animals we coexist with, and the environment we inhabit, from toxic chemical exposures. And one of the worst of those chemicals is pesticides.

In 1976 the Toxic Substances Control Act (TSCA) charged the

EPA with assessing the safety levels of new commercial chemicals before they were marketed to the public. The agency also was to regulate all existing chemicals (except for those that fell under the auspices of other government agencies, like the FDA), to ensure they were safe for use as well. If the EPA deemed a chemical "an unreasonable risk to health or the environment," the agency was empowered to either regulate the chemical's distribution and application or to ban it.

The TSCA was enacted to prevent consumers from interacting on a daily basis with chemicals that posed a danger. But this simple and important concept was never fully implemented. According to a March 2015 *Washington Post* article, nearly four decades after passage of the act, the EPA has banned only 5 chemicals and it has required tests in less than 1 percent of the 62,000 chemicals on the market before 1976.

In defense of its glacial review rate of older chemicals, the EPA contends that the chemical companies cover their manufacturing information in secrecy, making it difficult for the agency to get sufficient data to assess the potential risks of a given chemical. EPA officials also say proving that a chemical presents unreasonable health risks by TSCA standards is nearly impossible. The *Washington Post* article notes that the EPA has only 90 days to make a determination that a chemical poses an "unreasonable risk," and "rarely does it have all the toxicity data it needs. As a result, nearly all substances the industry wants to make and sell are allowed to go on the market."

And when the EPA finished its ten-year, $10 million study in 1989 and issued a rule to phase out and ban asbestos products, its efforts were overturned two years later by the U.S. Court of Appeals for the Fifth Circuit, which ruled that the agency had insufficient evidence to issue such a ban.

Whether at fault or not, the EPA has let 22,000 chemicals come to market since 1976 with "little or no information ... regarding their potential health or environmental impacts," according to the Natural Resources Defense Council. In 2014, recognizing the need for reform in the TSCA, Congress began working on a draft of the Chemicals in Commerce Act, which both the House and the Senate eventually passed by the end of 2015. Unfortunately, early drafts of the act drew heavy criticism from the Sierra Club, public health groups, and the EPA for being more concerned with shielding trade secrets than protecting consumers from potentially dangerous chemicals.

SUPER WEEDS

The most deadly chemicals in use today are pesticides, and crops that have been genetically modified require tons of them. Farmers who buy Monsanto's genetically modified seeds are contractually bound to use the company's pesticide. So after fields have been periodically doused with the Roundup herbicide, plants that develop resistance to the pesticide—called super weeds—pop up and threaten crops.

By 2011, farming consultant Jay Holder said one variety of super weed had spread to cotton crops in 76 counties in Georgia. "It got to the point where some farmers were losing half their cotton fields to the weed," Holder told *Nature* in 2013. The proliferation of super weeds immune to the pesticide drives growers to apply larger quantities of Roundup, as well as other weed-killing chemicals. A study published in 2012 in the journal *Environmental Sciences Europe* estimates an additional 404 million pounds of secondary pesticides were applied to U.S. fields between 1996 and 2011.

A Washington State University agriculture professor compared farms raising GM crops to farms planting non-bioengineered crops. The former, facing herbicide-resistant super weeds, used 24 percent more pesticides than the latter. Alarmingly, the industry's response is to bioengineer seeds that will be resistant to increasingly toxic pesticides.

Currently waiting in the wings—and recommended for full deregulation by the EPA and the USDA—are Dow AgroScience's corn and soybean seeds. These seeds have been genetically altered to be resistant to the herbicide 2,4-D, which is a component of Agent Orange. And after the super weeds become resistant to 2,4-D? Then the biotech scientists will continue running in place on what Rachel Carson termed the "pesticide treadmill," trading up for the next, more-lethal weapon in what has come to be termed their "arms race against nature."

MORE SENTINELS: FISH

According to a report published in January 2016, there will be more waste plastic in the sea than fish by 2050. The Ellen

MacArthur Foundation produced the report. Dame Ellen is aware of this firsthand: She is a retired, award-winning solo round-the-world sailor.

Along with the World Economic Forum and analytical support from McKinsey & Company, the foundation's initiative is to accelerate business-driven innovations to get the world to a circular (no-waste) economy. Ellen MacArthur warns that plastics production has increased twentyfold since 1964, and projections have it doubling again in the next 20 years.

The North Pacific Gyre, aka the Great Pacific Garbage Patch, covers an area of nearly 5 million square miles—located 700 miles northeast of the Hawaiian Islands and 1,000 miles west of California. It is estimated that it currently contains 11 million tons of floating plastic. And it is only one of five major garbage patches in the oceans around us.

FOOD ADDITIVES: A FREE-FOR-ALL

Food additives are used to enhance the flavor and consistency of food, to add color, or to preserve nutrients. They range from the familiar (baking soda to make batter rise) to the unexpected (a touch of bovine horn in baked goods to prolong shelf-life). The de facto FDA policy is to let the food industry regulate itself on the question of which additives are safe for public consumption. Once the federal agency grants food additives "Generally Regarded As Safe" status, they are added to the food chain without regulatory testing and usually packaged with generic labels, such as "artificial flavoring" or "artificial coloring."

Dozens of new chemical combinations flood the food market each year, sometimes carrying unknown risks to consumers. One of those high-risk additives is azodicarbonamide (ADA or Azo), used by the food industry to bleach flour and develop dough. The chemical is found in hundreds of packaged foods—breakfast cereals, bread, bagels, pizza crust, and other baked goods—produced by dozens of manufacturers, including Sara Lee and Pillsbury. ADA can even be found in some products labeled as "natural" and "whole grain."

One place you won't find ADA is Subway fast-food restaurants. As of April 2014, the company removed the leavening agent after a food blogger's petition about the additive went viral and Subway suffered a substantial financial loss in response. What was all the fuss about? It turns out that one of the byproducts of ADA is urethane, which is used by the ceramics, plastics, and rubber industries to, among other things, manufacture products such as yoga mats and flip-flops.

According to the World Health Organization, ingesting urethane is known to increase the risk of skin reactions, allergies, respiratory issues, and asthma. In addition, based on experiments in which urethane caused cancerous tumors in laboratory animals, the National Institutes of Health declared ADA as "reasonably anticipated to be a human carcinogen." Because of health risks, ADA is banned as a food product in Europe, the United Kingdom, and Australia.

Chemicals deemed safe for inclusion in food in our country range from emulsifiers used in puddings to pesticides found on fruits. ADA is just one of nearly 4,000 additives in the FDA's database called EAFUS (Everything Added to Food in the United States). Yet, as of 2016, about 1,000 of the chemicals in this database had not undergone any toxicology testing. Also, once food additives are approved, manufacturers are not required to track their safety or report findings to the FDA if health risks are revealed. When concerns about already approved additives are raised by scientific studies, nutritionists, or consumers, the FDA usually reacts slowly, if at all. According to Michael Jacobson, nutrition watchdog and head of the Center for Science in the Public Interest, the FDA "requires virtually absolute proof—as in dead bodies with toe tags identifying the chemical cause of death—that a substance is deadly before it dares reverse a previous approval."

Despite evidence, the opinion of government and industry stays the same: There is no substantiation that food additives pose a threat to the health of humans. Subway's removal of the "yoga mat chemical" from its bread is a small victory. According to the Environmental Working Group, "**ADA turns up in nearly 500 items and in more than 130 brands** of bread, bread stuffing and snacks, including many advertised as 'healthy.' "

If it does nothing else, the controversy about ADA can help consumers become more aware of the issue of chemical additives in the foods they buy every day. But this is not a new problem, nor does it have a particularly hopeful solution. Artificial dyes and chemical additives once considered safe have been removed repeatedly from the food chain because of people's adverse reactions. In fact, ADA was substituted for potassium bromate, a chemical approved by the FDA in 1958. According to the Environmental Working Group, potassium bromate is added to "flour used in commercial baked goods." However, science, health, and government organizations, including the EPA, had established that a byproduct of potassium bromate causes cancer. It has been banned for decades in several countries, including Brazil, Canada, China, and the United Kingdom.

But in the United States it is a different story. Remember, the FDA is reluctant to ban previously approved products, so in 1991 the agency requested that bakers voluntarily stop using potassium bromate. Did they comply? Well, in California, foods made with potassium bromate must have a warning label, but let's just say you might want to rethink taking a bite out of that commercially produced pastry the next time you want a snack. It seems that if we want wholesome, decent food, we need to stand up and be heard. We must stop the influence of the lobbyists on the FDA and our elected officials.

THE FUTURE
Until we get an administration and Congress that stands up to the lobbying efforts of the chemical industry, our food will continue to be filled with potentially harmful chemicals—all in the name of profits.

7

The Big Pill: A Drugged Nation

"Rogue internet pharmacies continue to pose a serious threat to the health and safety of Americans. Simply put, a few unethical physicians and pharmacists have become drug suppliers to a nation."
> **—Senator Dianne Feinstein (D-CA)**

"No group is immune to it—it is happening in our inner cities, rural and affluent communities."
> **—Timothy R. Rourke, New Hampshire Governor's Commission on Alcohol and Drug Abuse Prevention, discussing illegal drugs**

"[In 2013] U.S. giant Pfizer, the largest drug company by pharmaceutical revenue, made an eye-watering 42 percent profit margin. As one industry veteran understandably says, 'I wouldn't be able to justify [those kinds of margins].' "
> **—BBC News, November 2014**

According to a Kaiser Family Foundation poll in June 2015, 50 percent of Americans take at least one prescription drug. That's a big number. So when that same poll found "1 in 5 … say they or a family member have skipped doses or cut pills in half due to cost or that they have a hard time affording them—rising to about a third among those with lower incomes"—that's a big problem because it involves billions of dollars to Americans.

Which, Kaiser found, is just what much of the country thinks: "Nearly three-quarters of the public think that the cost of prescription drugs is unreasonable … . Americans place much of the blame with the drug companies, saying they set prices too high and that company profits are a major factor in drug pricing."

And the public is right. Drug costs in this country are out of control and few elected officials are going to take on Big Pharma—they dominate with lobbyists.

Big Pharma rules the roost in Washington as set forth below. One prime example is when the Obama Administration first proposed the Affordable Care Act back in 2009. The only way the legislation was going to get through Congress (then Democrat controlled) was to get Big Pharma on board. They told Pharma that Medicare would NOT negotiate drug prices if they fell in line and supported the Act. They call it the Big Pharma Exemption—and it costs the American taxpayers almost *$15 billion* and climbing every year. Few people in our nation's capital have the power of Big Pharma—it doesn't matter what political party you represent!

THE INDUSTRY: PLAYERS AND PROFITS

> *"More than half the world's population will live in countries where medicine use will exceed one dose per person per day by 2020, up from 31 percent in 2005."*
> **—IMS Institute for Healthcare Informatics**

Worldwide, prescription drug sales are forecast to clock in at around $734 billion in 2015 and nearly $1 trillion by 2020. Five of the biggest pharmaceutical companies in the world are American. They enjoy the highest profit margins of any industrial sector, topping banks and Big Oil.

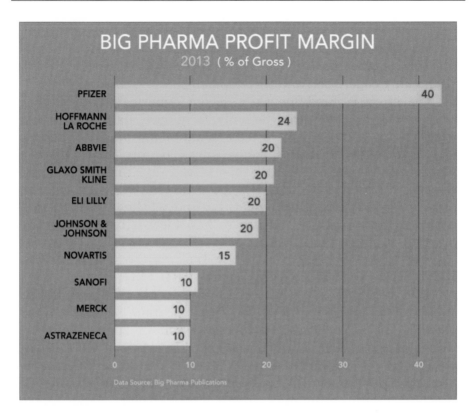

In 2013 according to *BBC News*, pharmaceutical companies enjoyed higher average profit margins than car makers, oil and gas companies, and media companies. Only banks had a profit margin comparable to Big Pharma's. And as you can see on that chart, in 2013 six pharmaceutical companies rang up profit margins of 20 percent or greater. Three years later the picture is even rosier ... for Pharma.

HOW THEY DO IT, PART 1: PRICE CONTROL ... OR PRICES CONTROLLED?

Prescription drug prices in America are expected to continue to rise by double-digit percentages over the next several years, according to the IMS Institute and other industry researchers. That's across the board, not just the name brands but the generics that do the same job at what is supposed to be a far lower price.

As Wendell Potter, former Cigna executive-turned-whistleblower and author, wrote in a commentary for the Center for Public Integrity, "We pay exactly 100 percent more per capita for pharmaceuticals than the average paid by citizens of the 33 other developed countries that comprise the Organization for Economic Cooperation and Development."

The story is fundamentally "about America's unique drug pricing policies. We are the only developed nation that lets drugmakers set their own prices—maximizing profits the same way that sellers of chairs, mugs, shoes, or any other seller of manufactured goods would," reports Sarah Kliff for *Vox*. "In Europe, Canada, and Australia, governments view the market for cures as essentially uncompetitive and set the price as part of a bureaucratic process—similar to how electricity or water are priced in regulated US utility markets."

HOW THEY DO IT, PART 2: DRUG PRICING

As we talked about in the beginning of the chapter, if the astronomical price for hepatitis C medication Sovaldi ignited outrage and a congressional investigation in 2014, why does Gilead Sciences sell this drug at such an extreme price in the United States while peddling it at $11 a pill in Egypt, the country with the highest rate of hepatitis C? And why did 30 capsules of cycloserine go for more than $10,000, or even $500, when a generic version made overseas costs roughly $20 for 100 capsules?

"Amir Attaran, an expert on pharmaceutical access issues and a professor at the University of Ottawa, said it would have made much more sense to just import the drug [cycloserine] from abroad, rather than have it produced in America for so few patients at such high cost. Mr. Hasler [president of the foundation now distributing the drug] said this was probably not done because foreign manufacturers were not willing to bear the expense of applying for regulatory approval in the United States," reported the *New York Times* in September 2015.

"Unfortunately, the process of proving to the FDA that what you are producing is equivalent to the original drug (a process called ANDA—Abbreviated New Drug Application) is expensive and time consuming, thereby reducing the incentive for pharma companies to do so," Ed Miseta wrote on *ClinicalLeader.com,* which reports on news and trends in the clinical research industry, in September 2015

In his Center for Public Integrity piece, whistleblower Potter went on to say that President Obama also once supported drug re-importation, as did Senator John McCain. "In 2012, two years after the passage of the Affordable Care Act, McCain teamed up with Senator Sherrod Brown (D-Ohio), in another attempt to get Congress to pass a drug re-importation bill," said Potter. "When it became clear that his bill would not pass, McCain took to the floor to denounce the ability of well-financed special interests to control the federal government."

" 'What you're about to see is the reason for the cynicism that the American people have about the way we do business in Washington,' " said McCain. '[The pharmaceutical industry] … will exert its influence again at the expense of low-income Americans who will again have to choose between medication and eating.' "

And as the *Wall Street Journal* noted, the "voracious deal making" that has enabled giant drug companies "to wield outsize influence in the pharmaceutical industry," is one of the reasons generic drug prices are rising.

A side note on pricing is the packaging of drugs for sale. A study of cancer drugs usage has shown that billions of dollars are spent on certain cancer drugs that are not used because they are sold only in large quantities because the FDA fails to act on regulating packaging or quantities sold. Some cancer drugs are sold in only one quantity and the waste of unused drugs could be greatly reduced. Two U.S. senators, both Democrats, Amy Klobuchar and Jeanne Shaheen, have proposed such intervention by the FDA.

HOW THEY DO IT, PART 3: BIG PHARMA LOBBYING EFFORTS

In 2014 the pharmaceutical industry spent $230 million on lobbying. That's $40 million less than the record high in 2009, when the fight over the Affordable Care Act was at its peak. According to Potter, Big Pharma's spending total of $3.3 billion from 1998 to 2015 surpassed that of financial services, Big Oil, defense contractors, and other major industries.

Former physician turned Congressman Andy Harris of Maryland was very vocal in his opposition to the Affordable Care Act, and in 2014 he was a leader in blocking the Washington,

D.C., marijuana decriminalization bill. In spite of the fact that approximately 70 percent of Washington, D.C., residents voted in favor of legalizing marijuana for recreational use, Harris was able to introduce an amendment to a congressional spending bill that effectively blocked the new law from taking effect.

Shortly thereafter, media reports revealed that health professionals and Big Pharma donated more than $300,000 to Harris for the 2014 election cycle. Most of the donations came from pain-physician groups. Harris's third largest campaign donor was Emergent BioSolutions, based in Rockville, Maryland. Emergent produces Episil, "a fast-acting treatment that reduces the pain associated with oral mucositis," a common complication of cancer chemotherapy treatment.

Marijuana has widely been accepted in a number of states for its therapeutic potential for pain-management in cancer patients as well as treating nausea and vomiting from chemotherapy. In states where medical marijuana has been legalized, the number of pharmaceutical pain killers prescribed has dropped significantly. Coincidence? Feel free to draw your own conclusions about the connection.

HOW THEY DO IT, PART 4: THE BIG GIVEAWAY AND THE REVOLVING DOOR

The Medicare Prescription Drug Improvement and Modernization Act of 2003 has been called a huge giveaway to drug makers because it prohibited the government from negotiating lower drug prices and banned the importation of identical, cheaper drugs from Canada and elsewhere. The bill, also known as the Medicare Modernization Act (MMA), was passed in an unusual early-morning congressional session under heavy pressure from the drug companies. Billy Tauzin of Louisiana was chairman of the House Committee on Energy and Commerce, which oversees the drug industry, and he played a key role in the passage of the bill.

Big Pharma's big coup in the MMA was the creation of the government-funded prescription drug program for seniors, known as Medicare Part D.

"As I learned from talking to pharmaceutical company lobbyists, the industry had for years been opposed to a prescription drug benefit," Lee Drutman wrote in his book, *The*

Business of America is Lobbying: How Corporations Became Politicized and Politics Became More Corporate. "They were convinced that such a benefit would mean government bulk purchasing. But at some point industry leaders realized they could push for a prescription drug benefit *without* bulk purchasing."

The *Economist* called the MMA a "classic case of selfish lobbying wrapped in a cloak of selflessness."

In 2004 Tauzin resigned from Congress and became head of PhRMA, a powerful trade group. It was a lucrative next step for the former congressman.

As *BloombergBusiness* picked up the thread, "In 2009 ... he brokered a deal capping at $80 billion the amount drugmakers would contribute to the overhaul in return for his organization's support of the law. ... The $80 billion contribution, to be made over 10 years, helped the Obama administration close a gap in Medicare funding, called the donut hole, and allowed health-law supporters to say they were lowering seniors' costs for prescription drugs." The health overhaul was signed into law in March 2010 after more than a year of debate. Tauzin seemed to be earning his keep with his $11.6 million salary.

Meanwhile the total net profits for Big Pharma's top 11 global companies from the year of Medicare Part D's passage to 2012: $711 billion, according to company filings analyzed by Health Care for America Now, a political group that advocated for health reform from 2008 to 2013. The $130 million Big Pharma laid out in lobbying expenses in 2003 turned out to be money well spent.

HOW THEY DO IT, PART 5; PAY FOR DELAY

Seeing that its patent on cancer drug Gleevec would be running out, Novartis put its chips on a replacement, Tasigna (annual price: $102,000, sales in 2013: $1.27 billion worldwide). But Novartis didn't entirely forgot about Gleevec. Although its patent expired in July 2015, a much cheaper generic wasn't available in the United States until February 2016.

That sleight of hand was accomplished under a so-called patent infringement settlement with a generic drug maker, in this case Sun Pharmaceuticals Industries, a subsidiary of a Mumbai pharmaceutical company. The sham suit was effectively a way for Novartis to pay Sun to delay bringing a competing drug to market. Lawsuits have been filed against what is known in the trade as a "pay-for-delay" deal, and these deals have recently come under government scrutiny. However, the courts are starting to use the laws that could stop pay to delay.

BIG PHARMA FIGHTS THE LAW

In the court of public opinion, the tide is starting to turn against Big Pharma's big prices and the tide may be starting to turn in the courts.

One of the first cracks in Big Pharma's armor came in response to the OxyContin story. "In 2007, in *United States of America v. The Purdue Frederick Company, Inc.*, Purdue and its top executives pleaded guilty to charges that it misled doctors and patients about the addictive properties of OxyContin and misbranded the product as 'abuse resistant,' " as Mike Mariani told the story in *Pacific Standard* in February 2015. "Prosecutors found a 'corporate culture that allowed this product to be misbranded with the intent to defraud and mislead.' Purdue Pharma paid $600 million in fines," in 2007, one of the largest fines for a drug company at the time.

A good example of recent price gouging is Daraprim, a small white pill that looks a bit like an aspirin. After more than six decades of quiet existence as a treatment for toxoplasmosis, a parasitic disease, Daraprim got its 15 minutes of fame last year when its price went up. Not double. Not triple. Daraprim became *55 times* more expensive from one day to the next. As the *Huffington Post* explained it, "a startup company called Turing Pharmaceuticals AG bought the exclusive marketing to Daraprim ... . Led by CEO Martin Shkreli ... Turing jacked up the price of this humble yet life-saving drug from $13.50 per pill to $750 per pill."

The *Los Angeles Times* reported Shkreli saying, "There's this expectation that drug companies should act differently from other companies, because you have to buy their products. That notion needs to disappear." *Newsweek*'s headline quoted him as saying, "I Think Profits Are a Great Thing."

After firing back at critics on Twitter (quoting rapper Eminem's lyrics), Shkreli backed down on the price hike and made his Twitter account private. In November 2015 he announced that hospitals will get discounts of up to 50 percent, but, as of February 2016, the price is still $750 a pill for everyone else.

Shkreli's rationale was that the "market" would be better off if he made a profit and was able to fund more research and development (R&D) for "new" drugs (note his focus on the "market" rather than the "patient" and his assumption that a newer drug will be better). Such brash and boorish behavior probably made some other Big Pharma execs wince as these antics trained a white-hot spotlight onto an industrywide get-rich scheme. Shkreli has since resigned as CEO and has been indicted on securities fraud charges (related to a previous job).

Daraprim can save the life of a person with a weakened immune system, if the patient can afford it.

ORPHAN DRUGS
Orphan drugs treat rare diseases that affect only a small number of people. Daraprim and medicines like it are referred to as "orphan drugs." (For example, about 2,000 patients a year in the U.S. take Daraprim.) And not long after Turing Pharmaceuticals' blatant act of price gouging, another orphan drug was in the news for similar reasons.

Cycloserine has been around since the 1950s and is used to treat "multidrug-resistant tuberculosis." As the *New York Times* tells the story, "In 2007 [the manufacturer] gave the rights for the United States and Canada to the Chao Center ... which is under the auspices of the Purdue Research Foundation." But after the center lost "about $10 million on the drug since 2007 because of the small number of patients and high regulatory costs ... Cycloserine was acquired ... by Rodelis Therapeutics, which promptly raised the price to $10,800 for 30 capsules, from $500."

Sound familiar? But this time, post-Turing, the story had a different ending. Dan Hasler, president of the Purdue Research Foundation, told the *Times,* "We said this was not what we had intended." And following the outcry about this price increase, Rodelis returned the drug to the Chao Center. "The foundation now will charge $1,050 for 30 capsules, twice what it charged before, but far less than Rodelis was charging. Mr. Hasler said the new price was needed to stem losses.

Cycloserine may not seem like a very important, but it means the world to the small group of people for whom it's a life-saving medicine.

THE NEW BLOCKBUSTER DRUGS

On the other end of the medical spectrum from the orphan drugs are the blockbusters. Take Solvadi, a breakthrough medicine for the hepatitis C virus that is highly effective for the three million Americans suffering from the disease.

"Their lives, in short, will be transformed," said Pharmaceutical Research and Manufacturers of America (PhRMA)'s then-president and -CEO John Castellani, at the group's 2014 annual meeting in Washington. "The value to these patients, and to their loved ones and society—you can't put a price tag on it."

Except the California biopharmaceutical company, Gilead Sciences, did just that—and a hefty price tag at that. Gilead more than doubled the price of Sovaldi after acquiring its developer Pharmasset in 2011. The new price: $84,000 for a 12-week treatment, or about $1,000 per pill. (Gilead's profit margin turned out to be pretty hefty as well: 57 percent in March of 2015, with projections that it would hit $30 billion in sales by the end of 2015.)

So what determines a morally justifiable price for a drug? You would think that a reasonable drug price could maintain healthy pharmaceutical company profits without venturing into the realm of profiteering. And pharmaceutical company profits *are* quite healthy:

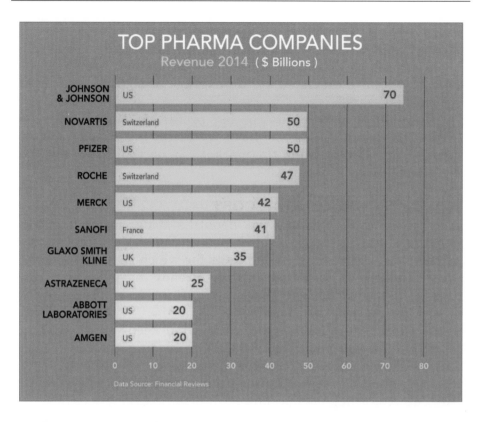

In a 2013 open letter in *Blood,* the journal of the American Society of Hematology, more than 100 oncologists from around the world cited prices of $100,000 and more for drugs targeted at a specific type of cancer, chronic myelogenous leukemia. The letter pointed to the price of Imatinib (marketed as Gleevec), whose price has tripled from $30,000 per year when it was introduced in 2001 to $92,000 in 2012 and which has generated billions in sales and profits for its Swiss manufacturer, Novartis.

"If you are making $3 billion a year on Gleevec, could you get by with $2 billion?" asked Dr. Brian Druker, who helped develop the drug and is now director of the Knight Cancer Institute at Oregon Health & Science University, in an interview with the *New York Times.*

Two years later, more than 100 oncologists wrote another open letter, which appeared in the journal *Mayo Clinic Proceedings,* stating, "There is no relief in sight because drug companies keep challenging the market with even higher prices. This raises the question of whether current pricing of cancer drugs is based on reasonable expectation of return on investment or whether it is based on what prices the market can bear."

According to an academic study cited in that letter, cancer drug prices have escalated by "an average of $8,500 a year over the past 15 years."

There is huge potential for big profits on new drugs—the blockbusters. But unlike the movie business, Big Pharma makes money at the other end of the market too, on the "indie" orphan drugs and on the greatest hits.

A HUMAN COST OF HIGH COST

Let's go back to Solvadi, the hepatitis drug, for a moment. Because it is so expensive, Medicare and private insurers have placed strict limits on the conditions for which they approve the drug, limiting it to patients who already have severe liver damage. As Olga Khazan reports in an article in the *Atlantic,* posted on its website September 25, 2015, "It [Solvadi] was supposed to be a miracle, but now it's what keeps Laura Bush, a nurse-practitioner near Albuquerque, awake at night. ...

"Bush's clinic, First Choice Community Healthcare, is a federally qualified health center in the rural town of Los Lunas, New Mexico, which means she sees a disproportionate number of patients who are uninsured, underinsured, and on Medicaid, the government insurance program for the poor. In other words, they can't afford Sovaldi.

"The state's Medicaid program rations access to Sovaldi and other blockbuster Hep C drugs to only the sickest patients. Even with those limitations, the drugs will likely cost the state an estimated $140 million this year. At various points since Sovaldi became available last year, Bush said, Medicaid has required her to perform risky liver biopsies on patients to prove how sick they are, or wait until patients have late-stage liver disease before they can be eligible for coverage. Each day, Bush juggles seeing patients with writing appeal letters and filing pre-authorizations that are often denied. ...

"Those who don't get the medication can die 'some of the worse deaths I've ever seen,' Bush said. ... 'At the end you die not knowing who you are, your belly looks 12 months pregnant, you're malnourished, and you're bleeding to death.' "

PRESCRIPTION DRUG OVERDOSES AND ADDICTION

The price Americans pay for Big Pharma's greed goes well beyond dollars. According to the Centers for Disease Control and Prevention, in 2014 the number of deaths associated with prescription drug overdoses hit a peak: About 128 Americans were dying from overdoses of painkillers each day—and most of these cases involved prescription medications. And today, roughly 7,000 people are treated in emergency rooms every day for overdosing on painkillers—mostly opiates.

Surprisingly, in the United States, rural deaths by overdose have exceeded deaths in metropolitan areas. For example, the deaths in New Hampshire made it a top campaign issue in the 2016 primary election. In 2014, there were 334 deaths from opioid overdose in that small state. Most of those deaths involved a version of fentanyl, a synthetic opiate that can be deadlier than heroin.

New Mexico is another example of a rural population dealing with an increase in drug addiction. The state has seen high death rates from heroin overdoses since the early 1990s. A nonprofit organization formed to fight heroin addiction, Healing Addiction in Our Community, said that heroin addiction is now being passed down from generation to generation. A state epidemiologist said addiction is as prevalent in poor communities as well as affluent ones.

But maybe there isn't any place hit harder than Kentucky, and Ground Zero in Kentucky might well be rural Bell County. The *Boston Globe* (looking to learn lessons that might help Massachusetts cope with its own opiate problem) reported on the story last summer:

"Nearly two-thirds of the adults in [Bell] county do not have jobs, and addiction to opioid painkillers has metastasized. Miners often turned to painkillers after injuries, and many of their children became dependent on opioids stashed as close as the medicine cabinet. ... The opioid death rate in 2013 was 93.2 per 100,000 in Bell County, nearly double that of any other Kentucky county. ... [Statewide, almost 1,100 Kentuckians died of an opiate overdose in 2014.]

"Micky Hatmaker, a former state trooper and [Bell County] native, put much of the blame on big pharmaceutical companies for aggressively marketing painkillers, and on unscrupulous doctors and pharmacists who dispense them. ...

"As he walked through a small professional building, Hatmaker glanced at a pharmaceutical saleswoman waiting outside a dental office. 'You see her?' Hatmaker asked a visitor... 'That's the enemy.' "

How did all this happen to rural America? For that answer, we turn to urban America, and turn back the clock.

ADVERTISING, PROMOTION, AND ADDICTION

"In 1952, brothers Arthur, Raymond, and Mortimer Sackler purchased Purdue Pharma, then called Purdue Frederick Co.," as Mike Mariani reported in *Pacific Standard,* a print and digital magazine that covers the intersection between private behavior and public policy. The article appeared in February 2015. "The eldest brother, Arthur, was a brilliant polymath, contributing not only to psychiatric research but also thriving in the fledgling field of pharmaceutical advertising. It was here that he would leave his greatest mark. ... Sackler expanded the possibilities of medical advertising by promoting products in medical journals and experimenting with television and radio marketing. Perhaps his greatest achievement, detailed in his biography in the Medical Advertising Hall of Fame, was finding enough different uses for Valium to turn it into the first drug to hit $100 million in revenue. ...

"On December 12, 1995, the Food and Drug Administration approved the opioid analgesic OxyContin. ... In its first year, OxyContin accounted for $45 million in sales for its manufacturer ... Purdue Pharma. By 2000 that number would balloon to $1.1 billion. ... Ten years later, the profits would inflate still further, to $3.1 billion. How did they do it?

"According to an article published in *The American Journal of Public Health,* 'The Promotion and Marketing of OxyContin: Commercial Triumph, Public Health Tragedy,' Purdue increased its number of sales representatives from 318 in 1996 to 671 in 2000. By 2001, when OxyContin was hitting its stride, these sales reps received annual bonuses averaging over $70,000, with some bonuses nearing a quarter of a million dollars. In that year Purdue Pharma spent $200 million marketing its golden goose."

And there was more.

"Long before the rise of big data, Purdue was compiling

profiles of doctors and their prescribing habits into databases. ... The idea was to pinpoint the doctors prescribing the most pain medication and target them for the company's marketing onslaught. ...

"Between physician databases, incentive-happy sales reps, and an aggressive blitz package of promotional ephemera, Purdue's multifaceted marketing campaign pushed OxyContin out of the niche offices of oncologists and pain specialists and into the primary care bazaar, where prescriptions for the drug could be handed out to millions upon millions of Americans."

But if Arthur Sackler and Purdue paved the way, many have followed that path. Expenditures on direct-to-users advertising have more than quintupled in the eight years between 1997 and 2005 since the FDA changed the guidelines, from over $1 billion in 1998 to over $4 billion in 2005, a 300 percent increase according to government figures.

Nine of the world's ten biggest pharmaceutical companies now spend more on marketing drugs than developing them, according to data collected by GlobalData. Marketing of drugs is the new opportunity, whether you are wearing a tie or a sweatshirt.

DIRECT CONSUMER MARKETING
Big Pharma spends billions to advertise directly to consumers and in 2014, it is estimated they spent almost $5 billion in direct consumer advertising. As mentioned, almost every other country in the world bans direct advertising.

Gray Humphreys described this famous Lipitor ad in a 2009 article in the *Bulletin of the World Health Organization:*

"The distinguished doctor who has been introduced as the 'inventor of the artificial heart' turns to the camera and says, 'Just because I'm a doctor doesn't mean I don't worry about my cholesterol.' He then recommends people use an anti-cholesterol drug, Lipitor, and to show just how confident he is in his own ticker, he rows across a lake. It was a killer advertisement, part of a campaign put together at a cost of US$ 260 million for drug company Pfizer. But it relied on the audience being unaware of several important facts: Robert Jarvik, the distinguished 'doctor' in the boat, had never been licensed as a medical doctor, could not legally prescribe anything and was not the inventor of the artificial heart (at least according to three former colleagues at the University of Utah). It later turned out that he hadn't even rowed the boat. Welcome to the world of direct-to-consumer advertising."

According to Humphreys, "direct-to-consumer advertising of drugs has been legal in the USA since 1985, but only really took off in 1997 when the Food and Drug Administration (FDA) eased up on a rule obliging companies to offer a detailed list of side-effects in their infomercials (long format television commercials)." (Mass marketing to consumers of pharmaceuticals is banned in more than 30 industrialized nations, but not in the United States as the FDA has been useless in policing drug advertising. You can buy anything you want on the internet.)

BATHTUBS, BLADDERS, AND SIDE EFFECTS

We've all seen the scenes of happy couples—smiling from their his-and-her bath tubs overlooking the ocean. The visuals promise sex, satisfaction, love, and health while the voice-over and fine print at the end murmur of side effects and "serious complications."

As Julia Belluz notes in her health column on *Vox,* a news website:

> "Drug companies are not required to tell patients how well their drugs actually work or really give any context all. Companies don't have to say how many people will actually benefit from the drug, or how many might be harmed. They also don't need to mention cost, or whether there's a cheaper generic version of the drug, or whether improved diet and exercise could help a person's condition more than their medication.
>
> "This means drug companies have no incentive to spell out the fact that their new insomnia pill will probably only grant you 15 minutes more sleep a night, while delivering a 70 percent chance that you'll be drowsy to the point of potentially crashing your car the next day.
>
> " 'These ads are out there for a reason, which is to try to sell the drug,' said Harvard's Aaron Kesselheim, 'and as a result, there have been a lot of instances where they tend to

overstate positive components and understate or present negative ones in ways that aren't necessarily as strident as they could be.' "

Recent moves on the political chessboard in the United States include the FDA issuing a draft of new guidelines that feature recommendations that "companies would be required to deliver information about their products in plain language, and they wouldn't need to mention every side effect of a drug, only the 'most serious and the most common' ones," reports Belluz.

But in a counter move, Belluz also mentioned that two drug companies had sued the FDA over the rule that they're "not allowed to advertise 'off-label uses,' claiming that it violates their First Amendment right to free speech." ("Off-label" means uses of a drug that aren't listed on the FDA-approved label for that drug.) Don't expect the FDA to take on the drug companies with any determination as many people at the FDA do not want to create waves.

DOCTORS AS PUSHERS

The great majority of doctors are really concerned only with the health and treatment of their patients. Unfortunately, there are a number of doctors that buy into the song of drug companies. We can turn a deaf ear to those TV enticements for new drugs that will improve our lives, but drug companies aim even more money at enticing our doctors. Doctors are wined and dined, researchers write favorable pieces in medical journals, "medical leaders" are hired to expound on the drugs' wonders, and sales people use an arsenal of dubious claims in their pitches in doctor's offices.

Endo Pharmaceuticals sales representatives made 72,000 visits to doctors pushing the narcotic Opana ER, according to court documents published by *Bloomberg,* citing company records. It was money well spent, noted *FiercePharma*, an online trade publication, stating, "The doctors [those] reps visited wrote three times as many scripts for the drug as those who weren't on the call list. The most heavily targeted docs prescribed the drug an average of 30 times a month."

Just about every other line of business believes that sex sells, so why would Big Pharma be any different? That's how GlaxoSmithKline (GSK) saw it when it decided to sell its antidepressant Wellbutrin for off-label uses such as libido enhancement and weight loss. Whistleblower Blair Hamrick testified that he was encouraged to tell doctors: Hey Doc, remember Wellbutrin is the happy, horny, skinny drug."

Radio personality Dr. Drew Pinsky praised the virtues of Wellbutrin to his listeners, saying he prescribes it and other medications to depressed patients because it "may enhance or at least not suppress sexual arousal" as much as other antidepressants do, according to a 2012 *Wall Street Journal* article. Listeners didn't know that Pinsky received $275,000 from GSK for "services for Wellbutrin." For this and inappropriate marketing of other drugs, GSK agreed to pay a *$3 billion* penalty in 2012.

In 2010 Allergan made off-label marketing "a top corporate priority to maximize sales of Botox," according to the Justice Department, no matter how bogus the off-label claims were.

"Allergan held workshops to teach doctors and their office staffs how to bill for off-label uses, conducted detailed audits of doctors' billing records to demonstrate how they could make money by injecting Botox," says a Justice Department press release. Allergan also "directed physician workshops and dinners focused on off-label uses, paid doctors to attend 'advisory boards' promoting off-label uses, and created a purportedly independent online neurotoxin education organization to stimulate increased use of Botox for off-label indications."

The company paid $600 million in civil and criminal penalties for its "off-label" marketing of Botox injections for pain, headaches, spasticity, and even juvenile cerebral palsy.

Many other doctors are on the Big Pharma payroll in one way or another. Between August 2013 and December 2014, 1,617 drug and medical device companies made $3.53 billion in "general payments," according to ProPublica, drawing on a federal database, part of the Physician Payments Sunshine Act, which requires drug and medical device manufacturers to report payments they make to doctors.

It is estimated that over 500,000 doctors have had some type of suspension in California alone—many for the over prescription of drugs. It is in the millions across the country and getting worse every day for the prescribing of pain pills.

OUR MEDICAL SCHOOLS

Leaders of prestigious medical schools are on the payroll as well. According to a study in the April 2014 *Journal of the American Medical Association*, some of the largest U.S. drug companies have on their boards of directors at least one member who is a senior executive of an academic medical center or a teaching hospital, a position with "considerable influence over research, clinical, and educational missions."

Among those listed in the *JAMA* article are medical schools at Yale, Harvard, Johns Hopkins, and the University of Southern California; and hospitals and medical centers including New York Presbyterian, Massachusetts General, and Memorial Sloan-Kettering Cancer Center. Johnson & Johnson reimbursed directors between $275,000 and $310,000 a year. Gilead Sciences, Valeant, Novartis, and Celgene had directorial reimbursements ranging between $350,000 and $500,000 per year.

So when the pharmaceutical companies say that bringing a new drug to market is expensive, and that high prices on existing drugs pay for the research that makes future drugs possible, your antenna should go up. And when those companies want us to picture that money spent on test tubes and beakers and scientists in lab coats, you will know now to erase that image and picture instead brochures, free samples, sales people hosting lunches, and beautiful television ads. The reality is that the big companies are spending far more on marketing than on research.

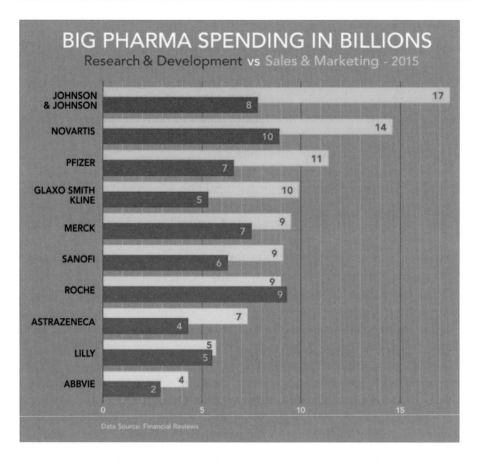

RESEARCH AND DEVELOPMENT OUTSOURCED

With all those payments to doctors and ad agencies, even Big Pharma has to cut costs somewhere. An increasingly popular cost-control measure is outsourcing for work "historically held as core pharmaceutical functions"—researching, developing, and making drugs. That is, the work you might naturally assume a pharmaceutical company would do. This, according to a 2010 report by researchers from ICON, a clinical research and biotech company based in Ireland.

The pharmaceutical outsourcing market reached about $130 billion in 2015, and it is projected to grow to $215 billion in 2020, according to Research and Markets, an online market research database. According to BBC Research, the fastest growing segment is contract research, which accounted for $42 billion in 2014 and is estimated to reach $72 billion in 2019.

Already, the majority of U.S. drug company clinical trials are carried out overseas. As of February 2016, according to the NIH, of 209,000 registered studies, only 38 percent were conducted exclusively in the U.S., with 46 percent taking place wholly outside the country. Of the 37,000 studies in the recruiting stages, 54 percent are happening overseas.

"The hiring company benefits by saving costs and eliminating the stresses related to operating and managing a production facility and related research," according to the BBC Research report. Which raises the question—what do pharmaceutical companies do in this country? And we've seen the answer—advertising and sales.

BIG PILL SWALLOWS LITTLE PILLS (AND LEAVES THE COUNTRY)

Since more and more companies outsource more and more research, it's probably not surprising that R&D tax credits don't do much for the industry, saving maybe a paltry $5 billion a year. But "tax inversions" offer a tremendous upside.

Here's an example: An American pharmaceutical company, Horizon Pharma of Lake Forest, Illinois, buys a foreign drug company, in this case, Vidara Therapeutics of Dublin, Ireland, and presto! Horizon declares it's no longer based in the United States and thus no longer subject to U.S. corporate taxes. Its new official headquarters are in Ireland, where corporate tax rates are far lower.

But that change was child's play compared to the challenge of following this transformation: In 2012, U.S.–based Watson Pharmaceuticals bought Actavis (a Swiss company), and then changed its name to—Actavis. In 2013, Actavis bought Warner Chilcott (based in Ireland). This time, Actavis kept its name, but moved its location—"inverting" itself to Dublin. Then Actavis, now an Irish company, bought Forest Laboratories, a U.S. company, in a relatively simple transaction. Finally (for the moment, at least) Actavis bought Allergan (the maker of Botox)—and after the dust settled from that transaction, in 2015 Actavis changed its name to—Allergan!

But wait, there's more. Also last year, Allergan sold off its generic drug business (which, if you're keeping score, was the original Actavis's business) to Israel's Teva Pharmaceutical

Industries for $40.5 billion.

The Obama Administration finally stepped up to the plate in late 2015when the Treasury Department announced new steps to stop the tax inversions (loopholes). Pfizer had planned a $150 billion merger with Allergan for a lower tax bill and then abandoned it in 2016 when the Treasury put out new rules to stop the Wall Street tax scams with Big Pharma.

STOPPING GENERICS

In May 2015, Teva Pharmaceuticals agreed to pay $1.2 billion to settle a Federal Trade Commission (FTC) antitrust suit filed in 2008 against Cephalon, a Pennsylvania biopharmaceutical acquired by Teva in 2011. The case involved the drug Provigil. Most often prescribed for sleep disorders, Provigil is also popular with stock traders, college students, and others who choose to keep their eyes wide open for considerable periods of time. Cephalon had paid generic drug makers more than $300 million to hold off manufacturing and selling cheaper versions for six years.

As reported by the *New York Times* on May 28, 2015, "Michael A. Carrier, a professor at the Rutgers School of Law, who specializes in anti-trust and patent law, said Teva may have decided to settle after a judge ruled that the F.T.C. could seek disgorgement of Cephalon's profits from Provigil between 2007 and 2012 if it prevailed in the trial that was scheduled. Had the trial proceeded, Mr. Carrier said, 'they could have been looking at billions.' Still, he said, the settlement amount would catch the attention of companies that engage in similar practices and would be a powerful deterrent.

" 'A billion is a big figure,' he said. 'That will wake people up.' "

The *Times* story continued, "The government wants more generics in the market, more quickly, in order to cut health care costs," said Erik Gordon, a professor at the University of Michigan's business and law schools who focuses on the pharmaceutical industry. "Anyone doing anything to slow the flow of generics should expect trouble.

MISLEADING THE PUBLIC

In 2014 five major drug companies—Actavis, Endo Health

Solutions, Johnson & Johnson's Janssen Pharmaceuticals, Purdue Pharma, and Teva Pharmaceutical Industries' Cephalon— were sued by Orange and Santa Clara counties for improperly spending tens of millions of dollars on marketing narcotic painkillers as safe—safer even than over-the-counter drugs like aspirin and ibuprofen (because nobody is going to get rich if people just take aspirin).

Other industry leaders caught misleading the public about their wares, and fined a total of about $20 billion in the past decade, include Merck (Vioxx), GlaxoSmithKline (Avandia), Pfizer, Johnson & Johnson, Eli Lilly, and Abbott Laboratories.

Beyond false advertising infractions, thousands of major civil lawsuits and criminal investigations alleging insurance fraud and other misdeeds have been filed. The lawsuits being filed by teams of prosecutors against Big Pharma calls to mind the decades-long legal onslaught against the tobacco industry.

Novartis is one of Big Pharma's repeat offenders. The U.S. Justice Department and 11 states are going after the company. A whistleblower suit alleges the maker of two drugs—one to treat iron overload in the blood, the other to prevent organ rejection in transplant patients—engaged in a multimillion dollar kickback scheme with doctors and specialty pharmacies to keep prescribing and refilling prescriptions for the drugs, at a cost of $700 million in reimbursements from Medicare and Medicaid.

A 2010 report from Public Citizen found: "Four companies (GlaxoSmithKline, Pfizer, Eli Lilly, and Schering-Plough) accounted for more than half (53 percent or $10.5 billion) of all financial penalties imposed over the past two decades [1991 to 2010]. These leading violators were among the world's largest pharmaceutical companies."

The pharmaceutical industry has been taken to court for violations ranging from defrauding Medicare and Medicaid, to illegally promoting drugs for "off-label" uses, to shoddy manufacturing.

TAKING ON DRUG COMPANIES

Many private law firms have taken on Big Pharma and Cotchett, Pitre & McCarthy has successfully sued Big Pharma on behalf of thousands of patients and investors (and acquired a first-hand familiarity with the industry's violations of the law). For example, the firm was co-lead trial counsel in a class-action lawsuit against Pfizer alleging that painkillers Bextra and Celebrex led to heart attacks and strokes. Pfizer agreed to settle the case for $894 million in 2008 for the benefit of consumers.

Given their immense profits, even the "big" fines levied against Big Pharma may not have a big impact. But the government does have a weapon in its arsenal that might be effective: banning a company from future federal contracts, that is, selling drugs to Medicare and Medicaid. In the Bextra case, Pfizer arranged for a subsidiary—which, as a CNN investigative report noted, was "nothing more than a shell company whose only function is to plead guilty"—to take the fall for the criminal conviction.

To some, these drug company crimes are not just symptoms of something wrong with the system. They are a disease—an addiction—that has infected the industry at the highest levels. Medicare spent $103 billion on prescription drugs in 2013, according to the Centers for Medicare and Medicaid Services. Big Pharma wants to protect Part D and not negotiate drug prices with the government. That accounts for approximately one-third of all prescription drug sales in that year. Big Pharma wants to keep it that way. *Big Pharma wants no reduction on new drug patents from 12 years to 7.* Protect Big Pharma's ability to charge for a drug as long as possible before it becomes generic. Big Pharma wants no *restrictions on pay to delay.* Let them make its side deals without intervention. They want no *easing of importation rules.* Keep low-cost competitors out of the marketplace with no *restriction on pricing.* Big Pharma wants to set prices to whatever the market will bear.

WHAT CAN BE DONE—BETTER REGULATION

All of this is pretty one-sided in favor of Big Pharma, but that's the way it has been in the gold rush of the past 20 years. That's what they've come to expect and that's what they pay good money for. It's possible though, that the good times are waning and they have become too greedy for their own good. Public concern is growing and becoming louder.

We've seen that the courts have acted in some cases to hold Big Pharma accountable for stretching, bending, and outright breaking the law.

A July 2015 Kaiser Family Foundation poll on Medicare found that 87 percent of those surveyed want the federal government to negotiate with Big Pharma on drug prices.

The Veterans Health Administration can negotiate on drug prices and pays significantly less than Medicare does. If Medicare, with its immense purchasing power, could do the same, and negotiate the cost of drugs used by its subscribers, the potential savings could reach $540 billion over a ten-year period. The NIH (National Institutes of Health) comes up with a more moderate estimate of $22 billion. But a billion here, a billion there—pretty soon you're talking real money. "The magnitude of these savings cannot be ignored," said the NIH.

"People don't understand why these drugs cost so much, and they don't understand why, in America, you can't negotiate for a better price," said Mollyann Brodie, the executive director of public opinion and survey researching at the Kaiser Family Foundation.

A number of states are also trying to come to grips with the issue. One tool is a "transparency" law that forces manufacturers to post the production costs of expensive drugs on a public website. Bills have been introduced in several states, but with the drug lobby coming down hard, none have passed yet. That includes California, the bluest of blue states.

But with the latest revelations in the news, this could change. It seems investors and Wall Street are having second thoughts. As Gretchen Morgenson wrote in the *New York Times* on October 5, 2015, "Until recently, investors were positively star-struck by drug companies that could raise prices indiscriminately, letting their patients struggle to pay the freight. Lauded for a laserlike focus on shareholder returns, companies like Valeant Pharmaceuticals International, a multinational specialty drug company based in Quebec, received high marks and even higher valuations from besotted shareholders.

"Now, however, investors are beginning to see the peril in such a business model. Sure, price jumps may generate earnings and stock gains, but when the enrichment of a few comes at the cost of many, unwanted scrutiny often follows. ...

"Valeant caught the eye of Congress this year after it increased the price of two heart medications it had just bought the rights to sell ... [one by 212 percent and the other by 525 percent].

"Democratic members of the House Committee on Oversight and Government Reform ... have been investigating rocketing drug prices. This year they asked Valeant to provide documents about the increases; it declined."

It is possible to make affordable medicines and to make a profit, but not the obscene profits some drug makers seem to seek. And the other stakeholders—patients, employees, the community—are most likely to be thrown under the bus when big profits are on the line. Greed is the most contagious disease of all.

Big Pharma argues that the costs of drugs in the United States is only 10 percent of health spending. But some major drug companies increase prices by almost 10 percent a year, all to the detriment of the public. One thing is clear: Prescription drugs must be regulated by a Congress that cannot take contributions from drug companies, their executives, or their agents. Republicans and Democrats alike have to step up to the public bar. Nancy Reagan once said "just say no to drugs" — unfortunately that will not stop Big Pharma and the outrageous profits they make at the expense of the public. Almost every major country legislates drug policies and bans direct consumer ads—why not in the United States?

Let's close with a look at the bigger picture. Our pharmaceutical industry is the healthiest in the world, number one; we've seen that. But how about our healthcare? All the industry's pills and potions aren't an end in themselves—they are part of our healthcare system. And are we number one when it comes to healthcare? No. Number five? No. Number ten? No. According to general sources, it is as follows for general healthcare.

HEALTHCARE AROUND THE WORLD

1	FRANCE	7	NORWAY	13	SWITZERLAND	19	CANADA
2	ITALY	8	MONACO	14	IRELAND	20	AUSTRALIA
3	SINGAPORE	9	LUXEMBOURG	15	SWEDEN	21	FINLAND
4	SPAIN	10	ICELAND	16	BELGIUM	22	CHILE
5	AUSTRIA	11	NETHERLANDS	17	GERMANY	23	DENMARK
6	JAPAN	12	ENGLAND	18	ISRAEL	24	U.S.A

Data Source: Financial Health Organizations

BETTER USE OF OUR LAWS AND REGULATIONS

We are behind many other countries according to World Health organizations. There's no pill for that, but there is a prescription that will help: the legal and political actions to "just say no" to obscene pharmaceutical profits and prices. We have to enforce the laws on the books with courageous prosecutors and elected people in Washington, D.C. We have to ban the direct advertising, the buying up of generics and better regulate Big Pharma.

In 2013, United States Supreme Court Justice Stephen Breyer wrote a decision that gives hope to the public on stopping the "pay for delay" use of a generic drug that is as good as a brand-name drug. The case involved a "reverse payment" where a brand-name drug company sued a generic manufacturer of an equivalent drug for violating its patent. The case then settled with the drug company paying the defendant generic manufacturer millions of dollars to stop selling the generic. The lower courts have been split on this which has caused the FTC to be wary of taking on Big Pharma. The lower court in *FTC v. Actavis* allowed the settlement to stand and Justice Breyer reversed in a 5-3 split decision saying that the Circuit Court should have allowed the FTC case to move forward. Justice Breyer said in essence that you had to look at the total economic picture of the deal.

While the case isn't the answer to stopping the outrageous conduct of buying up generics, it now allows courts to dig into the economics and monopoly aspects of the alleged lawsuit. There are many other actions that private lawyers, the FTC and the Department of Justice can bring—it just takes the courage to stand up to Big Pharma.

It is not only Pharma that contributes to this but the over-prescription by thousands of doctors of pain medication—all because they are hustled into repeated and excessive prescriptions of controlled substances—most notably opioids. States have to enforce laws to remove these doctors from practicing and unfortunately, in many states, the public doesn't know their names. People in California are pushing a law to make doctors notify their patients when they are put on probation by medical boards. Notification is fine but removal is what is needed to protect the public.

8

Big Oil Is King

"Drill, baby, drill!"
—Sarah Palin, former Governor of Alaska

"The meek shall inherit the earth, but not its mineral rights."
—J. Paul Getty

"And *up from the ground came a bubblin' crude. Oil that is, black gold, Texas Tea.*"
—Theme song from *The Beverly Hillbillies*

John D. Rockefeller was born in a small village in rural upstate New York into a world without electricity, cars, or airplanes. By the time President Theodore Roosevelt moved to break up his company, Standard Oil—"busting the trust"—the modern world was in high gear, and the name Rockefeller had become synonymous with wealth thanks to the ruthless monopoly he had established. The 1911 breakup of Standard Oil might have reshaped the corporate landscape, but Teddy Roosevelt and the trustbusters could not stop the oil industry's drive to rule our economy, ruin our environment, and buy public officials.

OIL, ROADS, AND AUTOMOBILES
In the early 1940s and 50s, the City of Los Angeles was thriving and so did its local small railways. A network of streetcars took workers all over the sprawling City of Angels. By 1963, the last electric Yellow Car trolley had made its final run, and the automobile's took over Los Angeles.

Most historians agree that L.A.'s change was primarily the result of commuters deciding they preferred to ride in their own cars instead of antiquated, crowded, clanging trolleys that didn't reach the suburbs. One persistent theory is that the decline of the streetcar had support from an unholy consortium of oil, gas, and automotive companies with a vested interest in the outcome—profit.

A subsidiary of National City Lines, a company whose investors included Standard Oil, Phillips Petroleum, Firestone Tires, and General Motors, bought the Yellow Car system from the heirs of Henry Huntington as well as 45 other public transit networks in the West and Midwest. According to an article in the *Los Angeles Times,* National City "began scrapping these electric systems and replacing them with diesel buses that—surprise— used fuel and rubber."

In 1946, the U.S. Justice Department filed an antitrust suit, charging National City with conspiracy to monopolize the transit industry. The *Los Angeles Times* wrote, "Before the suit came to trial in Chicago, the consortium of big companies bailed out, selling their holdings in National City Lines. That essentially left it as an empty corporation."

The *Times* reported, "In 1949, the case finally came to trial. The verdict was mixed, with acquittals and convictions. Although they no longer owned National City Lines, the companies in the consortium were fined the wrist-slapping amount of $5,000 each, while individual company officials were fined $1 each, for a total of $37,007." An incredible result for the oil, gas, auto, and tire industries.

"By then," the *Times* piece continued, "the far-flung suburbs were already crisscrossed by cars, highways, and a few freeways, and the so-called conspiracy plot simply applied the coup de grâce to a dying system"—public transit.

Within a few years, public transit was dealt another significant blow when in 1956, at President Dwight Eisenhower's request, Congress approved significant funding for the National System of Interstate and Defense Highways. When Eisenhower was a lieutenant colonel in 1919, he participated in the first transcontinental motor convoy, and later, during World War II, he saw the advantages that the autobahn (Germany's highway system) gave to the Germans. "The bill was lobbied for heavily by a coalition of vehicle, oil, tire, cement, steel, and union interests," according to the University of Vermont's Landscape Change Program. Eisenhower's secretary of defense was Charles

Wilson—a former president of General Motors who is famously remembered for saying, "I thought what was good for our country was good for General Motors and vice versa." An incredible but true statement.

THE THREAT OF THE ELECTRIC CAR

By 1990 there were almost 200 million cars on the road in the United States. That's when the California Air Resources Board (CARB) issued a mandate: If you want to sell cars in California, some of them must be electric. This wasn't a particularly far-fetched or futuristic vision. General Motors had already touted its progress in designing the EV1 electric vehicle. GM, Ford, and Chrysler, along with Japanese automakers Honda, Toyota, and Nissan, all began making electric cars. Their drivers loved them, according to the 2006 documentary *Who Killed the Electric Car?*, and demand began to grow.

Rather than embrace their new product, one that could propel their business in a post-oil future and appeal to a populace increasingly concerned about climate change, GM, along with other automakers began a campaign against CARB's mandate. The oil industry helped out by quietly funding such phony "grassroots" groups as The Clean Air Alliance, which presented technical and economic arguments against electric cars. With former CEO of the American Automobile Manufacturing Association Andrew Card firmly ensconced in the White House as President George W. Bush's chief of staff, the federal government joined a lawsuit against California seeking to stop electric cars. The mandate was removed. Automakers reclaimed more than 5,000 electric cars—which had been leased—and destroyed them. The last EV1s were removed in 2005 from a GM lot in Burbank, California, and crushed.

Big Auto's timing was terrible. The price of oil soared as the war in Iraq dragged on and the entire Arab world plunged into yet another period of turbulence. Global warming, which to many had been an abstract notion, started to become a reality: People were noticing that the world around them was changing. Al Gore's documentary about global warming, *An Inconvenient Truth,* which premiered in 2006, also contributed to bringing climate change to the public's attention.

Toyota introduced the hybrid Prius in 1997 as a kind of low-key experiment. But it caught on, and sales in the first year exceeded projections. And when some Hollywood stars started driving Priuses, owning a Prius became a status symbol.

The 2003 Toyota Prius was fully redesigned, with more power and even better gas mileage than previous generations boasted. The car became a stylish and green option for buyers, and sales took off. Sales of the Prius doubled in 2004 and then doubled again in 2005. People were on waiting lists for months to buy it.

As of today, the Prius is one of the best-selling hybrid vehicles in the country, but automobile companies are still lobbied by the oil industry to go slow, all in the name of profits.

Still, the appeal of the electric car is very real and persistent. On Earth Day, April 22, 2011, a documentary film, *The Revenge of the Electric Car,* a sequel to *Who Killed the Electric Car?,* debuted. One of the heroes of that film is Elon Musk, the face and co-founder of Tesla Motors. When the Tesla S sports car hit the road in June 2012, electric cars got a whole lot sexier. And Detroit has decided to get back on the electric bandwagon, with current offerings from Ford and Chevrolet; international options from Nissan, Kia, Renault, Mitsubishi, Honda, Fiat, and BMW are also available. The electric car is finally on its way, notwithstanding the opposition of Big Oil.

Ironically, the weak economy and high gas prices of 2008 to 2012 pushed people to seek more economical and environmental cars, or to keep driving their old ones. Car sales dropped off in the post–Great Recession years, but now that the oil companies are looking at reduced profits from falling gas prices, auto sales are creeping back up and America is in danger of relapsing into its oil addiction. Through the first half of 2015, auto sales hit levels not seen in 15 years, and the oil industry is again pushing sales of gas-using cars.

Back in L.A., the poster-child for automobile-centric cities, citizens who drive have suffered through two rounds of "Carmageddon," the enormous traffic jams caused by road construction on the notorious 405 Freeway. The construction of a light rail system is L.A.'s attempt to get back to where it was before the trains went away, but the process has been slowed by the auto industry and their lobbyists in Sacramento.

OIL: THE BIG AND RICH

Thanks to cornering the oil market, Rockefeller became one of the first U.S. billionaires, but J. Paul Getty also had an instinct about oil as the key to amassing great wealth. Showing remarkable foresight in 1949, Getty paid Ibn Saud, the first monarch and founder of Saudi Arabia, $9.5 million in cash and $1 million a year for a 60-year concession on a tract of land not far from the border of Kuwait and Saudi Arabia. Although no oil had ever been discovered in that area, four years later, after an investment of $30 million, Getty's gamble paid off to the tune of 16,000,000 barrels a year.

In 1997, 60 years after the death of Rockefeller and eight decades after the breakup of his company, four of Standard Oil's successor firms—Exxon, Mobil, Amoco, and Chevron—ranked among the 50 largest companies in the world, according to Ron Chernow's biography, *Titan: The Life of John D. Rockefeller, Sr.* In 1998, when that book was published, Exxon and Mobil merged, creating the largest U.S. company by market capitalization; Amoco now is part of BP, and Chevron has gobbled up Texaco. Environmental writer, Bill McKibben, says in his book, *Eaarth,* that the planet has changed so much, it needs a new spelling for its name. He also notes that ExxonMobil "made more money in 2006, 2007 and 2008 than any company in the history of money." Since that time, its net income has increased from $19.2 billion in 2009 to a peak of more than $44.8 billion in 2012, dropping to $32.5 billion in 2013—mostly paid for by U.S. citizens, in their cars, on our roads.

"It's the world's greatest company, period," said Arjun N. Murti, a former Goldman Sachs oil analyst, in the *New York Times* in 2008. "I would put Exxon up against any other company at any other period of time." On *Fortune's* list of the largest companies on earth, ranked by revenue, more than one-third of the top 56 companies are oil and gas companies, and 8 are automotive companies. And from the second quarter of 2013 to the second quarter of 2014, the 5 largest Big Oil companies—BP, Chevron, ConocoPhillips, ExxonMobil, and Shell—raked in more than $100 billion in profit, according to figures compiled by the Center for American Progress. That's not revenue, that's profit—and much of it at the expense of U.S. citizens.

Two of the top oil barons in 2015 were the Koch brothers,

David and Charles, with a net worth in February 2015 of $100 billion, according to *Bloomberg*.

OIL AND WAR: OFTEN THEY GO TOGETHER

"Greed for petroleum has produced plenty of war. War can be defined narrowly, as conflict between nations, or broadly, as large-scale violence in pursuit of gain," said writer, historian, and activist Rebecca Solnit in a December 2015 article in the *Guardian*. She pointed to activities in the Middle East:

"In the fossil-fuel era, some oil corporations became powers equal to states, and some states became petroleum corporations in drag, and both were willing to fight horrific wars over resource control. ... Consider that the legitimately elected prime minister of Iran was deposed in a 1953 coup because he had nationalized the oil industry. BP wasn't going to give up its profits without a fight, and the dirty fight was carried out by the United States and Britain. That Iran coup was just one of many interventions in the Middle East driven by oil."

Author and columnist Dean Henderson wrote in his first book, *Big Oil & Their Bankers in the Persian Gulf*:

> "Under the ... rule of the US puppet Shah of Iran—who came to power after a BP-sponsored ... coup—Chase Manhattan, which later merged with JPMorgan to become JPMorgan Chase, issued letters of credit for all Iranian oil exports and monopolized deposits from the National Iranian Oil Company (NIOC).
>
> "Chase controlled the Pahlavi Foundation which owned an oil company, twelve Iranian sugar refineries, electronics firms, cemeteries, mines, industrial bakeries, the country's General Motors franchise, and a slew of banks—including the Shah's personal piggy bank—the Bank Omran. While 'Omran' means 'development', the Pahlavi Foundation focused only on developing the fortunes of both the Shah and Chase Manhattan."

David Rockefeller, whose family controlled the majority interest in Chase Manhattan, was the chairman of the bank, and the Rockefellers increased the family fortune during the reign of Shah Mohammed Reza Pahlavi while the average Iranian lived in poverty—which led to the revolt in Iran.

Henderson calls the Big Four oil companies (ExxonMobil, Chevron, BP, and Royal Dutch Shell) the Four Horsemen, as in the apocalypse and all that that implies. He points to a web of interlocking directorates with international megabanks: ExxonMobil shared board members with JPMorgan Chase, Citigroup, Deutsche Bank, Royal Bank of Canada, and Prudential. Chevron Texaco had interlocks with Bank of America and JPMorgan Chase. BP Amoco shared directors with JPMorgan Chase. Shell had ties with Citigroup, JPMorgan Chase, N. M. Rothschild & Sons, and the Bank of England. Is there any question about how Big Oil and Wall Street dominate Main Street and the citizens of our great country?

But this is not just a case of rich guys being chummy in boardrooms. These relationships can affect things on the world diplomatic stage that then go on to affect our citizens. Terence Smith wrote in the *New York Times* that it was David Rockefeller and Henry Kissinger (once a director of special projects for the Rockefeller Brothers Fund and chairman of Chase's international advisory committee), along with John J. McCloy, lawyer for both the Pahlavi family and Chase Manhattan Bank, who convinced a strongly resistant President Jimmy Carter to allow the Shah to seek medical treatment in the United States. This was much more than a humanitarian judgment call. Smith calls the decision "the proximate cause of the takeover and all that followed"—the Iran hostage crisis and the regime change in Iran, which became an Islamic republic after the Shah left the country.

Fast forward about two decades: The U.S. presence had been greatly increased in the Middle East after the 1990 war that George H. W. Bush pursued, in part to defend Kuwait and (to a lesser extent) Saudi petroleum. And Iraq invaded Kuwait, partly to retaliate against Kuwait for undermining the price of oil. One of al-Qaida's biggest objections was the U.S. presence in Saudi Arabia before 9/11—which was also oil-related.

The invasion of Iraq in 2003 was led by George W. Bush (the Second) and Dick Cheney, politicians with deep ties to the petroleum industry. After years of sanctions, Iraq oil was up for grabs, and they grabbed, and profited at the expense of many of our young men and women in the armed services, soldiers who died or were wounded in Iraq.

BIG, GLOBAL, AND DANGEROUS

"If revenue were counted as gross domestic product, the corporation would rank among the top 30 countries," wrote Adam Hochschild in his *New York Times* review of *Private Empire: ExxonMobil and American Power* by Pulitzer Prize–winning journalist Steve Coll. Hochschild continued, "It's a picture of a corporation so large and powerful—operating in some 200 nations and territories—that it really has its own foreign policy."

Oil barons have long roamed the world and made deals anywhere they could find oil. This sometimes made for strange bedfellows and did not always overlap with the interests of the U.S. government. Conversely, many dictators knew they could get away with all sorts of plunder and human rights abuses so long as they stayed on Exxon's good side.

THE LONG AND LUCRATIVE REIGN OF PRESIDENT OBIANG

Around the world, corruption reigns as two-bit dictators do business with Big Oil. Equatorial Guinea gained little traction with the Clinton administration because of its abysmal human rights record, Coll reported in *Private Empire*. However, after the 9/11 terrorist attacks in 2001, it found a friendlier ear in the Bush administration, which opened an embassy in the tiny West African nation. Coll noted that ExxonMobil had initially established drilling platforms off the coast, much to the delight of the country's dictator, President Teodoro Obiang Nguema Mbasogo. ExxonMobil made those rigs highly productive, and to ensure their success, it funneled business to companies controlled by Obiang's friends.

Even though U.S. law normally prohibits such dealings through the Foreign Corrupt Practices Act, the government apparently believed ExxonMobil's rationale that there were no other entities it could engage with in that tiny nation. Leaving the country was not an option because by the early part of this century, ExxonMobil was pumping more than 300,000 barrels a day in Equatorial Guinea. The money from that operation kept Obiang—one of the longest-serving heads of state in the world—in power.

In its 2014 World Report on Equatorial Guinea, Human Rights Watch called out Obiang's regime for "corruption, poverty, and repression," and noted that "vast oil revenues fund lavish lifestyles for the small elite surrounding the president, while a large proportion of the population continues to live in poverty." The nonprofit NGO's report continues, "Mismanagement of public funds and credible allegations of high-level corruption persist, as do other serious abuses, including arbitrary detention, secret detention, and unfair trials."

ExxonMobil also had investments in a Chad-Cameroon oil project. According to the *New York Times* review of Coll's book, after quoting a cable from the U.S. Embassy in Chad complaining that Exxon was ignoring American diplomats there, Coll asked, "And why should it be otherwise? ... Annual aid to Chad from the United States was only about $3 *million*." ExxonMobil's investment was about $4 billion.

ExxonMobil epitomizes the corporation as nation-state much as the East India Company did in the glory days of British colonization.

SOUTHEAST ASIA: AN OIL PROBLEM

In taking over Mobil Oil in 1998, Exxon inherited a thorny situation in Indonesia. Separatists in the province of Aceh were waging an armed uprising that threatened ExxonMobil's productive and lucrative Arun oil fields. ExxonMobil needed to protect its operations and wound up paying Indonesian soldiers as its security force. Although this put it in the middle of a civil war, the corporation's main focus was getting oil out of the ground.

ExxonMobil's conduct included letting the Indonesian military use its land, and its earth-moving equipment, possibly for burials of people. To be sure, the rebels of the Free Aceh Movement—known in Indonesian as Gerakan Aceh Merdeka, or GAM—were also guilty of horrible abuses and crimes. Rebel attacks on ExxonMobil's plant and its workers—in which GAM denies any involvement—led the company to suspend operations for a time.

The nonprofit group International Rights Advocates helped some Indonesians sue Exxon in U.S. district court, a case that has taken more than a decade to litigate. In a 2008 ruling, a U.S. district judge denied ExxonMobil's summary judgment motion, citing "evidence that these security forces committed the alleged atrocities" and found that plaintiffs had sufficiently tied the conduct of ExxonMobil's paid security forces to the villagers' injuries. In July 2015 a federal court ruled the Alien Tort Statute claims against ExxonMobil for human rights violations can finally proceed, according to the *GlobeNewswire*.

SHELL SETTLES IN NIGERIA

Lawsuits, however, can be effective even if they don't get to court, by bringing pressure on companies to act responsibly. In 2009, Royal Dutch Shell agreed to pay $15.5 million on the eve of trial to settle claims that it had conspired in the death of writer and activist Ken Saro-Wiwa and eight other leaders of the indigenous Ogoni tribe of southern Nigeria. Saro-Wiwa organized nonviolent protests on behalf of the Ogoni people against the rape of the land by Royal Dutch Shell and other corporations.

Britain's *Guardian* called it "one of the largest payouts agreed by a multinational corporation charged with human rights violations." Shell still denied culpability, saying in a statement that it made the payment out of compassion, "in recognition of the tragic turn of events in Ogoni land, even though Shell had no part in the violence that took place." A 2009 report from Amnesty International found that "the oil industry in the Niger Delta of Nigeria has brought impoverishment, conflict, human rights abuses and despair to the majority of the people in the oil-producing areas."

Two years later, in 2011, the United Nations Environment Program (UNEP) reported that groundwater in Ogoni land contained 900 times the recommended amount of benzene, a carcinogen. This estimate suggests that it could take 20 to 30 years to the land.

THE BRAVE AND CREATIVE WOMEN OF UGBORODO

The villagers of Ugborodo, Nigeria, might not have lawyers to defend them, but after Chevron Texaco moved in with its oil terminal, they felt they needed to take some action.

Sonia Shah told the incredible story of Ugborodo in her 2011 book *Crude: The Story of Oil*. It is mandatory reading for understanding Big Oil. The village didn't have indoor plumbing, let alone a gas station, noted Shah. Chevron had widened local creeks to build their facilities and Ugborodo was slowly being flooded. Meanwhile, Chevron's buildings had air conditioning, microwave ovens, and fresh produce to make life more comfortable for the staff. So the villagers began to protest.

"When men and boys protested ... they set off a chain of violence. ... In the village of Ugborodo, the women decided to get organized," said Shah. "First they sent a letter to Chevron officials, which received ... no response at all. In July 2002, hundreds of women hijacked a boat and occupied Chevron's facility... . The women stayed put, trapping more than seven hundred Chevron staff in the facility and blocking the arrival of helicopters, planes, and boats that might bring fresh supplies to the oil workers. If Chevron didn't listen, the unarmed singing protesters said, they would humiliate the men in the worst way possible. The women would take their clothes off. Stunned security staff didn't know what to do."

After ten days of occupation, Chevron agreed to "share some of its plentiful electricity and clean water, and might build a few buildings amidst the rubble of the lands they had devastated. They would even, perhaps, start to construct a new place for the villagers to live, once the flooding they had unleashed submerged the village entirely."

In the movie version this would make for a fine happy ending. But environmentalists who saw internal company documents about such community development projects, according to Ike Okonta and Oronto Douglas in *Where Vultures Feast: Shell, Human Rights, and Oil in the Niger Delta*, found that Shell executives "had no sympathy for the plight of the Niger Delta communities, generally saw them as indolent, and also regarded the whole exercise as a waste of time."

Shell in Nigeria, a "briefing for Shell stakeholders" published in part by the antipoverty charity Christian Aid, reported that Christian Aid's 2003 study about a community development program in Niger found it was "dysfunctional" and the Niger delta was "a veritable graveyard of projects, including water systems that do not work, health centers that have never opened and schools where no lesson has ever been taught."

THE U'WA OF COLUMBIA: MORE PRECIOUS THAN MONEY

The U'wa tribe hold that "Oil is the blood of Mother Earth ... to take the oil is, for us, worse than killing your own mother. If you kill the earth, then no one will live," according to Amazon Watch.

The U'wa, no more than a few thousand people living in the remote Andes of northeast Columbia, have been stewards of the cloud forest for centuries, says Amazon Watch. When Occidental Petroleum took the first steps toward oil exploration there in 1988, it discovered that the inhabitants had no interest in financial payoffs and were desperately serious about protecting the land. The U'wa threatened to commit mass ritual suicide by throwing themselves over their sacred cliffs. The world took notice and it became a public relations nightmare for the company. In 1998 U'wa leader Berito Kuwaru'wa received the Goldman Environmental Award, and after more media coverage, in 2002 Occidental pulled out.

But in February 2014 the U'wa were again threatened with oil exploration, when an "avalanche of heavy machinery" arrived and armed forces moved into the zone where Ecopetrol S.A. had decided to situate its pipeline, known as the Magallnes gas project, according to an Amazon Watch update. By then the U'wa had improved their public relations skills: They nonviolently occupied a bombed oil pipeline site on their territory for two months and got quoted by such international news heavyweights as *Reuters*, the *Wall Street Journal* and the *Guardian*.

According to Amazon Watch, a number of Colombian organizations stepped forward to support the U'wa cause, and international networks led by groups like Amazon Watch and EarthRights International joined in. Amazon Watch also says that 28 international organizations signed a letter calling for the U'wa's demands for their rights as an indigenous people to be respected. A mere three months after their machinery rumbled onto U'wa land, in May 2014, Ecopetrol decided to dismantle the project.

ECUADOR TRIES TO MAKE A DEAL

In 2007, President Rafael Correa told the world he was willing to leave vast oil deposits in the ground in Ecuador's Yasuni National Park if the world would help his country shoulder the costs of the lost opportunity—the estimated value of the untapped oil beneath Yasuni, then valued at $7 billion, according to the economics journal *Dollars & Sense*. At the 2007 United Nations General Assembly, Correa said if the world would pay

Ecuador $350 million over ten years—a figure his government would match—it would put a halt to plans to drill. In August of 2013, having received only a fraction of those commitments, Correa pulled the plug on his plan. With the oil now said to be worth an estimated $18 billion, China is eyeing that oil hungrily and is financing Ecuador's efforts to tap it, according to Bloomberg. Ecuador is going forward even though it has seen the darkest downside of Big Oil. Each year, according to *Dollars & Sense,* 198,000 hectares of land in the Amazon are deforested for oil production.

In 2012, an Ecuadorean court granted $19 billion to 30,000 victims of Chevron Texaco's drilling operations from 1964 to 1990 in the area northwest of Yasuní. According to *Dollars & Sense,* the lawsuit alleged that "thousands of cancers and other health problems were caused by Texaco's use of outdated and dangerous practices, including the dumping of 18 billion gallons of toxic wastewater into local water supplies." Some environmental activists have referred to it as a "Rainforest Chernobyl."

But the money had to be collected in the United States, as Chevron has almost no assets in Ecuador. In 2014, the $19 billion verdict was overturned by a New York federal judge who found that the lead attorney for the Ecuadoreans had worked to rig the outcome of the case, even allegedly bribing the Ecuadorean judge.

Then, in 2015, it was revealed that Chevron had paid more than $360,000 to another Ecuadorean judge to provide testimony in the case. The dramatic legal maneuvering sparked the book *Law of the Jungle,* by Paul Barrett.

According to a *New Yorker* article, in 2008, a Chevron lobbyist in Washington, D.C., told *Newsweek,* "We can't let little countries screw around with big companies like this." One Chevron spokesman has said, "We're going to fight this until Hell freezes over—and then we'll fight it out on the ice." And so it continues with the Ecuadoreans no better off.

CLOSER TO HOME: A HISTORY OF SPILLS

You can't have drilling without a spilling of some kind. Almost forgotten is the Lakeview gusher that erupted in March 1910 in California's Kern County, spewing 378 million gallons of oil over a vast area in an eruption that gushed for more than 17 months.

Cleanup workers were "covered from head to foot with the black sticky stuff, standing in a shower of hot oil that caused the skin to blister and peel off wherever it stuck," the *Los Angeles Times* wrote, quoting a contemporaneous account published in *California Oil World*. The piece also quotes a preacher from Pennsylvania who warned drillers that the oil was meant to remain underground to "kindle the fires of Hell." Californians ignored the preacher's warnings of hellfire and damnation and the site became a tourist attraction.

Even without an accident, the everyday business of drilling produces spills. Oil operations on land require drilling fluids (sometimes called "mud") that are injected into the wellbore to lubricate the drilling bit. These fluids are supposed to be captured in lined pits for disposal, but very often they spill and splash around the well pad. In a press release, Western Resources Advocates, a conservation group that focuses on seven western states, reported that one oil production company in La Plata County, Colorado, was spilling drilling fluids so frequently that its target was to reduce the spills to only every other day.

Offshore oil production involves oil spills from oil tankers transporting oil from the platform, as well as leaks and accidents on the platform itself. The January 1969 blowout at a Unocal rig, which spilled 3 million gallons of petroleum off the coast of Santa Barbara, California, resulted in drilling bans in offshore California and Florida.

Then came the *Exxon Valdez,* the infamous tanker that ran into a reef in Prince William Sound, Alaska, in 1989. Eleven million gallons were spilled there. Making this spill especially damaging and difficult to clean up, however, was its remote location and the ease with which oil spreads across water. Exxon says it spent $2.1 billion cleaning up the mess. Not so easily cleaned up, however, was the company's reputation, though that stain has rarely seemed to interfere with the company's bottom line.

PERILOUS PIPELINES: THE LEAKS OF BIG OIL
A less dramatic but more consistent problem are leaks and spills from pipelines. The *Dallas Morning News* reported in 2013 that more than 600 oil pipeline spills occurred in the United States since 2010. Many of these spills took place far from the oil fields of Texas or Oklahoma:

- 2010: An Enbridge Energy pipeline burst, sending more than 840,000 gallons into the Kalamazoo River and Talmadge Creek near Marshall, Michigan, in what the *New York Times* reported as the largest oil pipeline failure in U.S. history.
- 2011: During flooding on the Yellowstone River in Montana, federal pipeline authorities warned Exxon and WBI Energy that their pipelines in the river were in danger. WBI shut down, but Exxon closed its pipeline for only a few hours before starting up again. Debris from the raging river caused a "guillotine break" in the line, and ultimately more than 60,000 gallons of oil contaminated the river, according to the *Dallas Morning News*. Exxon was fined $1.7 million.
- 2013: ExxonMobil's Pegasus pipeline burst and spilled an estimated 210,000 gallons of heavy crude oil in Mayflower, Arkansas.

These leaks affect thousands of people, but to Big Oil, they are just a cost of doing business and nothing more.

BP STANDS FOR BIG PROBLEMS

British Petroleum traces its origins to 1908 in Iranian oil fields and was once partly owned by the British government. It merged with Amoco (in 1998) and Arco (in 2000) and went on an acquisition spree in the 1990s, perhaps in response to predictions of dwindling reserves. They pursued a course of risk taking and cost slashing, which was to have negative payoffs in multiple ways.

In 2005, a Galveston, Texas, refinery that had once been part of Amoco's operations was sorely in need of maintenance. Instead of investing in safety, BP cut costs. When the company brought a tower closed for maintenance back into operation, the tower, and the backup unit, overflowed, sending gasoline shooting into the air. The vapor cloud ignited into one of the worst industrial explosions in U.S. history, killing 15 workers and injuring 180 other people. According to *Reuters,* BP confessed to ignoring safety procedures and paid more than $2 billion to settle legal claims, $71.6 million for worker safety violations, and $100 million in pollution fines.

In 2006, in Prudhoe Bay, Alaska, corroded pipe problems caused the largest oil spill in the biggest oil field in the country.

The first leak, in March, spilled more than 200,000 gallons of crude oil over the tundra; after a second, smaller leak in August, BP shut down production on part of the oil field. BP was charged with failing to heed warning signs and has paid dearly in both fines and a civil settlement.

In 2007, BP agreed to pay a criminal fine of $12 million, community service payments of $4 million, and criminal restitution to the tune of another $4 million.

In April 2010, the Deepwater Horizon drilling rig in the Gulf of Mexico caused a full-scale televised disaster with the world watching in horror as it exploded. Eleven workers died and a gusher of oil mushroomed into the largest marine oil spill in history. Over nearly three months, when it seemed nearly impossible to cap the flow of the well, located in the Macondo oil prospect, 4.9 million barrels of oil, or 210 million gallons, spewed into the gulf. Economic losses numbered in the tens of billions of dollars.

BP pleaded guilty to criminal conduct in the incident, agreeing to pay $4.5 billion—*the biggest criminal penalty in U.S. history*. Three of its executives were charged criminally as well. Of the settlement money, about $2.4 billion was designated for acquiring, restoring, preserving, and conserving the marine and coastal environments in the gulf. Another $350 million will aid in the development of state-of-the art oil spill prevention and response technologies, education, research, and training. And $525 million went to settle fraud charges with the Securities and Exchange Commission, which said that BP had hidden the extent of the damage from its investors.

"The explosion of the rig was a disaster that resulted from BP's culture of privileging profit over prudence," said Assistant Attorney General Lanny A. Breuer of the Justice Department's Criminal Division at a press conference in November 2012. And that was just the start of the effort to hold BP accountable. With the criminal charges settled, the government took BP to civil court. In 2014, U.S. District Judge Carl Barbier in New Orleans ruled that the company was liable for gross negligence and could face up to $18 billion in fines under the Clean Water Act.

In 2012, the state of Alaska won $255 million in arbitration, mostly for lost royalties and interest suffered when the lucrative oil field had to shut down; $10 million of the award was penalties for environmental damage. BP was able to pass some of the costs on to ExxonMobil and ConocoPhillips, part owners of the pipeline, but it still had to pay $66 million.

GROSS NEGLIGENCE BY BIG OIL

Drilling the Macondo well involved problems from the start, earning the project the nickname "the well from hell," noted Judge Barbier. According to court documents, drilling into fragile sandstone, BP repeatedly endured what is known as "kicks," or fluid flowing into the wellbore—events that can cause explosions, fires, and blowouts. Yet during and after these kicks, BP kept drilling, despite damning analysis from BP's own engineers only a month before the disaster.

According to findings of fact published by Judge Barbier, one engineer said the accelerated speed of the drilling exceeded the ability to recognize, communicate, and act on the data. A BP geologist produced a particularly incriminating memo, saying, "I'm not sure it was a lack of communication or awareness as much as a 'we can get away with this' attitude."

"The immediate causes of the Macondo well blowout can be traced to a series of identifiable mistakes made by BP, Halliburton, and Transocean that reveal such systematic failures in risk management that they place in doubt the safety culture of the entire industry."
—The National Commission on the BP Deepwater Horizon, 2011

These astounding errors led Judge Barbier to bring the hammer down on BP. Although the company sought to place significant blame on Transocean, which owned the Deepwater Horizon rig, and Halliburton, a subcontractor, Barbier found BP 67 percent responsible, giving Transocean 30 percent of the blame and Halliburton 3 percent. Only BP was found to be grossly negligent; BP "had a hand in" most of Transocean's failures, Barbier wrote. He used the word "reckless" to describe BP, which he found was driven by profit and convenience rather than any desire to do the right thing or protect the environment.

A COST OF DOING BUSINESS

At the end of the court cases BP will be forced to pay over $20 billion, the largest settlement ever reached with a single entity. "BP is receiving the punishment it deserves," U.S. Attorney General Loretta Lynch announced in October 2015.

"But is it really?" asked Charles Kennedy of OilPrice.com days after the announcement. He continued: "BP will be able to write-off three-quarters of the total, taking a tax deduction on $15.3 billion ... . Only $5.5 billion out of the $20.8 billion total is not eligible for a tax deduction ... [and] those charges stem from a Clean Water Act violation.

"Due to quirks in the tax code, the "historic" settlement is not as significant ... as the U.S. government is making it out to be. It is normal for companies to deduct the business costs. Even litigation costs are often tax deductible. ... Sometimes there needs to be explicit language in settlements that bars companies from writing off penalties paid to the government.

"It appears that BP will be able to deduct quite a bit of its settlement with the U.S. government ... [and] it is essentially treated as any other cost of doing business ... . The $32 billion that BP spent to clean up the Gulf area was also tax deductible, costing U.S. taxpayers $10 billion."

THE NEW DEVELOPMENT—FRACKING

"The amount of oil under the ground in any region is finite, therefore the rate of discovery which initially increases quickly must reach a maximum and decline."
—M. King Hubbert, Shell Oil scientist

Years ago, Hubbert presented a paper to the American Petroleum Institute based on his theory that oil production in the United States would reach its peak in the 1970s. He was correct. Looking at Hubbert's dire prediction, the oil companies knew that they would not only have to find new ways to get oil out of the ground but also new types of oil.

Ronald Bailey's 2015 book, *The End of Doom: Environmental Renewal in the Twenty-first Century,* takes another look at Hubbert's predictions. Bailey penned a June 2015 article for *Reason,* a magazine covering politics, culture, and ideas, positing, "So how is it that going into 2016 Goldman Sachs is suggesting that the price of oil could fall as low as $20 per barrel during the next few years?" He continues, "Keep in mind that back during the last peak oil craze in 2008, Goldman was predicting $200 per barrel oil ... . So why might crude prices drop to $20 per barrel? Two reasons. First, vast new supplies of petroleum have been accessed by fracking and horizontal drilling. Fracked oil is now swing production that can come quickly online whenever prices to start to rise. And second, oil states like Russia, Nigeria, Venezuela, Iran, and Saudi Arabia must keep pumping even at low prices in order to generate the cash they need to buy off their restive citizens."

Hydraulic fracturing, aka fracking, involves using a high-pressure combination of water, chemicals, and sand to drill deep into the earth to access the gas trapped there. This process creates fractures in rock, which are then kept open to allow petroleum to be drawn up into a well. Needless to say, energy companies have been eager to use this technique, which lets them reach petroleum they had never been able to extract before. But fracking is also controversial because it uses enormous amounts of water and there are concerns that the process may cause earthquakes and contaminate groundwater.

Last fall, *Agence France-Presse* reported that since fracking started in Oklahoma, which is not near any major fault lines, the state has seen a huge increase in earthquakes. While Oklahoma previously experienced perhaps two earthquakes a year, in 2014 it experienced 585 earthquakes that registered 3.0-magnitude or greater—three times the 180 quakes felt by California in 2014, according to the *Agence France-Presse* article. Oklahoma has 4,500 injection wells.

CLIMATE CHANGE DOES NOT EXIST ACCORDING TO BIG OIL

After the conduct of ExxonMobil over the years, it seems a bit minor league that the big case against them is for allegedly lying to the public about the risks of climate change, and for lying to investors about how such risks might hurt oil business profits.

And yet in November 2015, New York State Attorney General Eric Schneiderman opened an investigation into whether Exxon misled investors by supporting groups that question the danger of climate change, even as its own scientists briefed executives on the risks. Schneiderman has subpoenaed documents from

Exxon, the world's biggest oil explorer, dating back to the 1970s, a person familiar with the probe told several news outlets.

ExxonMobil now faces the prospect of civil lawsuits, and possible criminal penalties, for allegedly suppressing its internal awareness about the serious risk to the environment as well as to shareholder value, from climate change caused by the burning of fossil fuels. "In New York," Schneiderman said in an interview on PBS NewsHour, "we have laws against defrauding the public, defrauding consumers, defrauding shareholders."

Various facts and accusations are emerging. According to company documents obtained by both *InsideClimate News* and a joint project between Columbia University Graduate School of Journalism and the *Los Angeles Times,* ExxonMobil executives were informed by their own scientists of the serious threat of climate change as far back as the 1970s, with ExxonMobil using this data to inform its own long-term planning.

Despite this apparent knowledge, ExxonMobil provided significant funding to climate change denial groups such as the Heartland Institute and CFACT (Committee for a Constructive Tomorrow), according to the investigatory pieces.

According to a July 2015 report by the Union of Concerned Scientists, the company was aware as early as 1981 that climate change as a result of greenhouse gas emissions was going to be an issue. Internally, it understood the science. Yet its public-facing strategy over the decades that followed was one based on denial—a strategy backed by millions of dollars in spending. Exxon, in response, asserted that it no longer funded climate change denial groups. In fact, the company swore to quit that habit eight years ago—and then went ahead and kept doing it. According to the *Guardian*, Exxon has given more than $2.3 million to climate-change-denying members of Congress and to that monster of anti-climate science lobbying groups, the American Legislative Exchange Council (ALEC).

Salon reported that Exxon made a promise "in response to pressure from shareholders" in its 2007 Corporate Citizenship report, which read: 'In 2008 we will discontinue contributions to several public policy groups whose position on climate change could divert attention from the important discussion on how the world will secure energy required for economic growth in an environmentally responsible manner.' " But according to the

Guardian, "here's the breakdown, per its financial and tax records, of what it's done since: it's given $1.87 million to members of Congress who are on the record denying the scientific reality of man-made climate change, and $454,000 to ALEC."

In October 2015, the *Los Angeles Times* wrote: "In 1992, Exxon joined the Global Climate Coalition, an association of companies from industries linked to fossil fuels, which vigorously fought potential climate change regulations by emphasizing scientific uncertainty and underscoring the negative economic impact of such laws on consumers. From 1998 to 2005, Exxon contributed almost $16 million to at least 43 organizations to wage a campaign raising questions about climate change, according to the Union of Concerned Scientists, an environmental activist group. Greenpeace has estimated that Exxon spent more than $30 million in that effort."

Columbia's study with the *Los Angeles Times* also points out that "Exxon reinforced pipelines buried in Northern tundra to withstand permafrost melt and bid on Arctic oil leases in permanently frozen offshore locations that they suspected would eventually thaw (and thaw they did)."

According to another *L.A. Times* story, "Exxon's executives also publicly questioned climate change science. In 1997, Exxon's chairman and chief executive, Lee Raymond, derided potential regulations on carbon emissions at a meeting of the World Petroleum Council in Beijing.

" 'Many people—politicians and the public alike—believe that global warming is a rock-solid certainty,' Raymond said at the meeting, according to the *Times.* 'But it's not.' " That being said, Exxon engineers still planned for certain global warming.

GOING FORWARD WITH OIL

What is the takeaway from the conduct of the oil industry over the past years? It's simple really. Big Oil: Bigger than the law, bigger than oil company stockholders, bigger than the United States, bigger than science, and bigger than the truth. It all goes back to the ability of big oil and the overwhelming desire for profit. If the environmental movement can gain ground in the face of huge donations of millions of dollars to our government officials, our country may be saved—along with our globe.

9

In Defense of Our Country

"The ugly truth is virtually all of the major defense contractors in this country for years have been engaged in systematic fraudulent dealing, while receiving hundreds of billions of dollars of taxpayer money."
—Senator Bernie Sanders (D-VT)

"We are still having to procure systems we don't need."
—General Raymond Odierno, Army Chief of Staff

"We lead the world in only three categories: number of incarcerated citizens per capita, number of adults who believe angels are real, and defense spending..."
—Will McAvoy, *Newsroom*

THE U.S. IS NUMBER ONE
The U.S. spends as much money on defense as the next seven countries—combined. That's $600 billion a year, every year. That's a lot of money in absolute numbers, and a lot of money compared to the rest of the world.

And when you add up all the different categories of U.S. defense spending, which encompasses spending not reflected in the chart, the Center for Defense Information at POGO (the Project on Government Oversight) says, "The proposed [2017] budget continues a trend of Pentagon spending well above historical norms, with our total national security spending for next year at nearly $1.1 trillion."

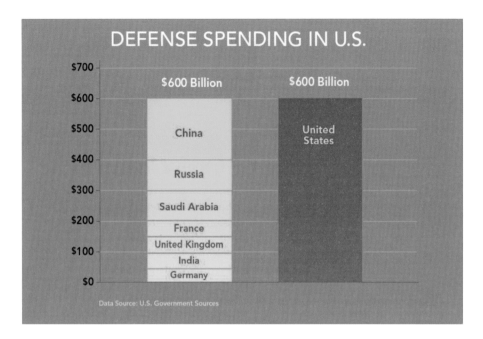

WHO KNOWS WHERE THE MONEY GOES?

Early in my life, I enlisted in the U.S. Marine Reserves with the intent of going to Officers Candidate School following college. Instead, after ROTC, I was commissioned in the U.S. Army Intelligence Corps and went on to become a Special Forces Officer—an airborne parachute officer and after many jumps, I transferred into the Judge Advocate General Corps. I spent over thirty years in a uniform of the Army Reserves, eventually as Commander of a Senior JAG Unit. Since then, I spent time on the board of the Army War College Foundation, which supports the Army War College at Carlisle Barracks, the graduate school for the senior commanders of all branches of the service, including officers from foreign allies. I have been involved with veterans for years.

Although not an expert on the Pentagon, I believe I know something about how military budgets work. I recall the first time I was notified that I didn't use all my budget for my Detachment for the year so I quickly had to send some people on an extended "Reserve Duty." The full use of your budget is almost mandatory and that said, nothing has changed in years. As General Ray Odierno said recently, "we still have to procure systems we don't need" and that was true in Vietnam, Iraq and

Afghanistan.

In February 2015, *The Hill* reported, "Since 1997, the Government Accountability Office (GAO) has been required to audit the federal government's consolidated financial statements, but the watchdog agency has repeatedly said its reviews of the Pentagon are not based on accurate data. ... In 2010, it was determined that nearly $6 billion spent to improve the agency's financial information was unsuccessful and GAO could not predict when the DOD [Department of Defense] would be able to provide these financial statements."

The armed services are facing a September 2017 deadline to have their books ready for a successful audit. According to *The Hill,* when Senator Joe Manchin asked the heads of the armed services about meeting the 2017 deadline, Army Chief of Staff General Ray Odierno said, "We're not where we need to be yet, but we're making progress and we should be prepared by '17 to meet that goal." Chief Naval Officer Admiral Jonathan Greenert said the Navy was "on track."

Defense News provided a status report on the Air Force and the Marines: " 'We will be 100 percent ready to undergo an audit,' [Associate Deputy Assistant Secretary for Financial Operations of the Air Force, Stephen] Herrera said. 'That should not imply that we will have corrected every potential finding that may occur in an audit. Our strategy is to address high risk, material areas sufficient to demonstrate Air Force auditability.' " But "a Pentagon watchdog agency is withdrawing a clean audit report it gave the US Marine Corps in 2013, an embarrassing snag for the Defense Department's endeavor to become auditable, and one which drew head-shaking in Congress," *Defense News* wrote. "The episode hints at the difficulty for DoD as [it] strives to become audit-ready by 2017, an undertaking the ... GAO described as making mixed progress."

WHERE THE MONEY WENT: A HISTORY LESSON

In wartime, especially in the time of a "good war," you might expect that patriotism comes first: everyone sacrificing and working together for the common good. But that's not always the case. In fact, there's a long history of working in wartime for the good of the personal bank account, instead of the public trust.

Take the American Civil War, fought to keep the country

together and (in the end) to bring an end to slavery. You can't get much better than that.

And yet, John Pierpont (J. P.) Morgan bought his way out of military service by paying another man $300 to serve in his stead, which was then legal. But avoiding service didn't mean avoiding the war. "During the Civil War he bought five thousand rifles for $3.50 each from an army arsenal, and sold them to a general in the field for $22 each," Howard Zinn wrote in his seminal work, *A People's History of the United States*. "The rifles were defective and would shoot off the thumbs of the soldiers using them. A congressional committee noted this in the small print of an obscure report, but a federal judge upheld the deal as the fulfillment of a valid legal contract." And for Morgan, as we know, it only got better after the war.

Or take this story (from the *New York Times*'s Disunion series, on the 150th anniversary of the Civil War). Elisha Brooks was head of a company that "was awarded an initial contract for the fabrication of 12,000 uniforms just two weeks after war was declared; in 1861 alone, it filled 36,000 orders. The company had obtained the contract through questionable means, and proceeded to fill the order in much the same way: turned out in a matter of weeks, the uniforms were so ill-fitting—many lacking buttons and button holes—that the New York Volunteers who wore them suffered humiliation from other outfits. ... But that was not the worst of it: facing a paucity of wool, [the company] glued together shredded, often decaying rags, pressed them into a semblance of cloth, and sewed the pieces into uniforms. Far from protecting the soldiers from inclement weather, these uniforms would fall apart in the first rain."

Did that start hinder Elisha Brooks on his upward climb to wealth and fame? Well, we know his company today as—Brooks Brothers, where I buy my shirts and ties.

WWI, OR HOW MUCH IS THAT GUNPOWDER IN THE WINDOW?

Of course sometimes, even in wartime, a quality product is delivered to soldiers in the field. For a price. A good price.

U.S. Marine Corps Major General Smedley Butler saw a lot of war firsthand. Here's a little of what he saw during World War I, from his book, *War Is a Racket:* "Take our friends, the du

Ponts, the [gun]powder people—didn't one of them testify before a Senate committee recently that their powder won the war? Or saved the world for democracy? Or something? How did they do in the war? They were a patriotic corporation.

"Well, the average earnings of the du Ponts for the period 1910 to 1914 were $6,000,000 a year. It wasn't much, but the du Ponts managed to get along on it. Now let's look at their average yearly profit during the war years, 1914 to 1918. Fifty-eight million dollars a year profit we find! Nearly ten times that of normal times, and the profits of normal times were pretty good. An increase in profits of more than 950 per cent."

COME FLY WITH ME, FOR A FEW BILLION DOLLARS
Lockheed Martin is the world's largest defense contractor, and like the giants of yesteryear, it's no surprise that Lockheed Martin also goes big when it goes boondoggle. For example, in July 2014, Paul Waldman wrote in the *Washington Post* about Lockheed Martin's F-35 fighter plane: "If you'd been following it you know that [the F-35] has been one of the most remarkable boondoggles we've ever seen, not only the most expensive weapons system in history, but one that has been plagued by one disastrous problem after another (the latest of which came last month when an F-35 caught fire when taking off and the whole fleet of them were grounded).

"...the F-35 has been a disaster. Bursting into flames is just the latest mishap—it's been so unreliable that at various points the planes have been forbidden from flying at night, or in the rain, or too fast, or too steep. There have problems with hardware and software and everything in between.

"The F-35 Joint Strike Fighter was supposed to extend American air superiority deep into the 21st century. The F-35 was designed to evade not just enemy fighters, but political accountability as well."

Well into its second decade of development, the F-35 continues to have serious problems, and the concerns of a lot of Air Force officers who put their lives on the line for good aircrafts. Even a tremendous amount of lobbying by Lockhead can't get people in line to accept this billion dollar potential debacle. This, when we can't even our VA hospitals money to help our men and women who served and now need medical treatment.

IT'S WHO YOU KNOW

Our military and elected officials find plenty of ways to spend our money on defense. But not just anybody gets a piece of the pie. It helps to be somebody who knows somebody.

Lockheed Martin knows how to play *that* game, and Paul Waldman explained how it played out with the F-35, in the *Washington Post*: "Its subcontracts were spread out over 1,300 separate companies in 45 states, ensuring that members of Congress from throughout the land have an interest in keeping the project going. It's an incredibly poor way to create jobs (depending on how you count, a single job supported by the F-35 costs the taxpayer as much as $8 million). We'll spend around $400 billion to build the planes—nearly twice what the program was supposed to cost when it began."

Lockheed Martin was far from the first, or the only, company to milk the cash cow. Back in the 1940s, "a Texas firm called Brown & Root constructed a massive dam project near Austin. The company's founders, Herman and George Brown, won the contract to build Mansfield Dam thanks to the efforts of [Lyndon] Johnson, who was then a Texas congressman," as NPR recounted the story.

When Lyndon Johnson became president in 1963, Brown & Root went on a run of landing "contracts for huge federal construction projects," the NPR story continued. "By the mid-1960s, newspaper columnists and the Republican minority in Congress began to suggest that the company's good luck was tied to its sizable contributions to Johnson's political campaigns. More questions were raised when a consortium of which Brown & Root was a part won a $380 million contract to build airports, bases, and other facilities for the U.S. Navy in South Vietnam."

Various corporate mergers and acquisitions later, we come to Kellogg, Brown & Root (KBR), the single largest contractor with the Pentagon during the Iraq War ($39.5 billion). Up until 2007, KBR was a subsidiary of Halliburton. And if the name Halliburton sounds familiar, that might be because one of the people Halliburton "knew" was Dick Cheney, who went from his post as Secretary of Defense in the administration of President George H. W. Bush, to CEO and chairman of military contractor

Halliburton, and then back to Washington as George W. Bush's vice-president.

DO WE REALLY NEED THAT TANK?

In the modern era, the old military-industrial complex has come up with new and improved ways of emptying the public treasury. Sometimes the problem isn't the quality. Sometimes it isn't the price. Sometimes it's just we don't need the damn thing.

In December 2014, *Military.com* reported this story:

> "The new defense spending bill includes $120 million for tanks that the Army has repeatedly said it doesn't want.
>
> "For three years, the Army ... has pushed a plan that essentially would have suspended tank building and upgrades in the U.S. for the first time since World War II. ... Each time, Congress has pushed back. Last week, Congress won again in the National Defense Authorization Act ... for Fiscal Year 2015.
>
> "The tank debate between the Army and Congress goes back to 2012 when [Army Chief of Staff General Raymond] Odierno testified that 'Our tank fleet is two and a half years old on average now. We're in good shape and these are additional tanks that we don't need.'
>
> "Odierno lost then too. Congress voted for another $183 million for tanks ... . He told the *Associated Press* at the time that 'if we had our choice, we would use that money in a different way.' "

And no, it isn't just an Army thing. "There are too many people involved in the process," said Chief of Naval Operations, Admiral Jonathan Greenert in *Military.com*. "If I say 'I need a thing' ... there are a whole lot of people telling us 'no, this is what you really need.' "

ALICE IN AFGHANISTAN

> *"My auditors tell me things [about spending plans] and I say, 'you have to be making this up, this is Alice in Wonderland.' "*
> **—John Sopko, U.S. Special Inspector**
> **General for Afghanistan**
> **Reconstruction (SIGAR)**

Here's a sampling of what Inspector General Sopko found in Afghanistan:

- "A half-million-dollar U.S.-built training center in Afghanistan was so badly constructed that it is literally 'melting' and is such an 'embarrassment' that the Afghan government is rebuilding the complex itself, U.S. investigators said in a report released Thursday," reported NBC News in January 2015. "[It] began to disintegrate just four months after it was completed."
- "The U.S. military has erected a 64,000-square-foot headquarters building on the dusty moonscape of southwestern Afghanistan that comes with all the tools to wage a modern war … at a cost of $34 million," noted the *Washington Post* in July 2013. " 'Unfortunately, it is unused, unoccupied, and presumably will never be used for its intended purpose,' Sopko wrote."
- "The U.S. Government has spent $3 million on eight inflatable boats that were intended to be used in Afghanistan but never once saw water," according to a June 2014 *Daily Mail* article. "The landlocked nature of Afghanistan—not to mention the fact that they have been sitting in a Naval warehouse in Virginia ever since they were purchased … are two of the biggest reasons why they went unused. … [Sopko] expects the boats to be stripped for parts or 'sold for pennies on the dollar.' "

In February 2016, Sopko issued a report to Congress in which he described, "significant instances of waste and squandered opportunities in the critical area building up the Afghan Air Force. One of the most egregious was … [the] $486 million purchase of 20 G222 medium-lift cargo planes. … The program was ended in March 2013 after experiencing continuous and severe operational difficulties … . Sixteen of those 20 aircraft were sold for scrap metal for six cents a pound or $32,000."

VANISHING ACT—100 DOLLAR BILLS
In Iraq, on the other hand, the U.S. didn't even bother spending the money badly. We just gave away the cash. Picture about $12 billion (that's almost 281 million $100 bills—for visualization

purposes), neatly bundled in shrink-wrapped packages, put onto planes and flown into Iraq. Now, if you can picture what happened to that money, you've just figured out "one of the great unsolved mysteries of the Iraq war," as James Risen describes it in his book, *Pay Any Price: Greed, Power, and Endless War*.

"Another $5.8 billion was sent from the New York Federal Reserve to Baghdad by electronic funds transfers," Risen writes. "All told, approximately $20 billion was sent to Iraq without any clear orders or direction on how the money was to be used. The controls on the money were so lax that few credible records exist of exactly how much cash there was or where the cash went once it arrived in Baghdad."

And what we do know about some of the money doesn't give you a good feeling about the rest of it. In February 2007, the *Guardian* hit some of the "highlights," taken from "a memorandum prepared for ... the House committee on oversight and government reform":

- "One contractor received a $2 million payment in a duffel bag stuffed with shrink-wrapped bundles of currency."
- "One official was given $6.75 million in cash, and was ordered to spend it in one week before the interim Iraqi government took control of Iraqi funds."
- "...$774,300 in cash had been stolen from one division's vault. Cash payments were made from the back of a pickup truck, and cash was stored in unguarded sacks in Iraqi ministry offices."
- "The minutes from a May 2004 CPA (Coalition Provisional Authority) meeting reveal 'a single disbursement of $500 million in security funding labeled merely 'TBD,' meaning 'to be determined.' "

CONTRACTING OUT—EVERYTHING

"Civilian contractors working for the Pentagon in Afghanistan not only outnumber the uniformed troops," reported the *New York Times* in September 2009, "according to a report by a Congressional research group, but also form the highest ratio of contractors to military personnel recorded in any war in the history of the United States." In Iraq during the war, that ratio was roughly one-to-one.

In March 2013 the *Financial Times* published an article with the headline "Contractors reap $139bn from Iraq war." One of the people interviewed was Daniel Gouré, a vice president of the Lexington Institute, a small public policy think tank that focuses on defense, education and tax reform, and the environment, and is partly funded by defense contractors. He said, " 'This is not my grandfather's military industrial complex. There's not a single munitions producer in this list.' Instead, the US had created a fifth branch of the military, he said. 'It's called the private sector.' "

Here is the *Financial Times*'s list of "Top 10 Corporate winners in Iraq":

KBR (Kellogg, Brown & Root): $39.5 billion
Former subsidiary of Halliburton, the military's largest contractor in Iraq

Agility Logistics: $7.4 billion
Food supplier

Kuwait Petroleum Corp.: $6.3 billion
Oil refining company

ITT: $4.4 billion
Maintained battle gear and made jammers to block roadside bombs

Dyncorp: $4.1 billion
Private security company contracted to train Iraqi police officers

Combat Support Associates: $3.4 billion
Provided logistical support to U.S. troops in Kuwait

International Oil Trading Co.: $2.1 billion
Transported fuel from Jordan to U.S. forces in Iraq

Triple Canopy: $1.8 billion
Large private military contractor; former Delta Force

personnel

Fluor Corp.: $1.5 billion
Logistics and reconstruction

Blackwater: $1.3 billion
Private security firm (changed name to Xe, then Academi)

FEAR GETS CONTRACTED OUT (AND FUNDED)

The fear unleashed by the 9/11 attacks opened the floodgates to spending on counterterrorism and also created opportunities for a completely new group of private intelligence contractors. Tim Shorrock reported in *Salon* in June 2013 that "about 70 percent of our national intelligence budgets [are] being spent on the private sector" and that "contractors have become essential to the spying and surveillance operations of the NSA. ... If the 70 percent figure is applied to the NSA's estimated budget of $8 billion a year ... NSA contracting could reach as high as $6 billion every year."

Who's leading the rush to monetize fear? *AlterNet,* an activist news service, identified the top three private security contractors in an August 2013 article:

The Chertoff Group

Created in 2009, this private firm is hired by companies "to consult on best practices for security and combating terrorism." The "Chertoff" in the name is former Homeland Security chief Michael Chertoff. Also working for the company is Michael Hayden, a former director of the National Security Agency (NSA). After the failed 2010 attempt by the "underwear bomber" to blow up a plane, Chertoff suggested the Transportation Security Agency "use full-body scanners like the ones Rapiscan, one of the Chertoff Group's clients, made," said *AlterNet*. "After the Christmas Day plot, the TSA ordered 300 Rapiscan machines."

Booz Allen Hamilton

This is where Edward Snowden worked. "Thousands of [Booz Allen] employees provide services to the NSA, like analyzing the massive amounts of data the government agency collects every day," according to *AlterNet*. "The company is also the shining symbol of the government-private security complex's revolving door: its vice president is the former director of national intelligence, while the current director of national intelligence is a former employee of Booz Allen. ... And they're making a lot of money from the U.S. In the last fiscal year, the company made $1.3 billion from working in U.S. intelligence."

Science Applications International Corp.
"Sometimes referred to as 'NSA West' because so many former NSA employees go on to work for ... SAIC, this firm makes a ton of cash off government contracts. ... [SAIC] boasts 42,000 employees—20,000 of whom hold U.S. government security clearances, It is the NSA's largest contractor, according to CorpWatch, [a research group that reports on corporate transgressions, environmental violations, fraud, and corruption] and is deeply involved in the NSA's collection of intelligence. [In 2012] it reported a net income of $525 million."

"WAR IS GOOD BUSINESS"
—General Bull Right (a character on TV's *Laugh-In*)

Pope Francis has spoken out against war profiteers, reported the *National Catholic Register,* telling thousands of children last spring, "This is serious. Some powerful people make their living with the production of arms and sell them to one country for them to use against another country ... . It's the industry of death ... . The economic system orbits around money and not men, women. ... This is why some people don't want peace: They make more money from war... ."

The United States, as we saw at the beginning of this chapter, spends far more money on the military than any other country on Earth. And this country also *makes* far more money from war than any other country on Earth. According to a 2015 *Fast Company* article, "40 of the top 100 arms-producing companies in the world are based in the United States, with Lockheed Martin and Boeing being the biggest of the bunch. ... In Lockheed Martin's case, it's 78% of total sales, resulting in nearly $3 billion worth of arms profit in 2013 alone. Boeing, comparatively, only made 35% of its money on arms in 2013, but that 35% was big money: Boeing made $4.5 billion in profits in 2013 just from selling arms and weaponry." The article used 2013 data from the Stockholm International Peace Research Institute.

WHAT IS BEING DONE

There are some modest steps being taken in the right direction. One is in the courts, where we have seen some prosecutions, and some fines, for punishing fraud, waste, and wrongdoing by private contractors and by military personnel.

In Iraq, for example, where former CPA in South Central Iraq comptroller Robert Stein pleaded guilty to charges including conspiracy, bribery, money laundering, possession of machine guns, and being a felon in possession of a firearm. He forfeited $3.6 million and was sentenced to nine years in prison. In addition, an investigation by the Special Inspector General for Iraq Reconstruction resulted in former Army Major John Cockerham pleading guilty to conspiracy, money laundering, and bribery and being sentenced to 17 years in prison for taking more than $9 million in bribes to award contracts for services for troops in Iraq.

Also in Iraq, where three KBR (Kellogg, Brown & Root) employees pleaded guilty to a scam committed in 2003 and 2004 in which KBR awarded a subcontract to a Kuwaiti firm in exchange for a huge kickback—in one case, $1 million. Then KBR over-billed the U.S. military, for example, charging three times the value of fuel tankers, or billing for truck leases when it had already stopped leasing the trucks.

Here at home in 2014, the Justice Department announced that "Lockheed Martin ... has agreed to pay $27.5 million to resolve allegations that it violated the False Claims Act by knowingly overbilling the government for work performed by ... employees who lacked required job qualifications. ... 'U.S. forces rely on the goods and services provided by defense contractors, so it is imperative the government be able to rely on those contractors to adhere to the rules,' said U.S. Attorney [Paul] Fishman. 'This settlement should remind all who do business with the government that there is a price to pay for fudging the truth.' "

WHAT CAN BE DONE

So long as war is a matter of business, big business, the business of war has to be conducted in a businesslike fashion. That trillion dollars a year we spend on defense can't remain a mystery. Whether the money goes for fighter planes or tanks, secret agents or software, it has to be accounted for and justified openly. Whether it's spent by generals or bureaucrats, if that money— our money—is spent foolishly or carelessly, those people shouldn't be in those jobs. And when that money, our money, is taken by companies that deliver weapons that don't work or aren't needed, the people running those companies should be prosecuted. The defense budget cannot be an open container for public money without accountability.

General Ray Odierno, former Army Chief of Staff, said, "We are still having to procure systems we don't need." That statement is repeated every day by our responsible service members.

10

Your Privacy for Sale

"Nothing is out of bounds. No list is too obnoxious to sell. Data brokers sell lists that allow for the use of racial, ethnic and other factors that would be illegal or unacceptable in other circumstances... If a consumer learns that he or she is on a list, there is usually no way to get off the list."
> **—Pam Dixon, Executive Director, World Privacy Forum**

"Americans deserve policies that protect both their security and their liberty—this bill fails on both counts."
> **—Senator Ron Wyden (D-OR), voting against the Cybersecurity Act of 2015**

"It is a mistake to consider tracking benign …. It's both an opportunity for amazing connections of data, as well as a time bomb of revealing personal information you assume will be kept private."
> **—Sagi Leizerov, Executive Director, Ernst & Young's Privacy Services**

BIG DATA'S BIG TRADE OFF: PRIVACY VERSUS SECURITY

I am a total novice when it comes to the new internet age of information. When looking at cases that come into our law firm, I am amazed at what can be found on the internet. One can never understand the extent of information available or the privacy we have lost. There is a balance that we must recognize in today's world of terrorism and that is the big policy question of the day facing all Americans as well as citizens of the world. It is privacy versus security. The issue of the iPhone in San Bernardino is a classic example but it is not as clear as each side makes it. When

I started doing the research on this subject, I was amazed at the money involved.

It started out as a convenient service and we didn't realize what was really happening. While you are shopping on Amazon, a message popped up saying something like, "if you like this you may like that," and a selection of items similar to the search appeared on the screen. How smart of them. The alternative offerings are like having a personal shopper who saves you time and guides you through an overabundance of choices. Here are more conveniences: Amazon remembers your prior searches, Google remembers your prior searches, your browser remembers your passwords (of which you by now have more than a dozen). And with each "convenience" you unwittingly surrender a sliver of your privacy.

Every day, we go online and generate mountains of data that is correlated and triangulated to create a dossier of untold value that reveals who we are, how we feel, what we want, and even, to a degree, what we think. The mass accumulation of these profiles is well under way. Many of the conveniences resulting from these seemingly innocuous privacy invasions may seem worth the trade-off. After all, you may ask yourself, "Who wants to know about boring old me?"

Everyone wants to know about you. You are a commodity to marketers, the government, and criminals. But mostly, you are important to "big data" corporations that reap millions of dollars by selling information about you: you as an individual, you as a target market, and you in the aggregate. Everything about you is up for sale to the big payers and we have to position this against the security of our country.

For that reason, tech companies who are concerned about data that is now being stolen from consumers are seeking to put encryption tools on their devices that no one can break. Apple is the best example of this position.

0WE KNOW WHO YOU ARE AND WE KNOW WHAT YOU WANT

> *"Half the money I spend on advertising is wasted; the trouble is I don't know which half."*
> **—John Wanamaker, John Wanamaker & Co. department store**

Gerald Chait, the CEO of Marketing by Objectives said, "Gone are the days when we would define roughly segmented target audiences and place an ad hoping someone would purchase something. Today's inbound marketing approaches enable us to identify who to work with to make a sale, right down to [the] individual level. What's more, we can personalize and customize our advertising and messaging to each specific person, no matter how many people there are. We can even customize and personalize website pages depending on who's viewing them."

We live in a lucrative new world for marketers, where unseen data points abound, metrics are in control, and big data analytics serve to let commerce invade your innermost thoughts. Every day new data patterns are generated to sell you something. And it's not just online anymore.

BIG DATA TO TARGET EXPECTANT MOTHERS

A classic example of using data collection is Target stores from new parents. And it spends a lot of time and money figuring out the best way to capture them as customers. Charles Duhigg interviewed one of the retailer's statisticians, Andrew Pole, for the *New York Times Magazine* in February 2012. The retailer wanted to send tailored ads to pregnant women in their second trimester, in hopes of selling them baby products among other things.

Pole told Duhigg that Target has a sophisticated system that tracks your credit card and coupon use, plus any other kind of interaction you might have with the store. It all links to an internally assigned guest identification number. These statistics are augmented by bought data that can reveal your ethnicity, place of employment, financial history, favorite websites, and consumer preferences. Target can find out about your politics and the books you read; it can find out the brand of cereal you like. All kinds of information about you is now for sale.

According to Duhigg, Target's data specialists are so good that they can predict a woman's due date based on the products she is buying. This in turn allows Target to send coupons to match up with what a woman might want to buy as her pregnancy progresses. When someone pointed out that women might get upset if they receive an advertisement making it obvious Target was studying their reproductive status, the marketing department ran a test.

Sure enough, "we learned that some women react badly," a Target executive told Duhigg. One father was incensed that the store was sending his teenage daughter advertisements for baby gear. He later called to apologize to the store when he found out that the retailer's information was more accurate than his own.

THE FIGHT FOR PRIVACY RIGHTS

In 1890, a 34-year-old Boston lawyer named Louis Brandeis and his law partner Samuel Warren published "The Right to Privacy" in the *Harvard Law Review,* the first major article to advocate for a legal right to privacy. Brandeis wrote, "Recent inventions and business methods call attention to the next step which must be taken for the protection of the person, and for securing to the individual ... the right 'to be let alone.' " The invention he referred to was the portable camera and the business method he sought to highlight was celebrity journalism.

Twenty-six years later, Brandeis became a Supreme Court justice, and he soon gained another opportunity to advocate for a constitutional right to privacy. In *Olmstead v. United States,* in 1928, the U.S. Supreme Court held that the warrantless wiretapping of a suspected bootlegger's telephone conversations did not violate his right to privacy under the Fourth or Fifth Amendments to the Constitution. Brandeis vehemently disagreed, and in his dissent to the *Olmstead* decision, which has become a famous passage, he argued, "The progress of science in furnishing the Government with means of espionage is not likely to stop with wire-tapping. Ways may someday be developed by which the Government, without removing papers from secret drawers, can reproduce them in court, and by which it will be enabled to expose to a jury the most intimate occurrences of the home."

Brandeis was the first justice to identify how technology could put people's privacy at risk. He is considered such a hero among privacy rights advocates that a privacy rights award is given in his name.

WE'RE THE GOVERNMENT, WE WANT TO PROTECT YOU

Justice Brandeis's definition of an individual's right to privacy was reinforced by other Supreme Court decisions throughout the 20th century. Even today, his eloquent and prescient arguments form the legal bulwark restricting government snooping. Spying on people, even for the presumed greater good, invariably leads to abuses of power. Brandeis knew this and proved to be far-sighted about the likelihood that new inventions, i.e., technology, could enable the government to reproduce incriminating evidence.

Indeed, the probing of private matters that Brandeis sought to preempt is precisely what the data collecting industry is all about. The deployment of new technologies to spy on the citizenry has come to pass.

The spies at the National Security Agency are no dummies. They were quick to realize that the mountains of consumer data collected to sell online advertising might also be helpful to flush out suspected terrorists. And as we now know, thanks to whistleblower Edward Snowden, the NSA received only a modicum of resistance from the corporate sector when the agency's officials came calling for access to consumer data. Snowden released tens of thousands of pages of documents showing that the NSA had taken possession of the telephone records, email messages, and social media postings of hundreds of millions of ordinary Americans.

This private information, handed over to the NSA by Verizon, AT&T, Google, Microsoft, Facebook, Apple, and others, should have been sacrosanct. And for nearly a hundred years, it was: The citizens of the United States had been able to stand confidently behind the Constitution as a protective shield against undue government surveillance.

But Snowden's disclosures of the NSA's PRISM surveillance program, which collected communications by foreigners from U.S. Internet companies shed light on how the agency maneuvered around constitutional protections. Instead of challenging constitutional limits on directly spying on citizens, why not simply tap into commercial surveillance?

THE POWER TO PROTECT AND THE POWER TO COERCE
No one should expect the NSA or any law enforcement agency to curtail their efforts to obtain and sift through consumer data. In fact, the FBI has already shown the strategy that authorities will pursue next. As part of assisting the investigation of Snowden, FBI agents obtained a court order requiring a small Texas provider of secure emails, Lavabit, to turn over encryption keys that the agents needed to unscramble messages Snowden had sent using Lavabit's services.

"The most powerful tool the Department of Justice has is not the ability to hack but the ability to coerce," said Chris Soghoian, principal technologist and senior policy analyst at the American Civil Liberties Union, in a talk in 2014. "You can fix the hack, but you can't patch away the coercion."

Lavabit founder Ladar Levison refused to comply with the order, instead shutting down his company and fighting the government in court. It seems clear that federal and state officials will accelerate the use of court orders and other legal methods to gain access to wide swaths of consumer data if authorities believe it will help them catch criminals and terrorists.

Soghoian says the government almost certainly will exercise any advantage it gains in the Lavabit case and use those tactics elsewhere. "The precedent that the government can go to a private company and demand the keys to the kingdom to get at one user's data threatens the entire Internet," said Soghoian.

WHOSE PHONE IS IT?
That threat emerged in December of 2015, when terrorists struck the small city of San Bernardino in California, killing 14 people, with many others injured. The police found an iPhone used by one of the terrorists and went to Apple to "open the phone." Apple said no, the government sued, but before the court said anything, the FBI found a way to break into the phone without the company's help. But while the legal case is now moot, that case sparked a national debate not only over the level of coercion

a government can exert, but also the level of privacy companies owe their customers and the degree of security the government owes its citizens.

COOKIES: THE POWER TO TRACK ONLINE CONSUMERS

In 1994, a bright young programmer named Louis J. Montulli came up with a way to upload a tiny coding routine to an Internet browser that enables websites to "remember" each returning visitor. Montulli was a founding engineer at Netscape, the company that introduced the web browser to the public. He had heard the programming term "magic cookie" in a college computing course, so he dubbed his snippet of coding a "cookie."

Montulli wanted to make it more convenient for Internet users to return quickly to a favorite website. He did not anticipate that using cookies would propagate a global consumer spying empire. Now co-founder and chief scientist at the Silicon Valley tech company Zetta.net, Montulli says his aim was, in fact, "to discourage tracking across websites … . The idea of a trail of breadcrumbs is, ironically, the opposite of what we were trying to accomplish with cookies."

Not long after Montulli came up with cookies, an advertising startup called DoubleClick latched onto his invention and widely dispersed cookies as a stealth tracking mechanism. Instead of deploying cookies as Montulli had intended, DoubleClick, and other large advertising companies, began to orchestrate the mass distribution of third-party cookies via any website interested in participating in online advertising. It developed a sophisticated system for identifying a unique visitor using cookies dispersed from multiple websites. This allowed DoubleClick to keep track of each visitor as he or she navigated to other websites.

This new capacity to cross-correlate numerous cookies that glom onto the browser of each individual Internet user is the core of online tracking. It has empowered online advertising agencies—of which Google is by far the largest—to scrutinize every move each Internet user makes in a way unlike anything ever dreamed of in broadcast or print advertising.

Montulli now laments that "the third-party cookie, combined with the referrer field, is an unintended consequence of multiple technologies combining to allow something that should not have been possible."

In 1999, DoubleClick announced that it intended to execute a $1.7 billion merger with data broker Abacus Direct, a supplier of consumer data to offline catalog companies. Privacy advocates immediately protested. DoubleClick would be able to correlate Internet behaviors culled from tracking cookies with the sensitive Personally Identifiable Information, or PII, contained in Abacus's database of more than 2 billion consumer catalog transactions, including names, addresses, phone numbers, and email addresses.

Jason Catlett, a consumer-privacy advocate, sent letters of protest to Abacus, DoubleClick, the Federal Trade Commission (FTC), and members of Congress, urging them to suspend or block the merger. "By synchronizing cookies with name and address from email, registrations and ecommerce transactions, the merged company would have a surveillance database of Orwellian proportions," Catlett warned. The FTC investigated and called on Congress to ensure a minimum level of privacy for online consumers, but the merger was consummated in 1999.

DoubleClick subsequently made a number of moves to avoid further protests. In March 2000, CEO Kevin O'Connor promised that the company would not "link personally identifiable information to anonymous user activity across Web sites." Then, in February 2006, DoubleClick announced the sale of its email solutions division to data broker Epsilon; that December, the company announced that it was spinning off Abacus to Epsilon, for $435 million in cash. This was all a prelude to a move that would result in a quantum leap for consumer surveillance—and the complete destruction of individual privacy envisioned by Justice Brandeis.

GOOGLE: CROSSING THE LINE TO INVADE PRIVACY

In 2007, search giant Google agreed to acquire DoubleClick for $3.1 billion. Once again, privacy advocates howled in protest. Marc Rotenberg, the outspoken executive director of the Electronic Privacy Information Center, warned of dire consequences should the combined companies be allowed to control consumer data. Regulators in the United States, Canada, Australia, and Europe "appear to be in agreement that there is no merger that poses a more significant threat to online privacy than Google's proposed acquisition of DoubleClick," Rotenberg said at the time. "This is going to be a real problem for the Internet if it's allowed to go forward."

But the merger did indeed go forward, despite intense lobbying from Microsoft and Yahoo. Google's top rivals pleaded with the FTC and congressional leaders to block the merger, to stop Google from securing a monopoly on online advertising. But in 2007, Google completed its acquisition of DoubleClick, and the surveillance of consumer behavior online soon kicked into overdrive.

Google accelerated the correlation of data from DoubleClick's tracking cookies to user data scraped from its numerous online services, including Google search queries, YouTube video viewing, and Android smartphone apps. It extracted, analyzed, and cross-referenced text from Gmail users' email.

It didn't help Google's standing with privacy advocacy groups that Eric Schmidt, the company's CEO during much of this period, tended to thump his chest in public about the company's engineering prowess and bold pioneering mindset. In an *Atlantic* magazine interview, Schmidt volunteered that company executives and chief engineers referred to something called the "creepy line." "Google policy is to get right up to the creepy line and not cross it," Schmidt told *Atlantic* editor James Bennet.

But competition has a funny way of clouding judgment. With Facebook's Mark Zuckerberg commanding the media's admiration and his company attracting more and more advertising revenue, Google vaulted across the creepy line. In February 2010, the company launched Google Buzz, which was its attempt at creating a social network with Facebook and Twitter features. But Google made the mistake of integrating Buzz into people's Gmail without asking permission. And Buzz did a few pretty invasive things by default, such as choosing contacts from Gmail users' accounts, automatically making them Buzz followers, and making the list public. As complaints rolled in, Google was compelled to terminate Buzz, only to replace it a little more than a year later with the social website Google Plus.

In another act of overreaching, beginning on 2007, Google dispatched fleets of cars into 33 countries equipped to take photographs for Google's Street View maps. No one raised a fuss until 2010 when German authorities discovered that the vehicles also were intercepting data moving across unprotected Wi-Fi networks, including emails, medical records, and other sensitive personal information. The Google street view cars had gathered this data as they cruised by houses and businesses snapping photos in Germany. Google's automobile data-pilfering touched off an international furor. Google officials contended it was all a big mistake and agreed to turn over about 600 gigabytes of personal Wi-Fi data to German authorities.

"Google's culture is demonstrably hostile to privacy, yielding the world's worst privacy record," according to Scott Cleland, an analyst at and president of the consultancy Precursor and author of a book lambasting the search giant, *Search & Destroy: Why You Can't Trust Google Inc.* He said the company's monopoly power "creates a unique global privacy problem" that "exponentially exacerbated the global surveillance of private information."

Ever since introducing Street View in 2007, Google has been crossing that creepy line and laying waste to its original corporate philosophy, "Don't be evil."

FACEBOOK: SACTIONED FOR DECEPTIVE PRIVACY PRACTICES

Over at Facebook, Mark Zuckerberg has yet to publicly acknowledge he sees a line at all. Facebook assumes its users are comfortable with everything it wants to do to extract more clues about their interests, preferences, and friends. Facebook continually concocts tricks to get users to divulge more detailed personal information and only vaguely discloses whom it might share it with and how it intends to profit from it. Once you create a Facebook account, good luck trying to permanently delete it.

In November 2011, after a two-year investigation, the FTC barred Facebook from deceiving consumers about the company's privacy practices and required the company to submit to monitoring for 20 years. The sanctions stemmed from changes in privacy settings Facebook made in December 2009 without asking users' permission.

It was a slap on the wrist. While not unwelcomed by privacy advocates, the FTC's action highlighted everything that's fundamentally wrong with how corporations are allowed to dictate privacy standards in the digital age. Privacy policies should be transparent and understandable to everyone, and consumers should have an easy-to-understand way to opt out of sharing information to protect their privacy while using Facebook's Timeline pages.

Virtually every Facebook user has been annoyed at one time or another by ads popping up revealing products from a recent search, or worse, ads that reveal that Facebook is tracking your age and now thinks you need wrinkle cream or Viagra.

PRIVACY: NO LONGER THE SOCIAL NORM

In what has become an infamous TechCrunch video interview, Facebook's Zuckerberg posited that "people have really gotten comfortable not only sharing more information and different kinds, but more openly and with more people." He then declared that individual privacy was no longer a "social norm."

It's not the professional norm either. A May 2015 article in the *Cleveland Plain Dealer* reported on polling data findings that, "Fifty-two percent of employers use social networking sites to research candidates. That figure is up from 43 percent last year and 39 percent in 2013."

Clearly, job applicants who have an online presence have an edge over those who don't use social networks. "The survey found that 35 percent of hiring managers who use social media to screen applicants have sent friend requests or the equivalent," according to the *Plain Dealer*. "Eighty percent said job seekers have accepted such requests."

TRACKING: THE NEW SOCIAL NORM

Julia Angwin covered technology companies from 2000 to 2013 for the *Wall Street Journal*, giving the Pulitzer Prize–winning investigative reporter a ringside seat to observe how corporate greed has led to the commercialization of the Internet. As part of the research for her 2014 book, *Dragnet Nation: A Quest for Privacy, Security and Freedom in a World of Relentless Surveillance,* Angwin—later a reporter at ProPublica—carried out an arduous experiment. She tried for a year to dodge as much indiscriminate online tracking as humanly possible.

She quit Googling and terminated her LinkedIn account. To mask her identity, Angwin used a prepaid cell phone under a pseudonym, which she used to set up a new email account and other online accounts. In short, she made a concerted effort to do what corporations engaging in consumer surveillance proactively make it very difficult for average U.S. citizens to do: opt out of getting tracked.

Of her experience, Angwin told newsman Bill Moyers on his PBS program: "What I learned was that I had been accepting all this technology, you know, just taking Gmail at face value and thinking, 'This is the way it has to be.' Or using Google search and thinking, 'This is the way it has to be.' And what I learned was that by spending a little time and effort, I could change the rules of the game. I was able to find another search engine, DuckDuckGo, that was privacy-protecting. And at first, I found my searches weren't as good, but when I figured out how to use it, I was able to do it. And I felt very proud of myself. Because I thought, you know, in the end, as we become more of a technology society and more machine-based, my ability to control the machines is important, because otherwise they're going to control me, right? And so I felt very empowered by my ability to switch off of these services."

But Angwin learned something else of profound consequence: She told Moyers she did not believe it was practical for ordinary citizens to do what she had done. She estimated that she was only 50 percent successful in avoiding tracking and that finding privacy-protected alternatives for many indispensable services, such as email, was a challenge. Angwin's experiment underscored a troubling reality of our Internet-dependent society as it has been shaped by corporate greed: Relentless tracking has become the norm.

ESPIONAGE IN REAL TIME

A stunning graphic display of the scale and scope of consumer surveillance conducted on each individual—you and me—is available for you to see—for free.

It is a nifty tool called Lightbeam, an add-on to Firefox, the popular browser developed by Mozilla. Firefox, ironically, derives from the Netscape browser that Louis Montulli, the inventor of tracking cookies, originally worked on.

The tool is a free download. In 2012, Gary Kovacs, then Mozilla's CEO, unveiled the prototype for Lightbeam. He conducted a public demonstration as part of a TED talk that has become one of the most watched of all time, with more than 1.9 million views. Kovacs put up a slide showing a web of interconnected dots representing 25 entities voraciously tracking his presence on the Internet in real time—moments after he clicked open only four websites—as he sat down to breakfast with his nine-year-old daughter.

Kovacs continued, "So let me fast-forward through the rest of my day. I go to work, I check email, I log onto a few more social sites, I blog, I check more news reports, I share some of those news reports, I go look at some videos, pretty typical day ... and at the end of the day, as my day winds down, look at my profile. The red dots have exploded. The gray dots have grown exponentially. All in all, there's over 150 sites that are now tracking my personal information, most all of them without my consent."

Mozilla hopes a lot of folks start using Lightbeam. It asks Firefox users to contribute data showing who is tracking them to a central database to be analyzed. Mozilla wants to assemble a big-picture view of Web tracking and put a spotlight on the third parties doing the most tracking.

So this is the first thing that you can do—watch back. Hopefully, campaigns like WebWeWant, a public service campaign to raise awareness about an open Web, will continue to come along to help pull back the curtain of secrecy that corporations have draped around the expanding machinery spying on us. This espionage is launched with every connection to the Internet we make on computing devices every day, on the go, in homes and offices.

It is empowering to be able to look up helpful information anytime, anywhere, and to communicate with friends, loved ones, and colleagues. And, yes, there is a convenience factor for shopping and banking online and receiving relevant advertisements. But we must find a better way to pay for the access and connections that the Internet bestows, a system that honors the right to be left alone and doesn't, by default, convey the full value of our valuable personal information to the corporate sector.

EUROPEAN PRIVACY REVOLUTION

In America, we consumers are seduced by convenience and complacent about corporate control of the intimate details of our lives. Edward Snowden's disclosures of the NSA's surveillance program revealed the extent to which the Web giants will readily hand over sensitive consumer data to government snoops. In reaction to Snowden's whistleblowing, Google, Microsoft, Facebook, Yahoo, and Apple scrambled to distance themselves from this practice and to cast themselves as staunch resisters of government data sweeps. Many of these data gatherers have since encrypted consumer data that comes in via their main servers. A recent example is the resistance Apple and its CEO Tim Cook put up against the FBI's effort to get the company to break its password encryption on the iPhone used by one of the San Bernardino terrorists.

In contrast, Europe's citizenry and political leaders haven't forgotten the atrocities wrought by despots who trampled on everyone's personal privacy. Europe is continually refining policies built around the concept of keeping the individual in firm control of his or her personal information.

Members of the Europe Union are serious about data privacy. For 15 years, a Safe Harbor agreement had been in place between the United States and the European Union that let U.S. companies transfer personal data on E.U. citizens if the data protection protocols met E.U. privacy standards. However, in October 2015, the E.U.'s Court of Justice invalidated the Safe Harbor agreement, ruling that the existing agreement didn't "ensure an adequate level of protection" of personal data.

Two months later, four Dutch privacy organizations and some individuals demanded that Facebook find a way to store personal information about its Dutch users without transferring the data to the United States. According to *Forbes,* Facebook stated that the company "uses the same mechanisms that thousands of others [sic] companies across the EU use to transfer data legally from the EU to the US, and to other countries around the world. We believe that the best solution to the on-going debate around transatlantic data transfers is for there to be a new Safe Harbor agreement with appropriate safeguards for EU citizens."

Privacy is a critical issue for European citizens, who have been advocating for "the right to be forgotten"—in other words, to be able to ask search engines to remove private information that they say is irrelevant—upon request. It's often embarrassing or misleading personal information that people want removed, such as revealing images. In 2014 the E.U.'s

Court of Justice issued a groundbreaking decision that gave its citizens this right, with the stipulation that the information must no longer be pertinent. According to the Electronic Privacy Information Center, the court found that "the fundamental right to privacy is greater than the economic interest of the commercial firm and, in some circumstances, the public interest in access to information." We're seeing a privacy revolution in Europe and may be at the beginning of a privacy revolution here in America.

BIG DATA FOR SALE: CRIMINALS APPRECIATE THE HELP

The tracking giants, led by Google and Facebook, have begun to partner with the Big Three credit bureaus, Experian, TransUnion, and Equifax, and with huge data brokerages, led by Acxiom and Epsilon, to accelerate spying on consumers to gather data. A glimpse at how this is done comes from a U.S. Senate staff report delivered to Senator Jay Rockefeller of West Virginia, in December 2013.

Senate staff investigators found a mind-boggling level of comingling of online and offline personal data—credit histories, tax and property records, vital statistics, voting records, driving records, and criminal histories. Data brokers blend offline information with Web-surfing patterns. They then put consumers into groupings referred to as "buckets." These buckets are used for discriminating, redlining, and conducting "differential pricing," the practice of charging different prices for the same products based on invasive profiling of buyers.

Pam Dixon, executive director of the World Privacy Forum, testified about these practices at a Senate hearing chaired by Rockefeller:

"Data brokers sell lists of people suffering from mental health diseases, cancer, HIV/AIDS, and hundreds of other illnesses. ... Data brokers sell lists of people who are late on payments, often to those who make predatory offers to those in financial trouble. Data brokers sell lists of people who are impulse buyers or 'eager senior buyers.' All in all, there are millions of lists."

The Senate staffers who put together the report offered no concrete solutions, just this stark conclusion: "The responses the Committee received in its inquiry into the data broker industry provide a snapshot of how data brokers collect, use, and share consumer data for marketing purposes.

"This information makes clear that consumers going about their daily activities—from making purchases online and at brick-and-mortar stores, to using social media, to answering surveys to obtain coupons or prizes, to filing for a professional license—should expect that they are generating data that may well end up in the hands of data brokers.

"They should expect that this data may well be amassed with many other details about them data brokers already have compiled. And they should expect that data brokers will draw on this data without their permission to construct detailed profiles on them reflecting judgments about their characteristics and predicted behaviors."

And these are the companies that are collecting your data legally. Criminals really appreciate the help.

DATA BREACHES: NO INDUSTRY OR CONSUMER IS PROTECTED

"Throughout 2015, industries of all types were hit again and again by data breaches," wrote Sarah Kuranda for *CRN,* a computer-industry online publication. "From health care to education to the public sector, no industry was exempt in 2015 from the eye of attackers. While the number of breaches overall was down from 2014 (190 total reported breaches in 2015, as opposed to 297 in 2014, according to the Privacy Rights Clearinghouse), the tone of many of the breaches this year was much more sinister. 2015 saw mega-breaches compromising more extensive personal information than ever before."

Here were some of the biggest data breaches of 2015 according to *CRN:* The Army National Guard; Starwood Hotels; Anthem; Blue Cross Blue Shield affiliates in New York, Washington, and Alaska, and the U.S. Office of Personnel Management. Hackers also targeted credit service provider Experian. Kuranda reported, "In October, the credit company said that information on 15 million T-Mobile customers who had applied for the telecom vendor's postpaid services, which are handled by Experian, had been compromised after unauthorized access was discovered to a company server ... . Information compromised could include names, addresses, Social Security numbers, dates of birth, and identification numbers, the company said at the time."

THERE'S MORE: YOUR APPLIANCES ARE WATCHING YOU

As consumers in the Internet age, we are immersed in a world of digital devices and clever online services. We use our smartphones, touch tablets, e-readers, laptops, and desktop PCs to shop, bank, invest, socialize, learn, work, and play. Our ability to instantly access endless caches of content, and to make connections with individuals and organizations around the globe, is simply astounding. And the future suggests that it's not going to slow down.

We are confronted with the Internet of Things—where our household appliances are able to sense when we want to change temperature, lighting, or window and security settings. Even kids' toys are Internet connected, leading to a new layer of paranoia that your child's Barbie may be eavesdropping on you. Oh, and your neighbor may have gotten a drone for Christmas.

AUTOMATED LICENSE PLATE READERS: GET A DEAR "JOHN" LETTER

"The Los Angeles City Council is considering a controversial plan that would involve tracking license plates and automatically issuing letters to the homes of 'Johns' suspected of visiting sex workers," according to a *MintPress News* article in December 2015. The article continued:

"Denounced by both the Electronic Frontier Foundation and the ACLU, the plan would allow automated license plate readers to generate letters informing households that the specific car was observed habituating certain areas known for prostitution. ... While privacy advocates are criticizing the plan as an unconstitutional breach of civil liberties, others say such measures are necessary to reduce street prostitution ... ."

"Police departments in Minneapolis, Des Moines, and Oakland have utilized similar automated license plate readers. Each of these cities has also sent letters to the alleged 'Johns,' informing them, their wives, or whoever happens to open the mail that the city knows where they've been and that there may be cause for alarm."

To issue a warning based on the perceived intent of someone doing nothing more than legally driving down the wrong street surely transgresses both the creepy line and civil liberties.

CYBERSECURITY INFORMATION SHARING ACT OF 2015: ALL OF THE SHARING, NONE OF THE SECURITY

"[A] new surveillance bill masquerading as cybersecurity legislation," is how the ACLU described the Cybersecurity Information Sharing Act (CISA) of 2015.

The cybersecurity in this case wasn't directly for us. The stated purpose was to encourage businesses to pass on "cyber threat indicators" to the federal government, to help fight hacking.

So why did the opposition to the Cyber Act include a dizzying array of big tech names, from Amazon and Apple to Google and Salesforce, from the American Library Association and the ACLU to Decide the Future, Freedom Works, Human Rights Watch, and a list that goes on and on?

Decide The Future breaks it down this way on its website: the new law "Removed prohibition of information being shared automatically with [the National Security Agency and Department of Defense] ... . Removes prohibition on using CISA for 'surveillance' activities. Removes limitation that government can only use collected info for cybersecurity purposes ... . Removes requirement that government scrub personal information unrelated to a cybersecurity threat before sharing information."

Oh, and the bill also protects companies from liability if they pass on a bit too much information—while doing nothing to improve cybersecurity measures that might prevent hacking in the first place.

Senator Ron Wyden of Oregon summed it up in explaining his opposition: "Americans deserve policies that protect both their security and their liberty. This bill fails on both counts."

PRIVACY v. SECURITY: THE ISSUE OF OUR TIMES

There are three groups that want a resolution to privacy versus security. The first is the government, which wants total access for security. The second would be terrorists and criminals. They want to keep secrets. And the third would be the citizens. We have secrets too, but we also want to be safe in the world.

Here's a roundup from CNET of some polling done earlier in

the year:

"The poll, conducted by [the] Wall Street Journal and NBC News [found that overall,] 47 percent said they feared the government wouldn't go far enough in protecting national security, while 44 percent feared it would intrude too far into citizens' privacy. ...

"A Pew study found about 51 percent of those surveyed believed Apple should comply with the court order, while 38 percent said the tech giant shouldn't unlock the iPhone. However a Reuters poll had opposite results. About 46 percent actually agreed with Apple's stance and 35 percent disagreed."

If we knew an attack was imminent, and we knew the information to stop it was on an iPhone—most of us would probably say, "hack that phone." But that same "most of us" would probably not want the government to be able to look at anything, anywhere, anytime—just on the say-so of the police or the FBI.

And what made this iPhone more than just the ongoing story of privacy versus security is that today's phone is one-stop shopping for the details of our lives.

Getting access to someone's phone now is like tapping their landline, reading their mail, looking at their medical records, opening up their safe, peeking under their mattress, discovering their decoder ring and following them around town—all at once. Which means, if our phones are open secrets to our government, our lives are open secrets. And we can't count on the government to always distinguish between a terrorist's secret that might endanger us and the secrets that are legitimately private.

Most likely, Apple (or others) and the government will face off in court again, the next time the FBI runs up against the next set of security measures Apple creates for its phones. Because there won't be a one-size-fits-all answer to the privacy versus security question; there will be laws, and there will be human judgment about how to apply those laws, case by case.

WHAT CAN BE DONE

Can you be private in public? When "public" means the online world of the Internet, the answer is ... sort of.

As we saw in Julia Angwin's year of trying to become e-invisible, she de-Googled and de-LinkedIn herself. She created pseudonyms for herself. She used a burner phone (basically a prepaid phone) to have an anonymous number. She encrypted herself.

And yet, "After spending a year doing this, I felt this is not something any normal person would do or should do," Angwin told NPR's *All Things Considered*. "It's too much work, and I didn't actually achieve many of my goals."

In his *Huffington Post* column from January 23, 2015, privacy maven Mark Weinberg offered up "7 Cool Ways to Have Fun Online While Protecting Your Privacy." His suggestions include using Tor for your web browser, DuckDuckGo for your search engine, and Wickr for your messaging app.

Or for the deluge of information we've come to expect from Internet searches, you could go to CNET and search terms like "privacy tools."

We do want more privacy in our online lives. When the Pew Research Center polled Americans last year about online privacy, here's what they heard:

"93 percent of adults say that being in control of *who* can get information about them is important; 74 percent feel this is 'very important,' while 19 percent say it is 'somewhat important.'

"90 percent say that controlling *what* information is collected about them is important—65 percent think it is 'very important' and 25 percent say it is 'somewhat important.' "

But at present, the only way to be truly invisible online, is to go offline. To make the future different from that present, we need to change more than just our Internet browsers or our messaging apps. We need to change the rules about what corporations and governments are allowed to do on the Internet when it comes to following us. And that means we need elected officials that understand the policy debate and recognize the balance between privacy and national security—it is not an easy question. One thing is for sure, billions of dollars are being spent on collecting your data.

U.S. Senator Dianne Feinstein, Democrat of California, and U.S. Senator Richard Burr, Republican of North Carolina, have tried to cobble together legislation to address encryption. The legislation is very simple in concept—protect privacy but allow courts to make appropriate orders to protect the security of our country. It is an easy concept but one that will be debated for years. As world terrorism increases, the policy will become clear.

11

Lawyers and the Rich Man's Justice

"You [sir], were a dirty lawyer for many, many years."
—**Colleen McMahon, U.S. District Judge, sentencing a New York lawyer, 2015**

"You were the linchpin of the whole thing … You gave it an air of legitimacy."
—**James Mahan, U.S. District Judge, sentencing a Las Vegas lawyer, 2015**

"Certainly, when I was a boy, people liked to believe that lawyers were kind of pillars of goodness of the likes of Atticus Finch in To Kill a Mockingbird.*"*
—**Scott Turow, lawyer and author**

You only have to read the previous chapters to understand that most frauds and scams would not be possible without the assistance of lawyers. It takes a lot of high priced attorneys to keep Wall Street running, to make Big Pharma deals, to counsel how to get around regulations, to advise how to move money offshore, and to help corporations skirt laws. Corporate boardrooms across the country are filled with lawyers of all stripes giving them all kinds of advice, including how to avoid taxes and get around our laws.

Scams and kickback opportunities become abundant when big money transactions go down. Lawyers rubbing elbows with politicians, bankers, and financiers may find themselves invited to sit at tables filled with temptation and many will give in to it. Of the roughly 1.3 million lawyers in the United States, the great majority are professional and honest; but, unfortunately, some lawyers see a law degree as a license to steal. It all comes down to billing and greed.

The sad fact is that for many lawyers today, the quest for the dollar bill contributes to insatiable materialism and unbridled egotism—to live in the big house, drive the big car, and be on the right invitation lists. Thankfully, we still have a profession where many law graduates want to work in public interest firms and for legal aid across the country. I have been in practice over 50 years and have tried cases around the country. I have also seen everything in our practice from honest, decent lawyers, to people who should not have a license. Unfortunately, our bar associations are very lax in removing bad lawyers from practice and our courts are equally as lenient. The following are just a few recent examples of where a great profession has gone wrong. Thankfully, the honest, decent lawyers far out-number the bad ones.

OFFICERS OF THE COURT ... SOMETIMES

Getting admitted to the bar to practice law includes its own set of criteria, part of it ethical. According to the American Bar Association:

"In order to obtain a license to practice law, almost all law school graduates must apply for bar admission through a state board of bar examiners. ...

"Licensing involves a demonstration of worthiness in two distinct areas. The first is competence ... ordinarily established by a showing that the applicant holds an acceptable educational credential ... from a law school that meets educational standards, and by achieving a passing score on the bar examination. ...

"The second area of inquiry by bar examiners involves the character and fitness of applicants for a law license. In this regard, bar examiners seek background information concerning each applicant that is relevant to the appropriateness of granting a professional credential. Because law is a public profession, and because the degree of harm a lawyer, once licensed, can inflict is substantial, decisions about who should be admitted to practice law are made carefully by bar examining boards."

You only need to glance at a list of lawyers who've been

disbarred or suspended to know that these ethical standards are there for a reason.

LAWYERS USED TO BE HEROES
Scott Turow, lawyer and author of *Presumed Innocent, The Burden of Proof,* and *The Laws of Our Fathers*, remembers Atticus Finch. Many of us remember Raymond Burr as Perry Mason and Andy Griffith as Ben Matlock. For the prosecution there was Sam Waterston as District Attorney Jack McCoy on *Law & Order* or his colleague DA Arthur Branch played by real lawyer Fred Thompson, who began acting on the long-running TV series at the end of his last term as a U.S. Senator. Thompson first gained notice as minority counsel on the Senate Watergate Committee.

Today even fictional lawyers are more likely to be known for clever but quasi-ethical behind-the-scenes maneuvers than they are for their courtroom prowess. Deals more than justice are the meat of today's legal dramas.

In various dictionaries you will find terms for a group of lawyers. Collective nouns can often be amusing—like a gaggle of geese or murder of crows. For lawyers you will find a few choices—an eloquence of lawyers, an argument of lawyers, or a disputation of lawyers may all aptly apply. One might also picture a huddle or a quarrel of lawyers. But the most cautionary label, and one that is too often the case—a greed of lawyers is the popular collective noun of the day.

BILLABLE HOURS: A BROKEN BUSINESS MODEL
Steven J. Harper, former partner at Kirkland & Ellis and author of *The Lawyer Bubble: A Profession in Crisis,* wrote about the problem of the billable hour in an op-ed piece in *The New York Times* in March 2013.

"It typically takes at least 50 hours a week to bill an honest 40 hours to a client. Add commuting time, bathroom breaks, lunch, holidays, an annual vacation and a little socializing, and most associates find themselves working evenings and weekends to 'make their hours.' "

Associates may be expected to bill 2,000 hours a year to retain their jobs and get raises, and 2,500 to get bonuses and be in line for partnerships. Most firms increase financial rewards as an associate's billable hours move beyond the stated threshold. This isn't easy, or even humanly possible.

Sometimes law firms sue for unpaid legal fees. They are surprised when the client countersues accusing the firm of overbilling. It didn't help a case brought against DLA Piper that emails revealed one DLA Piper lawyer describing to another DLA Piper lawyer how a colleague had "random people working full time ... in standard 'Churn that bill, baby!' mode," and another lawyer from the firm writing, "I hear we are already 200k over our estimate—that's Team DLA Piper!"

Harper mentions that "a partner in a prominent Chicago law firm got into trouble when someone wondered how he could bill almost 6,000 hours annually over four consecutive years. He couldn't."

There's no question that the billable hour can be an incentive to overcharge or over research a project. More is more, and when that's what is being measured, some people will overachieve. We inhabit a culture of "more."

In 2015, some law firms reached hourly billing rates of $1,500 per hour. "We just raise them every year," said a lawyer at one of the large New York firms in a February 2016 *Wall Street Journal* article. "Lots of lawyers will charge whatever the market can bear"—all of this when our country is trying to make an economic recovery from the 2008 financial crisis. Middle-class Americans cannot afford lawyers anymore—only the rich, and corporations that write them off as business expenses, can pay that much.

2015: A BANNER YEAR FOR LAWYER CRIME

In recent years, crimes committed by lawyers grabbed the headlines in New York, Dallas, Houston, Boston, Las Vegas, among other places. Almost every media outlet in the country covered these front-page stories. And the tales of misdeeds went way beyond the imaginings of TV writers. Here are a few of the most egregious.

THE IMPOSTER INVESTOR

According to a December 2015 *New York Post* article by Keith Kelly, "New York lawyer Harvey Newkirk was saddled with two mortgages and hoped to dig himself out from under the mountain of debt by earning a bonus from the transaction fees connected to the sale of ... [a men's] magazine, federal prosecutors told a Manhattan federal court jury. ... [B]y notching such a deal, Newkirk, then a lawyer with the prestigious Bryan Cave firm, could potentially get promoted to partner, the jury was told during the government's closing arguments at the trial."

Newkirk's client, Calvin Darden, Jr., had a big dream. He saw himself as the owner of *Maxim* magazine. Unfortunately, his bankroll did not match his aspirations. But his father's did. On the phone and in emails, Darden Jr. pretended to be Darden Sr. His act was so successful that he "tricked lenders into providing him more than $8 million for the acquisition of ... Maxim, while trying to con another investor out of $20 million," when he got caught, reported *Bloomberg*.

Needless to say there were plenty of fake emails and faked documents. Newkirk was found guilty of wire fraud; he might have been a bit more wary of partnering with Darden, a former stockbroker, who admitted stealing nearly $6 million from securities firms and investors, including former New York Knicks star Latrell Sprewell.

A DEVELOPER'S DILEMMA

According to the U.S. Attorney's office of the Southern District of New York, a developer wanted to develop a parcel of land in Yonkers called the Longfellow Project. But city councilwoman Sandy Annabi was against it, stating: "Even if the entire community supported [it], I would be opposed." She also said that the project was "outrageous" and a "slap in the face to the taxpayers of Yonkers."

Despite considerable effort, the developer was unable to move the project forward in the face of Annabi's opposition. Then he hired New York attorney Anthony Mangone to help "persuade" Ms. Annabi to change her position. As the FBI relates, "Developer No. 1 gave Mangone tens of thousands of dollars in cash for Annabi and paid Mangone a cash fee for his services. Shortly after receiving the money, Annabi made several substantial cash and credit card purchases—including airline ticket upgrades, a Rolex watch, and a diamond cross necklace. Then, at a City Council meeting in September 2006, Annabi reversed her long-held opposition to the Longfellow Project and voted in favor of awarding the project to Developer No. 1." Problem solved by a lawyer just doing his job.

Mangone also got a little sloppy with his paperwork, acknowledging that he failed to report legal fees from clients from 2003 through 2007. He pleaded guilty to charges of conspiracy, bribery, extortion, and tax evasion. Mangone was disbarred, and he later cooperated with the government to bring down a number of corrupt New York public officials. The prosecution recommended probation, and Mangone hoped that his cooperation would get him leniency with the sentencing judge, Judge Colleen McMahon. She told him his 18-month sentence would have been longer if he hadn't cooperated, saying, "You, Mr. Mangone, were a dirty lawyer for many, many years."

THE CRIMINAL'S CASH
Attorney Abraham Fisch of Houston made his living as a criminal defense lawyer for folks such as drug dealers and Medicare fraud operators. It was a pretty lucrative practice, as criminals frequently knew other criminals they could refer to Fisch.

According to a *Houston Chronicle* article in October 2015, when Joey Herrera was charged in a federal drug trafficking case, his mother heard that Fisch was a good lawyer. Fisch told her that for $80,000 cash, he would get her son probation by using the Washington contacts of a former FBI informant (and used car financier) named Lloyd Glen Williams. She sold her house to come up with the money for Fisch. Imagine her dismay when her son was sentenced to 15 years in prison and taken into custody in the courtroom, right before her eyes.

Fisch told drug trafficker Edilberto Portillo and his wife that they would need to pay him $1.1 million to have their charges dismissed. Umawa Oke Imo, a defendant in a complex health care fraud case, testified that Fisch and Williams quoted him $3 million to get a dismissal of the charges against him. In all of these cases, Fisch told clients he would use the money to bribe his government contacts. Instead, Fisch and Williams kept the money for themselves.

Perhaps he thought that people charged with crimes and involved in bribery themselves wouldn't reveal his backroom dealings. Or maybe he thought they wouldn't be believed. He was wrong: They were happy to testify against him.

The case dragged on for four years after Fisch's initial 2011 indictment due to a string of legal maneuvers by Fisch. He went through five different lawyers—and, at times, represented himself.

In May 2015, he was found guilty on more than a dozen counts that included conspiracy, obstruction of justice, money laundering, and failure to file tax returns; he was sentenced to 15 years. "I hope he feels exactly the anxiety, the loss and the helplessness that my son felt when they took him," said Joey Herrera's mother.

THE CONDO CAPERS

Condo, land, and real estate transactions involve a lot of paperwork, and where's there's paperwork there are lawyers. Sovereigns of the fine print and manipulators of clause and effect, more than one lawyer decided that this is where to find big payoffs. Making money from someone else's deal—priceless.

Boston attorney Michael R. Anderson worked with a developer to sell condos to investors. He helped find straw buyers to, among other bogus things, put their names on mortgages and say that the condo was going to be their primary residence so they could qualify for the loans. And then he officiated over the disbursement of the loan funds, making sure that he, himself, was very well paid.

In October 2015 he was convicted of wire fraud, bank fraud, and engaging in unlawful monetary transactions for his role in what the U.S. Attorney's office in Massachusetts called a "massive mortgage fraud scam." The court ordered Anderson to pay more than $11 million in restitution and to forfeit more than $7 million, on top of spending two years in prison.

Then there's the case of Las Vegas attorney Keith Gregory and partner Leon Benzer, a former construction company boss, who swindled millions of dollars from homeowner associations (HOAs) for construction-defect work that was mostly left incomplete. Condo associations and some subdivision neighborhoods with HOAs often set aside insurance or money for new construction to deal with any legal action related to potential construction defects—leaks, faulty wiring, etc.

Gregory and Benzer's scheme was to take control of the

HOAs and then send litigation to Gregory and any repairs to a construction company owned by Benzer. Gregory acted as general counsel to help "puppet" HOA boards steer big contracts to Benzer. Gregory got paid by both Benzer and the condo development. One HOA got taken for more than $7 million. In March 2015, Keith Gregory was sentenced to ten years in federal prison.

Judge James Mahan told Gregory, "You were the linchpin of the whole thing," reported the *Las Vegas Review-Journal*. "You gave it an air of legitimacy."

Lead Justice Department prosecutor Charles La Bella called the scam "massive," according to the article, telling the judge, "This conspiracy standing alone constituted its own crime wave."

MEANS, MOTIVE, AND OPPORTUNITY

The malfeasance of New York attorney Marc Dreier goes a little further back in time, but it was so big and audacious that it is a classic example of lawyer arrogance. A graduate of Yale and then Harvard Law School, Dreier was founder and senior partner of a 270-lawyer Park Avenue firm, representing hedge funds, investment firms, and others with the right degree of panache.

Money is everywhere and it always looks like someone has more of it than you do. And with lawyers, competition can be fierce not only in the courtroom but for the big bucks. Dreier paid his lawyers big money, sponsored charity golf tournaments, had a 120-foot yacht with a full-time staff, and lived in one of the most expensive condominiums in New York. To support this lifestyle, he needed money, so he created all kinds of phony financial documents to get access to it and to cover his tracks. His primary source was a client's realty company.

He started out small—if you call $20 million small. Using the name of one of his best clients, he created fake financial statements and got a hedge fund to agree to loan the money—ostensibly for expansion of the realty company. That worked so well that he did it over and over again.

Dreier subscribed to the idea that if you looked prosperous, people would want to do business with you and the top people would want to work for you. He wasn't wrong, though in retrospect many would say he went way over the top acquiring high-end art, cars, and real estate.

As the economic crash was bringing his Ponzi scheme to an end, Dreier doubled down: He went to hustle Arab investors. When that failed he had one last, desperate scheme up his sleeve. Next stop Canada.

"He was attempting at the time to sell a $44 million note to a hedge fund located in New York," said Assistant U.S. Attorney John Streeter. The false note was on behalf of the Ontario Teacher's Pension Plan (OTPP), a one-time client. But the hedge fund insisted that its representative meet with a representative of the pension plan for the signing of the documents at their Toronto headquarters.

Dreier flew to Toronto to meet the hedge fund representative in the OTPP offices. But first he met with a pension lawyer and got his business card. He then asked to use a conference room for a while, saying that his return flight had been delayed. When the hedge fund representative arrived, Dreier spotted him in the lobby and quickly ushered him into the conference room. He presented the attorney's business card as his own and hurriedly signed the papers. But the hedge fund representative smelled something fishy. He asked the receptionist if the person he just met with was the attorney whose card he had. The receptionist said no.

Dreier was arrested and put in jail in Toronto, where he reportedly was still able to move enough money from one of his client's accounts to cover bail. Ultimately he pleaded guilty to stealing over $380 million from his clients and friends, according to *Vanity Fair* in a November 2009 story. "All he ever wanted, Dreier says, was to be viewed as a success, and when he wasn't, he began to steal to get the things he craved," said *Vanity Fair*.

Judge Jed Rakoff, one of the outstanding U.S. District Court Judges in the Southern District of New York, called Dreier a "master of deceit and doyen of dishonesty," telling him he would not "get much sympathy from this court." And he didn't. Dreier was sentenced to 20 years.

THE CORRUPTION OF WALL STREET LAWYERS

Wall Street financial institutions cannot exist without lawyers looking over all their practices to give them an air of legality. One such lawyer was Joseph Collins. This is how U.S. Attorney Preet Bharara for the Southern District of New York described him in a Justice Department statement: "Joseph Collins was a lawyer deeply and corruptly enmeshed in coordinating and concealing the massive accounting fraud that ultimately led to Refco's collapse." Refco was "once the nation's largest commodities firm," according to the DOJ statement, and "the accounting fraud at Refco ... cost investors and lenders more than $2.4 billion in losses." Bharara's characterization of Collins continued: "By aiding and abetting the commodities firm's executives, Collins not only shirked his duties as an officer of the court and violated the ethical obligations of his profession—he broke the law."

Collins falsified loan transactions and financial statements to help the firm hide debt in what amounted to a multi-billion-dollar scam. He was convicted in 2009 and sentenced to prison, but a courtroom error, fueled by improper jury instructions, changed the outcome, and the Court of Appeal reversed. He was convicted again in 2012. Collins stole from the rich and famous; other lawyers steal from the less fortunate.

STEALING FROM THE POOR

Indian immigrant Anish Patel hired Dallas lawyer Sherin Thawer and put down a $2,000 retainer to represent him in removal proceedings to determine whether he would be deported. In a hearing, Thawer tried to have the case administratively closed, according to the *Dallas Observer*. Patel recalled what happened:

"After her motions were denied by the Judge, Attorney Thawer requested a five-minute recess, which was granted," according to the affidavit quoted in the *Dallas Observer* in December 2014. "We went into the hallway and Attorney Thawer instructed me to leave the hearing with her, saying 'We are leaving the Courthouse because I can't deal with this.' "

In an email shortly thereafter, the *Dallas Observer* reported, Thawer told Patel, "Yes, it's done—I'm getting paperwork done," which he took to mean that the case was resolved. But eight months later, "his brother, who had signed the bond allowing Anish to be released, was served with a notice that Anish was to be delivered to the U.S. government for immediate deportation. Thawer, according to the State Bar, had not gotten the case closed. When Patel didn't show up after the five-minute recess, the judge tried him in absentia and ordered him deported."

In November 2015, Thawer was sentenced to two years in federal prison for conspiracy to commit fraud in connection with immigration documents, mail fraud, transfer or use of the identification of another person, and aggravated identity theft, reported the *Dallas Morning News* in November 2015.

According to court documents, Thawer represented immigrants who were applying for various visas to enter or remain in the United States, including through U-Visas. To be eligible for a U-Visa, an immigrant must have been a victim of a crime, suffered from it, and helped law enforcement investigate and/or prosecute it. That gives you an idea of the extent of the harm some of her clients suffered and for which they sought her help. Thawer then used credentials from law enforcement officers and submitted forged law enforcement certification forms to obtain the U-Visas, according to the *Dallas Morning News* article. This is just one example of how immigrants are prime targets for unscrupulous lawyers.

THE NEW LAW ENFORCEMENT SQUAD

The year 2015 may have been the turning point when we moved beyond the mild wrist slap and fines for white-collar crime. Here are a few of the new prosecutors—and judges—who truly represent the best of our profession:

Attorney General Loretta Lynch came out with a statement about going after individuals as much as corporations shortly after taking office. A breath of fresh air.

Deputy U.S. Attorney General Sally Q. Yates put Wall Street on notice when she authored the memo that promised new policies suggesting an end to the pay-a-fine-and-move-on way of doing things.

Eric Schneiderman, New York Attorney General and former state senator. While he was a Harvard Law grad, he started his career in law enforcement as a Deputy Sheriff. He made headlines for investigating ExxonMobil for fraud in concealing climate change information from the public and investors.

Preet Bharara, U.S. Attorney for the Southern District of New York. *Time* magazine featured him on the cover with the headline "This Man Is Busting Wall St." He had an impressive run of 85 wins in insider trading cases before he lost even one. He has brought down corrupt city and state politicians, including Sheldon Silver, the former New York State Assembly speaker, and Dean G. Skelos, the former State Senate majority leader. (See Chapter 4.) Bharara traces his desire to be a lawyer back to the seventh grade, when he read the play *Inherit the Wind*, about the famous 1925 Scopes monkey trial in which a Tennessee school teacher fought for the right to teach evolution in a public school.

Barbara McQuade, U.S. Attorney for the Eastern District of Michigan. When she was awarded a "Shining Light" award for leadership, the *Detroit Free Press* noted McQuade's prosecution of former Detroit Mayor Kwame Kilpatrick (who received a 28-year sentence) and more than 30 others on public corruption charges in 2010. Her office also got a 45-year sentence for Dr. Farid Fata for health care fraud and swindling cancer patients. (See Chapter 1.)

There are also many judges who have let it be known that they are not going to go easy on folks just because they have political friends, rob only from the rich, or help prosecute their fellow conspirators. Jed Rakoff and Colleen McMahon, both judges in the U.S. Southern District of New York, are just a few of the judges who have led the way when it comes to reviewing the lawyers before them. There is justice in the land and prosecutors and judges are starting to speak out.

THE REVOLVING DOOR OF GOVERNMENT LAWYERS

The revolving door between large law firms and government lawyers is spinning at an accelerated pace. Republican or Democrat—it doesn't matter. If they don't move from government to a large law firm, they move to K Street—the home of many Washington, D.C., lobbyists.

One of the most recent examples of this revolving door is former Attorney General Eric Holder returning to Covington & Burling. C&B is known for representing most of the big banks in the country and Holder was the attorney general charged with making the big Wall Street banks accountable during the 2008 financial crisis. Very few executives went to jail and while Holder was the attorney general, white-collar or C-level executive prosecutions hit record lows. Shortly after Holder returned to

Covington & Burling, Margaret Richardson, his chief of staff at the Department of Justice, went with him, along with others who had been at Covington. Parenthetically, one of the partners now at Covington, Lanny Breuer, who was responsible for prosecutions of financial fraud as assistant attorney general in the Obama administration through 2012, came out of Covington and went back to the firm. It is a revolving door at C&B and many Washington, D.C. firms.

In the 1980s, I represented 23,000 victims, mostly senior citizens, who were defrauded in the savings and loan (S&L) crisis. It resulted in one of the largest verdicts in history—$3.3 billion in the civil case. Hundreds of S&L executives, lawyers, and accountants, including CEOs of large S&Ls, were convicted in the various criminal cases brought around the country by Department of Justice lawyers that I had the opportunity to work with.

In the financial crisis of 2008, not a single CEO or Chief Operating Officer of a major bank went to jail—they were represented by lawyers from major law firms who had connections to the U.S. government and specifically the Department of Justice. Former U.S. Senator Ted menendez of Delaware, Chair of the Congressional Oversight Committee, reviewed the multi-billion-dollar taxpayer bailout of the big banks. In August 2015 *Vice News* reported Kaufman saying, "[W]e're looking at a gigantic built-in conflict of interest revolving in and out of the attorney general's office."

Holder gave interviews after he left the DOJ on why he didn't seek criminal actions against several executives of banks that got our country into the 2008 financial crisis, which involved phony mortgage-backed securities and other banking scams. He reasoned that rather than putting people in jail, it was better to get large financial settlements, often without any admission of guilt from the banks! Why make examples of people by putting them in jail? Senator Kaufman, along with many other senators, were dumbfounded by this attitude. However, some in Congress didn't want to offend Wall Street—why not just bail them out with the public's money.

Covington & Burling is not alone in being part of the revolving door of good government, good practice. Many major New York law firms do the same thing with rotating law partners, which raises serious questions as to the degree of influence peddling in our court system. Not only do these firms boast an influential legal team, but they also regularly market the fact to corporate America. You only have to read the webpage for Covington's white-collar defense and investigations section: "Our team includes former senior SEC officials, a former Secretary of Homeland Security, three former heads of the Justice Department's Criminal Division, former federal judges, numerous former federal prosecutors with extensive criminal trial experience, as well as former senior Treasury Department, State Department, and EU officials."

Pretty much says it all.

THE FUTURE OF THE LEGAL PROFESSION

We rarely teach civics classes anymore in our schools, and we are more interested in the newest app for our smartphones than we are in making our students smart about their world. Do our young citizens know, for example, about the roles and responsibilities enumerated in the Constitution about the separation of powers, and how that might impact their futures? If you look at the comments of our elected officials following the death of Supreme Court Justice Antonin Scalia, you would have to wonder seriously whether we have an independent judiciary. Nearly every Republican senator or candidate for federal office made statements to the effect that President Obama should not make any appointment (as called for by the Constitution) and wait for the next president to do the job. Why? Politics.

The great majority of people do not understand how politicized our country is becoming. They do not believe they have any voice in our society. However, you do not have to be a rocket scientist to understand that the stealing of America is only possible when the courts fail to operate in an independent way. People look to the courts to be a guardian against those who break our laws, create financial scams, sell adulterated and untested food, and pollute our air.

Lawyers play a major role in determining who sits on our courts—both federal and state. And when lawyers go astray, our court system does not provide people with the equal rights they should have under our Constitution. When lawyers go bad, so does our entire society, and going bad means abusing the legal system—*prosecuting wrongly or failing to prosecute are the same thing.* Both are failures of the system and both have devastating effects on society.

Thankfully, we have a number of judges who have been speaking out recently on what they see as a failure of our system. U.S. District Judge Jed Rakoff, has become something of a bête noire in the financial world because of his role as a sitting judge in the Southern District of New York and questioning the conduct of the SEC in settling cases.

Wall Street, the center of the financial world, occasionally ends up before Rakoff. He refuses to approve SEC consent judgments drawn by SEC lawyers because they do not require guilty pleas from individuals. In one case, Rakoff said the court has become a "mere handmaiden" to enforcing the law and he voiced his opinion on the practice of letting corporate executives or others off the hook by paying a fine.

A March 2014 *Law360* article quoted Rakoff saying, "When I was a white-collar prosecutor, it was considered a failure to go after the company without going after the individual. ... Prosecuting individuals has a much greater deterrent effect than prosecuting companies, which is essentially an expense the company has to bear, ... but it's essentially in the framework of the cost of doing business."

GOING FORWARD

With a number of judges and lawyers concerned with the legal profession, we can clean up the abuses caused by lawyers who want to distort and use the law for their personal gain. Unfortunately, it is not clear that our politicians are going in that direction. Lawyers and the courts have to stand up and speak out to remove lawyers who have put personal financial gain above the law. Only then can we have a profession that gives rise to one that serves all of the public—not just those who can buy justice.

One of the major problems is that the judiciary—as the third branch of government—is treated like a step child. It is underfunded by the other two branches. In a recent article in *The Green Bag*, Judge Richard Posner, a Judge on the U.S. Court of Appeals for the Seventh Circuit and a lecturer at the University Of Chicago Law School, talked about the judicial process and described our current legal system as follows:

"Chief Justice Roberts in his annual reports likes to describe the American legal system as the envy of the world. Nonsense. The system has proved itself ineffectual in dealing with a host of problems, ranging from providing useful (as distinct from abstract theoretical) legal training at bearable cost to curbing crime and meting out rational punishment, providing representation for and protection of the vast number of Americans who are impecunious or commercially unsophisticated (so prey to sharpies), incorporating the insights of the social and natural sciences (with the notable exception of economics, however), curbing incompetent regulatory agencies such as the immigration and social security disability agencies, and limiting the role of partisan politics in the appointment of judges. The system is also immensely costly (more than $400 billion a year), with its million lawyers, many overpaid, many deficient in training and experience, some of questionable ethics."

Some may minimize the extent of our problems in the legal system, but it is clear that our third branch of government is the system that separates our country from all others in the world. It is the one legal system in the world where citizens can, and do, sit on juries in both civil and criminal actions. It is the one where due process flows from a written document—the Constitution. Courts may not get it right all the time, but to the average citizen, there is always hope that the system will work.

The key is to get rid of those who abuse it and elect public officials who will stand up to the abuses for all of our citizens, not just the wealthy and powerful.

EPILOGUE

"Our lives begin to end the day we become silent about things that matter."
—Dr. Martin Luther King, Jr.

Big changes have happened in the past several years—women earning equal jobs in the military, same sex marriage, a black president being inaugurated. There have also been small changes brought about by citizen action and outcry: the minimum wage has been increased; whistleblowers have helped law enforcement bring crooked doctors to judgment; Corporations have backed down from moving headquarters overseas. Change can happen but it takes the involvement of leaders who are concerned about our future to promote evolution and revolution.

WE THE PEOPLE—MORE POWERFUL THAN YOU KNOW

Our forefathers created a document—the Constitution—beginning with three words, "We the people... ." Billionaires and the members of Congress they own may think that money and fear will keep the people in their place and leave them too demoralized and pessimistic to vote or fight back. They may think that they can distract and confuse people with side issues and false outrage. But they would be wrong. We the People are made up of many groups with a strong collective public will.

A new generation of multicultural and immigrant consumers and entrepreneurs are the economic and political salvation of America, according to business consultant and journalist Guy Garcia. He calls them "the new mainstream." The spending power of U.S. minorities soared to over $2 trillion in 2015, outpacing all consumers. If it were a separate nation, the Hispanic market would be larger than the economies of all but fourteen countries. Rather than hurting our economy, immigration reform that welcomes new citizens and employees would boost American GDP by 3 percent and hundreds of billions of dollars by 2023, according to the Congressional Budget Office.

Meanwhile, women are quickly becoming the richest demographic in U.S. history. They hold one-third of professional and middle-management jobs and they make household decisions on buying retail goods. Women may also be the ones to help spread new business values—altruistic capitalism and more consumer-friendly, socially responsible companies—that could reshape the economy. "The change is coming," says broadcast journalist Claire Shipman, author of *Womenomics.*

Baby boomers still hold a lot of spending clout, despite advertisers who only seem to try to sell them drugs, "Depends" diapers and "Life Alert" alarms. They hold 70 percent of all the wealth in the nation and spend hundreds of billions of dollars as they near retirement, according to Merrill Lynch. Older consumers over 60 have no plans to dodder into senility. They are smashing stereotypes by working longer, launching businesses, and leading active lifestyles.

Millions of gay Americans boast multibillion-dollar buying power. Contrary to old stereotypes, they not only live in cities, but in suburbs, and rural regions as well. They own homes and raise children. The advocacy group GLAAD calls them "a confederation of individuals with identities as diverse as the general population" and are now allowed to openly serve in the military and show their great patriotism.

HOW MANY PEOPLE DOES IT TAKE TO MAKE A DIFFERENCE?

George Bush's final winning margin in the official Florida vote in the 2000 Presidential race against Al Gore was 537 votes. Do you want to be one of the 537 who didn't show up?

As 2016 Presidential candidate Bernie Sanders has noted, *"Nowadays you don't need to be a senator or a CEO or a celebrity to have a voice in the media, and if you happen to be a senator, a CEO or a celebrity, you have a thousand people each with their own respective audiences to hold you accountable."*

From our nation's founding, patriotic voices of change have spurred on social and political revolutions that have changed the course of America. Today is no different, and such voices of change and reformers from all political quarters are desperately needed in the wake of the Great Recession in 2008. The range and depth of people speaking out is growing. The previously silent who were busy with their careers are now lending their voices for change.

IT'S BEEN DONE BEFORE – IT CAN HAPPEN AGAIN

America was nearly crippled during the *Gilded Age* of the late 1800s and the *Roaring Twenties* of the 1920s, noted economist Joseph Stieglitz. Each troubled period was marked by political corruption, rampant speculation, and vast economic inequality between the poor and wealthy.

Stieglitz pointed out that government intervention and regulation helped to save our country from economic ruin. The Gilded Age was followed by the Progressive Era, in which public outrage and political reformers reined in the power of corporate monopolies. And the *Roaring Twenties* was followed by the New Deal and federal programs that uplifted the economy and the status of workers.

Look outside the United States and you will see that other countries are solving many of the problems that we consider impossible to fix. Look at how many common sense rules exist in other countries (like no direct drug advertising to consumers) that only the U.S. and one or two other countries allow.

THE ACTIONS OF OUR FEDERAL AND STATE AGENCIES

Our federal agencies including the U.S. Department of Justice try to do whatever they can to protect our citizens. They are hampered by politicians who are influenced by money and personnel that are subject to political ambition and the desire to look the other way. The stories of inaction are replete with scenes of the revolving doors of personnel that move between the Federal agencies and the lobbyists' offices on K Street in Washington, D.C.

The future is in the heads of state agencies and the attorneys general of the various states. They have a much closer view of the corruption, scams, abuses and fraud than Washington because they are closer to the people. They are on the so-called street level and usually have the ability to move quicker and have the opportunity to operate under various state laws that can be used effectively in the fight. For this reason, corporate lobbyists promote pre-emptive federal laws in Washington, D.C. to stop the enforcement of or to nullify local state laws.

The new move is the use of state consumer laws that give state attorneys general the ability to step in and utilize local consumer protection laws for the benefit of the public. A recent example is the use of state consumer protection laws to go after drug companies for charging outrageous prices set forth previously in Chapter 7. The Attorney General of Massachusetts, Maura Healey, has attempted to use state consumer laws to go after big pharma and specifically Gilead for charging outrageous prices for its Hepatitis C drugs. The laws are designed to prohibit unfair trade practices as set forth in Massachusetts state consumer laws. Along with state attorneys general, there are a number of non-profit foundations going after drug companies as well as local scam artists selling securities, cars, products and all types of frauds under state laws designed to protect consumers.

In many instances, corporate America goes to Washington to promote the passage of federal laws to preempt state laws. The good news is that state and local legislators are fighting back and taking the battle to the local courts—a development that has Wall Street and big corporations and their lawyers worried.

THE INVESTIGATIVE PRESS AND SOCIAL MEDIA

As repeated throughout this book, only a free press and the open exchange of information can keep our country honest. A great American expressed the importance of open access to information when he said,

> *"Information is the oxygen of the modern age. It seeps through the walls topped by barbed wire, it wafts across electrified borders."*
> **—Ronald Reagan**

Ronald Reagan was the "Great Communicator" and he understood media. The irony is that just as newspapers are going out of business and media outlets are being consolidated under the ownership of a few mega-moguls with their own political agendas, information, like water, has found a way. Blogs, Facebook, Twitter—people are finding new ways to pass on information, opinion and keep tabs on who's doing what. Teenagers and "millennials" today are all involved in social media—they know Snapchat, Instagram and record and post videos using their smart phones.

This book opened with the value of the investigative press and should close with the same. Without the press—in whatever form, print or electronic—to inform the public about the issues affecting them—nothing will change—in fact, without the investigative press, the status quo will continue to hide behind a wall of secrecy.

THOSE AT THE FOREFRONT OF CHANGE

There are many good people working daily to change the direction away from greed in our society—from local public officials, police, firemen, teachers, prosecutors, lawyers, business, labor leaders, and non-profit people. Thousands of people have spoken out and are continuing to act. People today like Elizabeth Warren, Robert Reich, Bernie Sanders, Al Gore, Hillary Clinton, Barbara Boxer, Dianne Feinstein, Tammy Duckworth, Nancy Pelosi, Jackie Speier, Jerry and Anne Brown, Warren Buffett, Gavin and Jennifer Newsom, as well as many judges and prosecutors like California Attorney General Kamala Harris, New York Attorney General Eric Schneiderman, Massachusetts Attorney General Maura Healey and local county district attorneys across the country, and especially two friends, Steve Wagstaffe and Nancy O'Malley, district attorneys from California who are standing up every day against those who want to corrupt and defraud our society

From several new faces of technology, finance, medicine and the entertainment field—Mark Zuckerberg and his wife Priscilla Chan, Bill and Melinda Gates, Marc and Lynne Benioff, Ron and Gayle Conway, Steve and Janet Wozniak, Larry Ellison, Tom and Kat Steyer who have opened a bank that is mandated to contribute to social justice and the environment, Jerry Yang and Akiko Yamazaki, Tony and Rosina Sun, Steve and Jamie Chen, Tim Cook of Apple, Oprah Winfrey, George Clooney, Leonardo DiCaprio for his untiring work for the protection of our oceans, Dr. Larry and Lenore Horowitz and the Save the Children Federation and Dr. Frank and Anne Longo who work tirelessly to develop a treatment for Alzheimer's disease. These are just a few who give back so much to benefit society and assist those in need and make our society better through education, philanthropy, research and development, including Diana Natalicio for her work at the University of Texas, El Paso, to help Mexican-American students.

From the world of non-profits, people like Joan Claybrook who helped found Public Citizen with Ralph Nader over 45 years ago to help oversee the three branches of our government. With Joan's guidance, Public Citizen has pushed for public policies necessary for the health and welfare of citizens such as litigation to force the transportation agencies to impose safety requirements on cars and trucks on our highways, including airbags and safety devices. They have been fought every step of the way by the auto industry. Morris Dees of the Southern Poverty Law Center who continues to take on discrimination against minorities every day. People like Jamie Court and Harvey Rosenfield of Los Angeles fight every day to take on big business on behalf of the consumer.

Those who are concerned about our environment—Albert Huang and David Doniger of the Natural Resources Defense Council, Michael Brune and Sarah Hodgdon of the Sierra Club, Lawrence Selzer and Chris Kelly of the Conservation Fund, Adelaide Gomer and Tracy Sturdivant of Greenpeace, and Michael Regan of the Environmental Defense Fund—are helping to keep our environment healthy for our children and future generations.

This book could not describe the battle of our environment without mentioning Pete and Helen McCloskey. A Marine and Korean War hero, he and Helen battle daily for a clean environment. As a Congressman for fourteen years, he co-founded Earth Day in 1970 with Senator Gaylord Nelson and Denis Hayes of Stanford. As a lawyer and partner at CPM, he represents the very best of our profession and society. Pete and Helen continue to lead the charge on climate change, organic pollutants, oil drilling, pollution and are is still battling for all of us.

People like professor Marc Edwards, who alerted residents of Flint, Michigan to the dangers of lead in the water and Dr. Mona Hanna-Attisha who alerted the dangers of lead to children. Art Pulaski and many union leaders who work every day for working people along with local union people like Shelly Kessler who give their entire lives to see that there is safety in the work place.

Even people like Donald Trump tell people of his passion for making America great again and surprised many by his stand against Wall Street—all from a billionaire developer. As stated many times in this book, the key to exposing the moral corruption in our society is a free and open expression of ideas and information, as mentioned in the Acknowledgements of this book—our national and local newspapers and their developing electronic platforms.

WHERE WILL YOU BE AND WHAT CAN BE DONE

Only those who cherish America's greatest values—fairness, equality, liberty, prosperity for all—can save America from itself. This isn't a Hollywood movie starring Harrison Ford. The troops won't come to our rescue. It's our calling as citizens of the world's best democracy and most-admired economy. Those who abuse wealth and power, as they toss fellow Americans on the trash heap, will get away with the hijacking of our nation only if we ignore the crisis and do nothing. For the sake of our country and future generations, we cannot let it happen.

Only a strong honest government run by strong honest elected public servants can stop the rampant fraud and scams we see every day in our media. Benjamin Disraeli said "the greatest of all evils is a weak government." There are those in our country that detest our federal and local governments and do so only to act in their own interest. All you had to do was listen to some of the Republican candidates for office in 2016. A strong government told its citizens that slavery was not moral, that drugs were killing our youth, that Wall Street barons had to be regulated, and seniors deserved health care regardless of income—the list goes on and on. Those countries that do not have strong honest leaders fail—pick up any newspaper—any day of the week or talk to those who lived through World War II. As said by Will Rogers, **"even if you're on the right track, you'll get run over if you just sit there,"** or as my sister Pat said, **"Get your ass out there and make a change."**

Your time, your voice, your knowledge, your vote, your participation. Talk to your friends about the different issues in the book and talk to friends you don't agree with. People must get involved in the process, whether it is at the school board, city council, state, national or non-profit levels—everything counts.

END NOTES

CHAPTER 1

Maria Gonzales is a fictional name for a real person involved in a court case.

Mary Ann Roser. "State Medical Board accuses well-known cardiologist of unnecessary heart procedures and patient's death." *American-Statesman*. Nov. 21, 2010. http://www.statesman.com/news/news/local/state-medical-board-accuses-well-known-cardiolog-1/nRTHX/

Peter Waldman, David Armstrong, and Sydney P. Freedberg. "Deaths Linked to Cardiac Stents Rise as Overuse Seen." *Bloomberg*. Sept. 25, 2013. http://www. Bloomberg.com/news/articles/2013-09-26/deaths-linked-to-cardiac-stents-rise-as-overuse-seen

Peter Eisler and Barbara Hansen. "Doctors perform thousands of unnecessary surgeries." *USA Today*. June 20, 2013. http://www.usatoday.com/story/news/nation/2013/06/18/unnecessary-surgery-usa-today-investigation/2435009/

Daniel Armstrong. "The Cardiologist Who Spread Heart Disease." *Bloomberg*. Oct. 23, 2013. http://www.bloomberg.com/news/articles/2013-10-24/the-cardiologist-who-spread-heart-disease

Journal of the American College of Cardiology. "Only 36% of angioplasty patients meet the procedure's criteria." *Advisory Board Company Daily Briefing*. May 25, 2012. www.advisory.com/daily-briefing/2012/05/25/only-one-third-of-angioplasty-patients-meet-procedures-criteria

Anna Wilde Mathews and Lisa Schwartz. "Medicare Paid One Doctor More Than $20 Million in 2012." *Wall Street Journal*. Apr. 9, 2014. http://www.wsj.com/articles/medicare-paid-one-doctor-more-than-20-million-in-2012-1397054458

Kent Cooper. "Top Dollars Go To Health Care Lobbying." *Roll Call*. Feb 10, 2014. blogs.rollcall.com/moneyline/top-dollars-go-to-health-care-lobbying/

Jim McElhatton. "Sen. Menendez pal Salomon Melgen collected $20 million from Medicare." *Washington Times*. Apr. 9, 2014. http://www.washingtontimes.com/news/2014/apr/9/sen-menendez-pal-salomon-melgen-collected-20-milli/

Brent Johnson. "Who is Salomon Melgen? Doctor is at center of Menendez corruption case." *NJ Advance Media for NJ.com*. Apr. 1, 2015. http://www.nj.com/politics/index.ssf/2015/04/who_is_salomon_melgen_doctor_is_at_center_of_rober.html

Anna R. Schecter, Kathryn Nathanson and Tracy Connor. "Dr. Fata Case: How a Broken Leg Ended One Woman's 'Cancer' Nightmare." NBC News. July 9, 2015. http://www.nbcnews.com/health/cancer/monica-n389321

Laura Berman. "Whistle-blower: How doctor uncovered nightmare: Oncologist's discovery leads to the downfall of a cancer treatment empire." *Detroit News*. June 10, 2015. http://www.detroitnews.com/story/news/special-reports/2015/06/10/whistle-blower-doctor-uncovered-medical-nightmare/71027690

Laura Berman. "Berman: One nurse's gutsy effort to protect patients." *Detroit News*. Feb. 6, 2015. http://www.detroitnews.com/story/opinion/columnists/laura-berman/2015/02/05/berman-gutsy-nurse-whistle-blower/22964301/

Ed Cara. "How Did Dr. Farid Fata, America's Greatest Cancer Fraudster, Get Away With It For So Long?" *Medical Daily*. July 7, 2015. http://www.medicaldaily.com/how-did-dr-farid-fata-americas-greatest-cancer-fraudster-get-away-it-so-long-341478

Carol Peckham. *Medscape Physician Compensation Report 2015*. Medscape. Apr. 21, 2015. http://www.medscape.com/features/slideshow/compensation/2015/public/overview

Elizabeth Rosenthal. "After Surgery, Surprise $117,000 Medical Bill From Doctor He Didn't Know." *New York Times*. Sept. 20, 2014. http://www.nytimes.com/2014/09/21/us/drive-by-doctoring-surprise-medical-bills.html?_r0

Helen Adamopoulos. "100 things to know about Medicare reimbursment." *Becker's Hospital CFO*. Aug. 19, 2014. http://www.beckershospitalreview.com/finance/100-things-to-know-about-medicare-reimbursement.html

Tod Aronovitz. "Port St. Lucie Dermatologist Applied Medicare Code for Radiation Treatment Not Used by Many Doctors." Aronovitz Law. June 6, 2014. http://www.aronovitzlaw.com/port-st-lucie-dermatologist-applied-medicare-billing-code-radiation-treatment-used-many-doctors/

Matthew P. Lungren, MD, et al. "Physician Self-Referral: Frequency of Negative Finding at MR Imaging of the Knee as a Marker of Appropriate Utilization." *RSNA Radiology*. Radiological Society of North America. Dec. 2013, Vol 269, Issue 3. http://www.pubs.rsna.org/doI/full10.1148/radiol.13130281

Office of the Inspector General. "Special Fraud Alert: Physician-Owned Entities." U.S. Department of Health and Human Services. Mar. 26, 2013. http://oig.hhs.gov/fraud/docs/alertsandbulletins/2013/POD_Special_Fraud_Alert.pdf

Karen Foshay. "Selling the Spine: Doctors profit in the OR, but at whose expense?" KPCC (Southern California Public Radio). June 17, 2015. http://projects.scpr.org/longreads/selling-the-spine/

"Detroit-Area Neurosurgeon Admits Causing Serious Bodily Injury to Patients in $11 Million Health Care Fraud Scheme." Department of Justice. May 22, 2015. http://www.justice.gov/opa/pr/detroit-area-neurosurgeon-admits-causing-serious-bodily-injury-patients-11-million-health

Crystal Hernandez. "Unnecessary surgeries." *CareClub News*. Sept. 25, 2013. http://www.careclubusa.com/News/unnecessary-surgeries/

Terri Langford. "Private ambulances take Medicare, taxpayers for a ride." *Houston Chronicle*. July 26, 2013.
http://www.chron.com/news/Houston-texas/article/Some-Ems-companies-taking-medicare-for-a-ride-2220817.php

Terri Langford. "Largest Medicare fraud takedown includes multiple Houston companies." *Beaumont Enterprise*. May 2, 2012.
http://www.beaumontenterprise.com/news/article/Largest-Medicare-fraud-takedown-includes-multiple-3528062.php

Cindy George. "Feds target ambulance service providers." *Houston Chronicle*. July 26, 2013.
http://www.houstonchronicle.com/news/houston-texas/houston/article/Feds-target-ambulance-service-providers-4690050.php

Thomas H. Stanton. "Fraud-And-Abuse Enforcement In Medicare: Finding Middle Ground." Health Affairs. July 2001. Vol. 20, No. 4 28-42.
http://content.healthaffairs.org/content/20/4/28.full

Milt Freudenheim. "Dialysis Provider to Pay $486 Million to Settle Charges." *New York Times*. Jan. 20, 2000.
http://www.nytimes.com/2000/01/20/business/dialysis-provider-to-pay-486-million-to-settle-charges.html

"United States Awarded $82.6 Million Against Renal Care Group & Fresenius Medical Care in Medicare Fraud Case." Middle District of Tennessee, U.S. Attorney's Office. May 26, 2011.
https://www.justice.gov/archive/usao/tnm/pressReleases/2011/5-26-11.html

Jeff Glor. "Medicare fraud allegations: National nursing home chain accused of billing for excess care." CBS News. May 8, 2013.
http://www.cbsnews.com/news/medicare-fraud-allegations-national-nursing-home-chain-accused-of-billing-for-excess-care/

Associated Press. "25 Charged in Largest Medicaid Fraud Bust in D.C. History." CBS News DC. Feb. 20, 2014.
http://washington.cbslocal.com/2014/02/20/feds-to-announce-arrests-in-d-c-health-care-fraud-case/

Davis Voreacos and Sophia Pearson. "Amedisys to Pay $150 Million for Medicare False Billing." *Bloomberg*. Apr. 23, 2014.
http://www.bloomberg.com/news/articles/2014-04-23/amedisys-to-pay-150-million-for-medicare-false-billing

Brooks Egerton. "Medicare fraud case update: Most suspended agencies in northeast Dallas, Garland; many apparently based in private homes." *Dallas Morning News*. Mar. 20, 2012.
http://watchdogblog.dallasnews.com/2012/03/federal-health-officials-have.html/
U.S. Attorney's Office, Northern District of Texas. "Owner of Home Health Care Company Sentenced to 10 Years in Federal Prison for Role in Health Care Fraud Conspiracy." Federal Bureau of Investigation, Dallas Division. Sept. 5, 2013.
https://www.fbi.gov/dallas/press-releases/2013/owner-of-home-health-care-company-sentenced-to-10-years-in-federal-prison-for-role-in-health-care-fraud-conspiracy

"Dallas Doctor Arrested for Alleged Role in Nearly $375 Million Health Care Fraud
Scheme." Department of Justice. Feb. 28, 2012.
https://www.justice.gov/opa/pr/dallas-doctor-arrested-alleged-role-nearly-375-million-
health-care-fraud-scheme
CLEAR for Healthcare Fraud Investigations, "White Paper: From Drugs to Wheelchairs:
New Technology Fights the Growing Menace of Organized Crime in Healthcare Fraud."
Reuters. June 2012.
https://static.legalsolutions.thomsonreuters.com/index/pdf/from-drugs-to-wheelchairs-
new-technology-fights-the-growing-menace-of-organized-crime-in-healthcare-fraud-
whitepaper.pdf

"Attorney General Lanny A. Breuer of the Criminal Division Speaks at the Philadelphia
La Cosa Nostra Takedown Press Conference." May 23, 2011.
http://www.justice.gov/opa/speech/assistant-attorney-general-lanny-breuer-criminal-
division-speaks-philadelphia-la-cosa

"73 Members and Associates of Organized Crime Enterprise, Others Indicted for Health
Care Fraud Crimes Involving More Than $163 Million." Oct. 13, 2010.
http://www.justice.gov/opa/pr/73-members-and-associates-organized-crime-enterprise-
others-indicted-health-care-fraud-crimes

Allan Chernoff and Sheila Steffen. "Organized crime's new target: Medicare." CNN. Oct.
24, 2009.
http://www.cnn.com/2009/CRIME/10/22/medicare.organized.crime/

Brandon Bailey. "Medicare Fraud leads to Prison: San Jose Immigrants Exploited by
Criminals." *Silicon Valley MercuryNews.com.* Aug. 1, 2007.
http://www.mercurynews.com/search/ci_6514239?nclick_check=3D1

William K. Rashbaum. "A $250 Million Fraud Scheme Finds a Path to Brighton Beach."
New York Times. Feb. 29, 2012.
http://www.nytimes.com/2012/03/01/nyregion/dozens-said-to-be-arrested-in-health-care-
fraud-scheme.html

Associated Press. "Mafia, violent criminals turn to Medicare fraud." NBC News.com. Oct.
6, 2009.
http://www.nbcnews.com/id/33196132/us_news-crime_and_courts/t/mafia-violent-
criminals-turn-medicare-fraud/#.VlUqatDHt_k

Associated Press. "Feds going after Medicare fraudsters who fled." *St. Augustine Record.*
Nov. 11, 2013.
http://www.staugustine.com/news/2013-11-11/feds-going-after-medicare-fraudsters-who-
fled#.Vk6JB;vHt_k

Jim Landers. "Dallas area home to huge health care frauds." *Dallas Morning News.* Feb.
15, 2014.
http://www.dallasnews.com/business/health-care/20140215-dallas-area-home-to-huge-
health-care-frauds.ece

Chris Parker. "Thieves' Bazaar: Medicare Fraud." *HoustonPress.com.* Apr. 24, 2013.
http://www.houstonpress.com/news/thieves-bazaar-medicare-fraud-6597957

Jay Weaver. "FBI tracking down Medicare fraud fugitives from South Florida." *Miami
Herald.* Nov. 2, 2013.
http://www.miamiherald.com/news/local/community/miami-dade/article1957034.html

"Medicare Fraud Strike Force Charges 91 Individuals for Approximately $430 Million in False Billing." Department of Justice. Oct. 4, 2012.
http://www.justice.gov/opa/pr/medicare-fraud-strike-force-charges-91-individuals-approximately-430-million-false-billing
"Departments of Justice and Health and Human Services announce record-breaking recoveries resulting from joint efforts to combat health care fraud." HHS.gov. Feb. 26, 2014. http://www.hhs.gov/about/news/2014/02/26/departments-of-justice-and-health-and-human-services-announce-record-breaking-recoveries-resulting-from%20joint-efforts-to-combat-health-care-fraud.html

"Former Miami Clinic Director Sentenced to 70 Months in Prison for Role in HIV Infusion Fraud Scheme." Department of Justice. Jan. 23, 2013.
https://www.justice.gov/opa/pr/former-miami-clinic-director-sentenced-70-months-prison-role-hiv-infusion-fraud-scheme

Jay Weaver. "Miami federal jury convicts doctor, therapists at Medicare fraud trial." *Miami Herald.* Aug. 26, 2015.
http://www.miamiherald.com/news/local/crime/article32454567.html

Renee Cocchi. "Medicare strike force sets record for fraud prosecutions." Healthcare Business & Technology. Jan. 27, 2014.
http://www.healthcarebusinesstech.com/medicare-strike-force/

Scott Cohn. "Feds Crack Down in $450 Million Medicare Fraud Sweep." CNBC. May 2, 2012. http://www.cnbc.com/id/47266784?_source=msnbc%7C&par=msnbc

Peter Katz. "Federal Healthcare Fraud Sentencing After Obamacare: Analyzing Title 18 USC 1347." Crotty Saland New York Criminal Lawyer Blog. June 13, 2014.
http://www.newyorkcriminallawyer-blog.com/2014/06/federal-healthcare-fraud-sentencing-obamacare.html

Rep. Tim Murphy and House Committee on Energy and Commerce, Subcommittee on Oversight and Investigations Hearing on Medicare Program Integrity. *Roll Call.* June 27, 2014
http://www.insurancefraud.org/downloads/Murphy_6-25-14hearing.pdf

Steven Brill. "Bitter Pill: Why Medical Bills Are Killing Us." *Time.* Feb. 20, 2013.
http://healthland.time.com/2013/02/20/bitter-pill-why-medical-bills-are-killing-us/print/[2/26/2013%207:31:26%20AM]/

Uwe E. Reinhardt. "The Pricing Of U.S. Hospital Services: Chaos Behind A Veil Of Secrecy." Health Affairs. Jan. 2006. Vol. 25, No. 157-69.
http://content.healthaffairs.org/content/25/1/57.full

"Largest Health Care Fraud Case in U.S. History Settled: HCA Investigation Nets Record Total of $1.7 Billion." Department of Justice. June 26, 2003.
http://www.justice.gov/archive/opa/pr/2003/june/03_civ_386.htm

Kurt Eichenwald. "FBI agent on R. Scott: I recommend he be indicted." Tweet on Gov.
Rick Scott's note to staff, reported by *Daily Koz*. May 31, 2012.
http://www.dailykos.com/story/2012/05/31/1096215/FBI-agent-on-R-Scott-I-recommended-
he-be-indicted

Julie Creswell and Reed Abelson. "A Giant Hospital Chain Is Blazing a Profit Trail." *New
York Times*. Aug. 14, 2012.
http://www.nytimes.com/2012/08/15/business/hca-giant-hospital-chain-creates-a-windfall-
for-private-equity.html

Reed Abelson and Julie Creswell. "Hospital Chain Inquiry Cited Unnecessary Cardiac
Work." *New York Times*. Aug. 6, 2012.
http://www.nytimes.com/2012/08/07/business/hospital-chain-internal-reports-
found-dubious-cardiac-work.html

Gina Kolata. "What Are a Hospital's Costs? Utah System Is Trying to Learn."
New York Times. Sept. 7, 2015.
http://www.nytimes.com/2015/09/08/what-are-a-hospitals-costs-utah-system-
is-trying-to-learn.html?_r=0

Steven Brill. *America's Bitter Pill: Money, Politics, Backroom Deals, and the Fight to Fix
Our Broken Healthcare System*. 2015. Random House. New York.

Linda Peeno. "The Confession of a Managed Care Medical Director, as heard by a
Congressional Subcommittee, May 30, 1996." Citizens' Council for Health Freedom. May
1996.
http://www.cchfreedom.org/cchf.php/415#.VxL5KZMrLVo

Alex Wayne. "Insurers Face $1 Trillion Revenue at Stake in Health Law." *Bloomberg*.
May 14, 2012.
http://www.bloomberg.com/news/articles/2012-05-14/insurers-face-1-trillion-revenue-at-
stake-in-health-law

Brian Eastwood. "Top health insurance CEO pay exceeds $10 million in 2014."
FierceHealthPayer. Apr. 10, 2015.
http://www.fiercehealthpayer.com/story/top-health-insurance-ceo-pay-exceeds-10-million-
2014/2015-04-10

Scott Gottlieb. "Health Plan Premiums Are Skyrocketing According To New Survey Of
148 Insurance Brokers, With Delaware Up 100%, California 53%, Florida 37%,
Pennsylvania 28%." *Forbes*. Apr. 7, 2014.
http://www.forbes.com/sites/scottgottlieb/2014/04/07/health-plan-premiums-are-
skyrocketing-according-to-new-survey-of-148-insurance-brokers-analysts-blame-
obamacare/#2715e4857a0b83703c719394

Brian Eastwood. "Health insurance stocks hit all-time highs." *FierceHealthPayer*. Jan. 22,
2015.
http://www.fiercehealthpayer.com/story/health-insurance-stocks-hit-all-time-highs/2015-
01-22

Ariana Eunjung Cha. *Doctors cut from Medicare Advantage networks struggle with what
to tell patients. Washington Post*. Jan. 25, 2014.
http://www.washingtonpost.com/national/health-science/doctors-cut-from-medicare-
advantage-networks-struggle-with-what-to-tell-patients/2014/01/25/541bfbd8-77b4-11e3-
af7f-13bf0e9965f6_story.html

Ellen Shapiro et al. "Coverage Denied." *People*. July 23, 2007. Vol. 68, No. 4.
http://www.people.com/people/archive/article/0,,20061418,00.html

Murray Waas. "Corrected: WellPoint routinely targets breast cancer patients." *Reuters*.
Apr. 23, 2010.
http://www.reuters.com/article/2010/04/23/us-wellpoint-breastcancer-
idUSTRE63M5D423#Dr9a7hKeoPypPWg7.97

Lisa Girion. "State accuses Blue Shield of illegal cancellations." *Los Angeles Times*. Dec.
13, 2007.
http://www.latimes.com/business/la-fi-insure13-2007dec13-story.html

Lisa Girion. "Insurer sued over rescissions." *Los Angeles Times*. Apr. 17, 2008.
http://articles.latimes.com/2008/apr/17/business/fi-insure17

"United agrees to pay $350 million, scrap system that undercut fees." American Medical
News. Jan. 26, 2009.
http://www.amednews.com/article/20090126/business/301269997/1/

Ingenix Soon OptumInsight. American Academy of Professional Coders (AAPC). Apr. 15,
2011.
http://www.aapc.com/blog/11560-ingenix-soon-optuminsight/

Michael Moore. *Sicko*. 2007.
http://www.imdb.com/title/tt0386032/quotes

World Health Organization's Ranking of the World's Health Systems
http://thepatientfactor.com/canadian-health-care-information/world-health-organizations-
ranking-of-the-worlds-health-systems/

NBC News RSS. "U.S. Infant Mortality Rate Still One of the Highest in Developed World:
Report." *Chicago Sun-Times*. Aug. 5, 2015.
http://chicagobeta.suntimes.wordpress-prod-wp.aggrego.com/nationworld/7/71/856429/u-s-
infant-mortality-rate-still-one-of-highest-in-developed-world-report

Avik Roy. "Conservative Think Tank: 10 Countries With Universal Health Care Have
Freer Economies Than The U.S." *Forbes*. Jan. 27, 2015.
http://www.forbes.com/sites/theapothecary/2015/01/27/conservative-think-tank-10-
countries-with-universal-health-care-are-economically-freer-than-the-u-s/

Karen Davis et al. "2014 Update: Mirror, Mirror on the Wall: How the U.S. Health Care
System Compares Internationally." Commonwealth Fund. June 2014.
http://www.commonwealthfund.org/~/media/files/publications/fund-
report/2014/jun/1755_davis_mirror_mirror_2014.pdf

Jon Greenberg. "Bernie Sanders: U.S. 'only major country' that doesn't guarantee right to
health care." *Politifact*. June 29, 2015.
http://www.politifact.com/truth-o-meter/statements/2015/jun/29/bernie-s/bernie-sanders-
us-only-major-country-doesnt-guaran/

CHAPTER 2

Robert Reich. "If They're Too Big to Fail, They're Too Big Period." Oct. 21, 2008.
http://www.robertreich.org/post/257309894

"Transcript: Attorney General Eric Holder on 'Too Big to Jail.' " American Banker. Mar. 6, 2013.
http://www.americanbanker.com/issues/178_45/transcript-attorney-general-eric-holder-on-too-big-to-jail-1057295-1.html

Christopher Ketchum. "The Curse of Bigness." *Orion Magazine*. Mar. 3, 2010.
http://www.orionmagazine.org/article/the-curse-of-bigness/

Matt Taibbi. *The Divide: American Injustice in the Age of the Wealth Gap*. 2014. Spiegel & Grau. New York.

Andrea Tan, Gavin Finch, and Liam Vaughan. *RBS Instant Messages Show Libor Rates Skewed for Traders*. Sept. 25, 2012.
http://www.bloomberg.com/news/articles/2012-09-25/rbs-instant-messages-show-libor-rates-skewed-for-traders
Eddie Wrenn. "U.S. pensioner who had her home repossessed in credit crunch launches class action against 12 banks for 'rigging mortgage rates in Libor scandal.' "
DailyMail.com. Oct. 15, 2012.
http://www.dailymail.co.uk/news/article-2217963/American-woman-house-repossessed-launches-class-action-12-banks-rigging-mortgage-rates-Libor-scandal.html

Kit Chellel. "Ex-RBS Banker in Libor Probe Sues for Race Discrimination." *Bloomberg*. May 29, 2014.
http://www.bloomberg.com/news/articles/2014-05-29/ex-rbs-banker-in-libor-probe-sues-over-dismissal-discrimination

"CFTC Orders Barclays to pay $200 Million Penalty for Attempted Manipulation of and False Reporting concerning LIBOR and Euribor Benchmark Interest Rates." U.S. Commodity Futures Trading Commission. June 27, 2012.
http://www.cftc.gov/PressRoom/PressReleases/pr6289-12

Patricia Hurtado. "The London Whale." *Bloomberg QuickTake*. Oct. 16, 2013.
http://www.bloombergview.com/quicktake/the-london-whale

Bob Van Voris. " 'London Whale' Testimony Sought in JPMorgan Shareholder Suit." *Bloomberg*. Sept. 14, 2015.
http://www.bloomberg.com/news/articles/2015-09-14/-london-whale-testimony-sought-in-jpmorgan-shareholder-suit

Elizabeth Warren. *A Fighting Chance*. 2014. Henry Holt & Co. New York.

Lindsay Fortado. "Holder: big penalties changed bank culture." *Financial Times*. July 6, 2015.
http://www.ft.com/intl/cms/s/0/f87fd52e-2324-11e5-9c4e-a775d2b173ca.html#axzz3wtaKUYhz

Jason Karaian. "Good news! Big banks only have $65 billion in legal fines left to pay." *Quartz*. Aug. 26, 2015.
http://qz.com/488349/good-news-big-banks-only-have-65-billion-in-legal-fines-left-to-pay/

"Consumer Financial Protection Bureau: Enforcing Consumer Protection Laws." Consumer Financial Protection Bureau. July 15, 2015.
http://files.consumerfinance.gov/f/201507_cfpb_enforcing-consumer-protection-laws.pdf

"CFPB, 47 States and D.C. Take Action Against JPMorgan Chase for Selling Bad Credit Card Debt and Robo-Signing Court Documents." July 8, 2015. http://www.consumerfinance.gov/newsroom/cfpb-47-states-and-d-c-take-action-against-jpmorgan-chase-for-selling-bad-credit-card-debt-and-robo-signing-court-documents/

Gretchen Morgenson. "An S.E.C. Settlement With Citigroup That Fails to Name Names." *New York Times.* Aug. 28, 2015. http://www.nytimes.com/2015/08/30/business/sec-settlement-with-citigroup-holds-no-one-responsible.html

SEC Fraud Actions. Constantine Cannon. Ongoing compilation. http://constantinecannon.com/whistleblower/sec-fraud-actions/#

Jessica Silver-Greenberg and Susanne Craig. "Fined Billions, JPMorgan Chase Will Give Dimon a Raise." *New York Times.* Jan. 23, 2014. http://dealbook.nytimes.com/2014/01/23/fined-billions-bank-approves-raise-for-chief/

Charles P. Kindleberger and Robert Z., Aliber. *Manias, Panics, and Crashes: A History of Financial Crises, 6th Ed.,* 2011. Palgrave Macmillan. England.

Janis Joplin. "Mercedes Benz." *Pearl.* Columbia Records. Oct. 1, 1970.

Aaron Elstein. "Get ready for the first billion-dollar CEO: Stephen Schwarzman." *Crain's New York Business.* Mar. 8, 2015. http://www.crainsnewyork.com/article/20150308/FINANCE/150309875/get-ready-for-the-first-billion-dollar-ceo-stephen-schwarzman

"Equity Exits Reached Record High in Second Quarter." *ValueWalk.* July 30, 2015. http://www.valuewalk.com/2015/07/private-equity-exits-reached-record-high-in-second-quarter/

Devin Banerjee. "SEC Finds Illegal or Bad Fees in 50% of Buyout Firms." *Bloomberg.* May 6, 2014. http://www.bloomberg.com/news/articles/2014-05-06/sec-finds-illegal-or-bad-fees-in-50-of-buyout-firms

Marc Wyatt. Private Equity: A Look Back and a Glimpse Ahead. Securities and Exchange Commission. Speech. May 13, 2015. https://www.sec.gov/news/speech/private-equity-look-back-and-glimpse-ahead.html

"SEC Charges KKR With Misallocating Broken Deal Expenses." Securities and Exchange Commission. June 29, 2015. http://www.sec.gov/news/pressrelease/2015-131.html

Amy Fontinelle. "What is the Dodd-Frank Act? How does it affect me?" Investopedia. http://www.investopedia.com/ask/answers/13/dodd-frank-act-affect-me.asp

CEO to Worker Pay Ratios. *PayScale.* 2013. http://www.payscale.com/data-packages/ceo-income/full-list

Alyssa Davis and Lawrence Mishel. "CEO Pay Continues to Rise as Typical Workers Are Paid Less." Economic Policy Institute. June 12, 2014. http://www.epi.org/publication/ceo-pay-continues-to-rise/

"Executive Compensation: Paying High For Low Performance." *ValueWalk*. Sept. 2, 2015.
http://www.valuewalk.com/2015/09/executive-compensation-paying-high-for-low-performance/

"JPMorgan CEO faults company and shareholders for disagreements." *Reuters*. May 27, 2015.
http://www.reuters.com/article/us-jpmorgan-shareholders-dimon-idUSKBN0OC2P020150527

William Alden. "Private Equity Payouts Leave the Rest of Wall St. in the Dust." *New York Times*. Mar. 3, 2015.
http://www.nytimes.com/2015/03/04/business/dealbook/private-equity-payouts-leave-the-rest-of-wall-st-in-the-dust.html

Jonathan Alter. *Schwarzman*: 'It's a War' Between Obama, Wall Street". *Newsweek*. Aug. 15, 2010.
http://www.newsweek.com/schwarzman-its-war-between-obama-wall-st-71317

Amanda Becker. "Clinton: Unfair that fund managers pay lower tax rate than truckers." *Reuters*. Apr. 14, 2015.
http://www.reuters.com/article/us-usa-election-clinton-idUSKBN0N52FI20150414

Greg Sargent. "Morning Plum: Donald Trump wants to tax the rich. Will Republican voters agree with him?" *Washington Post*. Aug. 28, 2015.
https://www.washingtonpost.com/blogs/plum-line/wp/2015/08/28/morning-plum-donald-trump-wants-to-tax-the-rich-will-republican-voters-agree-with-him/

Ann Tenbrunsel and Jordan Thomas. "The Street, The Bull and The Crisis: A Survey of the US & UK Financial Services Industry." University of Notre Dame and Labaton Sucharow LLP. May 2015.
www.secwhistlebloweradvocate.com/LiteratureRetrieve.aspx?ID=224757

"Financial Services Professionals Feel Unethical Behavior May be a Necessary Evil and Have Knowledge of Workplace Misconduct, According to Labaton Sucharow Survey." Labaton Sucharow. July 10, 2012.
http://www.labaton.com/en/about/press/Labaton-Sucharow-announces-results-of-financial-services-professional-survey.cfm

Alan Pyke. "5 Numbers To Know As Dodd-Frank Wall Street Reform Celebrates Its 5th Birthday." *ThinkProgress*. July 21, 2015.
http://thinkprogress.org/economy/2015/07/21/3682696/dodd-frank-five-years-2/

Marco Rubio on Budget & Economy. *On The Issues*. Ongoing compilation.
http://www.ontheissues.org/2016/Marco_Rubio_Budget_+_Economy.htm

Christina Rexrode. "Bank of America's Brian Moynihan Survives Chairman-CEO Vote." *Wall Street Journal*. Sept. 22, 2015.
http://www.wsj.com/articles/bofas-moynihan-survives-chairman-ceo-vote-1442931646

Amanda Terkel and Ryan Grim. *Jamie Dimon Wants to Mansplain Banking to Elizabeth Warren*. Huffington Post. June 10, 2015.
http://www.huffingtonpost.com/2015/06/10/jamie-dimon-elizabeth-warren_n_7555204.html

Associated Press. "US Senate passes Warren bill to require settlement details". *Boston Herald*. Sept. 22, 2015.
http://www.bostonherald.com/news_opinion/local_coverage/2015/09/us_senate_passes_war ren_bill_to_require_settlement_details

Matt Apuzzo and Ben Protess. "Justice Department Sets Sights on Wall Street Executives." *New York Times*. Sept. 9, 2015.
http://www.nytimes.com/2015/09/10/us/politics/new-justice-dept-rules-aimed-at-prosecuting-corporate-executives.html?_r=0

Michael Rothfeld. "Firms Get Penalized, but Many Workers Don't." *Wall Street Journal*. Jan. 16, 2014.
http://www.wsj.com/articles/SB10001424052702304419104579324962459771186

Jonathan Stempel. "Judge OKs "half-baked" SEC-Bank of America accord." *Reuters*. Feb. 22, 2010.
http://www.reuters.com/article/us-bankofamerica-sec-idUSTRE61G4AY20100222

Joseph Lawler. 'Fed official: 'No substitute' for jailing bankers." *Washington Examiner*. June 25, 2015.
http://www.washingtonexaminer.com/fed-official-no-substitute-for-jailing-bankers/article/2567009

James W. Brock. "The real issue behind saving Bear Stearns: size." *Christian Science Monitor*. Apr. 7, 2008.
http://www.csmonitor.com/Commentary/Opinion/2008/0407/p09s01-coop.html

Robert Reich. "Hillary, Bernie, and the Banks." Oct. 9, 2015.
http://robertreich.org/post/130820178090

CHAPTER 3

Floyd G. Brown. *Slick Willie: Why America Cannot Trust Bill Clinton*. Annapolis-Washington Book Pub. 1992.

Richard L Berke. *The1992 Campaign: White House; Bush Rejects 'Sleaze' TV Ad That Assails Clinton. New York Times*. July 11, 1992.
http://www.nytimes.com/1992/07/11/us/the-1992-campaign-white-house-bush-rejects-sleaze-tv-ad-that-assails-clinton.html

Jeffrey Toobin. "Money Unlimited: How Chief Justice John Roberts orchestrated the Citizens United decision." *New Yorker*. May 21, 2012.
http://www.newyorker.com/magazine/2012/05/21/money-unlimited.

Stephanie Mencimer. "The Man Behind Citizens United Is Just Getting Started." *Mother Jones*. May/June 2011.
http://www.motherjones.com/politics/2011/03/james-bopp-citizens-united

U.S. Supreme Court. *Citizens United v. Federal Election Comm'n* (No. 08-205). Oral argument transcript. Mar. 24, 2009.
http://www.supremecourt.gov/oral_arguments/argument_transcripts/08-205.pdf

Adam Liptak. "Justices Are Pressed for a Broad Ruling in Campaign Case." *New York Times*. Sept. 9, 2009. http://www.nytimes.com/2009/09/10/us/politics/10scotus.html

U.S. Supreme Court. *Citizens United v. Federal Election Comm'n* (558 U.S. 310). Jan. 21, 2010.
http://www.supremecourt.gov/opinions/09pdf/08-205.pdf

Julie Bykowicz. "For Clinton, the Citizens United struggle is deeply personal." AP. Sept. 8, 2015. http://bigstory.ap.org./article/1500da677bfa453782a66e8a2ed4c49b/clinton-citizens-united-struggle-deeply-personal
Philip Rucker. "Citizens United used 'Hillary the Movie' to Take on McCain-Feingold." *Washington Post.* Jan. 22, 2010.
http://www.washingtonpost.com/wp-dyn/content/article/2010/01/21/AR2010012103582.html

David Carr. "Comic's PAC Is More Than a Gag." *New York Times.* Aug. 21, 2011.
http://www.nytimes.com/2011/08/22/business/media/stephen-colberts-pac-is-more-than-a-gag.html

Jamie Fuller. "From George Washington to Shaun McCutcheon: A brief-ish history of campaign finance reform." *Washington Post.* Apr. 3, 2014
https://www.washingtonpost.com/news/the-fix/wp/2014/04/03/a-history-of-campaign-finance-reform-from-george-washington-to-shaun-mccutcheon/

Gwen Ifill. "Court Upholds Campaign Reform." *PBS NewsHour.* Dec. 10, 2003.
http://www.pbs.org/newshour/bb/law-july-dec03-cfr_12-10/

Federal Election Commission. *SpeechNow.org v. FEC* (08-5223) (consolidated with *Keating v. FEC* (09-5342)). Mar. 26, 2010.
http://www.fec.gov/law/litigation/speechnow.shtml#ac_dc_decision

Vitaly Kats. "Because, the Internet: The Limits of Online Campaign Finance Disclosure." *Florida Law Review,* Vol. 67, July 2015, Number 4.
http://www.floridalawreview.com/wp-content/uploads/11-Kats

Sam Frizell. "The Alabama Engineer Who Made History At the Supreme Court." *Time.* Apr. 2, 2014.
http://time.com/47236/shaun-mccutcheon-interview-supreme-court-campaign-finance/

Trevor Potter. "Here's what I learned when I helped Stephen Colbert set up his Super PAC." *Washington Post.* Jan. 21, 2015.
http://www.washingtonpost.com/posteverything/wp/2015/01/21/heres-what-i-learned-when-i-helped-stephen-colbert-set-up-his-super-pac/

Wilson Andrews, Jeremy Bowers, Sarah Cohen et al. "Million-Dollar Donors in the 2016 Presidential Race." *New York Times*, Aug. 25, 201N.
http://www.nytimes.com/interactive/2016/us/elections/top-presidential-donors-campaign-money.html?_r=0%208.25.15

Kenneth P. Vogel. "Koch brothers' Americans for Prosperity plans $125 million spending spree." *Politico.* May 2014.
http://www.politico.com/story/2014/05/koch-brothers-americans-for-prosperity-2014-elections-106520_Page2.html

Peter Overby. "Koch Brothers Put Price Tag On 2016: $889 Million." NPR. Jan. 27, 2015.
http://www.npr.org/sections/itsallpolitics/2015/01/27/381954047/koch-brothers-put-price-tag-on-2016-889-million

Lisa Rosenberg. "U.S. Political Finance: Americans spend more on elections, but they lead from behind." Sunlight Foundation. Nov. 11, 2014
http://www.sunlightfoundation.com/blog/2014/11/10/u-s-political-finance-americans-spend-more-on-elections-but-they-lead-from-behind/

James Verini. "Show Him the Money: Tom Donohue scares millions of dollars out of corporations and Republicans. But is his U.S. Chamber of Commerce good for business?" *Washington Monthly.* July/Aug. 2010.
http://www.washingtonmonthly.com/features/2010/1007.verini.html

SourceWatch. "U.S. Chamber of Commerce." Updated May 7, 2015.
http://www.sourcewatch.org/index.php?title=U.S._Chamber_of_Commerce
Danny Hakim. "Big Tobacco's Staunch Friend in Washington: U.S. Chamber of Commerce." *New York Times.* Oct. 9, 2015.
http://www.nytimes.com/2015/10/10/business/us-chamber-of-commerces-focus-on-advocacy-a-boon-to-tobacco.html?_r=0
Eric Lipton, Mike McIntire and Don Van Natta Jr. "Top Corporations Aid U.S. Chamber of Commerce Campaign." *New York Times.* Oct. 21, 2010.
http://www.nytimes.com/2010/10/22/us/politics/22chamber.html

Jessica Silver-Greenberg and Michael Corkery. "Efforts to Rein In Arbitration Come Under Well-Financed Attack." *New York Times.* Nov. 15, 2015.
http://www.nytimes.com/2015/11/16/business/dealbook/efforts-to-rein-in-arbitration-come-under-well-financed-attack.html

Reclaim Democracy. "The Powell Memo (also known as the Powell Manifesto)."
http://reclaimdemocracy.org/powell_memo_lewis/

Peter H. Stone. "Super PACs dominate but don't guarantee success." *Sacramento Bee.* Sept. 25, 2015.
http://www.sacbee.com/opinion/california-forum/article36326277.html

Greg Stohr. *Bloomberg Poll: Americans Want Supreme Court to Turn Off Political Spending Spigot. Bloomberg.* Sept. 29, 2015.
http://www.bloomberg.com/politics/articles/2015-09-28/bloomberg-poll-americans-want-supreme-court-to-turn-off-political-spending-spigot

Monica Youn (editor), *Money, Politics, and the Constitution: Beyond Citizens United.* Century Foundation Press and Brennan Center for Justice. 2011.
https://www.brennancenter.org/publication/money-politics-and-constitution-beyond-citizens-united

Lawrence Lessig. "Campaign Finance and the Nihilist Politics of Resignation." *Atlantic.* Apr. 10, 2014.
http://www.theatlantic.com/politics/archive/2014/04/campaign-finance-and-the-nihilst-politics-of-resignation/360437/

Jared Keller. "Lawrence Lessig Will Never Be President—Here's Why He Needs to Run Anyway." *Pacific Standard.* Aug. 17, 2015.
http://www.psmag.com/politics-and-law/run-lawrence-run

Linda Greenhouse. "Speaking Truth to the Supreme Court." *New York Times.* Apr. 16, 2015.
http://www.nytimes.com/2015/04/16/opinion/speaking-truth-to-the-supreme-court.html

Zachary Roth. *John Paul Stevens: We need to level the playing field.* MSNBC. Apr. 30, 20140.
http://www.msnbc.com/msnbc/john-paul-stevens-money-politics

John Paul Stevens. *Six Amendments: How and Why We Should Change the Constitution.* Little, Brown and Company. 2014.

CHAPTER 4

Jim Dwyer. "Testimony at Sheldon Silver's Trial Suggests How Lucrative Mesothelioma Was." *New York Times.* Nov. 10, 2015.
http://www.nytimes.com/2015/11/11/nyregion/testimony-at-sheldon-silvers-trial-suggests-how-lucrative-mesothelioma-was.html

Susanne Craig and Benjamin Weiser. "Sheldon Silver Was Paid for Referrals, Not Legal Work, Law Firm Leader Says at Trial." *New York Times.* Nov. 10, 2015.
http://www.nytimes.com/2015/11/11/nyregion/sheldon-silver-was-paid-for-referrals-not-legal-work-law-firm-leader-says-at-trial.html

Margaret Hartmann and Katie Zavadski. "Why New York Assembly Speaker Sheldon Silver Has Been Arrested." *New York* magazine. Jan. 22, 2015.
http://nymag.com/daily/intelligencer/2015/01/sheldon-silver-arrested.html

David Klepper. "New York lawmakers slow to address corruption despite trials." AP Nov. 21, 2015
http://www.bigstory.ap.org/article/a03c47d0aff8472c816926b4c242d26b/new-york-lawmakers-slow-address-corruption-despite-trials
Paul Pringle, Corina Knoll and Kim Murphy. "Rizzo's horse had come in." *Los Angeles Times.* Aug. 22, 2012.
http://www.latimes.com/local/la-me-rizzos-horse-had-come-in-08222010-m-story.html

Jeff Gottlieb and Ruben Vives. "Rizzo's compensation totaled $1.5 million a year, Bell records show." *Los Angeles Times.* Aug. 7, 2010.
http://latimesblogs.latimes.com/lanow/2010/08/bell-robert-rizzo-compensation-million.html

CNN wire staff. "8 current and former officials from Bell, California, arrested." CNN. Sept. 21, 2010.
http://www.cnn.com/2010/CRIME/09/21/california.bell.arrests/

Richard Winton. "3 accused Bell officials want cash-strapped city to pay their legal bills." *Los Angeles Times.* Jan. 10, 2011.
http://latimesblogs.latimes.com/lanow/2011/01/accused-bell-officials-want-cash-strapped-city-to-pay-their-legal-bills.html

Jeff Gottlieb and Ruben Vives. "Bell's former police chief calls high pay a shock." *Los Angeles Times.* Nov. 6, 2013.
http://articles.latimes.com/2013/nov/06/local/la-me-1107-bell-randy-adams-20131107

Jeff Gottlieb, Jack Leonard and Ruben Vives. "Bell's Rizzo to serve prison time," *Los Angeles Times.* Oct. 3, 2013.
http://articles.latimes.com/2013/oct/03/local/la-me-rizzo-20131004

Corina Knoll and Jeff Gottlieb. "Rizzo gets 12 years in prison, marking end to scandal that rocked Bell." *Los Angeles Times*. Apr. 16, 2014.
http://www.latimes.com/local/lanow/la-me-ln-rizzo-set-to-be-sentenced--20140415-story.html

Jeff Gottlieb and Ruben Vives. "Angela Spaccia convicted in Bell corruption scandal." *Los Aneles Times*. Dec. 9, 2013.
http://articles.latimes.com/2013/dec/09/local/la-me-1210-angela-spaccia-20131210

David Folkenflik. "How The L.A. Times Broke The Bell Corruption Story." NPR. Sept. 24, 2010.
http://www.npr.org/templates/story/story.php?storyId=130108851

Ed Mendel. "CalPERS to Vernon pensioner: repay $3.5 million." Calpensions. Nov. 19, 2015.
http://calpensions.com/2015/11/19/calpers-to-vernon-pensioner-repay-3-5-million/

Sam Allen. "State pension agency slashes benefits for former Vernon officials." *Los Angeles Times*. May 31, 2012.
http://articles.latimes.com/2012/may/31/local/la-me-vernon-pensions-20120601

Esmeralda Bermudez and Hector Becerra. "Former Vernon official Eric T. Fresch found dead in park. *Los Angeles Times*. June 30, 2012.
http://articles.latimes.com/2012/jun/30/local/la-me-0630-fresch-20120630

Gene Maddaus. "The Corrupt Town in *True Detective* Is Based on Vernon, and Vernon Couldn't Be Happier." *LA Weekly*. June 22, 2015.
http://www.laweekly.com/news/the-corrupt-town-in-true-detective-is-based-on-vernon-and-vernon-couldnt-be-happier-5709057

Sam Ro. "9 Things From Warren Buffett's 2013 Shareholder Letter That Had Everyone Talking." *Business Insider*. Mar. 3, 2014.
http://www.businessinsider.com/highlights-warren-buffett-2013-letter-2014-3

Rebecca Rosenberg, Jamie Schram, and Daniel Prendergast. "FDNY, NYPD retirees who 'faked 9/11 illnesses in scam' not too sick to have fun." *New York Post*. Jan. 7, 2014.
http://nypost.com/2014/01/07/massive-social-security-fraud-probe-snares-scores-of-fdny-nypd-retirees/

Bob Fredericks and Philip Messing. "How the massive NY pension scam worked." *New York Post*. Jan. 7, 2014.
http://nypost.com/2014/01/07/how-the-massive-nypd-fdny-pension-scam-worked/

Donovan Slack and Walter V. Robinson. "US probes firefighter disability abuse." *Boston Globe*, Apr. 17, 2008.
http://www.boston.com/news/local/articles/2008/04/17/us_probes_firefighter_disability_abuse/?page=full

Milton Valencia and Brian MacQuarrie. "Ex-deputy fire chief acquitted in fraud case." *Boston Globe*. Oct. 22, 2011.
https:/www.bostonglobe.com/metro/2011/10/22/retired-deputy-fire-chief-aquitted-pension-fraud-case/Fd0WVCua63irBnk0PWAtRI/story.html

Peter Lattman. "Private Equity Firm Tied to New York Pension Scandal Raises $7.7 Billion From Investors." *New York Times.* June 19, 2013.
http://dealbook.nytimes.com/2013/06/19/in-wake-of-pay-to-play-scandal-riverstone-raises-its-largest-fund/

Danny Hakim and William Rashbaum. *Hevesi Pleads Guilty in Pension Case. New York Times.* Oct. 7, 2010.
http://www.nytimes.com/2010/10/08/nyregion/08hevesi.html

Mary Williams Walsh. *New York Is Investigating Advisors to Pension Funds. New York Times.* Nov. 5, 2013.
http://dealbook.nytimes.com/2013/11/05/new-york-is-investigating-advisers-to-pension-funds/?_r=0

John Eligon. "Hevesi Advisor Is Sentenced in Pension Scandal." *City Room* blog, *New York Times.* Feb. 17, 2011.
http://cityroom.blogs.nytimes.com/2011/02/17/hevesi-adviser-is-sentenced-in-pension-scandal/

Harry Enten. "Ranking the States From Most to Least Corrupt." *FiveThirtyEight.* Jan. 23, 2015.
http://fivethirtyeight.com/datalab/ranking-the-states-from-most-to-least-corrupt/
Oguzhan Dincer and Michael Johnston. "Measuring Illegal and Legal Corruption in American States: Some Results from the Corruption in America Survey." Center for Ethics, Harvard University. Dec. 1, 2014.

http://ethics.harvard.edu/blog/measuring-illegal-and-legal-corruption-american-states-some-results-safra

Cameron McWhirter. "New Orleans Ex-Mayor Ray Nagin Sentenced to 10 Years." *Wall Street Journal.* July 9, 2014.
http://www.wsj.com/articles/former-new-orleans-mayor-nagin-sentenced-to-10-years-for-corruption-1404919783

Lauren McGaughy. "Louisiana's rate of public corruption convictions highest in nation." *Times-Picayune.* Sept. 4, 2013.
http://www.nola.com/politics/index.ssf/2013/09/louisiana_corruption_business.html

Nick Madigan. "Arrests of 3 Mayors Reinforce Florida's Notoriety as a Hothouse for Corruption." *New York Times.* Sept. 1, 2013.
http://www.nytimes.com/2013/09/02/us/arrests-of-3-mayors-reinforce-floridas-notoriety-as-a-hothouse-for-corruption.html

Valerie Bauerlein. "Charlotte Mayor Resigns After Corruption Charges." *Wall Street Journal.* Mar. 26, 2014.
http://www.wsj.com/articles/SB10001424052702304418404579463590421140948

Michael Gordon. "Former Charlotte Mayor Patrick Cannon enters West Virginia prison". *Charlotte Observer.* Nov., 18, 2014.
http://www.charlotteobserver.com/news/local/crime/article9233498.html

Erica Perez, Matt Smith, and Lance Williams. "Calif. Sen. Leland Yee's collision course of political ambition and debt." *Center for Investigative Reporting.* Mar. 28, 2014.
http://cironline.org/reports/calif-sen-leland-yees-collision-course-political-ambition-and-debt-6204

John Coté. "Linking Sen. Yee's voting record to major donations". *San Francisco Chronicle/SFGate*. Mar. 31, 2014.
http://www.sfgate.com/politics/article/Linking-Calif-Sen-Yee-s-voting-record-to-major-5360391.php

Bob Egeiko and Evan Sernoffsky. "Former state Sen. Leland Yee pleads guilty in corruption case." *San Francisco Chronicle/*SFGate. July 1, 2015.
http://www.sfgate.com/crime/article/Former-Sen-Leland-Yee-changes-plea-to-guilty-in-6360935.php
Catalina Camia. "McDonnell to join infamous club of governors who've gone to prison." *USA Today*. Jan. 6, 2015.
http://onpolitics.usatoday.com/2015/01/06/governors-prison-bob-mcdonnell/

Associated Press. "4 of Illinois' Last 7 Governors Went to Prison." Jan. 30, 2013.
https://www.yahoo.com/news/4-illinois-last-7-governors-went-prison-001500522.html?ref=gs

Federal Policy. Sunlight Foundation. https:/sunlightfoundation.com/policy/federal/

Center for Public Integrity. "State Integrity 2015." Nov. 9 2015.
https://www.publicintegrity.org/accountability/state-integrity-investigation/state-integrity-2015
Yue Qiu, Chirs Zubak-Skees, and Erik Lincoln. "How does your state rank for integrity? The 2015 State Integrity Investigation finds it doesn't look good." Center for Public Integrity. Nov. 9, 2015.
https://www.publicintegrity.org/2015/11/09/18822/how-does-your-state-rank-integrity

Nicohlas Kusnetz. "Only three states score higher than D+ in State Integrity Investigation; 11 flunk." Center for Public Integrity. Nov. 9, 2015.
https://www.publicintegrity.org/2015/11/09/18693/only-three-states-score-higher-d-state-integrity-investigation-11-flunk

Marc Lifsher, Stuart Pfeifer, and David Zahniser. "Go-betweens got $125-million-plus from investment firms for arranging CalPERS deals." *Los Angeles Times*. Jan. 15, 2010.
http://articles.latimes.com/2010/jan/15/business/la-fi-calpers-crist15-2010jan15

Peter Lattman. "Former Calpers Chief Indicted Over Fraud." *New York Times*. Mar. 18, 2013.
http://dealbook.nytimes.com/2013/03/18/ex-chief-of-calpers-is-indicted-over-fraud/

Mary Williams Walsh. *New York Is Investigating Advisors to Pension Funds. New York Times*. Nov. 5, 2013.
http://dealbook.nytimes.com/2013/11/05/new-york-is-investigating-advisers-to-pension-funds/?_r=0

Evan Halper and Marc Lifsher. "Government pensions in cross hairs." *Los Angeles Times*. Apr. 23, 2010.
http://articles.latimes.com/2010/apr/23/business/la-fi-pension-reform-20100423

Aaron Elstein. "Stringer seeks placement agent ban." *Crain's New York Business*. Jan. 30, 2014.
http://www.crainsnewyork.com/article/20140130/BLOGS02/140139994/stringer-seeks-placement-agent-ban

"New York State Common Retirement Fund Pension Reform Agenda Overview." State of New York, Office of the State Comptroller.
http://www.osc.state.ny.us/pension/reform.pdf

Kenneth R. Gosselin. "Corruption Costs Jobs, Study Says." *Hartford Courant*. Feb. 25, 2004.
http://articles.courant.com/2004-02-25/news/0402250773_1_job-growth-political-corruption-connecticut-economy

CHAPTER 5

Joshua J. McElwee. "Francis: World close to suicide over climate change." *National Catholic Reporter*. Nov. 30, 2015.
 http://ncronline.org/news/vatican/francis-world-close-suicide-over-climate-change

Jim Yardley and Laurie Goodstein. "Pope Francis, in Sweeping Encyclical, Calls for Swift Action on Climate Change." *New York Times*. June 18, 2015.
 http://www.nytimes.com/2015/06/19/world/europe/pope-francis-in-sweeping-encyclical-calls-for-swift-action-on-climate-change.html?_r=0

Pope Francis."Laudato si'."*Encyclical Letter*. May 24, 2015.
http://w2.vatican.va/content/francesco/en/encyclicals/documents/papa-francesco_20150524_enciclica-laudato-si.html

"Transcript: Pope Francis's speech to Congress." *Washington Post*. Sept. 24, 2015.
 https: /www.washingtonpost.com/local/social-issues/transcript-pope-franciss-speech-to-congress/2015/09/24/6d7d7ac8-62bf-11e5-8e9e-dce8a2a2a679_story.html

Eric Holthaus. "Children Sue Over Climate Change." *Slate*. Nov. 16, 2015.
http://www.slate.com/articles/news_and_politics/jurisprudence/2015/11/children_sue_the_obama_administration_over_climate_change.single.html

Our Children's Trust.
http://ourchildrenstrust.org/federalplaintiffs

John Light. "21 Kids and a Climate Scientist Are Suing to Force Obama to Fight Climate Change." *Moyers and Company*. Nov. 24, 2015.
 http://billmoyers.com/2015/11/24/21-kids-and-a-climate-scientist-are-suing-to-force-obama-to-fight-climate-change/

"Petroleum Industry Joins US Government to Fight Teenagers in Climate Court."*SustainableBusiness.com*. Nov. 12, 2015.
http://www.sustainablebusiness.com/index.cfm/go/news.display/id/26467
Steve Mirsky. "Climate Skeptic Senator burned after Snowball Stunt." *Scientific American*. Mar. 2, 2015.
http://www.scientificamerican.com/podcast/episode/climate-skeptic-senator-burned-after-snowball-stunt/

James Inhofe. *The Greatest Hoax*. WND Books. 2012.

Brian Tashman. "James Inhofe Says the Bible Refutes Climate Change." *Right Wing Watch*. Mar. 8, 2012.
http://www.rightwingwatch.org/content/james-inhofe-says-bible-refutes-climate-change

Emily Atkin. "Politicians Who Say 'I'm Not a Scientist' On Climate Offer Their Advice On Ebola." *Climate Progress.* Oct. 20, 2014.
http://thinkprogress.org/climate/2014/10/20/3581897/climate-change-ebola-not-a-scientist/

"Morning Joe."*MSNBC.* Dec. 1, 2015.
http://www.msnbc.com/morning-joe/watch/christie-on-climate-change-577053763864

Marina Fang. "Jeb Bush: The Pope Shouldn't Discuss Climate Change Because 'He's Not A Scientist'." *Huffington Post.* Sept. 24, 2014.
http://www.huffingtonpost.com/entry/jeb-bush-climate-change-pope_56047a10e4b08820d91c57bc

Tiffany Germain. "The Anti-Science Climate Denier Caucus: 114th Congress Edition." *Think Progress.* Jan. 8, 2015.
http://thinkprogress.org/climate/2015/01/08/3608427/climate-denier-caucus-114th-congress/

Richard Schiffman. "Pope's call for action on climate change has shifted US views." *New Scientist.* Nov. 10, 2015.
https://www.newscientist.com/article/dn28472-popes-call-for-action-on-climate-change-has-shifted-us-views/

Giovanni Russonello. "Two-Thirds of Americans Want U.S. to Join Climate Change Pact." *New York Times.* Nov. 20, 2015.
http://www.nytimes.com/2015/12/01/world/americas/us-climate-change-republicans-democrats.html

Brandon Baker. "Survey Shows Americans Lead the World in Climate Denial." *EcoWatch.* July 22, 2014.
http://ecowatch.com/2014/07/22/americans-lead-world-climate-denial/
Eric Roston. "Unearthing America's Deep Network of Climate Change Deniers." *Bloomberg.* Nov. 20, 2015.
http://www.bloomberg.com/news/articles/2015-11-30/unearthing-america-s-deep-network-of-climate-change-deniers

Joby Warrick. "Why are so many Americans skeptical about climate change? A study offers a surprising answer." *Washington Post.* Nov. 11, 2015.
https://www.washingtonpost.com/news/energy-environment/wp/2015/11/23/why-are-so-many-americans-skeptical-about-climate-change-a-study-offers-a-surprising-answer/

James Hansen. *Storms of My Grandchildren: The Truth About the Coming Climate Catastrophe and Our Last Chance to Save Humanity.* Bloomsbury Press. 2009.

Christine Todd Whitman. *It's My Party, Too: The Battle for the Heart of the GOP and the Future of America.* Penguin Group (USA). 2005.

Mark Bowen. *Censoring Science: Inside the Political Attack on Dr. James Hansen and the Truth of Global Warming.* Dutton, 2007.

Ron Suskind. *The Price of Loyalty: George W. Bush, the White House, and the Education of Paul O'Neill.* Simon & Schuster. 2004.

Tim McDonnell. "Another State Agency Just Banned the Words 'Climate Change'."
Mother Jones. Apr. 8, 2015.
http://www.motherjones.com/blue-marble/2015/04/another-state-agency-just-banned-
words-climate-change

Eric Roston. "For Some Wisconsin State Workers, 'Climate Change'Isn't Something You
Can Talk About." *Bloomberg Business*. Apr. 8, 2015.
Katherine Bagley. "FEMA to States: No Climate Planning, No Money." *InsideClimate
News*. Mar. 18, 2015.
http://insideclimatenews.org/news/18032015/fema-states-no-climate-planning-no-money

James West. "These 14 States Have a Plan for Climate Change. The Rest of You Are
Screwed." *Mother Jones*. Oct. 10, 2014.
 http://www.motherjones.com/environment/2014/10/most-states-dont-have-plan-when-
climate-change-brings-its-predictable-destruct-0

James Hansen. "Why I must speak out about climate change." *TED Talks*. Feb 29, 2012.
https:/www.ted.com/talks/james_hansen_why_i_must_speak_out_about_climate_change/t
ranscript?language=en

John Light, "For the kids suing over climate change, things are going well so far." *Grist*.
(cross-posted from Moyers and Company). Nov. 27, 2015.
 http://grist.org/climate-energy/for-the-kids-suing-the-feds-over-climate-change-things-
are-going-well-so-far/

Vivienne Walt. "Robert Redford: We Have to Act on Climate Change Without
Washington." *Time*. Dec. 6, 2015.
 http://time.com/4137823/robert-redford-paris-interview/

Jenny Staletovich. "Far from Paris, South Florida climate talks begin in Key West."
Miami Herald. Dec. 1, 2015.
http://www.miamiherald.com/news/local/environment/article47358405.html

Coral Davenport. "The Marshall Islands Are Disappearing."*New York Times*. Dec. 1,
2015.
http://www.nytimes.com/interactive/2015/12/02/world/The-Marshall-Islands-Are-
Disappearing.html

Jeff Goodell. "Obama Takes on Climate Change: The Rolling Stone Interview." *Rolling
Stone*. Sept. 23, 2015.
 http://www.rollingstone.com/politics/news/obama-takes-on-climate-change-the-rolling-
stone-interview-20150923

Samantha Page. "The Paris Climate Talks Have Begun, And Obama Has Strong Words
For Fellow Leaders." *ThinkProgress*. Nov. 30, 2015.
 http://thinkprogress.org/climate/2015/11/30/3726324/obama-cop21-speech/

Charisse Jones. "Shell says it will end Alaska offshore Arctic drilling."*USA Today*. Sept.
28, 2015.

Amy R. Connolly. "U.S. halts Alaskan oil drilling for two years." *UPI*. Oct. 17, 2015.

Laura Barron-Lopez. "Obama vetoes Keystone XL bill." *The Hill*. Feb 24, 2015.

Issie Lapowsky. "Tech Billionaires Team Up To Take On climate Change." *Wired.* Nov. 30, 2015 http://www.wired.com/2015/11/zuckerberg-gates-climate-change-breakthrough-energy-coalition/

Scott Bixby. "Billionaire Tom Steyer Wants to Prove That Fighting Climate Change Can Save the Economy." *Mic.com.* Dec. 1, 2015. http://mic.com/articles/129324/billionaire-tom-steyer-wants-to-prove-that-fighting-climate-change-can-save-the-economy#.X9moJh1lX
Kerry A. Dolan. "Bill Gates, Mark Zuckerberg, & More Than 20 Other Billionaires Launch Coalition To Invest In Clean Energy." *Forbes.* Nov. 29, 2015. http://www.forbes.com/sites/kerryadolan/2015/11/29/bill-gates-george-soros-more-than-20-other-billionaires-launch-coalition-to-invest-in-clean-energy/
Natasha Geiling. "Indigenous Leaders In Paris Issue Declaration Calling For The End of Fossil Fuel Extraction." *Think Progress.* Dec. 6, 2015. http://thinkprogress.org/climate/2015/12/06/3728851/indigenous-leaders-paris-rally/

Jeremy Deaton. "America's Elders Flex Their Political Muscles On Climate Change." *Think Progress.* Sept. 23, 2015. http://thinkprogress.org/climate/2015/09/23/3704800/listen-to-your-elders-on-climate/

President Barack Obama. "Remarks by the President at the GLACIER conference – Anchorage, AK." Aug. 31, 2015. https: /www.whitehouse.gov/the-press-office/2015/09/01/remarks-president-glacier-conference-anchorage-ak

CHAPTER 6

America's Story from America's Library. "Rachel Carson's *Silent Spring.*" http://www.americaslibrary.gov/aa/carson/aa_carson_spring_1.html

Pennsylvania Department of Environmental Protection. "The Rachel Carson Connection." http://www.dep.state.pa.us/dep/falcon/rachelcarsonconnection.html

Rachel Carson. *The Sea Around Us.* Oxford University Press. 1951

Nancy F. Koehn. "From Calm Leadership, Lasting Change." *New York Times.* Oct. 27. 2012. http://www.nytimes.com/2012/10/28/business/rachel-carsons-lessons-50-years-after-silent-spring.html?_r=0

Mark Stoll. "Rachel Carson's Silent Spring, A book That Changed The World." 2012 http://www.environmentandsociety.org/exhibitions/silent-spring/silent-spring-television

Jonathan Norton Leonard. "Rachel Carson Dies of Cancer, 'Silent Spring' Author Was 56." *New York Times.* Apr. 15, 1964. https:/www.nytimes.com/books/97/10/05/reviews/carson-obit.html

Rex Weyler. "Rachel Carson—And the birth of modern environmentalism." Sept. 27, 2012. http://www.greenpeace.org/usa/rachel-carson-and-the-birth-of-modern-environmentalism/

Eliza Griswold. "How 'Silent Spring' Ignited the Environmental Movement." *New York Times Magazine.* Sept. 21, 2012. http://www.nytimes.com/2012/09/23/magazine/how-silent-spring- ignited-the-environmental-movement.html

Natural Resources Defense Council. "The Story of Silent Spring." Aug. 13, 2015.
http://www.nrdc.org/health/pesticides/hcarson.asp

Tom Philpott. "A reflection on the lasting legacy of USDA Secretary Earl Butz." *Grist.*
Feb. 8, 2008.
http://grist.org/article/the-butz-stops-here/
Kimberly B. Morland, editor. *Local Food Environments: Food Access in America.* CRC
Press. 2014.

Alex Rindler. "Forbes Fat Cats Collect Taxpayer-Funded Farm Subsidies."
Environmental Working Group. Nov. 7, 2013.
http/www.ewg.org/research/forbes-fat-cats-collect-taxpayer-funded-farm-subsidies

David Kirby. *Animal Factory: The Looming Threat of Industrial Pig, Dairy, and Poultry
Farms to Humans and the Environment.* St. Martin's Griffin. 2011.

Erik Marcus. *Meat Market: Animals, Ethics, and Money.* Brio Press. 2005.

Wenonah Hauter. *Foodopoly: the Battle Over the Future of Food and Farming in America.*
The New Press, 2012.

Factory-Farming.com. "U.S. Beef Production ... from Calf to Feedlot to Slaughter to
Supermarket."
http://www.factory-farming.com/beef_production.html
ASPCA. "The Truth About Chicken."
http://truthaboutchicken.org

Wil S. Hylton. "A Bug in the System." *New Yorker.* Feb. 2, 2015.
http://www.newyorker.com/magazine/2015/02/02/bug-system

U.S. PIRG. "Weak Medicine: Why the FDA's Guidelines Are Inadequate to Curb
Antibiotic Resistance and Protect Public Health. Sept. 10, 2014.
http://www.uspirg.org/reports/usf/weak-medicine

Lydia Zuraw. "Q&A: US Rep. Louise Slaughter Discusses Antibiotic Resistance." *Food
Safety News.* Dec. 3, 2013.
http://www.foodsafetynews.com/2013/12/qa-with-rep-louise-slaughter/#.VoNzVtDHu7U

Brian Krans. "Politics Stall Antibiotics Ban in Congress." *Healthline.* 2014.
http://www.healthline.com/health/antibiotics/politics-pork-and-poultry-why-legislation-
has-not-passed

Science News staff. "Where antibiotics go." *ScienceNews.* Mar. 1, 2014.
https:/www.sciencenews.org/article/where-antibiotics-go

Willy Blackmore. "Here's Another Way to Get Antibiotics off Farms: Tax 'Em." TakePart.
Jan. 17, 2014.
http://www.takepart.com/article/2014/01/17/case-antibiotics-tax

Consumer Reports. "Making the World Safe From Superbugs." Jan. 2016.
http://www.consumerreports.org/cro/health/making-the-world-safe-from-
superbugs/index.htm?utm_source=hootsuite

"Antibiotic Resistance Threats in the United States, 2013." CDC Centers for Disease Control and Prevention. 2013.
http://www.cdc.gov/drugresistance/threat-report-2013/

Samantha Bonar. "Foster Farms Finally Recalls Chicken. Sort Of." *LA Weekly*. July 7, 2014.
http://www.laweekly.com/restaurants/foster-farms-finally-recalls-chicken-sort-of-4829157

Jonel Aleccia. "Reps Urge USDA to Shut Down Foster Farms After Chicken Recall." *NBC News*. July 8, 2014.
http://www.nbcnews.com/health/health-news/reps-urge-usda-shut-down-foster-farms-after-chicken-recall-n149806

eMedicineHealth. "Methicillin-Resistant Staphylococcus Aureus (MRSA)."
http://www.emedicinehealth.com/methicillin-resistant_staphylococcus_aureus_mrsa-health/article_em.htm

Massachusetts Department of Health and Human Services. "Methicillin-resistant Staphylococcus aureus (MRSA)."
http://www.mass.gov/eohhs/gov/departments/dph/programs/id/epidemiology/providers/mrsa/methicillin-resistant-staphylococcus-aureus-mrsa.html

Joseph Mercola. "The Hidden Health Hazards of Eating CAFO Chicken." Mercola.com. May 30, 2015.
http://articles.mercola.com/sites/articles/archive/2015/05/30/cafo-chicken-hidden-health-hazards.aspx

Sarah Zhang. "Pig-manure fertilizer linked to human MRSA infections." *Nature*. Sept. 16, 2013.
http://www.nature.com/news/pig-manure-fertilizer-linked-to-human-mrsa-infections-1.13752

Factory-Farming.com. "Factory Farming: In The Beginning ... Unintended Consequences."
http://www.factory-farming.com/factory_farming.html

Christine Escobar. "The Tale of rBGH, Milk, Monsanto and the Organic Backlash." *Huffington Post*. Apr. 2, 2009, updated May 25, 2011.
http://www.huffingtonpost.com/christine-escobar/the-tale-of-rbgh-milk-mon_b_170823.html

Toxin Detective. "Chemical Additives Allowed by the FDA but Banned in Other Countries."
http://toxindetective.com/us-foods-full-ingredients-banned-countries/

ProCon.org. "Is It Misleading to Label Milk as Free of the Artificial Growth Hormone rBST/rBGH?" Oct. 13, 2010.
http://milk.procon.org/view.answers.php?questionID=000971

Keith Schneider. "F.D.A. Accused of Improper Ties in Review of Drug for Milk Cows." *New York Times*. Jan. 12, 1990.
http://www.nytimes.com/1990/01/12/us/fda-accused-of-improper-ties-in-review-of-drug-for-milk-cows.html

Health Canada. "Recombinantn Bovine Somatotropin (rbST)."
http://www.hc-sc.gc.ca/dhp-mps/vet/issues-enjeux/rbst-stbr/index-eng.php

Mike Ewell. "Bovine Growth Hormone: Milk does nobody good…" EJnet.org.
http/www.ejnet.org/bgh/nogood.html

James Baxter. "Monsanto Accused of Attempt to Bribe Health Canada for rBGH (Posilac)
Approval." *Ethical Investing*, excerpted *Ottawa Citizen*. Oct. 23, 1998.
http://www.ethicalinvesting.com/monsanto/news/10009.htm
Jeffrey Smith. "Whistleblowers, Threats, and Bribes: A Short History of Genetically
Engineered Bovine Growth Hormone." Council for Responsible Genetics. May 1, 2005.
http://www.councilforresponsiblegenetics.org/ViewPage.aspx?pageId=125

Libby Moulton. "Labeling Milk from Cows Not Treated with rBST: Legal in all 50 States
as of Sept. 29th, 2010." *Columbia Science and Technology Law Review*. Oct. 28, 2010.
http://stlr.org/2010/10/28/labeling-milk-from-cows-not-treated-with-rbst-legal-in-all-50-
states-as-of-september-29th-2010/

Eli Lilly and Company/PRNewswire. "Elanco Announces Acquisition of Posilac Dairy
Business". Aug. 20, 2008.
https:/investor.lilly.com/releaseDetail.cfm?releaseid=329001

Reynard Loki. "Why Did Gov't Give Big Thumbs Up to Notorious Monsanto Pesticide We
Now Believe Causes Cancer?" AlterNet.Mar. 26, 2015.
http://www.alternet.org/food/why-did-govt-give-big-thumbs-notorious-monsanto-pesticide-
we-now-believe-causes-cancer

Anthony Samsel and Stephanie Seneff. "Glyphosate, pathways to modern diseases II:
Celiac sprue and gluten intolerance." *Interdisciplinary Toxicology*. Dec. 2013.
http://www.ncbi.nlm.nih.gov/pmc/articles/PMC3945755/

Mary Ellen Kustin. "2.6 Billion Pounds of Monsanto's Glyphosate Sprayed on U.S.
Farmland in Past Two Decades." *EcoWatch*. Oct. 12, 2015.
http://ecowatch.com/2015/10/12/monsanto-glyphosate/

BeyondPesticides.org. "Pesticide-Induced Diseases: Learning/Developmental Disorders."
http://www.beyondpesticides.org/resources/pesticide-induced-diseases-
database/learningdevelopmental

James R. Roberts and Catherine J. Karr. "Pesticide Exposure in Children." *Pediatrics*.
Dec. 2012, Vol 130, Issue 6.
http://pediatrics.aappublications.org/content/130/6/e1765

Food Allergy Research & Education. "How Many People Have Food Allergies?"
https://www.foodallergy.org/facts-and-stats

Center for Disease Control and Prevention. "Trends in Allergic Conditions Among
Children: United States, 1997–2011," May 2013.
http://www.cdc.gov/nchs/data/databriefs/db121.htm
Veronique Greenwood. "Why Are Asthma Rates Soaring?" *Scientific American*. Apr. 1
2011.
http://www.scientificamerican.com/article/why-are-asthma-rates-soaring/

Christina Sarich. "GMOs may be to Blame for Spike in Kids Suffering from Inflammatory Bowl Disease." *Natural Society*. Oct. 25, 2014.
http://naturalsociety.com/kids-suffering-inflammatory-bowl-disease-eating-gmos/#ixzz3xvHt76AZ

Emily Main. "Genes from GMO Food Do Wind Up in People, Study Shows." *Rodale's OrganicLife*. June2, 2011.
http://www.rodalesorganiclife.com/food/genetically-modified-food

Leah Schinasi and Maria E. Leon. "Non-Hodgkin Lymphoma and Occupational Exposure to Agricultural Pesticide Chemical Groups and Active Ingredients." *International Journal of Environmental Research and Public Health*. Apr. 23, 2014.
http://www.ncbi.nlm.nih.gov/pmc/articles/PMC4025008/

Angela Ryan. "The Scientific Advice the FDA Ignored: A Compilation." Institute of Science in Society.
http://www.i-sis.org.uk/fda.php

Gary Ruskin. "The FDA does not test whether GMOs are safe." U.S. Right To Know, excerpt from *Seedy Business*.
http://usrtk.org/the-fda-does-not-test-whether-gmos-are-safe/

"Statement of Michael F. Jacobson, Ph.D., Executive Director, Center for Science in the Public Interest to the Food and Drug Administration Chicago, Illinois," Meeting on the Safety and Labeling of Genetically Modified Organisms. Center for Science in the Public Interest. Nov. 18, 1999.
https: /cspinet.org/new/genetics_fda.html

Monsanto. "Saved Seed and Farmer Lawsuits." Monsanto. As of Mar. 2016.
http://www.monsanto.com/newsviews/pages/saved-seed-farmer-lawsuits.aspx
Center for Food Safety. "Monsanto v. U.S. Farmers 2012 Update." 2012.
http://www.centerforfoodsafety.org/files/monsanto-v-us-farmer-2012-update-final_98931.pdf

Layla Katiraee. "A look at GMO policies in different nations." *Biology Fortified*. July 6, 2015.
http://www.biofortified.org/2015/07/a-look-at-gmo-policies-in-different-nations/

Melissa Healy. "FDA says GMO apple, potatoes are 'safe for consumption.' " *Los Angeles Times*. Mar. 20, 2015.
http://www.latimes.com/science/sciencenow/la-sci-sn-gmo-apple-potato-fda-approval-20150320-story.html

Jennifer Chaussee. California lawmakers reject bill requiring labeling on GMO foods. *Reuters*. May 29, 2014.

http://www.reuters.com/article/usa-california-gmo-idUSL1N0OF06D20140529

John Hart. "GMO labeling: Advocates like transparency, opponents dislike the cost." *Southeast Farm Press*. Dec. 17, 2014.
http://southeastfarmpress.com/markets/gmo-labeling-advocates-transparency-opponents-dislike-cost

Alison Kopicki. "Strong Support for Labeling Modified Foods." *New York Times*. July 2, 2013.
http://www.nytimes.com/2013/07/28/science/strong-support-for-labeling-modified-foods.html

Philip Shabecoff. *Earth Rising American Environmentalism in the 21st Century*. Island Press. 2001

Joseph Mercola. "Cheerios Go Non-GMO." Mercola.com. Jan. 18, 2014.
http://articles.mercola.com/sites/articles/archive/2014/01/18/gmo-free-cheerios.aspx

Hunter Stuart. "Ben & Jerry's Will Stop Using Genetically-Modified Ingredients, Company Says." *Huffington Post*. June 2, 2013.
http://www.huffingtonpost.com/2013/06/02/ben-and-jerrys-gmos-genetically-modified_n_3372451.html

Sourcewatch. "Monsanto."
http://www.sourcewatch.org/index.php/Monsanto

Mark Stevenson. "I am polluted." *Globe and Mail*. Updated Apr. 7, 2009.
http://www.theglobeandmail.com/life/i-am-polluted/article1115582/?page=all

Environmental Working Group and Mount Sinai School of Medicine. "Body Burden: The Pollution in People." 2000.
http://www.ewg.org/sites/bodyburden1/methodology.php

Mark Segal. "Toxic Substances Control Act and Genetically Engineered Microorganisms." U.S. Environmental Protection Agency. Oct. 30, 2015.
http://www.fda.gov/downloads/NewsEvents/MeetingsConferencesWorkshops/UCM472502.pdf

Katie Weatherford, Ronald White. "Reducing Our Exposure to Toxic Chemicals." Center for Effective Government Report.
http://www.foreffectivegov.org/reducing-chemical-exposure

Puneet Kollipara. "The bizarre way the U.S. regulates chemicals — letting them on the market first, then maybe studying them." *Washington Post*. Mar. 19, 2015.
https://www.washingtonpost.com/news/energy-environment/wp/2015/03/19/our-broken-congresss-latest-effort-to-fix-our-broken-toxic-chemicals-law/

Sandy Schubert. "EWG Letter in Support of the Ban Asbestos in America Act of 2007." Environmental Working Group. Oct. 9, 2007
http://www.ewg.org/news/testimony-official-correspondence/ewg-letter-support-ban-asbestos-america-act-2007

Sierra Club. "Sierra Club Position on TSCA Reform Legislation." Apr. 2014.
http://www.sierraclub.org/toxics/sierra-club-position-tsca-reform-legislation

Carey Gillam. "Pesticide use ramping up as GMO crop technology backfires: study." *Reuters*. Oct. 1, 2012.
http://www.reuters.com/article/us-usa-study- pesticides- idUSBRE89100X20121002

Natasha Gilbert. "A Hard Look at 3 Myths about Genetically Modified Crops." *Nature.*
May 1, 2013.
http://www.scientificamerican.com/article/a-hard-look-at-3-myths-about-genetically-
modified-crops/

Brian Clark. "Summary of Major Findings and Definitions of Important Terms."
Washington State University. Oct. 1, 2012.
http://cahnrs.wsu.edu/news-release/2012/10/01/summary-of-major-findings-and-
definitions-of-important-terms/

Laura MacCleery. "Why must FDA make its own job on food additives so hard?" *Hill.*
June 1, 2015.
http://thehill.com/blogs/congress-blog/the-administration/243460-why-must-fda-make-its-
own-job-on-food-additives-so
Food Babe. "Subway: Stop Using Dangerous Chemicals In Your Bread."
http://foodbabe.com/subway/

Steven Novella. "Eating Yoga Mats." Neurologica blog. 02.14.14.
http://theness.com/neurologicablog/index.php/eating-yoga-mats/

Michael F. Jacobson. "FDA Is Not Protecting Consumers From Unsafe Food Additives."
Huffington Post. July 11, 2012.
http://www.huffingtonpost.com/michael-f-jacobson/food-additives-_b_1654034.html

Melanie Haiken. "Latest Food Scare: What is the 'Yoga Mat' Chemical - And Why Is It In
Your Food?" *Forbes.* Feb. 27, 2014.
http://www.forbes.com/sites/melaniehaiken/2014/02/27/what-is-the-yoga-mat-chemical-
and-why-is-it-in-your-food/#1e495806337d3b7cf523337d

CHAPTER 7

Bianca DiJulio, Jamie Firth, and Mollyann Brodie. "Kaiser Health Tracking Poll: June
2015." Kaiser Family Foundation. June 16, 2015.
http://kff.org/health-costs/poll-finding/kaiser-health-tracking-poll-june-2015/

Anna Almendraia. "What The Daraprim Price Hike Actually Does To Health Care."
Huffington Post. Sept. 22, 2015.
http://www.huffingtonpost.com/entry/daraprim-price-turing-
shkreli_560063cee4b00310edf82060

Michael Hiltzik. "A huge spike in the cost of an old drug reignites the pharma pricing
debate." *Los Angeles Times.* Sept. 21, 2015.
http://www.latimes.com/business/hiltzik/la-fi-mh-a-huge-spike-in-the-cost-of-an-old-drug-
20150921-column.html

Zoë Schlanger. "Martin Shkreli on Raising Price of AIDS Drug 5,000 Percent: 'I Think
Profits Are a Great Thing.' "*Newsweek.* Sept. 21, 2015.
http://www.newsweek.com/martin-shkreli-daraprim-drug-prices-374922

Andrew Pollack. "Big Price Increase for Tuberculosis Drug Is Rescinded." *New York
Times.* Sept. 21, 2015.
http://www.nytimes.com/2015/09/22/business/big-price-increase-for-tb-drug-is-
rescinded.html

Linda A. Johnson. "Multiple factors cause high prescription drug prices in US."
Associated Press. Sept. 25, 2015.
http://bigstory.ap.org/article/5c265fadcd664eb0b9410785d65a24c8/multiple-factors-cause-high-prescription-drug-prices-us

Wendell Potter. "Presidential candidates in fantasy land over health care." Center for
Public Integrity. Sept. 28, 2015.
http://www.publicintegrity.org/2015/09/28/18071/presidential-candidates-fantasy-land-over-health-care

Olga Khazan. "The True Cost of an Expensive Medication." *Atlantic*. Sept. 25, 2015.
http://www.theatlantic.com/health/archive/2015/09/an-expensive-medications-human-cost/407299/

Susan Heavey. "U.S. drug industry group defends price of Gilead hepatitis drug." *Reuters*.
Apr. 10, 2014.
http://www.reuters.com/article/health-hepatitis-gilead-phrma-idUSL2N0N20YI20140410

Anne Harding. "Pros and Cons of New Hepatitis C Drugs." *Everyday Health*. Apr. 7, 2015.
http://www.everydayhealth.com/news/pros-cons-new-hepatitis-treatments-patients/

Abhijit Sen. "Exxon (XOM), LinkedIn (LNKD), Gilead Sciences (GILD), Time Warner
Cable (TWC), AIG—Earnings Preview." LearnBonds. Apr. 30, 2015.
http://learnbonds.com/117927/exxon-xom-linkedin-lnkd-gilead-sciences-gild-time-warner-cable-twc-aig-earnings-preview/

Deena Beasley. "UPDATE 2-Gilead hepatitis C sales beat Wall Street, sales outlook
raised." *Reuters*. July 28, 2015.
http://www.reuters.com/article/gilead-results-idUSL1N1082SI20150728

Editorial. "What price life? Pushback by OHSU's Brian Druker against high drug costs
should prod review." *Oregonian*. Apr. 29, 2013.
http://www.oregonlive.com/opinion/index.ssf/2013/04/what_price_life_pushback_by_oh.html

Andrew Pollack. "Doctors Denounce Cancer Drug Prices of $100,000 a Year." *New York
Times*. Apr. 25, 2013.
http://www.nytimes.com/2013/04/26/business/cancer-physicians-attack-high-drug-costs.html

Andrew Pollack. "Drug Prices Soar, Prompting Calls for Justification." *New York Times*.
July 23, 2015.
http://www.nytimes.com/2015/07/23/business/drug-companies-pushed-from-far-and-wide-to-explain-high-prices.html

David H. Howard, Peter B. Bach, Ernst R. Berndt, and Rena M. Conti. "Pricing in the
Market for Anticancer Drugs." American Economic Association. *Journal of Economic
Perspectives*. Vol. 29, No. 1, Winter 2015.
https://www.aeaweb.org/articles.php?doi=10.1257/jep.29.1.139&fnd=s

Ana Swanson. "Big pharmaceutical companies are spending far more on marketing than research." *Washington Post*. Feb. 11, 2015.
https://www.washingtonpost.com/news/wonk/wp/2015/02/11/big-pharmaceutical-companies-are-spending-far-more-on-marketing-than-research/

Wikipedia. "Pharmaceutical marketing." Last updated Feb. 4, 2016.
https://en.wikipedia.org/wiki/Pharmaceutical_marketing#cite_note-McGill04-5

Bulletin of the World Health Organization. "Direct-to-consumer advertising under fire." Vol. 87, No. 8. Aug. 2009.
http://www.who.int/bulletin/volumes/87/8/09-040809/en/

Julia Belluz. "Why prescription drug ads always have that absurd list of side effects at the end." *Vox*. Sept. 29, 2015.
http://www.vox.com/2015/9/29/9414145/direct-consumer-advertising-pharmaceutical-regulation

Tracy Staton. "Painkiller marketing secrets? Check Chicago's unredacted suit against Endo, Purdue, Cephalon, et al." *FiercePharma*. Nov. 18, 2014.
http://www.fiercepharmamarketing.com/story/painkiller-marketing-secrets-check-chicagos-unredacted-suit-against-endo-pu/2014-11-18

Mike Adams. "Exclusive: Glaxo whistleblower goes public with shocking details of bribery, marketing fraud and other pharma crimes." *Natural News*. July 17, 2012.
http://www.naturalnews.com/036499_glaxo_whistleblower_bribery.html

Gary Schwitzer. "Dr. Drew, sex advice, big $ and antidepressants." *HealthNewsReview.org*. July 5, 2012.
http://www.healthnewsreview.org/2012/07/dr-drew-sex-advice-big-and-antidepressants/

David Lee. "Allergan Gets $600 Million Botox Headache." *Courthouse News Service*. Sept. 7, 2010.
http://www.courthousenews.com/2010/09/07/30128.htm
Charles Ornstein, Lena Groeger, Mike Tigas and Ryann Grochowski Jones. "Dollars for Docs: How Industry Dollars Reach Your Doctors." *ProPublica*. Updated Mar. 17, 2016.
https://projects.propublica.org/docdollars/

Timothy S. Anderson et al. "Academic Medical Center Leadership on Pharmaceutical Company Boards of Directors." Journal of the American Medical Association, Vol. 311, No. 13. Apr. 2, 2014.
http://jama.jamanetwork.com/article.aspx?articleid=1853147

Janet Jones and Michael Minor. "New, strategic outsourcing models to meet changing clinical development needs." *PubFacts*. Apr. 1, 2010.
http://www.pubfacts.com/detail/21829788/New-strategic-outsourcing-models-to-meet-changing-clinical-development-needs.

"Global Markets for Contract Pharmaceutical Manufacturing, Research and Packaging." *PR Newswire*. July 6, 2015.
http://www.prnewswire.com/news-releases/global-markets-for-contract-pharmaceutical-manufacturing-research-and-packaging-300109079.html

Trends, Charts, and Maps. *ClinicalTrials.gov*. National Institutes of Health. Ongoing compilation.
https://clinicaltrials.gov/ct2/resources/trends#LocationsOfRegisteredStudies

Jason Smith. "Kingpins: Oxycontin, Heroin, and the Sackler-Sinaloa Connection."
Addiction Unscripted.com.
https://addictionunscripted.com/kingpinsoxycontin-heroin-and-the-sackler-sinaloa-
connection/

Scott Glover and Lisa Girion. "OxyContin maker closely guards its list of suspect doctors."
Los Angeles Times. Aug. 11, 2013.
http://articles.latimes.com/2013/aug/11/local/la-me-rx-purdue-20130811

Art Van Zee. "The Promotion and Marketing of OxyContin: Commercial Triumph, Public
Health Tragedy." *American Journal of Public Health.* National Institutes of Health. Feb.
2009.
http://www.ncbi.nlm.nih.gov/pmc/articles/PMC2622774/

Anjelina Pokrovnichka. "History of OxyContin: Labeling and Risk Management." Food
and Drug Administration. Nov. 13, 2008.
http://www.fda.gov/downloads/AdvisoryCommittees/CommitteesMeetingMaterials/Drugs/
AnestheticAndLifeSupportDrugsAdvisoryCommittee/UCM248776.pdf
Mike Mariani. "How the American opiate epidemic was started by one pharmaceutical
company." *The Week.* Mar. 4, 2015.
http://theweek.com/articles/541564/how-american-opiate-epidemic-started-by-
pharmaceutical-company

Peter Frost. "Horizon Pharma defies lawmakers, moves to Ireland." *Chicago Tribune.*
Sept. 20, 2014
http://www.chicagotribune.com/business/ct-horizon-inversion-0920-biz-20140919-
story.html

Ben Hirschler and Bill Berkrot. "Pfizer walks away from $118 billion AstraZeneca
takeover fight." *Reuters.* May 26, 2014.
http://www.reuters.com/article/us-astrazeneca-pfizer-idUSBREA3R0H520140526

Stuart Pfeifer. "Allergan sells generic drug unit to Israel's Teva for $40.5 billion." *Los
Angeles Times.* July 27, 2015.
http://www.latimes.com/business/la-fi-teva-allergan-20150727-story.html

Sarah Kliff. "Martin Shkreli raised his drug's price 5,500 percent because, in America, he
can." *Vox.* Dec. 17, 2015.
http://www.vox.com/2015/9/22/9366721/daraprim-price-shkreli-turing

IMS Health. "IMS Health Forecasts Global Drug Spending to Increase 30 Percent by
2020, to $1.4 Trillion, As Medicine Use Gap Narrows." Nov. 18, 2015.
https://www.imshealth.com/en/about-us/news/ims-health-forecasts-global-drug-spending-
to-increase-30-percent-by-2020

Gabriel Levitt. "Medicare Drug Prices Much Higher Than Other Countries and Other
Federal Programs, According to New Policy Paper." *PharmacyChecker.com.* July 31, 2015.
https:/www.pharmacycheckerblog.com/medicare-drug-prices-much-higher-than-other-
countries-and-other-federal-programs-according-to-new-policy-paper

Ethan Rome. "Big Pharma Pockets $711 Billion in Profits by Robbing Seniors,
Taxpayers." *Huffington Post.* Apr. 8, 2013.
http://www.huffingtonpost.com/ethan-rome/big-pharma-pockets-711-bi_b_3034525.html

Eric Palmer. "Big Pharma (and Big Biotechs) riding drug approval surge toward $1T in sales." FiercePharma. June 17, 2015.
http://www.fiercepharma.com/story/big-pharma-and-big-biotechs-riding-drug-approval-surge-toward-1-trillion-sa/2015-06-17

Jonathan D. Rockoff, Dana Mattioli and Liz Hoffman. "Teva Would Vault to Top With $40 Billion Deal." *Wall Street Journal*. July 27, 2015.
http://online.wsj.com/public/resources/documents/print/WSJ_-B001-20150727.pdf

Statista. 2015 ranking of the global top 10 biotech and pharmaceutical companies based on revenue.
http://www.statista.com/statistics/272717/top-global-biotech-and-pharmaceutical-companies-based-on-revenue/

Adrus Wagstaff Law Blog. "Big Pharma Has Higher Profit Margins Than Any Other Industry." Nov. 21, 2014.
https://www.andruswagstaff.com/blog/big-pharma-has-higher-profit-margins-than-any-other-industry

Todd Campbell. "3 Drugs That Make Gilead Sciences' Harvoni Look Cheap." *Motley Fool*. Nov.10, 2014.
http://www.fool.com/investing/general/2014/11/10/3-drugs-that-make-gilead-sciences-harvoni-look-che.aspx

Marta Falconi. "Novartis Manages to Push Back Competition to Leukemia Drug in the U.S." *Wall Street Journal*. May 15, 2014.
http://www.wsj.com/articles/SB10001424052702304908304579563560797460496

Tracy Staton. "Unions accuse Novartis of 'sham' patent fight to delay Sun's Gleevec generics." FiercePharma. June 25, 2015.
http://www.fiercepharma.com/story/unions-accuse-novartis-sham-patent-fight-delay-suns-gleevec-generics/2015-06-25

Rebecca R. Ruiz and Katie Thomas. "Teva Settles Cephalon Generics Case With F.T.C. for $1.2 Billion. *New York Times*. May 28, 2015.
http://www.nytimes.com/2015/05/29/business/teva-cephalon-provigil-ftc-settlement.html?_r=1

Jennifer Wadsworth. "County Sues Rx Drug Makers, Alleges 'Campaign of Deception.' " San Jose Inside. May 22, 2014.
http://www.sanjoseinside.com/2014/05/22/county-sues-rx-drug-makers-alleges-campaign-of-deception/
Alexander Gaffney. "Study: Regulatory Noncompliance Plays Big Role in Record-Setting Fines." Regulatory Affairs Professionals Society. Sept. 28, 2012.
http://www.raps.org/focus-online/news/news-article-view/article/2321/

Bob Van Voris. "U.S. Seeks $3.3 Billion From Novartis in Drug Kickback Suit." *Bloomberg*. June 30, 2015.
http://www.bloomberg.com/news/articles/2015-07-01/u-s-seeks-3-3-billion-from-novartis-in-drug-kickback-suit

American Medical News. "Medicare buoyed by demo success after audits collect $700 million." Aug. 25, 2008.
http://www.amednews.com/article/20080825/government/308259984/6/

"GlaxoSmithKline to Plead Guilty and Pay $3 Billion to Resolve Fraud Allegations and Failure to Report Safety Data." Department of Justice. July 2, 2012.
http://www.justice.gov/opa/pr/glaxosmithkline-plead-guilty-and-pay-3-billion-resolve-fraud-allegations-and-failure-report

"Justice Department Announces Largest Health Care Fraud Settlement in its History." Department of Justice. Aug. 25, 2012.
http://www.justice.gov/opa/pr/justice-department-announces-largest-health-care-fraud-settlement-its-history

"Abbott Labs to Pay $1.5 Billion to Resolve Criminal & Civil Investigations of Off-label Promotion of Depakote." Department of Justice. May 7, 2012.
http://www.justice.gov/opa/pr/abbott-labs-pay-15-billion-resolve-criminal-civil-investigations-label-promotion-depakote

"Eli Lilly and Company Agrees to Pay $1.415 Billion to Resolve Allegations of Off-label Promotion of Zyprexa." Department of Justice. Jan. 15, 2009.
http://www.justice.gov/archive/opa/pr/2009/January/09-civ-038.html

Drew Griffin and Andy Segal. "Feds found Pfizer too big to nail." CNN. Apr. 2, 2010.
http://www.cnn.com/2010/HEALTH/04/02/pfizer.bextra/
Brian Feroldi. "This Presidential Candidate is Big Pharma's Worst Nightmare." *Motley Fool.* Sept. 6, 2015.
http://www.fool.com/investing/general/2015/09/06/this-presidential-candidate-is-big-pharmas-worst-n.aspx

Wendell Potter. "Opinion: Big Pharma's stranglehold on Washington." Center for Public Integrity. Feb. 11, 2013.
http://www.publicintegrity.org/2013/02/11/12175/opinion-big-pharmas-stranglehold-washington

Jared Celniker. "Will the Grass Grow Greener in D.C.?" OpenSecrets.org. Feb. 25, 2015.
https://www.opensecrets.org/news/2015/02/will-the-grass-grow-greener-in-d-c/

Freedom of Medicine and Diet. "Rep. Andy Harris Pharma Conflict of Interest." Dec. 17, 2014.
http://freedomofmedicineanddiet.blogspot.com/2014/12/rep-andy-harris-pharma-conflict-of.html

Lee Drutman. *The Business of America is Lobbying: How Corporations Became Politicized and Politics Became More Corporate (Studies in Postwar Political Development),* 1st Ed. 2015. Oxford University Press. New York.
Economist. "The Washington wishing-well: The unstoppable rise in lobbying by American business is bad for business itself." June 13, 2015.
http://www.economist.com/news/business/21654067-unstoppable-rise-lobbying-american-business-bad-business-itself-washington

Institute For America's Future. "Billy Tauzin: Case Study in Corruption, How Industry Money and Personal Interest Shaped Part D." May 2006.
http://www.medicalsupplychain.com/pdf/Medicare%20Part%20D%20Reform%20&%20Corruption%20Issues.pdf

Alex Wayne and Drew Armstrong. "Tauzin's $11.6 Million Made Him Highest-Paid Health-Law Lobbyist." *Bloomberg.* Nov. 28, 2011.
http://www.bloomberg.com/news/articles/2011-11-29/tauzin-s-11-6-million-made-him-

highest-paid-health-law-lobbyist

Walid F. Gellad et al. "What if the Federal Government Negotiated Pharmaceutical Prices for Seniors? An Estimate of National Savings." *Journal of General Internal Medicine.* National Institutes of Health. Sept 23, 2008.
http://www.ncbi.nlm.nih.gov/pmc/articles/PMC2517993/

Kylie Gumpert. "Americans want Medicare to help negotiate down drug prices-poll." *Reuters.* July 17, 2015.
http://www.reuters.com/article/usa-medicare-drugprices-idUSL2N0ZW21W20150717

Topher Spiro, Maura Calsyn, and Thomas Huelskoetter. "Enough Is Enough: The Time Has Come to Address Sky-High Drug Prices." Center for American Progress. Sept. 2015.
https://cdn.americanprogress.org/wp-content/uploads/2015/09/15131852/DrugPricingReforms-report1.pdf

CHAPTER 8

Scott Harrison. "Tracking the slow decline of the Pacific Electric Railway Red Cars." *Los Angeles Times.* Jan. 22, 2016.
http://www.latimes.com/local/california/la-me-california-retrospective-red-car-20160103-story.html

University of Vermont. "History and cultural impact of the Interstate Highway system." Landscape Change Program.
http://www.uvm.edu/landscape/learn/impact_of_interstate_system.html

Steven M. Gillon. *The American Paradox: A History of the United States Since 1945.* Cengage Learning. 2012.

Craig Noble. *Memo to : E2 Members.* Natural Resources Defense Council.
https:/www.e2.org/ext/document.jsp?docId=1043

Marty Padgett. *Toyota Prius: A Brief History in Time.* Green Car Reports. Sept. 10, 2008.
http://www.greencarreports.com/news/1014178_toyota-prius-a-brief-history-in-time

Jerry Hirsch. "2015 U.S. auto sales on track to hit a record." *Los Angeles Times.* July 2, 2015.
http://www.latimes.com/business/autos/la-fi-peak-auto-sales-20150702-story.html

Alden Whitman. *J. Paul Getty Dead at 83; Amassed Billions From Oil. New York Times.* June 6, 1976.
http://www.nytimes.com/learning/general/onthisday/bday/1215.html
Bill McKibben. *Eaarth: Making a Life on a Tough New Planet.* St. Martin's Griffin. 2011.

Jad Mouawad. "At Exxon, Making the Case for Oil." *New York Times.* Nov. 15, 2008.
http://www.nytimes.com/2008/11/16/business/16exxon.html

Rebecca Solnit. "Oil fuels war and terrorists like Isis. The climate movement can bring peace." *Guardian.* Dec. 8, 2015.
http://www.theguardian.com/commentisfree/2015/dec/08/oil-fuels-war-terrorists-isis-climate-movement-peace-cop-21

Dean Henderson. *Big Oil & Their Bankers in the Persian Gulf.* Create Space. 2010.

Dean Henderson. *The Four Horsemen Behind America's Oil Wars.* Global Research. Apr. 26, 2011.
http://www.globalresearch.ca/the-four-horsemen-behind-america-s-oil-wars/24507

Terence Smith. "Why Carter Admitted the Shah." *New York Times.* May 17, 1981.
http://www.nytimes.com/1981/05/17/magazine/why-carter-admitted-the-shah.html?pagewanted=all

Adam Hochschild. "Well-Oiled Machine: 'Private Empire,' Steve Coll's Book About Exxon Mobil." *New York Times.* June 8, 2012.
http://www.nytimes.com/2012/06/10/books/review/private-empire-steve-colls-book-about-exxon-mobil.html

Steve Coll. *Private Empire: ExxonMobil and American Power.* Penguin Books. 2013.

Human Rights Watch. "World Report 2015: Equatorial Guinea."
https://www.hrw.org/world-report/2015/country-chapters/equatorial-guinea

Cohen Milstein. "ExxonMobil Indonesian Villagers Human Rights Abuse Case to Proceed in Federal Court." Globe News Wire. July 7, 2015.
http://globenewswire.com/news-release/2015/07/07/750294/10140847/en/ExxonMobil-Indonesian-Villagers-Human-Rights-Abuse-Case-to-Proceed-in-Federal-Court.html

Ed Pilkington. "Shell pays out $15.5m over Saro-Wiwa killing." *Guardian.* June 8 2009.
http://www.theguardian.com/world/2009/jun/08/nigeria-usa

Business & Human Rights Resource Centre. "Nigeria: Amnesty report says oil industry has brought pollution, poverty & human rights violation to Niger Delta." July 29, 2009.
http://business-humanrights.org/en/nigeria-amnesty-report-says-oil-industry-has-brought-pollution-poverty-human-rights-violation-to-niger-delta#c28247

United Nations Environment Programme. "UNEP Ogoniland Oil Assessment Reveals Extent of Environmental Contamination and Threats to Human Health." Aug. 4, 2011.
http://www.unep.org/newscentre/Default.aspx?DocumentID=2649&ArticleID=8827

Sonia Shah. *Crude, The Story of Oil.* Seven Stories Press. Kindle edition: 2011.

Ike Okonto and Oronto Douglas. *Where Vultures Feast: Shell, Human Rights and Oil in the Niger Delta.* Verso. 2003.

Amazon Watch. "The U'wa People of Colombia's Cloud Forests."
http://amazonwatch.org/work/uwa

Andrew E. Miller. "Victory! Gas Project in U'wa Territory Dismantled." Amazon Watch. Feb. 26, 2015.
http://amazonwatch.org/news/2015/0226-victory-gas-project-in-uwa-territory-dismantled

Elissa Dennis. "Keep It In The Ground." *Dollars & Sense* article published on *Common Dreams.* July 1, 2010.
http://www.commondreams.org/views/2010/07/01/keep-it-ground

Adam Vaughan. "Ecuador signs permits for oil drilling in Amazon's Yasuni national park." *Guardian*. May 23, 2014.
http://www.theguardian.com/environment/2014/may/23/ecuador-amazon-yasuni-national-park-oil-drill

Business & Human Rights Resource Centre. "Texaco/Chevron lawsuits (re Ecuador)."
http://business-humanrights.org/en/texacochevron-lawsuits-re-ecuador

ChevronToxico: The Campaign for Justice in Ecuador. "A Rainforest Chernobyl."
http://chevrontoxico.com/about/rainforest-chernobyl/

Corporate Social Responsibility Newswire. "In 2016, Chevron Faces Potential 'Litigation Catastrophe' Over Ecuador Pollution Liability". Jan. 4, 2016.
http://www.csrwire.com/press_releases/38590-In-2016-Chevron-Faces-Potential-Litigation-Catastrophe-Over-Ecuador-Pollution-Liability

Patrick Raddon Keefe. "Reversal of Fortune: A crusading lawyer helped Ecuadorans secure a huge environmental judgment against Chevron. But did he go too far?" New Yorker. Jan. 9, 2012.
http://www.newyorker.com/magazine/2012/01/09/reversal-of-fortune-patrick-radden-keefe
Mica Rosenberg. "Chevron's U.S. win in Ecuador case looms over cases elsewhere." *Reuters*. Mar. 7, 2014.
http://www.reuters.com/article/chevron-ecuador-canada-idUSL1N0M21JC20140307

Steve Harvey. "California's legendary oil spill." *Los Angeles Times*. June 13, 2010.
http://articles.latimes.com/2010/jun/13/local/la-me-then-20100613

Wilderness Society. "Seven ways oil and gas drilling is bad news for the environment."
http://wilderness.org/six-ways-oil-and-gas-drilling-bad-news-environment

Dan Duray. "The Santa Barbara Oil Spill of 1969: A Lesson In Offshore Drilling." *Huffington Post*. July 22, 2008.
http://www.huffingtonpost.com/2008/07/14/the-santa-barbara-oil-spi_n_112605.html

James Osborne. "Lawsuits against Exxon Mobil mount over big oil pipeline spills." *Dallas Morning News*. Sept. 14, 2013.
http://www.dallasnews.com/business/energy/20130914-suits-against-exxon-mobil-mount-over-big-oil-pipeline-spills.ece

Dan Frosch. "Amid Pipeline Debate, Two Costly Cleanups Forever Change Towns." *New York Times*. Aug. 8, 2013.
http://www.nytimes.com/2013/08/11/us/amid-pipeline-debate-two-costly-cleanups-forever-change-towns.html

Nora Caplan-Bricker. "This Is What Happens When a Pipeline Bursts in Your Town." *New Republic*. Nov. 18, 2013.
https://newrepublic.com/article/115624/exxon-oil-spill-arkansas-2013-how-pipeline-burst-mayflower

BP. "Our History."
http://www.bp.com/en/global/corporate/about-bp/our-history.html

Reuters. "A history of BP's US disasters." *Telegraph*. Nov. 15, 2012.
http://www.telegraph.co.uk/finance/newsbysector/energy/oilandgas/9680589/A-history-of-BPs-US-disasters.html

"BP Alaska Oil Spill Penalty To Cost Company $25 Million." *Reuters*. May 3, 2011.
http://www.reuters.com/article/us-bp-spill-penalty-idUSTRE7424DR20110503

Michael Muskal and Ronald D. White. "BP fined, charged in oil spill that showed 'profit over prudence.' " *Los Angeles Times*. Nov. 15, 2012.
http://articles.latimes.com/2012/nov/15/nation/la-na-nn-holder-bp-oil-spill-settlement-20121115

Ed Caesar. "Deepwater Horizon." *Sunday Times*. Sept. 12, 2010.
http://www.edcaesar.co.uk/article.php?article_id=50

Charles Kennedy. "Most Of BP's $20.8 Billion Deepwater Horizon Fine Is Tax Deductible." OilPrice.com. Oct. 7, 2015.
http://oilprice.com/Energy/Energy-General/Most-Of-BPs-208-Billion-Deepwater-Horizon-Fine-Is-Tax-Deductible.html

Ronald Bailey. *The End of Doom: Environmental Renewal in the Twenty-First Century*. Thomas Dunne Books. 2015.
"What is fracking and why is it controversial?" *BBC*. Dec. 16, 2015.
http://www.bbc.com/news/uk-14432401

Juliana Keeping, Agence France Press. "How one US state went from two quakes a year to 585." *Business Insider*. Sept. 19, 2015.
http://www.businessinsider.com/afp-how-one-us-state-went-from-two-quakes-a-year-to-585-2015-9

Jeffrey Ball. "Exxon Says 'Fracking' Safe as Industry Mounts Defense." *Wall Street Journal*. May 26, 2011.
http://www.wsj.com/articles/SB10001424052702304520804576345522519486578

Judy Woodruff. "Has Exxon Mobil misled the public about its climate change research?" *PBS NewsHour*. Nov. 10, 2015.
http://www.pbs.org/newshour/bb/exxon-mobil-mislead-public-climate-change-research/

Lindsay Abrams. "Exxon's lies go even deeper: How the oil giant broke its promise and spent millions supporting climate denial." *Salon*. July 15, 2015.
http://www.salon.com/2015/07/15/exxons_lies_go_even_deeper_how_the_oil_giant_broke_its_promise_and_spent_millions_supporting_climate_denial/

Katie Jennings, Dino Grandoni and Susanne Rust. "How Exxon went from leader to skeptic on climate change research." *Los Angeles Times*. Oct. 23, 2015.
http://graphics.latimes.com/exxon-research/

CHAPTER 9

Senator Bernie Sanders. "Fraudulent Defense Contractors Paid $1 Trillion." *BERNIE SANDERS, United States Senator for Vermont*. Oct. 20, 2011.
http:/www.sanders.senate.gov/newsroom/press-releases/fraudulent-defense-contractors-paid-1-trillion

Major General Smedley Butler. *War is a Racket*. Feral House (reprint edition). 2003.

"We Just Decided To." *The Newsroom*. HBO. Apr. 24, 2012.
http://www.hbo.com/the-newsroom/episodes/index.html

Mandy Smithberger. "Pentagon's 2017 Budget is Mardi Gras for Defense Contractors."
POGO (Project on Government Oversight). Feb. 11, 2016.
http://www.pogo.org/blog/2016/02/pentagons-2017-budget-is-mardi-gras-for-defense-
contractors.html

"$561bn Pentagon budget planned, advocates say real budget is $1trn." *RT.com*.
Jan. 30, 2015.
https://www.rt.com/usa/227679-obama-trillion-defense-budget/

Senator Bernie Sanders. "Bernie Sanders Addresses Specifics to Cut U.S. Deficit."
Bloomberg Politics. Sept. 18, 2015.
https://www.youtube.com/watch?v=IMMugKrqb-c

Martin Matishak. "Senators move to demand DOD audit penalties." *The Hill*. Feb. 4,
2015.
http: /thehill.com/policy/defense/231751-senators-move-to-demand-dod-audit-penalties

Joe Gould and Hope Hodge Seck. "USMC Reversal a Hitch in DoD Audit Plans."
DefenseNews. Mar. 30, 2015
http://www.defensenews.com/story/defense/policy-budget/2015/03/29/usmc-reversal-a-
hitch-in-dod-audit-readiness-plans/70444036/

Howard Zinn. *A People's History of the United States*. Harper Perennial Modern Classics.
2005.

Ron Soodalter. "The Union's 'Shoddy' Aristocracy." *New York Times* Disunion series. May
9, 2011.
http://opinionator.blogs.nytimes.com/2011/05/09/the-unions-shoddy-aristocracy/?_r=0

Paul Waldman. "How the F35 boondoggle shows that deficit hawkery is a sham."
Washington Post. July 25, 2014.
https: /www.washingtonpost.com/blogs/plum-line/wp/2014/07/25/how-the-f-35-boondoggle-
shows-that-deficit-hawkery-is-a-sham/

John Burnett. "Halliburton Deals Recall Vietnam-Era Controversy." *NPR All Things
Considered*. Dec. 24, 2003.
http://www.npr.org/templates/story/story.php?storyId=1569483

Richard Sisk. "Congress Again Buys Abrams Tanks the Army Doesn't Want."
Military.com. Dec. 18, 2014.
http://www.military.com/daily-news/2014/12/18/congress-again-buys-abrams-tanks-the-
army-doesnt-want.html

Alex Johnson. "$500,000 U.S. Training Center in Afghanistan Is 'Melting': Inspector
General." *NBC News*. Jan. 16, 2015.
http://www.nbcnews.com/news/world/500-000-u-s-training-center-afghanistan-melting-
inspector-general-n287256

Rajiv Chandrasekaran. "A Brand-new U.S. military headquarters in Afghanistan. And
nobody to use it." *Washington Post*. July 10, 2013.
https://www.washingtonpost.com/world/national-security/a-brand-new-us-military-
headquarters-in-afghanistan-and-nobody-to-use-it/2013/07/09/2bb73728-e8cd-11e2-a301-
ea5a8116d211_story.html

Meghan Keneally. "New report reveals massive taxpayer waste in Afghanistan citing $3million inflatable boats that were never even shipped to the landlocked country." *Daily Mail*. June 12, 2014.
http://www.dailymail.co.uk/news/article-2656600/Pentagon-reveals-massive-taxpayer-waste-Afghanistan-citing-3million-inflatable-boats-never-shipped-landlocked-country.html

John F. Sopko, Special Inspector General for Afghanistan Reconstruction. "Assessing the Capabilities and Effectiveness of the Afghan National Defense and Security Forces" (Testimony Before the Subcommittee on Oversight and Investigations, Committee on Armed Services, U.S. House of Representatives).
https://www.sigar.mil/pdf/testimony/SIGAR-16-17-TY.pdf

James Risen. *Pay Any Price: Greed, Power, and Endless War*. Houghton Mifflin Harcourt. 2014.

David Pallister. "How the US sent $12bn in cash to Iraq. And watched it vanish." *Guardian*. Feb. 7, 2007.
http://www.theguardian.com/world/2007/feb/08/usa.iraq1

James Glanz. "Contractors Outnumber U.S. Troops in Afghanistan." *New York Times*. Sept. 1, 2009.
http://www.nytimes.com/2009/09/02/world/asia/02contractors.html

Anna Fifield. "Contractors reap $138bn from Iraq war." *Financial Times*. Mar. 18, 2013.
http://www.ft.com/intl/cms/s/0/7f435f04-8c05-11e2-b001-00144feabdc0.html#axzz463ATmmvu

Tim Shorrock. "Meet the contractors analyzing your private data." *Salon*. June 10, 2013.
http://www.salon.com/2013/06/10/digital_blackwater_meet_the_contractors_who_analyze_your_personal_data/

Alex Kane. "5 Companies That Make Money By Keeping Americans Terrified of Terror Attacks." *AlterNet*. Aug. 16, 2013.
http://www.alternet.org/civil-liberties/5-companies-make-money-keeping-americans-terrified-terror-attacks

Travis Daub. "How a Reno casino con man duped the CIA and pulled one of the 'most dangerous hoaxes' in American history." *PBS NewsHour*. Oct. 14, 2014.
http://www.pbs.org/newshour/rundown/reno-casino-conman-pulled-greatest-hoax-american-history/

Victor Gaetan. "'Industry of Death': Pope Francis on Arms Dealers and Causes of World War III." *National Catholic Register*. Feb. 9, 2016.
http://www.newsjs.com/url.php?p=http://www.ncregister.com/daily-news/industry-of-death-pope-francis-on-arms-dealers-and-causes-of-world-war-iii/

John Brownlee. "Guess Which Country's Companies Profit Most From War?" *Fast Company*. Feb. 23, 2015.
http://www.fastcodesign.com/3042669/infographic-of-the-day/guess-which-countrys-companies-profit-most-from-war

SIGIR (Special Inspector General for Iraq Reconstruction) Investigations. "Report to Congress." Jan. 30, 2010.
http://www.globalsecurity.org/military/library/report/sigir/sigir-2010-01_section4d.pdf

Julie DiMauro. "KBR sued for kickbacks, false claims in Iraq subcontracts." *FPCA Blog.* Jan. 24, 2014.
http://www.fcpablog.com/blog/2014/1/24/kbr-sued-for-kickbacks-false-claims-in-iraq-subcontracts.html

"Defense Contractor Agrees to Pay $27.5 Million to Settle Overbilling Allegations." Department of Justice. Dec. 19, 2014.
https://www.justice.gov/opa/pr/defense-contractor-agrees-pay-275-million-settle-overbilling-allegations

CHAPTER 10

"Testimony of Pam Dixon, Executive Director, World Privacy Forum, Before the Senate Committee on Commerce, Science and Transportation. ' What Information Do Data Brokers Have on Consumers, and How Do They Use It?' " United States Senate Committee on Commerce, Science, and Transportation. Dec. 12, 2013.
https://www.commerce.senate.gov/public/_cache/files/e290bd4e-66e4-42ad-94c5-fcd4f9987781/BF22BC3239AE8F1E971B5FB40FFEA8DD.dixon-testimony.pdf
Byron Acohido. "Web tracking has become a privacy time bomb." *USA Today.* Aug. 8, 2011. http: /usatoday30.usatoday.com/tech/news/2011-08-03-internet-tracking-mobile-privacy_n.htm

Gerald Chait. "Half the Money I Spend on Advertising Is Wasted – The Trouble Is I Don't Know Which Half." *EzineArticles.* Feb. 23, 2015.
http:/ezinearticles.com/?Half-the-Money-I-Spend-on-Advertising-Is-Wasted-The-Trouble-Is-I-Dont-Know-Which-Half&id=8936126

Charles Duhigg. "How Companies Learn Your Secrets." *New York Times Magazine.* Feb. 2, 2012.
http:/www.nytimes.com/2012/02/19/magazine/shopping-habits.html?_r=0

Leah Burrows. "To be let alone: Brandeis foresaw privacy problems." *BrandeisNOW.* July 24, 2013.
https://www.brandeis.edu/now/2013/july/privacy.html

"*Olmstead v. United States:* The Constitutional Challenges of Prohibition Enforcement: Dissenting opinion of Justice Louis D. Brandeis in Olmstead v. United States." Federal Judicial Center. 1928.
http:/www.fjc.gov/history/home.nsf/page/tu_olmstead_doc_15.html

"Edward Snowden: Leaks that exposed US spy programme." BBC News. Jan. 17, 2014.
http://www.bbc.com/news/world-us-canada-23123964

Dennis Fisher. "'Our Threat Model Has Changed'.*" Threatpost.* Feb. 2, 2014.
https:/threatpost.com/our-threat-model-has-changed/104160/
Lou Montulli. "The reasoning behind Web Cookies." *The irregular musings of Lou Montulli.* May 14, 2013.
http: /www.montulli-blog.com/2013/05/the-reasoning-behind-web-cookies.html

Dan Lyons. "In (Partial) Defense of Tracking Cookies." HubSpot Blogs. May 16, 2013.
http: /blog.hubspot.com/marketing/in-defense-of-tracking-cookies

"DoubleClick Inc.—Company Profile, Information, Business Description, History, Background Information on DoubleClick Inc." Reference for Business.
http:/www.referenceforbusiness.com/history2/44/DoubleClick-Inc.html

"Jason Catlett quotes." Thinkexist.com.
http:/thinkexist.com/quotation/by-synchronizing-cookies-with-name-and-
address/940852.html

"Statement From Kevin O'Conner, CEO of DoubleClick." *Tech Law Journal*. Mar. 3, 2000.
http:/techlawjournal.com/privacy/20000302.htm

"Alliance Data's Epsilon to Acquire DoubleClick Email Solutions, a Global Leader in
Targeted Email Communications and Marketing Services for Leading Blue-Chip Brands."
PR Newswire. Feb. 14, 2006.
http: /www.prnewswire.com/news-releases/alliance-datas-epsilon-to-acquire-doubleclick-
email-solutions-a-global-leader-in-targeted-email-communications-and-marketing-
services-for-leading-blue-chip-brands-55316457.html

Wendy Davis. "DoubleClick Sells Abacus To Epsilon For $435M." *MediaPost*. Dec. 29,
2006.
http://www.mediapost.com/publications/article/53117/doubleclick-sells-abacus-to-epsilon-
for-435m.html?edition=

Grant Gross. "Microsoft, others protest Google's DoubleClick deal. *Washington Post*. Sept.
27, 2007.
http://www.washingtonpost.com/wp-
dyn/content/article/2007/09/27/AR2007092701900.html

Derek Thompson. "Google's CEO: 'The Laws Are Written by Lobbyists'." *Atlantic*. Oct. 1,
2010.
http:/www.theatlantic.com/technology/archive/2010/10/googles-ceo-the-laws-are-written-
by-lobbyists/63908/
"Introducing Google Buzz." Google. Feb. 2, 2010.
https:/googleblog.blogspot.com/2010/02/introducing-google-buzz.html

Byron Acohido. "Google Buzz fuels rising privacy, security concerns." *USA Today*. Feb.
18, 2010.
http://content.usatoday.com/communities/technologylive/post/2010/02/google-buzz-facing-
privacy-security-storm-1/1#.VxKklNUrKVM

Byron Acohido. "Critics call for Congressional hearings on Google's Wi-Fi data
harvesting." *USA Today*. Oct. 28, 2010.
http:/content.usatoday.com/communities/technologylive/post/2010/10/critics-call-for-
congressional-hearings-on-googles-wi-fi-data-harvesting/1#.Vq2HpynqcgU

Scott Cleland. "The Unique Google Privacy Problem." *Googleopoly.net* Oct. 25, 2012.
http:/googleopoly.net/wp-content/uploads/2012/07/Unique-Google-Privacy-Problem.pdf

"Facebook Settles FTC Charges That It Deceived Consumers By Failing To Keep Privacy
Promises." Federal Trade Commission. Nov. 29, 2011.
https://www.ftc.gov/news-events/press-releases/2011/11/facebook-settles-ftc-charges-it-
deceived-consumers-failing-keep

Bobbie Johnson. "Privacy no longer a social norm, says Facebook founder." *Guardian*.
Jan. 10, 2010.
http:/www.theguardian.com/technology/2010/jan/11/facebook-privacy

Olivia Perkins. "More than half of employers now use social media to screen job candidates, poll says; even send friend requests." *Cleveland Plain Dealer*. May 14, 2015. http:/www.cleveland.com/business/index.ssf/2015/05/more_than_half_of_employers_no_1. html

Julia Angwin. *Dragnet Nation: A Quest for Privacy, Security and Freedom in a World of Relentless Surveillance*. Times Books. 2014.

Julia Angwin interview. "No Escaping Dragnet Nation." *Moyers and Company*. Mar. 14, 2014.
http://billmoyers.com/episode/no-escaping-dragnet-nation/

Gary Kovacs. "Tracking our online trackers." *TED Talks*. Mar. 2012.
https:/www.ted.com/talks/gary_kovacs_tracking_the_trackers/transcript?language=en

Dillon Mann. "Announcing the Web We Want." World Wide Web Foundation. Dec. 5, 2013.
http:/webfoundation.org/2013/12/announcing-the-web-we-want/
"Dutch privacy groups threat Facebook with court over Safe Harbour treaty." *DutchNews.nl*. Dec. 16, 2015.
http:/www.dutchnews.nl/news/archives/2015/12/dutch-privacy-groups-threat-facebook-with-court-over-safe-harbour-treaty/

"Factsheet on the 'Right to be Forgotten' ruling (C-131/12)." European Commission.
http://ec.europa.eu/justice/data-protection/files/factsheets/factsheet_data_protection_en.pdf

"A Review of the Data Broker Industry: Collection, Use and Sale of Consumer Data for Marketing Purposes (Staff Report for Chairman Rockefeller)." United States Senate Committee on Commerce, Science, and Transportation, Office of Oversight and Investigation, Majority Staff. Dec. 18, 2013.
http://educationnewyork.com/files/rockefeller_databroker.pdf

Sarah Kuranda. "The 10 Biggest Data Breaches Of 2015." *CRN*. Dec. 21, 2015.
http:/www.crn.com/slide-shows/security/300079193/the-10-biggest-data-breaches-of-2015.htm

Jake Anderson. "Automated Police Tracking System Will Notify Your Wife If You Drive Past a Prostitute." *Anti-Media*. Dec. 4, 2015.
http:/theantimedia.org/automated-police-tracking-system-will-notify-your-wife-if-you-drive-past-a-prostitute/

American Civil Liberties Union (ACLU). "A Surveillance Bill by Any Other Name Smells Just As Foul." July 28, 2015.
https://www.aclu.org/blog/washington-markup/surveillance-bill-any-other-name-smells-just-foul

Decide The Future. "The U.S. Congress Just Made Us Less Safe."
https://www.decidethefuture.org/cisa/

Senator Ron Wyden. "Wyden Slams Latest, Worse Version of Cybersecurity Bill." Dec. 16, 2015.
https://www.wyden.senate.gov/news/press-releases/wyden-slams-latest-worse-version-of-cybersecurity-bill

Steven Musil. "Apple has support of independent voters in FBI iPhone battle." *CNET*. Mar. 8, 2016.
http://www.cnet.com/news/apple-has-support-of-independent-voters-in-fbi-iphone-battle/

Julia Angwin. "Privacy Tools: How to Safely Browse the Web." *juliaangwin.com*. Jan. 12, 2014.
http://juliaangwin.com/author/juliaangwin/page/7/

Mark Weinstein. "7 Cool Ways to Have Fun Online While Protecting Your Privacy." *Huffington Post*. Jan. 23, 2015.
http://www.huffingtonpost.com/mark-weinstein/7-cool-ways-to-have-fun-o_b_6519794.html

Pew Research Center. "Americans' Views About Data Collection and Security." May 20, 2015.
http://www.pewinternet.org/2015/05/20/americans-views-about-data-collection-and-security/

CHAPTER 11

Benjamin Weiser. "To Judge, Lawyer's Cooperation Doesn't Offset Corruption." *New York Times*. Dec. 7, 2015.
http://www.nytimes.com/2015/12/08/nyregion/prison-term-for-lawyer-who-cooperated-in-graft-cases.html

Jeff German. "Vegas attorney Gregory gets 10 years in prison for role in HOA fraud." *Las Vegas Review-Journal*. June 17, 2015.
http://www.reviewjournal.com/news/las-vegas/vegas-attorney-gregory-gets-10-years-prison-role-hoa-fraud

Steven J. Harper. *The Lawyer Bubble: A Profession in Crisis*. Basic Books. 2013.

Martha Neil. "'Churn that bill, baby!' email surfaces in fee dispute with DLA Piper." *ABA Journal*. Mar. 25, 2013.
http://www.abajournal.com/news/article/sued_by_dla_piper_for_675k_ex-client_discovers_lighthearted_churn_that_bill/

Sara Randazzo and Jacqueline Palank. "Legal Fees Cross New Mark: $1,500 an Hour." *Wall Street Journal*. Feb. 9, 2016.
http://www.wsj.com/articles/legal-fees-reach-new-pinnacle-1-500-an-hour-1454960708

Bar Admissions Basic Overview. American Bar Association.
http://www.americanbar.org/groups/legal_education/resources/bar_admissions/basic_overview.html

Keith J. Kelly. "Maxim 'scammer' was stuck in a pile of debt: prosecutors." *New York Post*. Dec. 10, 2015.
http://nypost.com/2015/12/10/maxim-scammer-was-stuck-in-a-pile-of-debt-prosecutors/

U.S. Attorney's Office, Southern District of New York. "Westchester County Attorney Anthony Mangone, Defendant in Yonkers Public Corruption Case, Pleads Guilty in White Plains Federal Court." Nov. 29, 2010.
https://www.fbi.gov/newyork/press-releases/2010/nyfo112910.htm

Cindy George. "Defense attorney sentenced to 15 years in bribery case." *Houston Chronicle*. Oct. 27, 2015.
http://www.chron.com/news/houston-texas/houston/article/Defense-attorney-sentenced-to-15-years-in-bribery-6594228.php

Erin Ailworth. "Lawyer pleads guilty in condo fraud." *Boston.com*. Jan. 28, 2011.
http://archive.boston.com/yourtown/framingham/articles/2011/01/28/lawyer_pleads_guilty_in_condo_fraud/

Bryan Burrough. "Marc Dreier's Crime of Destiny." *Vanity Fair*. Sept. 29, 2009.
http://www.vanityfair.com/news/2009/11/marc-dreier200911

U.S. Attorney's Office, Southern District of New York. "Joseph Collins, Principal Attorney For Former Commodities Firm Refco, Sentenced in Manhattan Federal Court To One Year And One Day In Prison For Securities Fraud." July 15, 2013.
https://www.justice.gov/usao-sdny/pr/joseph-collins-principal-attorney-former-commodities-firm-refco-sentenced-manhattan

Kevin Krause. "Dallas immigration lawyer gets 2 years in federal prison for visa fraud scheme." *Dallas Morning News*. Nov. 19, 2015.
http://crimeblog.dallasnews.com/2015/11/dallas-immigration-lawyer-gets-2-years-in-federal-prison-for-visa-fraud-scheme.html/

Avi Asher-Schapiro. "How Eric Holder's Corporate Law Firm Is Turning Into a 'Shadow Justice Department'." *Vice News*. Aug. 25, 2015.
https://news.vice.com/article/how-eric-holders-corporate-law-firm-is-turning-into-shadow-justice-department

William D. Cohan. "How Wall Street's Bankers Stayed Out of Jail." *Atlantic*. Sep. 2015.
http://www.theatlantic.com/magazine/archive/2015/09/how-wall-streets-bankers-stayed-out-of-jail/399368/

Gavin Broady. "The Merry Crusader: Judge Jed Rakoff." *Law360*. Mar. 18, 2014.
http://www.law360.com/articles/518684/the-merry-crusader-judge-jed-rakoff

INDEX